Debt in the Ancient Mediterranean and Near East

Debt in the Ancient Mediterranean and Near East

Credit, Money, and Social Obligation

Edited by

JOHN WEISWEILER

OXFORD
UNIVERSITY PRESS

OXFORD
UNIVERSITY PRESS

Oxford University Press is a department of the University of Oxford. It furthers
the University's objective of excellence in research, scholarship, and education
by publishing worldwide. Oxford is a registered trade mark of Oxford University
Press in the UK and certain other countries.

Published in the United States of America by Oxford University Press
198 Madison Avenue, New York, NY 10016, United States of America.

© Oxford University Press 2023

Library of Congress Cataloging-in-Publication Data
Names: Weisweiler, John, editor.
Title: Debt in the ancient Mediterranean and Near East : credit, money, and
social obligation / edited by John Weisweiler.
Description: New York, NY : Oxford University Press, [2023] |
Includes bibliographical references and index.
Identifiers: LCCN 2022018785 (print) | LCCN 2022018786 (ebook) |
ISBN 9780197647172 (hardback) | ISBN 9780197647196 (epub)
Subjects: LCSH: Debt—Mediterranean Area—History, | Credit—Mediterranean
Area—History, | Money—Mediterranean Area—History, | Debt—Middle
East—History. | Credit—Middle East—History, | Money—Middle
East—History,
Classification: LCC HG3701 .D3925 2022 (print) | LCC HG3701 (ebook) |
DDC 332.70956—dc23/eng/20220708
LC record available at https://lccn.loc.gov/2022018785
LC ebook record available at https://lccn.loc.gov/2022018786

DOI: 10.1093/oso/9780197647172.001.0001

1 3 5 7 9 8 6 4 2

Printed by Integrated Books International, United States of America

In memory of David Graeber (1961–2020)

Contents

Preface

IN 2014 AND 2016, I taught two undergraduate seminars on Greek and Roman debt at the Seminar für Alte Geschichte of the University of Tübingen. This book is inspired by the students who participated in these courses. The lively discussions in the Zeitschriftenzimmer of the top floor of the Hegelbau, taking place just as the Greek debt crisis reached its denouement, were a powerful reminder of what is at stake in thinking about the interplay between credit and coercion in world history.

Most of the chapters included in this volume were first presented at a workshop held in Schloss Hohentübingen in summer 2016. The stately surroundings of the Fürstenzimmer provided an appropriate backdrop for discussing the roles played by religion, state violence, and metal currencies in premodern Eurasia. Although Michael Hudson, Michael Jursa, and Reinhard Wolters did not participate in the project until the end, their observations and insights were crucial in moving it forward. So was the learning and good humor of Cliff Ando, who moderated the discussion. Finally, the manuscript greatly benefited from the comments of two anonymous reviewers. I would like to thank all of them for their contributions to this project.

It is a pleasure to acknowledge the generous financial support of the Fritz-Thyssen-Stiftung for the workshop from which this book originates. The unbureaucratic way in which this foundation awards and manages grant money is a model for institutions of its kind—the opposite of the "box tickers" and "task masters" who, according to David Graeber's apposite characterization, dominate so many organizations of higher education.

The delight about the appearance of this book is mixed with incalculable sadness. Two key contributors to this project did not live to see its conclusion. Michael Bonner's acumen and generosity greatly enlivened the Tübingen workshop. His contribution to this volume will be among the last publications of a scholar whose work has reconfigured our understanding of the early Islamic economy. David Graeber's learning and anarchic humor were a glorious spectacle to behold. It is still difficult to grasp that his youthful mind is no longer with us. This book is dedicated to his memory.

List of Contributors

Michael Bonner, University of Michigan, Ann Arbor †

Lisa Eberle, University of Tübingen lisa.eberle@uni-tuebingen.de

Keith Hart, The Memory Bank keith@thememorybank.co.uk

Moritz Hinsch, Humboldt University of Berlin moritz.hinsch@hu-berlin.de

Neville Morley, University of Exeter N.D.G.Morley@exeter.ac.uk

Arietta Papaconstantinou, University of Reading a.s.papaconstantinou@reading.ac.uk

Richard Payne, University of Chicago repayne@uchicago.edu

Reinhard Pirngruber, University of Vienna reinhard.pirngruber@univie.ac.at

Alice Rio, King's College, London alice.rio@kcl.ac.uk

Richard Seaford, University of Exeter r.a.s.seaford@exeter.ac.uk

John Weisweiler, St John's College, Cambridge jw439@cam.ac.uk

I

The Currency–Slavery–Warfare Complex

DAVID GRAEBER AND THE HISTORY OF VALUE IN ANTIQUITY

John Weisweiler

IN HIS *DEBT: The First 5,000 Years* (2011), David Graeber develops a new grand narrative of world history. Graeber argues that the roots of the current socio-economic order are located not in early-modern Europe but in antiquity. From the late Bronze Age onward, all across Eurasia, relationships of social obligation were transformed into quantifiable and legally enforceable debts. Graeber suggests that this transformation made possible new economic institutions, such as IOUs, coinage, and debt-slavery. At the same time, it also led to the emergence of new modes of thought, which have shaped Eurasian philosophical and religious traditions ever since.

This volume explores the implications of Graeber's work for the history of the ancient Mediterranean and Near East (roughly 700 BCE to 700 CE). This era, which Graeber dubs (following Karl Jaspers) the "Axial Age," plays a central role in his narrative.[1] He suggests that the territorial states of this period had a distinct political economy, marked by metal currencies, taxation, chattel slavery, and impersonal markets. All across Eurasia, old credit systems began to be replaced by new forms of coinage, and states and landowning elites accumulated unprecedented amounts of wealth. New cosmologies and philosophical practices enabled individuals to maintain a sense of autonomy and self-determination in these dynamic market societies. At the same time, inequality soared. Warfare led to the spread of chattel slavery, and debt enmeshed rural populations in webs of

John Weisweiler, *The Currency–Slavery–Warfare Complex* In: *Debt in the Ancient Mediterranean and Near East*. Edited by: John Weisweiler, Oxford University Press. © Oxford University Press 2023.
DOI: 10.1093/oso/9780197647172.003.0001

dependency and obligation. Adapting an expression coined by Geoffrey Ingham, Graeber calls this synergistic relationship between coinage, markets, fiscally intensive states and coercive labor practices the "currency–slavery–warfare complex."[2] On his reading, this constellation of power unraveled at the end of antiquity. After the highly monetized empires of antiquity had disintegrated, usury was outlawed in most regions of western Eurasia, chattel slavery ended, and non-market forms of exchange again became more important.[3]

The chapters assembled in this volume pursue two objectives. First, they test the accuracy of this grand narrative of ancient history. Specialists assess how well the interpretations advanced in *Debt* fit current understanding of the societies of the ancient Mediterranean and Near East. Does Graeber's concept of a "currency–slavery–warfare complex" shed new light on the political economy of western Eurasia in this period? Second, this volume offers a history of ancient credit systems which takes seriously the dual nature of debt as *both* a quantifiable economic reality *and* an immeasurable social obligation. By exploring the diverse ways in which social relationships were quantified in different ancient societies, it tries out a method of writing the history of ancient systems of exchange that departs from the currently dominant paradigm of neo-institutional economics.

Debt: The First 5,000 Years

When in 2011 David Graeber published his *Debt: The First 5,000 Years*, he was professor of anthropology at Goldsmith's College of the University of London. But he spent his academic leave in his home city, New York. There he quickly became one of the most influential voices of the Occupy Wall Street movement. Graeber had long mixed activism with scholarship. In addition to writing three influential works of ethnography and anthropological theory,[4] he was an active participant in the global justice movement and published a classic study of it, *Direct Action: An Ethnography*.[5] But none of his earlier books spoke as much to the concerns of the moment as *Debt: The First 5,000 Years*. Although it was published by a small independent press, it became an instant bestseller and has been translated into seventeen languages. In retrospect, this success may seem unsurprising. After all, *Debt* appeared at the height of the European debt crisis and in a moment when the social effects of the 2007 credit crunch had led to an upsurge of social protest across the globe. The book looked like the manifesto of the movements that seemed to challenge the established order in the summer of 2011. This impression was reinforced by the fact that Graeber was one of the most visible representatives of the protests in New York.

Yet this impression is misleading. Research for *Debt* had (of course) begun years before the uprisings of 2011. Already in 2009, Graeber published a paper in which he outlined the main contours of the argument that would later be elaborated in his book.[6] On closer inspection, it is also not clear whether *Debt* was quite so obviously predestined to become a publishing success as it would later appear. The book puts forward a complex and challenging argument. Although it is written in accessible style, it is deeply versed in anthropological theory. Entire chapters are taken up by technical arguments around the nature of money, definitions of modes of exchange, or explorations of credit systems in remote societies or distant periods of history. In this sense, one may suspect that the popular success of the book was more of a mirage than a reality. Like that other surprise bestseller, Thomas Piketty's *Capital in the Twenty-First Century* (2014), Graeber's *Debt* was probably more often cited than read from cover to cover. But for scholars interested in the shape of premodern economies, the book repays attention. It offers at least three insights that ancient historians may usefully incorporate into their work.

First, Graeber challenges the narrative (prevalent since at least Adam Smith and accepted as common sense in many quarters until today) according to which world economic history can be written in terms of a development to ever more efficient modes of exchange, from barter (allegedly prevalent in pre-monetized societies) through coinage (developed in classical antiquity) to the complex credit instruments employed in modern finance. Graeber shows that this story is empirically wrong. In the opening chapter of the book, he demonstrates that in reality the circulation of goods in most pre-monetized societies was determined by relationships of mutual obligation, not by exchanging fixed amounts of one commodity against fixed amounts of another.[7] The refutation of the myth of barter was probably the most influential section of *Debt*. Though it was long known among anthropologists that barter cannot have been the original form of exchange, it was only in the wake of Graeber's book that this conclusion began to be widely accepted outside of specialist scholarship.[8]

Second, Graeber shows that exchanges based on reciprocity are not as natural or ubiquitous as common sense might lead us to believe and as social scientists of different political persuasions since the nineteenth century have tended to think. He observes that cash purchases, credit contracts, and barter resemble each other in important ways. They are all based on an expectation that one party will give something in return for what the other party has given, and will do so in a precisely quantifiable way. Once the transaction is concluded, the relationship between the two parties ends. Graeber distinguishes this *reciprocal* logic from *non-reciprocal* forms of interaction. The latter fall into two subgroups. The first (which he calls "baseline communism") denotes interactions which operate without an expectation of reciprocity, such as giving somebody a lighter, lending somebody a tool, or giving somebody directions. The second (which Graeber calls "hierarchy") comprises forms of exchange between non-equals, such as the payment of protection money, euergetism, or gifts to a child. Though in some of these cases obligations are claimed to be reciprocal, in practice they follow the logic of precedent. Moreover, the relationship is constantly ongoing, rather than being broken off. In all societies these non-reciprocal forms of interaction are probably at least as widespread as market sales and other forms of reciprocal exchange.[9]

Here is an important difference between Graeber and Karl Polanyi. In his *Great Transformation*, Polanyi famously argues that market societies are products of modernity. In order to highlight how radically different they are from what went before, he emphasizes the wide gap that separated capitalism from earlier systems of exchange in which the allocation of resources was chiefly determined by networks of redistribution and reciprocity.[10] Graeber challenges these views. He observes that many forms of what Polanyi and others have called "reciprocity" follow dynamics that in crucial regards resemble market mechanisms. Whether a sale is conducted through the exchange of one commodity for another, through a credit contract, or by handing over physical coins, what matters is that in all those cases the value of the item is precisely calculated and that after the transaction is conducted, neither the buyer nor the seller has (in principle) any further obligations vis-à-vis each other. This perspective has interesting implications. By emphasizing the similarities between different types of quantified exchange, he cuts through the debate between "primitivist" and "modernist" conceptions of ancient economy. On the one hand, Graeber's insistence that the societies of the ancient Mediterranean and Near East developed dynamic market economies (even though they lacked the forms of rationality and technologies of exchange ancient historians have long seen as preconditions for the emergence of such economies) fits well with recent research which has decisively rejected "primitivist" views of the ancient economy. On the other hand, Graeber encourages us to see the emergence of commodity markets not as a natural development (as is sometimes the case in "modernist" scholarship) but to investigate for each society the precise reasons why some fields of life came to be organized according to a strictly economic logic.

Third, if it is recognized that commodity markets do not emerge naturally or inevitably, this raises the question of why they played an ever more important role in the societies of the ancient Mediterranean and Near East. The anthropological evidence discussed by Graeber is a useful reminder that in small-scale communities where people know each other reciprocal forms of exchange usually play only a limited role; in these "human economies," precise quantification of mutual obligations is generally only necessary in the context of trade with outsiders.[11] Why then did in the ancient Mediterranean and Near East unquantifiable moral obligations transform into precisely calculable debts? Graeber suggests that the rise of territorial states which collected their taxes and paid their soldiers in metal currency played a crucial role: "By insisting that only their own coins were acceptable as fees, fines, or taxes, governments were able to overwhelm the innumerable social currencies that already existed in their hinterlands, and to establish something like uniform national markets."[12] As will be seen in the final section of this chapter, it is too simple to ascribe the spread of coinage to efforts to finance mercenary armies and imperial warfare. Nevertheless, Graeber is correct that state formation, monetization, and the expansion of markets are processes that reinforce each other. They work hand in hand because they all operate by subjecting new fields of life to a quantitative logic. By pointing to the crucial role played by public institutions in promoting reciprocal exchange, he offers a useful counterpoint to theories which see markets as the natural outgrowths of private enterprise.

After Neo-Institutionalism

In seeking to understand ancient systems of exchange from the vantage point of Graeber's anthropological theory, this book departs from the now dominant approach in economic history. Since the early 2000s, an outpouring of sophisticated new work has applied the toolkit of new institutional economics (NIE) to the societies of the ancient Mediterranean and Near East. The most influential exponent of this theory was the US economist Douglass North, who in 1995 received the prize in economic sciences of the Swedish Riksbank (often referred to as the Nobel Prize in Economics). North ascribes differences in economic performance of different societies to the efficacy of the institutions—a term that encompasses both legal rules and informal understandings—that govern them. If institutions are well designed, they facilitate the free exchange of information and goods among economic actors. A positive feedback loop ensues; as trust among market participants increases, production and exchange intensify. By contrast, if institutions are inefficient, they create information and power asymmetries between buyers and sellers. Market participants are forced to expend resources to ascertain the quality of traded goods and to ensure the enforcement of contracts; these "transactions costs" hinder exchange and economic growth.[13] In the view of North and his followers, these dynamics explain the divergent trajectory of the economies of western Europe and North America since the Industrial Revolution.[14]

As more recent scholarship has pointed out, there are problems with this simple model of the relationship between institutions and economic growth. By seeing markets and private property rights as the most efficient mechanisms for allocating resources, North naturalizes the institutions of the liberal capital-ist nation-states of his own time. Effectively, the economic order prevalent in post–Cold War North America and western Europe becomes the transhistorical measuring stick by which other economic systems are assessed. Such a teleologi-cal view prevents understanding other periods and places on their own terms.[15] NIE also does not provide much help for understanding the more recent evolu-tion of the world economy. For instance, the recent rise of East Asia and espe-cially China, where markets are more tightly regulated and public institutions control a much larger share of national wealth than in contemporary Europe and North America, sheds doubt on the view that low transaction costs and the uncompromising defense of property rights play quite the central role in facilitat-ing economic growth, as neo-institutional theory suggests.[16] In retrospect, neo-institutional economics is all too visibly the product of the triumphalist high point of neoliberal globalization in the 1990s.[17]

It might thus be expected that the application of neo-institutional economics to ancient history had unambiguously deleterious effects. However, this would be a mistaken assessment. In a discipline concerned with the interpretation of source materials that were produced in cultures that radically differ from our own, the universalizing claims made by North and his followers were always unlikely to be adopted in full. On the contrary, by providing a simple framework to make sense of the relationship between institutions and economic performance in dif-ferent societies, NIE had some beneficial effects on ancient economic history. Two developments were especially welcome. First, neo-institutional economics motivated ancient historians to enter into a dialogue with specialists in related disciplines. Most importantly, Mediterranean and Near Eastern historians began to collaborate more closely with each other. In a landmark collection, *The Ancient Economy: Evidence and Models*, Joe Manning and Ian Morris exposed the ways in which cooperation between specialist in Greek, Roman, Egyptian, and Mesopotamian history might reconfigure each of those fields.[18] More recently, Michael Jursa has systematically applied the methods of quantitative history honed in the Mediterranean to the much more densely documented regions of ancient Mesopotamia.[19]

Second, the engagement with neo-institutional economics inspired a turn toward quantification. It motivated ancient historians to harvest the wealth of evidence provided by landscape surveys and archaeological excavations, in order to trace rhythms of intensification and abatement in ancient economies. The publications of the Oxford Roman Economy project have made an array of new data sets available, which greatly refined our understanding of the ancient economy.[20] Walter Scheidel in various publications revealed the use of models derived from other premodern societies for understanding the dynamics and scale of the Roman economy.[21] Alain Bresson, by combining neo-institutional theory with a careful analysis of literary, epigraphic, and archaeological evidence, expanded and refined our understanding of the Greek systems of exchange.[22] Overall, the new focus on measuring the performance of the ancient economy made possible a more rigorous comparison with other historical periods. Rather than asking whether ancient economies were "modern" or "primitive," scholars began to explore *the degree to which* their performance resembled later systems of production, consumption, and exchange. In the introduction to the *Cambridge Economic History of the Greco-Roman World*, Ian Morris, Richard Saller, and Walter Scheidel summarize the ways in which their interpretation of ancient economic history expands on previous analyses: "It improves on substantivist approaches by providing crude statistics of economic performance, but it also goes beyond both sides in the old primitivist–modernist debate by developing general theoretical models of ancient economic behavior and putting them in a global, comparative context. It recognizes that classical antiquity saw one of the strongest economic efflorescences in premodern history, but keeps this in perspective, refusing to confuse the ancient economy with the modern."[23]

It should also be noted that the application of neo-institutional models to ancient history did *not* produce the heavily ideological narrative readers of Douglass North's oeuvre might expect. To be sure, some celebrations of the efficacy of ancient institutions and the dynamism of ancient market economies may underplay the violence and inequality that sustained these systems.[24] Yet overall, the most influential work did not depict the development of ancient market societies as an unalloyed boon. For instance, Scheidel consistently emphasizes the double-edged effects of the Roman economic miracle. While empire facilitated an unprecedented expansion of exchange systems, it also escalated inequality and had deleterious effects on human well-being.[25] Similarly, Bresson and Jursa are acutely sensitive to the predation and exploitation that made possible the Greek and Near Eastern economic efflorescences, respectively.[26] Overall then, when ancient historians incorporated NIE into their own research, they did not inevitably adopt the ideological standpoint and teleology that are implicit in the founding texts of this theory—that market exchange and robust private property rights, backed by the institutions of a liberal capitalist state, are the natural and most efficient methods to allocate resources. On the contrary, by motivating a turn toward quantification and a renewed effort to situate the Mediterranean and Near East in a larger comparative context, scholarship inspired by NIE has added insight and nuance to our understanding of ancient economies.

Nevertheless, it is unlikely that neo-institutionalism will maintain its role as the dominant paradigm in the study of premodern economies for much longer. Global warming, the financial crisis of 2007, and the coronavirus pandemic have

shaken the faith in the market as the most efficient resource allocation mechanism. At the same time, the rise of China has demonstrated that the institutions
of liberal capitalism do not provide the only road to prosperity. These developments create a demand for theories that are better suited to describe the diversity
of ways in which human systems of exchange have been organized in the past.
By reconsidering the structure of ancient systems of exchange from the vantage
point of Graeber's theory, this book hopes to contribute to such a renovation
of the field of premodern economic history. There are at least three areas of
research that would benefit from renewed attention in such a reimagining of the
discipline.

The first is the problem of ancient economic thought. By focusing on performance, neo-institutionalists managed to sidestep the difficult question of the
relationship between ancient conceptions of the economy and ancient economic
practice. As Neville Morley points out in his contribution to this volume, the
expansion of markets was made possible not only by technological or political
change but also by the emergence of new ideas of a just economic order: "we need
to pay as much attention to the complex processes whereby certain ideas are made
thinkable, the world is represented and hence perceived in new ways, and as a
result new possibilities for action and change are created."[27] Graeber's insistence
on the fundamental importance of Axial-Age thought for understanding ancient
systems of exchange is a useful counterpoint to the tendency of neo-institutional
theory to naturalize market mentalities. Here he follows a long-standing tradition in classical scholarship; not coincidentally, his account of the "Axial Age"
is inspired by the work of Leslie Kurke, Sitta von Reden, and above all Richard
Seaford.[28]

Second, since neo-institutional theory sees the emergence of markets as natural, it does not give sufficient attention to the historical processes by which markets are created and sustained. By subsuming limitations on the free purchase and
sale of goods under the catch-all heading of "transaction costs," the theory does
not fully capture the purpose and logic of such limitations. Here, too, Graeber
offers a useful counterweight. His broader theory of exchange encourages us to
reconsider the relationship of market exchange to non-reciprocal forms of interaction. Ancient historians have already begun to approach this question from
new vantage points. Nicholas Purcell, in an important chapter, has sketched the
boundary of what could and could not be sold in different ancient societies.[29]
Brent Shaw, in various studies, has made a strong case that conventional models
of economic history (all of which ultimately derive from forms of social theory
developed in late nineteenth- and early twentieth-century Europe) are not well
suited to describe the distinctive ways in which ancient systems of exchange functioned and evolved.[30] Astrid Van Oyen has used thing theory to develop a more

nuanced understanding of the role played by strictly economic logics in the circulation of goods in the Roman world.[31]

Finally, the transformative role of money is undertheorized in neo-institutional economics. Since commodity exchange is taken as natural, the theory does not properly bring into focus the ways in which the introduction of a new medium of exchange such as metal coinage reconfigures social relations more broadly. Graeber's examination of the effects of metal coinage and virtual currencies offers an interesting new perspective on this question. Recent work on silverization in the Near East, the monetization of the Roman Republic, and the currency system of the Roman Empire reveals the potential of an anthropological approach to the history of coinage in antiquity.[32] Overall, by offering new perspectives on the problem of ancient economic thought, the nature of ancient markets, and the problem of monetization, Graeber invites us to reconsider some of the most important questions in ancient economic history.

Toward a History of Value in Antiquity

Subsequent chapters test to what extent the theoretical framework developed by Graeber is helpful for writing the history of debt, money, and social obligation in the ancient Mediterranean and Near East.[33] In this section, I will sketch the arguments these contributions develop and suggest that they tell a shared story. In the next, I will explore to what extent this story can be reconciled with the arguments put forward in *Debt*.

We begin at the dawn of what Graeber calls the "Axial Age." In the first millennium BCE, Mesopotamian society came to be heavily monetized. Not only did the scope of market exchange expand but the importance of silver as a medium of exchange steadily grew. Especially from the sixth century onward, cash payments were as ubiquitous in Mesopotamia as in the Aegean world.[34] In his contribution to the volume, Reinhard Pirngruber examines the ideological effects of these transformations. More specifically, he looks at Mesopotamian economic thought through the prism of literature and business letters. In a series of close readings of cuneiform texts, he shows that responses to the expansion of the market were diverse. Especially from the sixth century onward, what we might term the beginning of the "Axial Age" in Mesopotamia, extant texts become increasingly concerned with questions of economic justice. Some claimed to reject boundless accumulation in favor of alternative forms of the good life; others incorporate profit-thinking into a new business ethics. Yet these debates cannot unproblematically be taken as evidence that moral considerations constrained the free play of economic forces. On the contrary, in contemporary business letters and archives we see that profit considerations shaped relations even between temples and within tightly knit rural communities: "these texts attest to a rather harsh attitude toward those in need, shaped by expectations of equivalence (i.e., full and immediate repayment) and profit orientation (flexible interest)."[35] Pirngruber reveals the extent to which economic logics had colonized Babylonian society.

In the same period monetization also reshaped social relations and modes of thought in the Aegean and in India. In his contribution to this volume, Richard Seaford compares the impact of this invention in both regions. He shows that in Greek city-states the structure of the cosmologies created by philosophers such as Herakleitos, Anaximander, Parmenides, and Plato parallels the structure of the monetary system. The same can be shown for India. The relationship of the individual to the cosmos is conceptualized in terms of an eternal debt, to be paid off by sacrifices carried out through Brahmin priests. The accumulation of merit (*istapurta*) between different reincarnations is conceived of in economic terms, and karma (although conceptualized in ethical terms) functions as metaphysical money. In this sense, like early Greek philosophers, so also Indian thinkers conceptualize the cosmos on the analogy of a cycle of monetized obligation. But there are important differences. In India escape from the cycle of monetized obligation is achieved through the radical renunciation of all action (or at least of monetary exchange), while in Greece it is through an inner withdrawal from emotions and corporeal desire that can be reconciled with active engagement in public affairs. Seaford's chapter exposes the ways in which the invention of metal currency shapes modes of thought in different cultures. In particular, the ways in which coinage was embedded in city-state institutions left a lasting imprint on the ways in which exchange was conceptualized in Greek culture and its offshoots. It created a distinct form of subjectivity which linked individualism and membership in a wider political community: "In Greece the state had greater stability, power, and loyalty than it did in India; and the popular need for ultimate justice was eventually met not by ethicized money but by a cosmic tribunal. This fundamental difference between India and the West is still with us."[36]

With the next chapter, we move from the later seventh and sixth centuries BCE, when coins gradually became the main medium of exchange in the Aegean world, to the fifth and fourth centuries BCE, when nearly all Greek city-states had come to be monetized and deeply integrated into inter-regional commodity markets. Moritz Hinsch points out that debt crises were surprisingly rare in this period and largely occurred in remote and economically underdeveloped regions. By contrast, in the core of the Greek world, high levels of urbanization and more division of labor gave less well-off citizens an escape route from the cycle of peasant indebtedness. These observations lead Hinsch to reject Graeber's view that strong legal protections for creditors inevitably promote social conflict. On the contrary, in the context of a highly commercialized urban economy such as Athens, the legal enforceability of debt gave non-citizen artisans and merchants access to much needed capital and protected them from attempts by politically connected debtors to avoid repayment: "The same rulers and notables who coined the term 'debt of honor' when dealing with peers would intimidate, attack, or imprison their less powerful creditors to avoid repayment."[37] Hinsch's chapter exposes an empty space in Graeber's theory of a Eurasian Axial Age. While his idea of a link between coinage, state formation, and impersonal markets works well for large territorial states and empires, it is not clear whether it is equally applicable to the city-states of classical Greece. Outside of Athens, the small size of local economies ensured that debt remained embedded in a broader network of social relations. An ideology of equality may have alleviated the most disruptive effects of monetization, at least for freeborn male citizens.

At first sight, it might be expected in the more hierarchical society of the Roman Republic that no such limits on the free play of market forces existed. After all, in the period from the third to the first centuries BCE, the conquest by Roman armies of the Mediterranean world led to the enslavement millions of human beings, large transfers of wealth to Italy, and an unprecedented accumulation of capital among elite families. Yet, as Lisa Eberle shows in her contribution, some of the same ambiguities that characterized Greek understandings of debt recur in Rome. There is a surprising contrast between the harsh treatment of the debtor in Roman law, who in case of bankruptcy would suffer *infamia* and an immediate loss of all properties, and the fact that at several historical junctures creditors were strictly prohibited from lending at interest. Eberle shows that Roman authors distinguished between two spheres: one based on self-interested market exchange, the other on disinterested relations of friendship, in which (as the Romano-Syrian mime Publilius put it) "remembering a loan would be sufficient interest."[38] But the reason for the regulation of the credit market was different than in Greece. Whereas in Greek city-states citizen solidarity often prevented debt crises to spin out of control, in Rome patron–client relationships played a more important role in securing political stability. The fact that the Roman elite was both wealthier and more powerful than its Greek counterparts made it less concerned about the ways in which monetary exchange might undermine long-standing hierarchies of honor: "the biggest threat that such exchange posed for them and their social positions— potentially depending on others—did not in fact concern them; by contrast, everyone else was always dependent on them."[39] As a result, the Roman elite managed to subsume monetary debt as one part of a larger economy of gift-giving. The ideal Roman male would be involved in relationships of reciprocity with others but only on his own terms, in such ways as to prevent any dangerous loss of independence.

Morley continues the theme of the tension in Roman economic thought between the celebration of autarky and an interest in profit maximization. He looks at Varro's *De Re Rustica*, a treatise on agriculture written at the end of the Roman Republic. It is important to keep in mind the genre of this work, which was not a technical treatise but a complex literary creation. Yet precisely because it was the product of an exalted social milieu, it provides an insight into the changing ways in which the Roman ruling class conceived of estate management: "Varro's text offers evidence not only of how Roman ideas and practices were changing in response to new economic, political, and social conditions but also of the means—above all the literary means—by which such ways of thinking could be changed."[40] As might be expected, Varro exhibits a concern for the reduction of risk and extols the parsimony of the ancients over modern prodigality. More surprisingly, he also highlights the opportunities for profit-making the trade in luxury goods offers and sees the effective sale and marketing of goods as key duties of the good household manager. Remarkably, there is also a clear developmental narrative: Varro celebrates the superiority of modern civilization over earlier pastoral forms of life. Overall, Morley's chapter corroborates Graeber's contention that market rationality was not an invention of modern capitalism but was already present in the agrarian empires of the ancient Mediterranean and Near East.

My own chapter continues the story to late antiquity. In the third and fourth centuries CE, tax rates increased, and the size of the Roman administration expanded substantially. It has often been thought that this strengthening of state power reduced the scope for market exchange. Yet recent archaeological evidence has decisively refuted such theories. In many regions of the Roman Empire, monetization and inter-regional exchange reached levels not seen in previous periods of ancient history. How to explain this apparent paradox? Graeber's insistence on the link between state formation, metal currency, and the formation of impersonal markets may help to make sense of these developments. The late antique strengthening of state power did not curb the dynamism of the Mediterranean economy but promoted an extension of market logics to new fields of life. In particular, the introduction of a new "hard" gold currency, the *solidus*, and the imposition of a unified taxation system (which treated urban and rural lands equally) promoted an increase in monetization and a further expansion of commodity markets. On this reading, the later Roman state was not a departure from but the culmination of Axial-Age patterns of empire formation and economic intensification. Yet this alliance between state and markets had unequal effects. As recent osteological evidence suggests, under Roman domination Mediterranean populations were sicker and more poorly nourished than before conquest and after the dissolution of the empire. It seems that economic intensification did not improve human well-being.

Very similar developments took place in Sasanian Iran, which Richard Payne examines in his chapter. Politically, Zoroastrianism underwrote a highly unequal social order, in which a small group of families—the Iranian ethno-class—dominated a wide range of dependents (with the same deleterious consequences on human well-being as in Rome).[41] This relationship of exploitation was legitimized through an ideology of hierarchical exchange: Rural populations gave up a share of their surplus in return for military protection and daily food rations (attested in newly discovered leather documents from Qom). Economically, this polity was the culmination of earlier Mediterranean and Near Eastern empires: A silver currency of unprecedented purity promoted monetization of unmatched depth. Credit relations played a crucial role in sustaining elite dominance. Interest-bearing credit seems to have been widespread in Iranian society, and debts to fire temples were eternal and could never be forgiven. Ideologically, Zoroastrian religion encapsulated the dual face of Axial-Age religion, based on an artificial dichotomy between body and spirit. Next to warfare, debt bondage was probably the most important source of new slaves. Zoroastrianism also illustrates Graeber's contention that Axial-Age economies create the terms for radical oppositional movements. The objective of the Mazdakite revolt, led by a group of priest-scholars in the 520s, was the introduction of what has been called "Iranian communism," a new social order based on communal ownership of property and the abolition of marriage. And Islam's rejection of luxury garments, alcohol, and interest-taking in favor of an egalitarian community of believers might be seen as a response to an exposure to the social hierarchies and stark materialism which were the hallmarks of the Iranian social order: "In imagining the egalitarian convening of the Muslim community in shared submission to a single god, dressed in simple linen or cotton, undivided by patrilineage or patrimony, we should recall what was implicitly rejected: one particular solution to the contradictions of the Iron Age, in favor of a radical alternative."[42]

Accordingly, the next two chapters turn to the early Islamic economy. The view, outlined in *Debt*, of Islam as the dynamic center of the global economy in the early medieval period fits well with recent research which has decisively proven that the first centuries of Muslim rule witnessed a remarkable economic boom. Michael Bonner explores the contribution Islam's Arabian environment made to that success. Some modern neo-institutional economists argue that Islam inhibited economic growth because it did not feature familiar features of Western capitalism, such as interest-bearing loans and firms enjoying legal personhood. Others have made the case that religion made a significant contribution to the Islamic economic miracle. Yet ultimately, it is not clear to what extent the commercial zest of early Arabs can be ascribed to religious factors. Bonner emphasizes the continuity between the forms of non-monetized generosity praised in pre-Islamic poetry and the ethos of Islamic traders. By contrast, it is not clear whether the outlawing of debt bondage had pre-Islamic precedents. It is well possible that debt servitude was widespread in the world in which Muhammad grew up, though the fragmentary nature of our sources makes it difficult to be sure: "So while the early Islamic world featured bustling markets and trade, including large-scale traffic in persons, it also set clear limits on the commodification of persons."[43]

Arietta Papaconstantinou deals with the impact of Islamic conquest on the province of Egypt through the prism of papyri. She too emphasizes the continuity between the pre-Islamic and Islamic periods; in Graeber's terminology, the caliphate was an Axial-Age polity, a state run by a military elite whose wealth was based on the extraction of gold taxes. At the same time, there was a flourishing system of microcredit which tied together men and women and a broad range of social classes and professions. Enforcement of debts was backed up by complex webs of family relations and patronage, which were especially important in periods of state weakness. But the important role played by personal relations in negotiating credit did not mean that the end result was any less oppressive. As Papaconstantinou observes, face-to-face communities can be as exploitative as the impersonal institutions of the state: "They did not, at least in the period treated here, offer a safe haven against an oppressive state: where individuals and their debts were concerned they often even represented the opposite."[44] Strikingly, Egyptian villagers perceived the representatives of the distant imperial administration often as protectors against encroachments by neighbors, relatives, and other local strongmen. Drawing on the work of Miranda Joseph,[45] Papaconstantinou suggests that Graeber's emphasis on the ways in which personal relations alleviate oppression may underplay structural violence in small-scale communities.

This raises the question of how the history of debt continued in post-Roman Europe, the one area in western Eurasia in which the coercive ability of state institutions was severely weakened and the availability of metal currency sharply declined at the end of antiquity. This question is tackled by Alice Rio in her chapter. She shows that, in line with Graeber's model, in the early Middle Ages interest-bearing credit contracts no longer were as ubiquitous as in the Roman Empire. It also seems that fewer coins were produced and virtual currencies became more important; overall, the force of the non-commercial webs of exchange which Graeber calls "human economies" strengthened. Yet it is not clear whether this led to a decline in the intensity of exploitation, at least in areas for which written sources survive; the "social currencies" employed by these new "human economies" remained convertible into cash, and the lack of coinage frequently forced those who did not have access to metal currency to take out loans from those who had. Nor did the fact that relationships of debt were more deeply embedded into local social networks make it impossible to turn human beings into commodities. On the contrary, the end of Roman state institutions also ended legal protections against the enslavement of free persons. It seems that the heritage of Axial-Age institutions influenced the character of the post-Roman world more decisively than a superficial reader of Graeber's book might expect. Elites were able to make surprisingly effective use of the tools for domination developed by the Roman Empire centuries after that empire had ceased to exist: "The early medieval example shows that the mere memory of a strong state could sometimes give elites the ability to make some of its tools and instruments of domination survive, even in spite of a near-total absence of strong institutional backing."[46]

The Currency–Slavery–Warfare Complex in Antiquity

As the previous discussion has shown, the contributors to this volume do not agree with all aspects of Graeber's historical vision. In particular, his approach does not seem well suited to explain the political economy of Greek city-states. To the hesitations expressed by Hinsch in his chapter it may be added that Graeber's framework does not adequately explain the adoption and quick spread of coinage across the Hellenic world. It is true that this new technology of exchange was invented in a territorial state, Lydia. Here it may indeed have served the purpose to pay mercenary armies, as Graeber suggests. Yet from a world historical perspective, what mattered much more was that the new medium quickly traveled west. Soon, Greek city-states issued coinage in much higher quantities than the Lydian kings ever had. Here this new medium served redistribution within the civic community, the reassertion of local identities, and inter-regional exchange. By contrast, in the large territorial empires of Persia and Carthage, which *did* employ large numbers of mercenary soldiers, coinage played a more marginal role; in fact, it was predominantly used for interactions with Greek populations. The idea that the spread of coinage was the product of imperial warfare and taxation cannot fully explain the early history of that medium in the Mediterranean.[47]

Nor are we persuaded by Graeber's vision of the European Middle Ages as a decisive rejection of Axial-Age inequalities. To be sure, there is evidence that levels of human well-being increased after the dissolution of the Roman Empire.[48] Yet in other ways, early-medieval elites proved remarkably adept at constructing out of the ruins of Roman structures of exploitation new and equally effective instruments of oppression. As Rio points out, the legal protections granted by Roman law to freeborn persons evaporated, opening up new avenues for the commodification of human beings. Also, in Egypt, the temporary weakening of state power in the wake of the Islamic conquest may not always have been beneficial for subordinate groups; as Papaconstantinou reminds us, local bigwigs were often perceived as more oppressive masters than a distant imperial administration. Graeber likely underestimates the long-term effects of the structures of domination created in the Axial Age. The empires of antiquity did not leave "clean slates" in their wake.

Yet in other ways, the theoretical framework developed by Graeber advances our understanding of the trajectory of Near East and Mediterranean economies. Three features of his historical vision seem particularly illuminating. First, Graeber's emphasis on differences which separate the monetized market economies of the "Axial Age" from less intensive modes of exchange in the preceding period has been vindicated by recent research. Metal currency and a steep rise in the intensity of inter-regional exchange distinguish not only Greek city-states of the classical period from the dark-age polities that preceded them but also the Roman Empire from its successor states. As Michael Jursa, Robertus van der Spek, and Reinhard Pirngruber have shown, similar differences mark out the economy of the Neo-Babylonian and Achaemenian Empires from the much less monetized polities that preceded them.[49] However, the medium of exchange in these regions was not coinage but weighted silver; as Sitta von Reden points out, there were two cash traditions in ancient Eurasia, of which only one was based on coinage, the other on uncoined precious metal.[50] If this is recognized, it becomes clear that from the seventh century BCE onward Mesopotamian cities reached the same level of "deep" monetization as the most monetized Greek and Roman cities.[51] In this sense, Graeber was correct to observe that there is a link between the formation of impersonal markets, the creation of large territorial states, and the spread of metal currencies. Also, from the perspective of his theory, it is not surprising that many territorial states preferred bullion as a medium of exchange. Even more than coinage, which usually only served as legal tender in the restricted territory of a city-state, unstamped metal was the impersonal medium of exchange par excellence: "an object without a history, valuable because one knows it will be accepted in exchange for other goods just about anywhere, no questions asked."[52]

Second, the volume shows that Graeber's idea of a "military–slavery–currency" complex provides a useful analytic for highlighting key features which connect the political economy of different Axial-Age states. Recent research in the comparative history of ancient empires has rightly highlighted the role played by warfare and slavery in shaping not only the extractive but also the knowledge economies of ancient empires.[53] Graeber's theory encourages ancient historians to look more closely at the ways in which the introduction of metal currencies and the expansion of market exchange contributed to underwrite the capacity of ancient states. Among the polities examined in this volume, this process is particularly visible in the empires of Rome, Iran, and early Islam. But the same could be shown for the Near Eastern and Hellenistic states that preceded them. For example, in the Neo-Babylonian Empire of the sixth century BCE, the influx of silver from subject territories facilitated the emergence of a highly monetized market economy, powered by a mix of servile, dependent, and wage labor;[54] in third-century BCE Egypt, the imposition of Greek-style coinage, backed up by a complex credit and banking system, led to an explosion of debt among cash-poor rural populations but made the ruling dynasty and the state elite fantastically wealthy.[55] All of these economies featured the same potent combination of metal currencies, coercive labor practices, and dynamic systems of exchange. The recurrence of this pattern corroborates Graeber's suggestion that there is a deeper affinity between marketization and state formation.

Third, the contributors to this volume highlight the cultural consequences of the emergence of dynamic market societies. Across the Mediterranean and Near East, the invention of money and the intensification of exchange promoted the application of market-based rationality to new social fields. The quantification of social life promoted by monetization left a lasting imprint on Greek conceptions of the cosmos. The Roman Empire witnessed an intensification of this pattern. As microcredit and debt slavery became regular features of Mediterranean and Near Eastern countrysides, intellectuals developed new theories to allow landowners to reconcile profit-oriented management with long-standing ideals of autarky; as Morley observes in his chapter, "The rise of the impersonal market, integrated (however imperfectly) into wider regional and transregional networks and driven by the expansion of the Roman Empire, goes hand in hand with the rise of instrumental and profit-orientated thinking."[56] Also in Iran, a materialist cosmology justified wealth accumulation by an ultra-wealthy agrarian elite. By contrast, the rise of universal religions had an unequal impact on both empires. In Rome, Christianity (drawing on the language of Greek philosophy developed at the beginning of the Axial Age) accommodated itself surprisingly easily to imperial institutions, whereas the Iranian Empire and the Arabian Peninsula witnessed the emergence of oppositional movements which contested the economic order in the name of more egalitarian religious ideals.

Overall then, this volume suggests that Graeber's anthropological theory may deepen our understanding of the economic history of the ancient Mediterranean and Near East. By exploring the wider social and cultural effects of the vibrant commodity markets whose functioning recent ancient historical research has so clearly delineated, he extends our field of historical vision into new areas.

2
─────────

Beyond Debt

MARKETS AND MORALITY IN FIRST-MILLENNIUM BCE BABYLONIA

Reinhard Pirngruber

Introduction: The Rise of Markets in Babylonia, c. Sixth Century BCE

To this day, the role of the market as transactional mode and its impact on society is a contentious issue in the field of ancient Near Eastern studies. For Babylonia during the second half of the first millennium BCE, that is, the period of the Neo-Babylonian (626–539), Achaemenid (539–330), and Seleucid (c. 304–141) Empires, recent scholarships agrees on a comparatively important scope for markets. In particular, this is the case for the "long sixth century BCE," that is, the roughly 150 years between the establishment of the Neo-Babylonian dynasty in 626 and the failed uprisings against Achaemenid rule under King Xerxes (484), the repression of which led to significant changes in the country's socioeconomic configurations.[1] In a nutshell, the underlying dynamics can be characterized as follows: Military success in Syria and the Levant brought enormous quantities of booty and tribute in silver and (to a lesser extent) other precious metals into Babylonia. These spoils of empire—together with a stable and peaceful political situation, the Persian takeover in 539 BCE notwithstanding—were the basis for a period of sustained economic growth in the imperial center as they were immediately fed back into the economy. In the words of one authority, "[p]rofiting from state-controlled investment in the agrarian infrastructure and generally lavish state spending, population growth and a concomitant process of urbanization set in motion (and were in turn sustained by) a positive feedback cycle in the economy. This led to an increase in demand and to an increase in aggregate as well as per capita production.

Reinhard Pirngruber, *Beyond Debt* In: *Debt in the Ancient Mediterranean and Near East*. Edited by: John Weisweiler, Oxford University Press. © Oxford University Press 2023. DOI: 10.1093/oso/9780197647172.003.0002

Urbanization allowed an increasing division of labour and economic specialization, and thus led to higher productivity."[2] Thus, one central mechanism by which the (forcibly) accumulated capital was fed back into the economy was via salaries for labor power for state-financed building projects, including temple renovations and palace-building—a prime example being Nebuchadnezzar's magnificent buildings in Babylon—but also works of what one can (somewhat anachronistically) term public infrastructure, in particular canals, including the *nār šarri*, the "royal canal," connecting the Euphrates and Tigris Rivers. These canals not only were all-important for the country's agricultural regime—mainly barley farming and increasingly date horticulture—but also served as cheap transport routes for bulky goods, thus facilitating the region's economic integration. As regards taxation in Babylonia, the crown mainly resorted to those which it could rather easily target (in the sense of availability), urban elites, and especially temple households and was primarily interested in labor service for the aforementioned building projects as well as army service.[3] As it soon became practice to hire other persons (usually of modest social standing) to perform these corvée duties against remuneration, this system of taxation indirectly contributed to the increasing monetization of the country. In order to have enough liquid assets for hiring these substitute laborers, temples embarked on the course of agricultural specialization, increasing their productivity by producing cash crops for the market; the Ebabbar temple in the north Babylonian town of Sippar, for example, expanded its date orchards on a massive scale. One result of these processes was that silver was available in smaller denominations—the smallest unit attested in texts is the *hallūru* (lit. "[chick?] pea") of one-fortieth of a shekel (of 8.33 grams)—and even came to play a significant role in the temples' internal economy. Also, the institutional framework of the period fostered the development of a monetized market, with the emergence of new contract types, various provisions designed to protect creditors in case of default, and especially state guarantees for silver quality (e.g., in the form of stamp marks on ingots). The rich price data from Babylonia corroborate the comparative importance of the market in this period, exhibiting expected patterns such as seasonal fluctuation (i.e., rising prices throughout the harvest year, with peaks immediately preceding the new harvest, when prices dropped steeply) and reactions to political events, natural disasters, and the amount of specie in circulation.

David Graeber and the Economy of the Ancient Near East

While the existence of price-setting mechanisms shaping the interplay of supply and demand in particular in the sphere of commodities is no longer doubted, it is oftentimes asserted that the economic relevance of market exchange and the number of people affected by its mechanisms were ancillary at best. A good example is R. Nam's review of the present author's monograph on the Babylonian economy in the fourth to second centuries BCE. In this book, I analyzed a series of price observations for a standardized group of basic goods, including the food staples barley and dates, from a corpus of cuneiform records. One conclusion was that market efficiency—that is, the capacity of the market to respond to sudden shocks in supply or demand—was fairly high in Babylonia during the late Achaemenid and Seleucid periods by preindustrial standards. Yet, Nam cautions that these data convey "a very limited perspective of the ancient economy" only and that the economic realities they describe may not be representative for the everyday experience in particular in rural areas.[4]

This stance echoes earlier views expounded by scholars like Marc van de Mieroop, who advise against the use of contemporary economic theory to shed light on ancient economies because of the latter's embeddedness in society.[5] Of course, such assessments (as well as the terminology employed) reflect Karl Polanyi's influential typology of economic interaction preceding market exchange, viz. reciprocity prevailing among symmetrical peer groups and usually located with peasant communities beyond the reach of the market, on the one hand, and the redistribution of centralizing large-scale households, mostly temples and palaces, on the other. Polanyi's classification certainly has the potential to generate exciting insights when sensibly employed as a heuristic framework, rather than as a description of social realities.[6] Yet, as in the example given above, it is mostly in the latter sense that Polanyi's ideas are invoked and in contexts that aim at diminishing the importance of the market. It is hardly surprising, then, that outsiders to the field often tend to minimize the relevance of the market in the ancient Near East. In particular, this is the case with classicists pursuing the agenda of exalting the uniqueness of the Greco-Roman world. According to Alain Bresson, for example, the key difference between free-trading Greece and a largely tributary Near East was indeed the near absence of markets.[7]

It speaks volumes of David Graeber's historical acumen that he entirely sidesteps the rather sterile dispute between formalists and substantivists concerning which mode of exchange predominated during what period. His own classification of human interaction—laid out under the title "A Brief Treatise on the Moral Grounds of Economic Relations"—modifies Polanyi's scheme by shifting the focus away from principles of exchange and toward the underlying moral principles underlying social action conceived as a series of dyadic relationships.[8] He thus distinguishes between (baseline) communism, hierarchy, and exchange. These, importantly, cannot be mapped one by one on Polanyi's scheme.

"Communism" as a moral principle is "reciprocal only in the sense that both sides are equally disposed to help one another; there is no feeling that accounts ought to balance out at any given moment—in part, because there's no assumption that such relations will ever end."[9] "Hierarchy" governs unequal relationships; rather than reciprocity, the defining logic is that of precedent (although the relationship may be represented on the ideological plane as reciprocal, a case in point is spiritual guidance provided by priests or the protection granted by armed lords in exchange for a share in the harvest).[10] Finally, three key elements characterize "exchange": an assumption of a fundamental equality between the partners involved, the acceptance that the relationship is temporary and can be canceled at will, and, most importantly, equivalence as an underlying moral principle, implying a constant concern for quantification and valuation. A fourth element is the potential for competitive behavior that is inherent in exchange, which threatens to undermine the autonomous status of each partner. Market exchange is thus just one manifestation of the principle of exchange, "a certain form of immediate, balanced, impersonal, self-interested transactions that we call 'commercial exchange.'"[11] In his account of the origins of debt, the expansion of the logics of exchange during the Axial Age, which furthered trends such as commodification and rational calculation (including profit orientation) and was predicated on warfare on an imperial scale, plays a key role.

Graeber's paradigm shift has important consequences. When one starts conceiving of exchange as a "constant process of interaction tending toward equivalence," a whole new set of research perspectives emerges.[12] First, such an approach invites us to gauge the relevance of (market) exchange not merely by looking at the way business was conducted according to legal records or, conversely, according to their absence. A frequent "argument" for the restricted domain of (market) exchange in this regard is an alleged lack of monetization on the countryside—as if only specie were proper money as opposed to undoubtedly more frequent and sometimes informal credit arrangements.[13] Rather, one expects that if exchange indeed played a large role in everyday life, then its constituting morality—the expectations of equivalence, interaction characterized by competition, etc.—will find expression in a diverse array of textual sources, including letters and literary works. Second, Graeber's conceptualization of communism, exchange, and hierarchy as modes of social interaction, rather than successive stages of economic relations, each governed by its own moral rationale, allows for a fine-grained analysis of different logics exhibited by the same persons in varying social contexts. In particular, this is relevant in moments of crisis, when large-scale indebtedness brought about shifts in the mode of social interaction between debtors and creditors. Hence, while debt fundamentally has its roots in the logics of exchange, as an arrangement between persons of (at least in theory) equal standing, while the debt is outstanding, the relationship between debtor and creditor gravitates toward a relationship marked by hierarchy.[14]

Communal Values versus Ethics of Reciprocity in Literary Texts

In this contribution, I would like to test the implications of Graeber's approach by investigating the permeation of society with expectations of reciprocity and equivalence as well as the "radical simplification of motives" entailed by the diffusion of a mindset concerned with quantification and pursuit of self-interest in order to shed light on prevailing economic mentalities.[15] To this purpose, I will discuss the conception of modes of social interaction in a variety of textual sources from Mesopotamia, in particular literary texts. My approach to these hitherto underexplored sources is to read them as Geertzian "thick descriptions" of the societies from which they emanate, as "structures for the accumulation, transformation, representation, and communication of social energies and practices."[16] This contribution aims thus at providing a complementary perspective to the essays in a rather recent volume on the topic of debts (Hudson and van de Mieroop 2002), which provides a chronologically arranged overview and discussion of mainly archival sources (i.e., documents emanating from the sphere of economic practice) from the mid-third millennium BCE down to the Achaemenid period.

Before going in medias res, a word on chronology is in order. While most of the actual tablets discussed in this section date to the centuries between c. 800 and 200 BCE—roughly corresponding to the first half of the Axial Age that features so prominently in Graeber's account—it is clear that in some instances the texts, and the values reflected therein, have their roots in the (later) Bronze Age. As we will see, this is in particular the case with proverbs and popular sayings. Also, considering the social locus of literary production in Mesopotamia, tied to the structurally conservative institutional households of palace and temple, a favorable attitude toward the ethics of hierarchy as well as a hesitant stance toward the ethics of exchange can be expected.

A good starting point for our purpose is the disputation poem *iškar šēlebi*, the "Series of the Fox," which enjoyed high popularity in first-millennium BCE Babylonia and Assyria but likely was composed during the Old Babylonian period already.[17] Due to the fragmentary state of the text, the narrative is somewhat elusive. A recent reconstruction tentatively postulates that the fox has stolen something from the lion, subsequently incriminating the wolf with the deed.[18] The fox and the wolf seem then to stand trial before the god Šamaš, and a prominent role is assigned to the dog, who is clearly an enemy of both the wolf and the fox.

Interesting for our purposes is the description of the fox as a cunning rap-scallion. In addition to expected adjectives like *sarru* ("false," "dishonest") and *emqu* ("clever"), there is a curious passage on a fragment from the Nineveh library (c. seventh century BCE), which reads *ištēn šiqil tumtaṭṭi ebirka ana* [x], "you demand (payment of) even one shekel from your friend for/to [x]."[19] The context of this phrase is a negative characterization (likely) of the fox by (likely) the wolf, who in the preceding lines is accused as a slanderer and trickster. The line under discussion is a complaint about his miserliness toward friends (*ebru*). The underlying ethical rationale is evident: One was expected to be generous with one's immediate social peers, to exhibit the behavior Graeber characterized as (baseline) communism. The fox, conversely, keeps a record of every favor granted, of every loan extended no matter how petty the sum. Worse, he conceives of his favors in terms of debt and insists on repayment; he expects interactions even with friends to cancel out. This passage thus depicts thinking in terms of equivalences as inappropriate in the context of amicable relationships, yet it must have been current enough for the author to expect the audience to recognize the fox's violation of the social code.

A second passage on a tablet from the city of Babylon and dating to the Hellenistic period provides further food for thought.[20] The best-preserved section of the tablet contains an inner monologue of the fox; the setting is a narrow escape from the claws of the dog, who beleaguers the escapees in their hiding place:

14: ... lū īdêma lā ūṣâmma lū abīt ina hurrīa
　　Had I known . . . I would not have gone out, I would have stayed in my hole
17: ēteriška Enlil kī mešrê balāṭa
　　I implore you, Enlil, instead of riches give me well-being
18: kīma zitte kurummate napišta [qīša]
　　Instead of profit and rations, [give me] life.

In lines 17 and 18, the fox, happy to have come away with his life, prays to Enlil, the supreme deity of the Mesopotamian pantheon during the Old Babylonian period and vows to renounce prosperity in exchange for his life. The terminology employed is revealing, as is the entire set-up of the prayer. The fox identifies different sources of wealth. In line 18, *zittu* and *kurummatu* are named; these terms are not synonymous but describe the types of gain to be made beyond the confines of one's hearth (see the reference to the fox regretting having left his den in line 14). The latter designates income accruing to dependents of institutional households and usually takes the form of food allowances, mostly barley or flour and/or dates; additionally, sesame oil and clothing could be issued under this designation.[21] *Zittu*, on the other hand, literally translates as "share" (e.g., in an inheritance) and in this passage more likely refers to shares in profits from a business venture. It is in this sense that the word also regularly appears in another genre of literary texts, namely omen treatises. CT 40 48: 4–5 reads, for example, "If a man embarks on a business journey and a falcon passes from the man's left to the right and then turns back: wherever he goes, this man will make [lit.: eat] profit, the heart will be happy."[22] The word used in the preceding line, *mašrû*, is confined to literature and omen texts—contrary to *zittu* and *kurummatu*, which occur regularly in legal and administrative records—and is sometimes juxtaposed with *dumqu* ("good luck"; the absence of wealth is conversely marked by *lumnu*, "bad luck," "sadness"). *Mašrû* is often said to be bestowed upon someone by a god. The expression refers thus less to wealth that is earned by one's business proficiency or hard work and more to wealth that is gained by divine favor; it is the wealth that is allotted as one's fate and, as such, is distinct from *zittu* and *kurummatu*, rather than an umbrella term of sorts that is then defined more closely by these terms.[23] Summing up, the author of the fable was aware of different ways to make a living that each pertained to a different sphere of the social fabric. With a pinch of scholarly license, one may state that the terms employed in this story, *mašrû*, *zittu*, and *kurummatu*, are located in Graeber's categories of (baseline) communism, exchange, and hierarchy, respectively.

A second piece of wisdom literature, the "Dialogue of Pessimism"[24] between a master and his slave is, in spite of its satirical content, equally revealing as regards the reach of the logics of exchange. The text, which likely was composed in the late second or early first millennium BCE, shows a master considering several undertakings, each of which is encouraged by his slave. However, after each resolution, the master changes his mind and suggests engaging in an opposite venture, for which he likewise receives the slave's approval. The piece ends with a somber statement on life's futility. At one point in the dialogue, the master suggests engaging in credit lending:

> Listen to me, slave—Here I am, my master, here I am.—I will extend (loans) as a creditor.—Extend (loans), my master, extend (loans), (for) the man, who extends loans as creditor: his grain is still his grain, and his interest is abundant.—No, slave, I will not extend loans as a creditor.—Do not extend (loans), my master, do not extend (loans). Extending loans is like loving a woman, but getting them back is like giving birth to children. They will eat your grain and permanently revile you; and they will deny you the interest on your grain.

The passage contains one of the earliest instances of the literary motive of the urban usurer exploiting the hardship of peasants by making consumption loans at interest. This reading is confirmed by an alternative version of these lines, according to which the master loans explicitly "food allowances to the country" (*ipru ana māti*) at interest.

Above all, the passage illustrates the intrusion of profit-oriented thinking into small-scale agricultural economies of rural communities. The pernicious impact of this development is best exemplified by the famous debt remissions (*andurārum*) decreed by several Mesopotamian kings, in particular during the Old Babylonian period (c. first half of the second millennium BCE) but with forerunners in the Sumerian world already during the mid-third millennium BCE.[25] In the following section, I will discuss in more detail the ramifications of this trend under the changed circumstances prevailing in the first millennium BCE, namely increased monetization and concomitant greater reliance on market mechanisms as well as rule by a foreign dynasty, dispensing with these alleviations for the indebted peasantry.

For now, let us return to the role of the master and his mentality and consider the socioeconomic background of the text. It is significant that the one economic activity that comes to the mind of this urban notable is that of a moneylender/creditor to indebted farmers. During the economically vibrant "long sixth century BCE," moneylending was an ancillary activity only; according to one authority, "money-lending was [not] a ubiquitous economic phenomenon; in fact, evidence for money-lending as truly independent business, rather than an occasional activity is not very frequent."[26]

A couple of centuries earlier, on the other hand, at the turn of the second to the first millennium BCE—the approximate date of composition of the "Dialogue of Pessimism"—Babylonia had tumbled into an extended period of crisis, possibly as a consequence of worsening climatic conditions. Politically, the country was under the sway of its more powerful northern neighbor, Assyria, and had to cope with inner tensions between towns and countryside (i.e., semi-nomadic pastoralists). Economically, the period was marked by harvest failures and famines; an additional problem, and a grave one, seems to have been the shifting courses of important canals. All of these factors worked together to bring about a process of significant demographic decline and de-urbanization.[27] It comes as no surprise, then, that the master in the dialogue chose a rather conservative outlet for his surplus, rather than engaging in more risky operations such as long-distance trade, strategic cash crop production, or large-scale commercialization of agricultural goods.[28]

There is one reference to the world of trade in this dialogue, which confirms the impression of a stagnant economy at the time of its composition. When discussing with his slave the matter of whether or not to show reverence to the gods, the slave suggests that a devout man has "a happy heart, he will make loan upon loan" (*qīpta eli qīpti ippuš*). The word employed denotes a "commercial interest-bearing loan"; however, we are dealing with an anachronism here, as the *qīptu* (ŠU.LÁ) was prominent in particular in business records of the Old Babylonian and Old Assyrian periods.[29] Rather than describing actual economic practice, these lines refer to physical integrity, happiness, and prosperity in general terms.[30] Yet, the underlying sentiment shows the deep inroads commercial thinking had made into society already during the later Bronze Age: Proper behavior, in the sense of religious piety, came with the prospect of financial rewards.

What this reading of the dialogue thus implies is that, contrary to a recurrent assumption in particular in Marxist-inspired scholarship, times of weak states do not necessarily entail greater freedom for the rural population.[31] On the contrary, the dependence on wealthy urbanites whose power was no longer curtailed by a state authority—in the form of the above-mentioned *andurārum*-debt releases and similar others—may have rather exacerbated their economic plight. Rather than benign *doux commerce*, times of precarious external (economic as well as political) circumstances acted as catalysts in the process of the expansion of the logics of exchange. Incidentally, this also potentially bears on Graeber's chronological framework, in particular with regard to his all too neat distinction between the Axial Age, characterized by the preponderance of large predatory empires, and the ensuing Middle Ages, when the collapse of these empires "could only be seen as an extraordinary improvement over the terrors of the Axial Age" for most of the world's population.[32] This point is further elaborated in the contributions to this volume by Arietta Papaconstantinou (Chapter 10) and Alice Rio (Chapter 11), with the former (following the critical review of *Debt* by Miranda Joseph) taking issue with Graeber's overtly benign notion of "community" in her discussion of debt relations according to early medieval papyri from Egypt and the latter emphasizing the potentially grave risks of indebtedness in the absence of a regulatory state authority in medieval Europe.

As the third and final text, or rather text genre, I would like to discuss some of the current proverbs and popular sayings. Such texts rank among the most ancient examples of literary activity but enjoyed widespread popularity well into the first millennium BCE—cue the biblical book of Proverbs. The examples discussed below are found on cuneiform tablets recovered from the remnants of the famous library of the Neo-Assyrian king Assurbanipal (seventh century BCE) in Nineveh. The proverbs of this collection were recorded in both Sumerian and Assyrian,[33] and one important aspect they deal with is proper social behavior. Central values held in high esteem are modesty ("The wise man is girded with a loin-cloth. The fool is clad in a scarlet cloth"), piety ("Be you small or great, it is [your] god who is your support"), and loyalty ("Seeing you have done evil to your friend, what will you do to your enemy?"). The last aspect is of particular relevance, and some sayings betray a sense of Graeberian baseline communism: "When you are humiliated, let (your) friend act" is a reminder of one's embeddedness in a social web and of the importance of being able to rely on the latter in times of need.

Yet, also in these collections, profit-oriented thinking rears its head, attesting to the complex interplay of the different modes of social interaction. One saying from this collection resumes the juxtaposition of financial reward and religious piety: "When you have seen the profit of reverencing (your) god, you will praise (your) god and salute the king." The word translated as "profit," *nēmelu*, in its most frequent usage denotes specifically gains from business ventures. A proverb adopting the view of a woman puts the importance of affluence more bluntly: "Who is wealthy? Who is rich? For whom shall I reserve my vulva?"[34] And another saying uses a metaphor from the commercial world to caution against unnecessary expenses: "Do you pay out money [for] a pig's squeak?"[35] At the end of the day, however, adherence to society's mores trumps opulence: "It is not wealth that is your support. It is (your) god." Finally, also elements of hierarchy are present in this text, and the compilers leave no doubt that kingship is a desirable institution: "A people without a king (is like) sheep without a shepherd"; and obedience is owed to authorities: "Recognize the overlord; recognize the king; respect the vizier." To sum up, these sayings embody a worldview according to which wealth is desirable, yet the honoring of social conventions—both vis-à-vis government and in one's immediate social environment—is the indispensable glue that keeps society together.

Not addressed so far has been the question of chronology, to wit: Are there palpable differences between the proverb collections from the Neo-Assyrian period and their forerunners from the Middle Bronze Age, most prominently the Old Babylonian era? While an in-depth inquiry of the matter is beyond the scope of the present essay, a first glance at the source material at our disposal (Alster 1997) is promising and points indeed to an even stronger appreciation of "(baseline) communism," paired with reluctance toward the ethics of exchange for the earlier period. More than material riches, it is the family that emerges as the ultimate font of one's fortune: "He who does not support a wife, he who does not support a child, is not raised to prosperity."[36] The world of commerce is depicted in unanimously negative terms. Merchants are not only accused of greed for both produce and silver ("How the merchant carried the silver away, and how he carried the barley away") but, more strikingly, considered unsuitable for striking social relationships: "A man should not take a merchant for his friend."[37] Interesting from the perspective of cultural history is also Alster (1997,

19, no. 174), attesting to the primacy of producers over those engaged in distribution of basic necessities: "Things are traded in the city but (it was) the fisher-
men (that) caught the food supply." Conversely, greed in the face of friendship is
frowned upon: " 'Let my bread be left over, let me eat your bread!' Will this endear
a man to the household of his friend?"[38] Another important saying acknowledges
the impossibility of full equivalency and the dependence on one's social circle
in times of need: "You don't return borrowed bread." The opposition between
social value and purely economic costs is also inherent in another proverb: "He
who destroy houses destroys silver. He who destroy a house destroys gold."[39] In
my interpretation, the plural in the first sentence refers to houses as economically
valuable objects, while the singular refers to the household as the center of one's
identity, the destruction of which has graver consequences than mere financial
loss—expressed as the difference between silver and gold, the latter "a medium
capable of signalling qualities of purity and the sacred, highly valued in ancient
Mesopotamia" (Winter 2012, 161). A final example of this dichotomy I would
like to discuss reads "May you hold a kid [i.e., a young goat] in your right arm
and may you hold a bribe in your left arm." The proverb plays with the opposition between the positively connoted right side and the left side carrying negative
associations: While the former carries a ritually pure sacrificial animal, the latter
brings a profane payment, likely to the temple staff.[40]

Hence, as a conclusion to this exploratory investigation, one might suggest
that both the early second millennium and first millennium BCE proverb collections share a worldview that holds piety toward the divine and care for one's
immediate social surroundings in highest esteem. However, the earlier texts display a hostility toward the world of commerce that is absent from the later collections, where it is replaced by a tentative integration into society's social and
ethical framework. Tablets from the period in between, the Late Bronze Age,
show a similar tension between (baseline) communism and exchange. While
they do not outright condemn business activity, the few extant examples are still
rather suspicious in tone. A tablet from the Hittite capital Hattuša (Boghazköy),
for example, contrasts the stability of a life in one's *oikos* led in modesty ("My
well does not tire [of giving water]; my thirst is not excessive") with the perils
of trade ("I have gone shares in business; loss is unending").[41] To close this section, I would like to discuss a saying that is found in both the Old Babylonian
and the Neo-Assyrian corpora: "Friendship lasts only one day, but collegiality
is everlasting."[42] Rather than a celebration of an ethos based on purely rational
calculation—with morality replaced by impersonal arithmetic, in Graeberian
(2011, 14) terms—this proverb is an expression of a society in which social mobility is difficult to achieve: One's peer group is unlikely to change during one's
lifetime.

And in Letters and Business Archives from First-Millennium BCE Babylonia

The analysis of literary texts has shown that these writings provide us with unexpected insight into customs and norms regulating social interaction on the normative level. Although they are to some extent ahistorical (for lack of a better term), in that they are both difficult to pinpoint in time and consist moreover of several layers of transmission that are often difficult to isolate, it seems possible to make a case for a wider dispersion of the ethics of exchange during the first millennium BCE, that is, the Iron Age that plays such a seminal role in Graeber's account of the development of debts. In the current section, I wish to proceed to an investigation of current actualizations of the abstract principles formulated in the literature on the basis of the rich corpus of epistolographic and archival sources from Babylonia in the Neo-Babylonian and Achaemenid periods.

One point of concern here that echoes Graeber's "simplification of motive" is the occasional explicit reference to financial rewards in exchange for services rendered. The relevance of material wealth is also epitomized in sayings like "A man who owns silver counts it daily."[43] One of the terms employed, *šugarrû*, is of particular interest, also from the point of view of etymology.[44] *Šugarrû* is a so far unidentified product obtained from dates and originally designated a delivery that had to be paid by tenants of date orchards in addition to the rent payment. Yet over time the word acquired a secondary meaning of a gift that was payable to officials and intermediaries for the purpose of obtaining their favor. For example, in a letter from the Egibi business archive, the writer and current head of the family Iddin-Marduk instructs his son Marduk-rēmanni as well as two slave-agents with respect to their dealings with a certain Lū-ahū'a: "Whatever Lū-ahū'a tells you (to do), you will carry out against a *šugarrû*-gift (only)." It is also clear that some of the *šugarrû* payments mentioned are bribes.[45] Another example from a letter has an agent complaining to his superior about the latter's failure to provide one Nabû-balāssu-iqbi with a gift (*nuptû*), exhorting him to dispatch immediately barley or cress so that "my lord may have his wish granted."[46]

Letters from the first millennium BCE are also to a much stronger degree concerned with quantification, compared to their counterparts from the old Babylonian period. Texts dating to the reign of Cambyses show just how concerned temple officials of the Eanna temple in Uruk were with regional price differences, tracking the amounts of barley and dates one shekel of silver could buy throughout Babylonia.[47] Yet, the most striking aspect of these texts are the ethics of reciprocity that are quite clearly spelled out: Favors granted are stressed in often emotional language; the expectation of mutuality is evident.[48] The letter (Hackl, Jursa, and Schmidl 2014, no. 142) combines all of the elements just discussed: The writer, Nidintu, informs one Kidinnu concerning his designs as to a house in Babylon. To facilitate some unspecified upcoming proceedings, he offers the *sukkallu*, a high-ranking legal official, a "rich gift" (*šugarrû rabû*) and is assured in exchange of the latter's assistance. He then requests Kidinnu to appear in person before him with the conspicuous sum of twenty minas of silver. Anticipating resistance on the part of Kidinnu, he continues: "If you say: 'Why should I bow to your wish?'—I will hold your favour up to the heavens." Hence, the writer assumes, or rather makes explicit, that his correspondent will act first and foremost in expectation of his own benefits, rather than out of solidarity with a social peer (he is addressed as *ahu*, "brother," in the letter's introductory greeting formula). In the present instance, this advantage takes the form of increased reputation, hence social capital—the highest good in a society where social prestige and honor (and its opposite, shame) were the key determinants of one's social identity.[49]

I would like to conclude this contribution with a few remarks on the topic of rural indebtedness and the complex interplay between ethics of exchange, debts, and hierarchization. The archive of the Murašû family from the town of Nippur dating to the late Achaemenid period—roughly the last quarter of the fifth century BCE, hence the reigns of Artaxerxes I and Darius II—is our most informative witness in this regard.[50] The Murašûs, represented by Enlil-šum-iddin and his nephew Rēmūt-Ninurta, were a family of entrepreneurs with two distinct emphases in their business portfolio: first, the advancement of credit mainly for the purpose of tax payments to small-scale holders of agricultural "fiefs" and, second, the subletting of lands at their disposal, often pledges by insolvent debtors. A handful of documents explicitly sheds light on the highly commercialized ethics prevailing also in the rural economy. According to the promissory note BE 10 121, for example, a rather small quantity of barley (three *kurru*s and three *qa*, i.e., 543 liters) was given as a loan via middlemen to one Marduka, son of Rībat. The document further stipulates that the loan was to be squared according to the "tariff of the land" (*nishu ša māti*), very likely a standardized but potentially variable interest rate.[51] The dates recorded in the document are telling: The debt was contracted in month I in the seventh year of Darius II (c. April 417 BCE), that is, in the immediate pre-harvest period. Repayment was to take place not even a month later, in month II of the same year (i.e., May 417 BCE) and thus during the harvest period. This chronological pattern is shared by related documents (PBS 2/1 108, 110, 127 and 204; likely also Stolper 1985, no. 84), all of which are short-term (consumption) loans stipulating repayment according to the *nishu ša māti* in month II—the month of the barley harvest.[52] Also, the social locus of these texts is telling as in one instance (PBS 2/1 108) the creditor is Rībat, a slave-agent of the Murašûs. Hence, these loans also took place at the fringes of the Murašûs' activities, both socially—several steps further down the social ladder—and geographically. Far from solidarity within rural communities based on principles such as "From each according to his ability, to each according to his needs" (see Graeber 2011, 94), these texts attest to a rather harsh attitude toward those in need, shaped by expectations of equivalence (i.e., full and immediate repayment) and profit orientation (flexible interest). As I have dealt with the pertinent phenomena—forced labor of insolvent debtors in the *bīt kīli* (workhouse-prison), submission of debtors to a patron–client relationship in exchange for protection against exaggerated claims (*pirku*)—elsewhere in more detail (Pirngruber 2017, 59–66), suffice it here to point out that they fully vindicate Graeber's key point that such market relations predicated upon an assumption of (at least notional) equality have the potential to transform economic power into social power, thereby establishing relationships of hierarchy.[53]

Coda

It goes without saying that the present contribution is just a first step toward a more comprehensive approach to the influence of different modes of social interaction on economic mentalities, on society's social (and legal) framework, and on the creation and development of economic institutions. Yet I hope to have shown the potential inherent in an analysis of social norms and values and their manifestations in the spheres of production and distribution based on those texts that at first glance touch upon pertinent matters in only an ancillary manner. As one authority reminded us in a recent essay, the potential of approaching a literary text as a "true reflection of the social matrix . . . has not so far been used in a really focused manner."[54]

3

Cosmic Debt in Greece and India

Richard Seaford

IN SIXTH-CENTURY BCE Greece there occurred a revolution in metaphysics, in the thought of the so-called Presocratic philosophers. At about the same time there occurred a remarkably similar metaphysical revolution in India. The similarities and differences between these two revolutions are the theme of my recent monograph (Seaford 2020), in which I demonstrate that a key factor in both revolutions was pervasive *monetization*, which was in this era not yet occurring anywhere else in the world (except for China, which accordingly also underwent a metaphysical revolution). David Graeber in his book on debt discusses *cosmic debt* generally and in ancient India. My tribute to his memory consists of extending the argument of his book, and of mine, into the theme of cosmic debt in ancient Greece, which so far as I know has never been studied—unsurprisingly, for even its existence is not obvious.

A preliminary note on the ancient texts is in order. For Greece, my main focus is Presocratic philosophy (though I also adduce Plato), which was produced in the sixth and fifth centuries BCE. All that survives of it is in fragments (and descriptions) preserved by later authors. For India, I will use the Vedic texts known as Brahmanas and Upanishads, which derive from the tradition of comment on the performance of sacrifice, although the Upanishads in particular have developed for the most part into what we might call philosophy. Early Indian texts are notoriously hard to date, but the Brahmanas and Upanishads that I will use are probably roughly contemporary with Presocratic philosophy. Neither from Greece nor from India in this period does there survive a sustained discussion of debt. We depend on mentions of debt (cosmic and mundane) scattered throughout various texts.

Two concepts require preliminary clarification. The first is "debt" itself, which I use with the broad sense of *reified obligation to compensate* (whether by providing

Richard Seaford, *Cosmic Debt in Greece and India* In: *Debt in the Ancient Mediterranean and Near East.*
Edited by: John Weisweiler, Oxford University Press. © Oxford University Press 2023.
DOI: 10.1093/oso/9780197647172.003.0003

something or by suffering), of which commercial debt is one manifestation. All purchases (unlike, e.g., gift-exchange) involve debt, which is often paid immediately. The second concept requiring preliminary clarification is "cosmization." The sociologist Peter Berger notes that "there is an inherent logic that impels every nomos [meaningful human order] to expand into wider areas of meaning. If the ordering activity of society never attains to totality, it may yet be described as totalising." "Cosmization" is the process through which "nomos and cosmos appear to be co-extensive."[1] In the Indian god Indra war-leadership is cosmized, in Zeus patriarchal monarchy, in sacrifice to the gods gift-exchange. We will see that in both Greece and India the *two essences of money* are cosmized: *circulation*, which is driven by debt, and *abstract value-substance*. Circulation (and accordingly debt) is in the (Ionian) metaphysics of Anaximander and Herakleitos positively evaluated, whereas in the metaphysics of Parmenides of Elea, by contrast, it is abstract value that is cosmized. The contrast is, we shall see, *ideological*. Indian metaphysics is shaped by exactly the same opposition, between debt-driven circulation and abstract value, albeit with different results, reflecting differences between Greek and Indian society.

Greece

The man whom Athenians regarded as the founder of their polis, Solon, achieved this status by legislating to resolve a devastating general crisis caused by debt, in the first quarter of the sixth century BCE.[2] On Solon I confine myself to three briefly stated points. The first is the obvious one that the episode shows the importance of debt for the formation of the Athenian polis. The second is the likelihood that the depersonalization and quantification of debt were promoted by monetization and contributed to the crisis. The third is that Solon's poetry[3] indicates both the *subjective* and the *cosmic* dimension of the debt crisis: He recommends moderation in behavior, as well as maintaining that there is a "hidden measure (*metron*) of intelligence that holds the limits of all things."[4]

Various laws attributed to Solon indicate that Athens had been monetized (with silver as money),[5] although coinage was to be introduced probably not until a generation later. But if we cross the Aegean to Miletos, we find a polis that in the first quarter of the sixth century was not only already issuing coinage (one of the earliest coinages in history)[6] but also producing the first ever "philosophy," in the earliest surviving fragment of which we find a central role played by cosmic debt.[7] In the words of Simplicius (preserving Theophrastus),

> Anaximander said that the principle and element of existing things is the *apeiron* (unlimited or indefinite). . . . And from which (things) existing

things have their genesis, into those things also occurs their perishing κατὰ τὸ χρεών (according to necessity); for they give to each other δίκην (penalty) and τίσιν (retribution) for their injustice according to the τάξις (disposition/assessment) of time, describing it thus in rather poetical terms.[8]

The reference to poetical terms tends to confirm that the preceding words are Anaximander's.[9] The things giving penalty etc. are generally regarded as the opposites (hot and cold, etc.).

In this passage the cosmos is, on the one hand, imagined in terms of human society: more specifically, in terms of the judicial process by which the polis is constituted. But, on the other hand, there is the impersonal *apeiron*, from which things (including the opposites) emerge and into which they pass and which is unlimited, homogeneous, and abstract (or semi-abstract). And we know from other sources that it is in eternal motion and steers all things.[10] All of these characteristics of the *apeiron* are also characteristics of the monetary value embodied in coinage, by which Miletos was being pervaded in the lifetime of Anaximander, producing what was probably the first ever pervasively monetized society in history. I have shown this in detail elsewhere, as part of my demonstration that Presocratic cosmology in general is in its fundamental characteristics (e.g., there is a single entity of which everything consists) a cosmization of monetary value.[11] Its relevance here is that what is cosmized in Anaximander's *apeiron*, monetary value-substance, is—despite, or rather because of, its impersonality—a fundamental institution of the polis, like the judicial process that is also cosmized in these words of Anaximander.

What is more, the relation between *apeiron* and cosmized judicial process is exactly what we would expect from the relation of money and judicial process in the polis. From surviving laws (including those attributed to Solon) we can see reconciliation between opposed parties achieved by penalties in fixed quantities of money.[12] The opposition is transcended by the (necessarily impersonal) universality of money.

The payment and retribution occur, says Anaximander, according to necessity, κατὰ τὸ χρεών. This has not received the attention it deserves. Remarkably, the phrase occurs nowhere else and contains the earliest known instance of cosmic necessity. It is also the earliest known instance of the neuter noun χρεών, which is cognate with the impersonal verb χρή, meaning "one must" or "ought," with the neuter noun τὸ χρέος or χρεῖος (Attic χρέως) meaning "debt," and with the feminine nouns ἡ χρεώ (epic χρειώ) and ἡ χρεία meaning "need" or "want."

A new idea, (impersonal) cosmic necessity, is in the earliest surviving philosophical fragment created not out of the impersonal necessity on earth found in Homer (ἀνάγκη) but with a new neuter form (τὸ χρεών), cognate with the preexisting (neuter) noun for debt (τὸ χρέος). Moreover, the context is one of debt: The cosmic process occurring κατὰ τὸ χρεών is redescribed as the opposites giving the compensation that they owe to each other. We may infer that the new idea of (impersonal) cosmic necessity is created, in part at least, by cosmization of the human relation of debt: the metaphysical transition inherent in rapid monetization produces a phrase (κατὰ τὸ χρεών) that will never be used again. The addition of the τάξις ("disposition/assessment") of time adds the dimension of supervision, in the now somewhat depersonalized cosmos, by a third party (on earth the polis).

Anaximander was probably born at the end of the seventh century BCE. Moving forward two generations or so we find Herakleitos of Ephesos maintaining that the cosmos is an ever-living fire (B30) and that "all things are an exchange for fire and fire for all things, like goods for gold and gold for goods" (B90). All things happen according to the *logos* (B1), an abstract formula that could in this period have the meanings "monetary account,"[13] "reckoning," "proportion," "ratio." I will not repeat here my demonstration of the ways in which this monist cosmology is a cosmization of monetary circulation. My focus is rather on Herakleitos' statement that "war is communal, and justice is strife (ἔρις, and all things happen κατ' ἔριν καὶ χρεών (according to strife and necessity)" (B80). The cosmic process occurs according to necessity (χρεών), as in Anaximander, but also according to strife as well as according to the *logos*. Scholars are especially puzzled here by the role of war and strife.

Puzzlement dissolves only when we realize that the Herakleitean cosmos represents the advance of monetization. It is a projection not primarily of the power of money to reconcile conflict (as in Anaximander) but rather of the opposition inherent in *all* monetized exchange (in contrast to the reciprocal good will of gift-exchange). Commercial exchanges are universally ruled by the impersonal necessity (χρεών) of debt (typically paid immediately) and by the diametrically opposed interests (strife) of the exchangers, brought into harmony in each case by a communally agreed (B2, B114) numerical ratio (*logos*), so that justice is strife. Exactly similar is the Herakleitean cosmos, in which the opposites have lost the degree of autonomy they had retained in Anaximander: Instead, they are held together in unity or "harmony" (B8, B51), or constantly transformed into each other according to a fixed proportion (*logos*: B31) in the cycle of cosmic-monetized transformations of fire (B62, B67, B88, B126). The circulation of money is in Herakleitos cosmized (i.e., *universalized*): The all-pervasiveness of money becomes cosmic, debt becomes universal necessity, numerical formula (*logos*) becomes universal abstract principle (eventually "reason"), and transactional opposition becomes the universal unity of opposites.

The cosmic fire (like money) embodies the abstract *logos*,[14] and so does each soul (B45, B115), which—being an exhalation containing fire—is subject to the cosmic-monetized cycle and accordingly is expended by the spirit (*thumos*) that "buys what it wants at the price of soul (ὃ γὰρ ἂν θέλῃ ψυχῆς ὠνεῖται)" (B85).

The idea of loss of soul (ψυχή)—generally death—as *payment* occurs in several Greek texts.[15] In some, which indicate the doctrine of mystery-cult, the payment is a ποινά ("penalty" or "compensation"). In the mystic doctrine of reincarnation in Pindar's second Olympian the "helpless spirits of those who die pay ποινάς here immediately" (i.e., by dying), before then being sentenced beneath the earth.[16] Plato, in a passage of *Meno* (81ab) in which he attributes the doctrine of reincarnation to priests and priestesses (probably of mystery-cults), also quotes a statement of Pindar (fr. 133) that Persephone will return to the sun above, in the ninth year, the souls of those from whom she will receive ποινὰν) παλαιοῦ πένθεος: This may well mean "penalty consisting in ancient grief," which I take to be the defeat and confinement of the immortal Titans for their struggle against Zeus, with humankind imagined as Titans.[17] Whatever the truth of this, the ποινά may be the same as the "ποινά for unrighteous deeds" that—in a mystic formula inscribed on gold leaves (found in tombs) of the fourth century BCE[18]—the dead initiate claims to have paid as he supplicates Persephone to send him to the seats of the pure. On another gold leaf of the same period is written "enter the holy meadow, for the initiate is without ποινά (ἄποινος)."[19] These texts seem to imply a mystic doctrine of reincarnation,[20] in which a penalty has to be paid for transgression that is inseparable from being human. The idea of life itself as—or as inheriting— a metaphysical debt is in fact explicit in several non-mystic texts.[21]

We must now move from Ionia to the other end of the Greek world, southern Italy, and to the importance of debt (or rather of debtlessness) for a philosopher, Parmenides, whose vision of a temporal and spatially invariant abstract One (Being) represents the polar opposite to Herakleitos' vision of a constantly moving cycle.

First, we must try to understand this polar opposition. Money is money by being imagined as a *value-substance*, which is (ideally) ubiquitous and unchanging.[22] The other precondition or essence of money is its *circulation*: A society in which no money circulates is in effect moneyless. Money has therefore two essences, both of which are required for it to be money: value-substance and circulation. But, of course, in reality these two essences interact. Although money must be imagined as containing value (and so power) entirely within itself, it has value and power only by circulating. To the extent that it is imagined in absolute separation from circulation, it will seem to be an entity that is universal, abstract, and unchanging. Such an entity is the Being (or One) of Parmenides, separated ruthlessly from (communal) circulation by the ideology of individual economic self-sufficiency. The constantly circulating fire (embodying the abstract *logos*) of Herakleitos, on the other hand, is a projection of this (communal) circulation. This I have argued in detail in *Money and the Early Greek Mind* (Seaford 2004).

The Ionian cosmology of Anaximander and Herakleitos cosmizes the *communal* perspective of the polis on the (debt-driven) *circulation* of money. In what survives of Herakleitos we read that one should follow the communal and that the *logos* is communal (B2), that the people must fight for the law as for a wall (B44), and that "those who speak with intelligence (ξὺν νόῳ) must rely on what is communal (ξυνῷ) to all, as a *polis* relies on law, and much more strongly" (B114).[23] Parmenides, by contrast, cosmizes the perspective of the *individual citizen* on the imagined unchangingness of (individually owned) *abstract value* imagined as entirely separate from circulation (i.e., from debt). He is a wealthy aristocrat,[24] and it is to him alone that the goddess reveals the truth "away from the tread of men," whereas in the beliefs of mortals, who "know nothing," there is no true conviction.[25]

Subsequently, Plato of Athens belongs—metaphysically as well as geographically—between the Ionians and Parmenides. He maintains that the guardians of his ideal state should be told that they have in their souls divine gold and silver currency, which they should not mix with the polluting human currency of the majority (*Republic* 416e). But he also says that the soul (*psuchē*) succeeds in being "by itself" by gathering itself from all parts of the body, with wisdom (*phronēsis*) as the "only right currency (νόμισμα only), for which all those things [pleasures, pains, fears] must be *exchanged* [emphasis added]" (*Phaedo* 69a). In general, his attempt to formulate the relation of concrete particulars to the abstract unchanging form of the good, from which value derives,[26] cosmizes the relationship between circulating goods and abstract (ideally unchanging) value-substance. Analogously, he envisages the desirability of permanent escape, through philosophical absorption in the self-sufficiency of abstract Being, from the cosmic cycle (of reincarnation).[27]

We return to Parmenides. In arguing that the existent could not have come into being from the non-existent he says, according to the Penguin translation by Barnes, "what need would have impelled it, later or earlier, to spring up—if it began from nothing?" (fr. 8.9–10). The word translated as "need" here is χρέος. But the basic and most common meaning of χρέος is not "need" but "debt" or "obligation," which it frequently turns out to mean even when another translation is used.[28] Even in the (perhaps colloquial) expression "what (τί) χρέος?"[29] we cannot assume that the notion of obligation is absent. For the meaning "need" LSJ give only two passages, both of them with an object of the "need" in the genitive, but neither of them is convincing.[30] In the unusual abstract context of the

Parmenides passage, unqualified χρέος (without a genitive) cannot be detached from its normal meaning of debt or obligation.

However, it is usually mistranslated as "need,"[31] which seems more commonsensical: It is broader, not confined to the interpersonal relation of debt. The general mistranslation conceals the process through which the eternity of Being is imagined—a process involving not just reasoning but ideological preconception. *The fact is that the eternity of Being is associated with debtlessness.* The association is not as odd as it may at first seem.

The importance of ideology reappears a mere four lines later in the words "Justice has never loosed her fetters to allow it (Being) to come into being or perish, but holds it fast" (8.14–15). There was no debt (χρέος) to bring Being into being, and it was moreover prevented from coming into being (and perishing) by being imprisoned by Justice. And it was also held "in bonds of limit" by strong Necessity (Ἀνάγκη) supported by *Themis* (traditional law) (8.30–32). This is the earliest appearance of *cosmic ἀνάγκη*, a word which from Homer onward had often referred to no more than interpersonal constraint. True belief (πίστις) "drove away" coming-into-being and destruction (8.28). *Moira* (a notion of fate deriving from the idea of right distribution) fettered Being to be whole and unchanging (8.37–38). Being "is all inviolate (πᾶν ἐστιν ἄσυλον)" (8.48). The eternity and limitedness of Being is a product not just of reasoning but of justice maintained by force. We are reminded, despite the obvious differences, of the enforcement of justice at the heart of the cosmos imagined by Anaximander.

Those who assume that Parmenides proceeds mainly by deductive reasoning may claim that his new ideas of logical necessity and universal abstract Being are—because neither perceptible nor easily imagined—inevitably approached through ideas that are more familiar, such as justice, *themis*, imprisonment, inviolability, or debtlessness, which may accordingly be regarded as merely presentational or metaphorical.

But why, in order to approach logical necessity and the strange idea of universal abstract unchanging Being, would Parmenides use these particular (specific, striking, ethically charged) familiar ideas? They do in fact all fall into place only if we suppose that the logical or metaphysical necessity beloved of Parmenidean interpreters is a by-product of the combination of two other kinds of necessity. One is the universal abstract necessity inherent in money cosmized as universal abstract Being (abstractly shown to exist necessarily). The other is the ideological (and so ethical) necessity of monetized self-sufficiency, the limiting necessity that by separating abstract value from circulation ensures justice and debtlessness. Enclosure from within (inviolability) and from without (imprisonment), evoking, respectively, religious and social sanctions, emphasizes the just necessity of monetized self-sufficiency. This necessity has two aspects: the inviolable autonomy of individual wealth and the need—expressed by, for example, Solon and Aeschylus[32]—to limit the potential unlimitedness of money. Despite the crucial sociopolitical importance of this limit, the description of it in terms of fetters may seem too fierce but is in fact—Mourelatos observes—"significantly tempered by the language of πίστις [trust],[33] which is charged with connotations of civilised agreement and positive teleology . . . the real identifies with its limits or bounds and accepts them willingly."[34]

From the same fragment there is yet another passage that both looks like a purely logical argument and yet expresses the importance of debtlessness. Being is limited because unchanging (27) and because not lacking (i.e., self-sufficient); if it were lacking, it would lack everything (32–33). These three oddities of reasoning are explicable only in the light of the influence of the ideology of monetized self-sufficiency.[35] The vulgar circulation of money is unlimited, but abstract *ousia* ("wealth," "being"), from which Parmenides and other wealthy individuals live in the recently monetized polis, is ideologically imagined as unchanging and limited as well as self-sufficient—the three characteristics speciously welded together by Parmenides. He also maintains that Being, were it lacking, "would lack everything": This incorrect inference reflects, nevertheless, the reality that monetary value cannot enter (unlimited) circulation in a limited way, can circulate only as a means of *universal* exchange.

And so whereas in the Ionian cosmization of circulation necessity is associated with debt, in the Parmenidean cosmization of self-sufficient value it is associated with debtlessness. Rejection of my interpretation will be persuasive only if it provides a better explanation of why Parmenides chose the roles he did for (inter alia) Justice, Necessity, *Moira*, *Themis*, inviolability, and χρέος, as well as why he adopts the bizarre view, called by Aristotle "almost insane,"[36] that all that exists is abstract, eternal, and temporally and spatially invariant.

India

I begin with a passage from the *Śatapatha Brāhmana* (henceforth "SB"), which may well be from the sixth century BCE:

> Indeed, even in being born, man, by his own self (*ātman*), is born as a debt[37] to death. And in that he sacrifices, he thereby redeems[38] himself (*ātman*) from death.[39]

In Vedic sacrifice an individual goes to heaven, where they obtain a desirable place for eternity and then return to earth.[40] I call this a cosmic rite of passage. Greek mystic initiation too is a cosmic rite of passage, in which the initiands enter the next world temporarily as a way of ensuring their eventual eternal well-being there. And we have seen that the Greek ritual, like the Indian one, may involve absolution from cosmic debt.

The monetization of northern India, which was almost certainly occurring in the fifth century BCE, if not before, created a universal abstract power-entity that transcended—and could hardly fail to influence—the traditional power of sacrifice (Seaford 2020). The monetization of the Vedic cosmic rite of passage was facilitated by the fact that the ritual was already a context of substantial payment—required by cosmic debt and in exchange for salvation—to gods and to priests. Malamoud writes of the "general economy of debt and ransom which, in Brahminism, govern not only the individual life of men but also the whole organization of the world, and notably the sacrifice."[41]

With the monetization (and so depersonalization and quantification) of this debt, there emerges the idea of a store of sacred metaphysical money. Monetization encourages the individual storage of abstract value, which becomes a more valuable resource than the interpersonal good will created— among gods or humans—by the ancient code of reciprocal favors, gifts, and services. Accordingly, we find in certain Vedic texts, which are undateable but may well coincide with the process of monetization, the idea that the sacrifice creates for the sacrificer a store of (metaphysical) substance in the hereafter. The word *iṣṭāpūrta*, for instance, is etymologically connected with sacrifice and could refer to the result of sacrifice but eventually could mean material wealth in this world or the totality of merit accumulated in a life (not only by sacrifice).[42] It "appears to be a synonym for *nidhi* (treasure), deposit in heaven, consisting of religious merit, something on a man's credit side in the invisible world or in the life hereafter.'[43] Similarly, *karman*, which in its earliest occurrences refers to ritually correct action,[44] comes to refer to a metaphysical value-substance resulting from action in general. The good and evil done by the dead are *quantified* in heaven (*Jāiminīya Brāhmaṇa* 1.18), where there is a pair of scales (SB 11.2.7.33). And just as the store or result of offerings may *accumulate* in the afterlife, so too it may also *decrease* or be *exhausted*,[45] thereby creating the danger of repeated death.[46]

"May we be debtless in this, debtless in the other, debtless in the third, world! What paths there are trodden by the gods and trodden by the fathers—may we abide debtless on all (those) paths!" (*Taittirīya Brāhmarī* 3.7.9.8).[47] The same two paths reappear in the so-called two-path doctrine, which occurs (in different versions) in the earliest Upanishads—the *Bṛhadāraṇyaka Upaniṣad* (henceforth "BU") and the *Chāndogya Upaniṣad* (henceforth "CU"). The dead pass into the flame (on the *devayāna*, "path of the gods") or the smoke (on the *pitryāna*, "path of the fathers"). The *devayāna* is followed by "those who know this (the so-called

five-fire doctrine) and those there in the wilderness who venerate truth as faith"
(BU 6.2.15; similarly CU 5.10.1), whereas the *pitryāna* is followed by "those who
win heavenly worlds by offering sacrifices, by giving gifts, and by performing austerities" (BU 6.2.16) or by "the people here in the villages who venerate thus: gift-
giving is *iṣṭāpūrta*" (CU 5.10.3).

The *devayāna* leads ultimately to *brahman* (CU 5.10.2) or—for some "exalted
people"—"the worlds of *brahman*," from which "they do not return" (BU 6.2.15),[48]
whereas the *pitryāna* leads in both versions eventually to the moon, where the
dead are eaten by the gods (BU) or remain on the moon (which the gods eat) as
long as there is a *sampāta* (residue of sacrifice; CU 5.105); then in both versions
they return to earth and are reborn, and—the BU version adds—"rising up again
to the heavenly worlds, they circle round in the same way" (6.2.16).

Those who take the *pitryāna* fail to be permanently maintained in the hereafter by their austerities, gifts, sacrifices, and accumulated *iṣṭāpūrta*: When the
sacrificial residue (*sampāta*) runs out, they re-enter the rebirth cycle.[49] Sacrifices,
offerings, and austerities all "come to naught" (BU 3.8.10), and "in the hereafter
a world won by merit (*puṇyajītas*) comes to an end" (CU 8.1.6), whereas taking
the *devayāna* to permanently escape from the cycle into *brahman* occurs through
knowledge.

Neither metaphysical merit nor the cycle of reincarnation occurs in the earliest Vedic texts. The two-path doctrine is probably the earliest[50] known example of a widespread and persistent idea, that the hereafter takes the form of a
repeated cycle of reincarnation from which permanent escape is possible and
desirable. This new conception is a cosmization—I argue in my monograph—
of the desirability of permanent escape from the cycle of monetized obligation.
For people in general there is constant obligation to expend money, resulting in
its diminution, which necessitates constant activity in order to acquire it. (This
obligation is—until resolved—"debt.") This constant alternating acquisition
and diminution of money form a cycle from which escape is enabled by the historically unprecedented individual self-sufficiency created by the possession of
enough money.

But this is in fact not the only possible way of escape. Another is moneyless
(and homeless) withdrawal from the cycle of activity, renunciation, as we see in
the development of the *sramana* movements from about the fifth century BCE.
According to Richard Gombrich,

> Society with its web of obligations becomes an analogue for the entire
> cycle of *samsara*, and on the other hand the homeless life with no social
> ties becomes an analogue for that release from rebirth for which it is con-
> ceived to be literally a preparation.[51]

This insightful comment requires two modifications. Firstly, the implication that the social is based on the metaphysical ("becomes an analogue . . . ") should be reversed. Secondly, I would specify—as analogous to *samsara*—the *cycle* of *economic* obligations, which is cyclical in the way that I have just specified.

We have seen that there are various forms of accumulated metaphysical merit (*iṣṭāpūrta, sampāta, puṇyajitas, nidhi, karman*). But metaphysical merit may also diminish, resulting in repeated death or in re-entry into the cycle of reincarnation. This I regard as a cosmization of the accumulation and diminution of money that sustains the monetary cycle. But what is the significance of *brahman*, attained by those exalted people who escape the cycle?

Brahman and *karman* are exceptionally universal and will be exceptionally important. They both originate in the sphere of ritual performed on behalf of the individual. The earliest meaning of *brahman* is the *power* of the ritual; of *karman* it is its *correct practice*. But they both extend their meanings beyond the ritual sphere and from power/action to include entity/substance. Despite this extension, which is in my view driven in part by monetization, *brahman* and *karman* both retain their connection with individual access to metaphysical salvation.

But there is polarization between *brahman* and *karman*. *Brahman*, referring originally to ritual *power*, came to express *unchanging universal value*, from the perspective of individual *ownership* (separated from circulation, like Parmenidean Being). The "exalted people" who attain *brahman* have separated themselves permanently from cosmic circulation—analogously to those who have separated themselves from monetized circulation by accumulating or owning sufficient abstract value. But the exalted people have attained *brahman* not by accumulating metaphysical merit, which decreases, but rather by *knowledge* (we will return to this passage below).

By contrast karma, which referred originally to the *correct practice* of ritual, came to cosmize and *ethicize* money from the perspective of individual *practice*: The individual accumulation of money benefits its owner within the exchange cycle, just as the individual accumulation of karma benefits its owner within the reincarnation cycle. In contrast to *brahman*, which is comprehensive, indivisible, and unchanging, karma (*karman*) is accumulated by individuals for their future well-being and (like money driving the cycle of exchange) drives the cycle of reincarnation.

Comparison

In both India and Greece the cosmic rite of passage involved payment of cosmic debt. And in both cultures (and in no others[52]) we find the autonomous development, at about the same time, of what I call ethicized indiscriminate reincarnation (EIR), that is, reincarnation that may occur into any living being, depending on behavior in this life. The most important factor in this similarity is not influence (in either direction)[53] but the early development in both cultures of the cycle of monetized exchange, in which debt, which preexisted money, became as a result of monetization more objective and less personal. The new impersonal omnipotence of money is more powerful than ritual, trapping millions in an impersonal cycle of activity driven by the alternating need to acquire and expend money (monetized debt). This miserable cycle is cosmized as the miserable cycle of rebirth, in which the individual—unable to accept (or even imagine) the self-identical isolation imposed on them by monetization—finds other identities, as well as legitimation of the present and hope for the future. In the premonetary world of Homer and the Rigveda, by contrast, there is no cosmic debt, no cycle of reincarnation, and no desire to escape from life.

But there are also significant differences between the two cultures. In particular, in all religions originating in India, EIR was more lasting and widespread than in Greece. And Greece had nothing corresponding to karma. True, the Parmenidean One, the Platonic form of the good, and even the *logos* that inheres in Herakleitean fire[54] are—like karma—*ethicized* projections of money. But all four are projected and ethicized from different perspectives. The closest to karma is perhaps Herakleitean fire, which—like karma—drives circulation[55] as well as having both a subjective and an objective aspect.[56] But it is not very close: Karma is the projection of monetary *value-substance* from the perspective of *individual practice* (originally of ritual) and so can be accumulated for its owner's future well-being, whereas the circulation of Herakleitean fire is the projection of monetary *circulation* from the *communal* perspective.

As for *brahman*, it is in part shaped by the *individual ownership* of abstract value that is—ideally—universal, separated from circulation, and unchanging. In this respect it resembles Greek abstract Being, from which, however, it differs in its specificity and flexibility: For instance, it can—unlike Greek abstract Being—be identified with various things. This distinctiveness of *brahman* derives from its origin as the *power of ritual*, just as the distinctiveness of *karman* derives from its origin as the *right practice* of ritual.

This distinctiveness needs to be put in a broader context. Despite the basic similarity between the Indian and Greek cosmic rites of passage, there are also substantial differences. Greek mystic initiation typically incorporated the individual into a group, Greek animal sacrifice typically culminated in a communal meal, and both rituals could extend to dramatizing and reinforcing the solidarity of the polis.[57] The priests performing the Greek animal sacrifice were not members of a priestly caste but citizens. Early Greek philosophy was produced by citizens in a secular context under the influence of monetization.[58]

In Vedic ritual the state played no part.[59] The cosmic rite of passage (sacrifice) was performed on behalf of an individual (the *yajamāna*, "sacrificer")[60] by brahmin priests and had neither a communal organization nor a communal meal. But we have seen that it was—again, in contrast to the Greek cosmic rite of passage—the context of substantial debt-driven payment, by sacrificer to priests or gods. Vedic philosophy emerged from the monetized transformation (interiorization)[61] of the wealth-transferring cosmic rite of passage *within the priestly (brahminical) tradition.*

Monetization creates in this world a miserable cycle, from which there are two ways to withdraw. One is from above (ownership of sufficient money) and the other from below (renunciation, homelessness). Paradoxically, the Indian renouncer's withdrawal from below is (as metaphysically powerful) one way of attaining a universal but invisible entity (*brahman*) that is shaped in part by individual ownership of the universal but invisible entity money. We saw that in BU certain exalted people escape the reincarnation cycle and attain *brahman* by *knowledge*. Also in BU the sage Yajnavalkya, after expounding the self-knowledge required to attain *brahman*, becomes a renouncer (4.4.6–5.1).

The withdrawal recommended by Plato also involves attainment of such an entity (abstract Being) but is limited to *inner* withdrawal—from the disturbance created by certain emotions and sensations and by corporeal desire. In his will the aristocratic Plato bequeathed two estates, one of which he had bought, as well as slaves and a considerable amount of gold and silver; and he declared that he owed nothing to anybody.[62] The guardians of his ideal republic, although they own no private property and are forbidden from polluting the divine money in their souls by mixing it with monetary circulation, are nevertheless *citizens*, provided with an income (μισθός) by other citizens.[63]

The withdrawal of the Indian renouncer, by contrast, could be extreme. Inasmuch as actions (even eating) require money (i.e., create debt), which necessitates further action (work), the pure form of renunciatory escape from the monetary cycle is the rejection of *action* (even eating), as recommended by the Jains and the Ājīvikans. They reject all money, whether metaphysical (*karma*) or worldly, both of which are created by action, which accordingly they also reject.[64] Buddhist monks, on the other hand, though banned from handling money, are not banned from action: Just as there is both the owning and the owing of money, so there can be good as well as bad karma; and accumulated good karma may promote a better hereafter.

But for the millions of individuals (neither self-sufficiently wealthy nor renouncers) whose practice is constrained by monetized exchange, the answer is money from the perspective of *individual practice*, familiar but cosmized and ethicized, namely karma. A theme of Graeber's book on debt is the contradiction that payment of debt, though a moral duty, frequently produces an immoral result. Karma resolves the contradiction. The cosmic balance sheet of karma—unlike that of worldly money, which can be immorally accumulated—produces obligation that is entirely moral. The idea of right practice (*karman*)—ensuring metaphysical salvation—was detached from ritual, reified, and yet also (especially in early Buddhism) interiorized to the point of being identified with right intention (i.e., becoming subjective as well objective).[65] As such, it became ethicized metaphysical money, from the perspective of individual practice, available and familiar to all those trapped in the monetized cycle.

This near-universal currency of karma had no counterpart in Greece. On the one hand, the Parmenidean and Platonic ethicized projection of unchanging abstract value from the perspective of individual *ownership* (separate from practice) expressed an aristocratic ideology of monetized debtlessness, of withdrawal from the cycle from above, that could have little popular appeal, although it remained popular among (leisured) philosophers. And, on the other hand, the cosmic projection of *circulation* from the austerely *communal* perspective of Herakleitos was unlikely to engage the monetized *individual*, whether rich or poor, and soon died out. In Greece the state had greater stability, power, and loyalty than it did in India; and the popular need for ultimate justice was eventually met not by ethicized money but by a cosmic tribunal. This fundamental difference between India and the West is still with us.

Acknowledgment

I thank Malcolm Schofield for useful discussion.

4

Private Debts in Classical Greece

BOND OF FRIENDSHIP, CURSE OF HATRED?

Moritz Hinsch

Introduction

Debt is a large and complex topic in the history of ancient Greece. I will limit my discussion to three interrelated aspects of debt in the classical period (480–323 BCE): first, the pervasiveness of debt in Greek practice and thought; second, the apparent paradoxical evaluation of debt in contemporary ethics; and third, the absence of full-blown debt crises despite the pervasiveness of indebtedness.

The most famous ancient event linked to debts, today and in antiquity, is the so-called Solonian debt crisis, named after the Athenian lawgiver Solon. According to the sources, it took place in Athens at the beginning of the sixth century BCE, which makes it the earliest debt crisis reported for Greco-Roman antiquity. Its extent and the exact nature of Solon's reforms to solve it (remembered as the "shaking off the burdens," the *seisachtheia*) remain subjects of unending debate.[1] David Graeber cites the Solonian debt crisis as the first of "a series of debt crises"; in fact, it is the only debt crisis *ever* reported to have occurred in Athens.[2] If Graeber's picture of "Axial-Age societies," 800 BCE–600 CE, as being ridden by violent debt crises is correct, ancient Greece poses as a peculiar exception. The same holds true for debt bondage, the institution that together with debt slavery propelled the Solonian crisis. Even if debt bondage was not outlawed, contrary to what most scholars used to believe (see below), what is remarkable in comparative perspective is not its survival but its marginality in the classical period.[3] Both peculiarities call for explanations.

The reason for the absence of debt crises and debt bondage is not a lack of credit transactions in classical Greece. For Athens, the only city documented by

Moritz Hinsch, *Private Debts in Classical Greece* In: *Debt in the Ancient Mediterranean and Near East.*
Edited by: John Weisweiler, Oxford University Press. © Oxford University Press 2023.
DOI: 10.1093/oso/9780197647172.003.0004

a host of literary sources, monographic studies have delineated the pervasiveness and importance of credit in all spheres of life.[4] Against the background of this scholarship, I wish to test Graeber's claims about the role of debt in the Axial Age by surveying ancient Greek statements of the idea that "one must pay one's debt."[5] I will argue that the effective meaning of this notion depended on the prevalent structures of trust, power, and economic opportunity. I will draw on these factors to explain why Greeks thought of debt as both a bond of unity and a cause of hatred and why, despite the omnipresence of debt, violent debt crises are remarkably absent from Greece in the fifth and fourth centuries BCE.

The Omnipresence of Debt in Classical Greece

Paul Millett begins his study on lending and borrowing in classical Athens by noting the "pervasiveness of credit."[6] One may pick up a text from any genre and find at least some allusion to debt. Philosophical treatises discuss the problem in ethical and political terms. In comedies, the rich try to get rid of debt by going to court, while the poor lend tools or food to neighbors or pawn their household effects.[7] In forensic speeches, orators fight about who owes what to whom. This may be either a maritime loan, given to finance a trading voyage or an interest-free loan, called *eranos*, given to a friend in need.[8] Civic and social obligations were another reason to contract a debt: paying for a proper burial for the parents, paying the cash dowry for a daughter, and, among the rich, financing a war galley or a dramatic performance.[9]

Debt became a metaphor to describe and explain any social or even metaphysical relation.[10] In his *Laws*, Plato defines the order of pious honors to be paid. First come the gods, then *daimones*, then *hēroes*. Next come the deceased ancestors, then the living ancestors, one's parents. Plato elaborates on the last point:

> For established custom (θέμις) has is that the debtor should pay back the first and greatest of debts, the most primary of all dues (τὰ πρῶτά τε καὶ μέγιστα ὀφειλήματα, χρεῶν πάντων πρεσβύτατα), and that he should acknowledge that all that he owns and has belongs to those who begot and reared him, so that he ought to give them service to the utmost of his power—with substance, with body, and with soul, all three—thus making returns for the loans of care and pain spent on the children by those who suffered on their behalf in bygone years (ἀποτίνοντα δανείσματα ... δανεισθείσας), and recompensing the old in their old age, when they need help most.[11]

Themis, venerable, god-sanctioned custom, is exemplified by the terms of contemporary law on multiple creditors. The amount and the date of the debt define the order of settlement.[12] Taking care of one's parents becomes "paying back an interest-bearing loan" (*apotinonta daneismata*), making child care and filial piety two sides of a business transaction. Aristotle evokes a similar picture in his *Nicomachean Ethics*.[13] The debt owed to the gods or to one's parents is so great it may never be repaid. The indebtedness is eternal and any remittance an act of one-sided benevolence: "creditors can remit a debt; and a father can therefore do so too." In these descriptions of social obligation, the metaphor of debt is applied to a set of notions close to the original meaning. But debt also serves as metaphor or example in places where it arguably appears more far-fetched, at least to a modern reader. In Plato's dialogue *Politicus*, Socrates mockingly calls a lengthy answer "capital repaid with interest added."[14] In Aristotle's *Physics*, the first example to exemplify the notion of "coincidence" is a man who goes to the *agora* and there recovers a loan by chance.[15]

Classical Greece fits Graeber's general picture of "Axial-Age" thought and society as being materialistic and pervaded by notions of indebtedness quite well.[16] What is missing from his picture of ancient Greece are the effects of trust and power. Graeber himself considers them only for the Middle Ages.[17] Graeber stresses two important points in his discussion of Muslim and Christian commercial practices: first, that the rule to repay one's debts was integral to establish the necessary trust for mutual advantage business; second, that elite members who relied on power rather than trust presented a continuous threat because they felt entitled to disregard their obligations every now and then. In ancient Greece likewise, the effective meaning of the notion that "one must pay one's debts" depended on how trust and power shaped credit relations.

Must One Pay One's Debts? A Question of Trust and Power

In Graeber's descriptions of Axial-Age societies, the notion that "one must pay one's debts" appears almost as the prime cause for the emergence of hierarchies and domination, an "unmoved mover" propelling exploitation and dependency. Can a moral/legal notion accomplish so much on its own? Does enforceability necessarily result in domination? Most of Graeber's case studies on premodern debt crises describe what may be called "the vicious circle of peasant indebtedness," a process well attested in agrarian societies. Since peasant economies are local, all subsistence farmers are hit by the same calamities at the same time, while relief from other regions is out of reach. Larger households are better prepared to buffer agrarian risks like crop failure. Surpluses even allow them to bank on disaster by selling provisions to poorer neighbors. Since the demand for subsistence foodstuffs is inelastic, the poorer neighbors are competing as buyers in a seller's market. After the harvest, the small farmers must sell their produce all at once to honor their obligations. Now they compete as sellers in a buyer's market. The situation is reversed for the bigger households: They first sell at high prices and are later able to buy at low prices and accumulate new surpluses. The risks for small households increase with each turn of this vicious circle, as do the prospects for profit for bigger households. A series of crop failures may enable large households to first accumulate the means of production and then convert their control of them into more permanent, institutionalized forms of power, while small households descend into servitude.[18]

In the urban, polycentric societies of the Mediterranean things often have been different, both in antiquity and in the Middle Ages. In these societies, economic power was not as inseparably married to political and ideological power. Credit did not simply work as a tool of social subjugation. While it was an instrument of power, it also enabled people to earn a living apart from agriculture through trade and manufacture. In a diversified urban economy, "telling the truth and paying one's debts" was the foundation of mutual trust, the start of peaceful cooperation.

In Plato's *Republic* it is a non-citizen man of business, old Kephalos, who cites the notion of "telling the truth and paying one's debts" as his definition of justice.[19] Plato presents this definition as common and conventional, as indeed it was, and aims to demonstrate its insufficiency. Graeber cites this passage to show how commercialization and debt brought "extreme moral confusion" to the city of Athens.[20] I see nothing particularly confused about Kephalos' view, considering his social position. Kephalos introduces himself as a "moneymaker" (χρηματιστής) who values riches because they allow him to honor his obligations toward gods and humans.[21] Kephalos' self-portrait fits his biography. He resided as a metic (a resident alien) in Piraeus, Athens' emporium that during the fifth century BCE developed into the commercial hub of the Aegean world. Part of Kephalos' wealth stemmed from a slave-run workshop.[22] His ethics of honesty resemble the norms of Graeber's medieval merchants.[23] The ensuing debate in the *Republic* reveals that to Kephalos' son Polemarkhos, who takes up his father's argument, the just man is the man who treats his business partners honestly.[24] Polemarkhos' illustration for this is to guard a deposit (*parakatathēkē*) for the partner and return it undiminished, an example of goodwill that Greeks treated almost as the epitome of friendship.[25] Ideally, business becomes a matter of friendship, repaying a debt a question of honor. In terms of institutional economic analysis, mutual trust lowers both transaction costs and the risk of legal enforcement.

Not everyone was part of the Piraeus community, and not everyone was willing to play fair. Entrepreneurial non-citizens like Kephalos regularly dealt with people superior to them in power and status. This put them in a precarious position comparable to the situation faced by Italian traders abroad or by small artisans everywhere—not to mention the Jewish communities in Europe in the Middle Ages and early modern period. The same rulers and notables who coined the term "debt of honor" when dealing with peers would intimidate, attack, or imprison their less powerful creditors to avoid repayment. While economic and coercive powers reinforce each other in the vicious circle of peasant indebtedness, they may be separated in an urban credit economy. Communal statutes in medieval Italy outlawed the recourse to canon law to evade one's obligations; partnership contracts contained clauses forbidding the junior partner to make loans to princes and clerics.[26] These people, with power and morals on their side, could not be trusted.[27]

The Athenian banker Pasion and his son Apollodoros learned this lesson the hard way. We know about Pasion's exceptional career through a host of forensic speeches written for or by his litigious son.[28] A slave, Pasion was bought at a young age by two Athenian moneychangers-cum-bankers who trained him as a clerk. He managed to turn his business acumen into a rapid social climb. He was freed by his masters and gained citizenship in recognition of his outstanding donations to the city of Athens. When he died in 370/69, he left his two sons a substantial fortune.[29] While the Athenian citizen elite trusted and esteemed Pasion as a custodian of their money, their memory quickly faded after his death. This is at least what Apollodoros wanted an Athenian jury to believe when he sued for repayment of three interest-free loans of cash and silver plate which his father had granted to the renowned Athenian admiral Timotheus. Pasion had done so, Apollodoros explains, because he thought it wise to kindle the favor of a man of influence and standing. Eventually that very status made Timotheus question the notion that "one must pay one's debts" when dealing with a freedman turned citizen.[30] Apollodoros points out that the damage done by such opportunism goes beyond individual losses:[31]

> I should be glad, however, to ask you whether you feel anger against bankers who have failed. For, if you have reason to feel anger against them because they do you injury, is it not reasonable for you to support those who do you no injury? Surely it is through men like Timotheus that banks are caused to fail; for when they are in need, they borrow money, and think they should obtain credit because of their reputation; but when they are in funds, they do not make payments but seek to defraud their creditors.

As the relation of power is inversed, so is the situation of creditor and debtor. In the vicious circle of peasant indebtedness, the debtor goes bankrupt. In classical Athens, it may be the creditor. Apollodoros had a strong interest in smearing Timotheus, so he might have bent or altered the facts. But in order to convince the judges, several hundred ordinary Athenians elected by lot, he had to present them with arguments that matched their experiences and values.[32] Apollodoros obviously expected them to think it plausible that an elite citizen would take advantage of his position at the expense of a family of social climbers. And he expected them to take sides with the damaged creditor.

Likely, they did. Athenian law allowed anyone to sue for the enforcement of maritime contracts before a civic court of hundreds of citizens selected by lot, a procedure protecting foreigners and lower-class citizens from fraud and abuse. Athens did so for the same reason the maritime republics of Genoa and Venice insisted on fair proceedings in maritime matters: to promote trade and commerce. In 322 BCE, a metic plaintiff suing for the repayment of a maritime loan argued exactly this way:[33]

> Besides this, men of Athens, you must not forget that, while you are today deciding one case alone you are fixing a law for the whole port, and that many of those engaged in overseas trade are standing here and watching you to see how you decide this question. For if you hold that contracts and agreements made between man and man are to be binding, and show no leniency towards those who transgress them, lenders will be more ready to risk their money, and the business of your port will be increased.

This is not a unique statement.[34] The idea that legal security stimulates commerce is nowadays stressed by historians employing models of neo-institutional economics.[35] Max Weber had pointed it out a hundred years ago.[36] Plato himself made a concession to this view. In his *Laws*, he abolishes the enforcement of debts to shift the risk of a bad loan from debtor to creditor (see below). Contracts with artisans were a different matter. Plato stipulates a hefty fine for not paying an artisan after receiving the commissioned work. Plato explains that this law will "lend aid to the bonds that unite the city."[37]

Debts: Bond of Friendship, Curse of Hatred?

The idea that the obligation to pay one's debt created a bond of unity was a commonplace in oratory and political thought since the end of the fifth century. The first surviving comprehensive statement of it was written by the so-called Anonymous Iamblichi around 400:[38]

Trust (πίστις) is the first thing that comes about from good order (εὐνομία); it greatly benefits (or: "brings profit to," ὠφελοῦσα) all people, and belongs among the great good things. For because of this, resources (or: "money," χρήματα) are shared in common, and in this way, even if they are scarce, nonetheless they suffice because they circulate (κυκλούμενα), while, without this, they would not suffice even if they were abundant. And the most suitable way for people to navigate the uncertainties of fortune that affect money and life, both those that are favourable and those that are not, is for them to base themselves on good order: for those people who have good fortune enjoy it in safety and freedom from intrigues, while on the contrary those who have bad fortune receive assistance from the fortunate ones on the basis of intermingling and trust that come about from good order.

The Anonymous proposes two links between economic prosperity and social peace: First, trust raises productivity by easing the circulation of scarce resources and, second, the circulation of these resources contributes to a more equal distribution of wealth that in turn will promote social peace.[39] The Anonymous' general phrasing leaves it open whether he thinks of circulation of capital via cash sales or via credit transactions. His stress on trust makes the latter interpretation seem more likely. Similar statements from the fourth century BCE support this interpretation. In the *Areopagiticus*, a model speech written in 355 BCE, the Athenian orator Isocrates glorifies the mores of the Athenian ancestors. Prosperity and harmony reigned. Everybody got what was due to them, gods and humans. There was no enmity between rich and poor. The poorer citizens did not envy their betters but cared for their "great estates" like for their own because they considered the rich's well-being to be a precondition of their own prosperity (εὐπορία). Solidarity was reciprocal:[40]

Those who possessed wealth did not look down upon those in humbler circumstances, but, regarding poverty among their fellow-citizens as their own disgrace, came to the rescue of the distresses of the poor, handing over lands to some at moderate rentals, sending out some to engage in commerce, and furnishing capital (ἀφορμή) to others to enter upon various occupations; for they had no fear that they might suffer one of two things—that they might lose their whole investment or recover, after much trouble, only a mere fraction of their venture. . . . For they saw that in cases of contract the judges were not in the habit of indulging their sense of equity but were strictly faithful to the laws and that they . . . were indeed more severe on defaulters than were the injured themselves, since they believed that those who break down confidence in contracts do a greater injury to the poor than to the rich; for if the rich were to stop lending, they would be deprived of only a slight revenue, whereas if the poor should lack the help of their supporters they would be reduced to desperate straits.

Isocrates' golden age is a barely veiled rich man's fantasy of his own day. Like the vision of the world in the Mesopotamian letters discussed by Pirngruber (see Chapter 2), his glossy picture of interclass friendship throws a shadow of dominance and patronage. Isocrates suggested improvements to Athenian democracy that would have resulted in a shift toward oligarchy.[41] The image of upper-class citizens as patronizing investors who receive money—and reverence—in return for their generosity fits this picture. Isocrates suggests that all that is needed to escape poverty is a bit of initial help, diligence, and a righteous mind. He takes no account of the risks involved in Mediterranean agriculture and trade[42]—risks distributed in favor of creditors and aggravated by the absence of legal notions such as limited liability, legitimate bankruptcy, or insurance (in the modern sense).[43] Isocrates himself could, if rhetorical need be, bewail the plight of those who "fell into servitude for the sake of small contracts, working as hired laborers now."[44] The speechwriter Lysias uses almost the same phrase in a different context, which suggests that servitude through debts was a topos in Athenian oratory.[45] Obligations arising from enforceable contracts could become a heavy burden.

That debt and misery were familiar experiences to Athenian audiences is suggested by the opening scene of Menander's *Hero*, a comic play written toward the end of the fourth century BCE.[46] A slave who is asked whether a girl working in the household is a "slave" (δουλή) gives the curious answer "kind of." He relates the girl's story to clarify his answer. The girl's father was a non-citizen shepherd living in the Attic hinterland. He became a "household servant" (οἰκέτης) early in life. He fathered twins, the girl in question and a boy, who is a another dependent of the same household. Debt is the reason the twins are "quasi-slaves." Their father had to borrow a mina of silver (one hundred drachmae, about fifty to sixty-five daily wages at the time) from the head of the household to feed his children. He was never able to pay back a single installment of this loan. When the shepherd died, his son had to borrow another mina from the same creditor to pay for his father's burial. He told his sister "to work off the debt" (τὸ χρέος ἀπεργαζόμενος) in the creditor's household. Geoffrey de Ste. Croix could only explain this example of debt bondage by hypothesizing that after the downfall of democracy in 322, "forms of debt bondage could well have crept in and even received at least tacit legal recognition."[47] Edward Harris has argued that there is no need for such a hypothesis since Solon never abolished debt bondage in the first place.⁴⁸ I am skeptical about Harris' assumption that even citizens could become bondsmen in classical times (see below), but I agree with regard to non-citizen residents. Menander illustrates the reality of debt bondage: The legal line that divided chattel slavery and debt bondage could become all but invisible in everyday practice.

Menander's play gives some hints as to why poor households were threatened by debt. They lacked the means to buffer risks.⁴⁹ Small farmers had to deal with widely varying margins of crop returns; artisans and tradespeople were dependent on volatile markets for supplies and sales.⁵⁰ Because we lack archival records, tensions created by poverty and inequality only become visible when extraordinary events caught a historian's interest. In the summer of 428, Mytilene, the biggest city on the island of Lesbos, deserted the Delian league. The league, designed to counter the Persian king in 478, had since become an instrument of Athenian empire-building. The Spartans, at war with Athens and its allies, supported oligarchic Mytilene, which in turn was put under siege by an Athenian expedition force. Hard pressed, the Spartan commander in the city decided to hand heavy-infantry gear to the "the common people" (ὁ δῆμος), who until now had fought with light weaponry only. As soon as the commoners received the panoply, they stopped obeying their officers' commands. They banded together and told the "powerful" (οἱ δυνατοί) to "bring out the hidden corn and distribute it"; otherwise, they would surrender the city to the Athenians. Evidently, the poorer people were starving and suspected richer households of hoarding grain. The "powerful" lost hope and handed over the city to the Athenians themselves. The Athenians executed the members of the ruling elite who had instigated the revolt, more than a thousand people. They confiscated their estates and distributed it to Athenian citizens. Mytilene became a democracy.⁵¹

Sixty years later, around 370, civil strife in democratic Argos ended in a similar bloodshed. This time, no outside power was involved. The elitist literature of later antiquity memorialized the event as an example of the horrors of civil war and the excesses of the multitude. The first-century BCE historian Diodorus, our main source, labels the affair "the worst civil strife that ever happened among the Greeks" and blames "some demagogues" for it. They "inflamed the multitude against those of superior wealth and reputation to such a degree that the attacked conspired to overthrow the people." The plot was discovered, and "thirty of the most eminent citizens" were summarily condemned to death, their property confiscated. The demagogues pressed on, until in the end 1,200 of the "super rich" (μεγαλοπλούτων) and "powerful" were executed by clubbing (a procedure called *skutalismos*). The demagogues, frightened by the outburst of violence, wanted to stop the trials. Instead, the *dēmos*, fearing betrayal, summarily executed them as well.⁵²

These historiographical accounts seem to support Plato's vision of a general antagonism between "rich" and "poor" that ends in civil strife.[53] He remarks that oligarchs fear their poorer fellow citizens so much that they do not arm them even in the face of external threats. That observation neatly matches the events in Mytilene.[54] Plato identifies the greed of the ruling rich as the cause of the eventual downfall of oligarchy:[55]

> "And such negligence and encouragement of licentiousness in oligarchies not infrequently has reduced to poverty men of no ignoble quality." "It surely has." "And there they sit, I fancy, within the city, furnished with stings, that is, arms, some burdened with debt [οἱ μὲν ὀφείλοντες χρέα], others disfranchised, others both, hating and conspiring against the acquirers of their estates and the rest of the citizens, and eager for revolution." "Tis so." "But these money-makers with down-bent heads, pretending not even to see them, but inserting the sting of their money into any of the remainder who do not resist, and harvesting from them in interest as it were a manifold progeny of the parent sum, foster the drone and pauper element in the state."

The poor finally conspire against the rich, kill and exile them, and set up a democracy. Democracy eventually founders as well. A demagogue who pitches the masses against the rich will gain control. He becomes popular through the promise of "debt cancellation and the redistribution of land" (χρεῶν τε ἀποκοπὰς καὶ γῆς ἀναδασμόν). Instead of fulfilling these promises, the demagogue seizes power as tyrant and goes on to exploit the common people even worse than the oligarchs did.[56] At one point during his gloomy narrative, Plato offers a solution to the problem of accumulating bad debts. If the law placed the risk with the creditors, "money making would become less shameless in the city."[57] The idea is stated more fully in the *Laws*. Buying and selling shall only take place in the marketplace and only by cash payment. If anyone makes exchanges elsewhere and based on trust (i.e., through sale by credit), the contract is not legally enforceable.[58] This arrangement would not outlaw lending and borrowing so much as shift it from the law courts to the sphere of trust. The idea is well considered but contrafactual.[59] In the classical period, the principle of enforceability was firmly entrenched in practice and thought.[60]

Plato's view of sociopolitical crisis seems supported by more descriptive accounts of the role of debt in civil strife. The historian Thucydides reports how during the bloody civil war in Corcyra in 427, some participants used the chaos to settle older accounts, killing creditors and other personal enemies.[61] The military writer Aeneas Tacticus, writing in the 350s, gave the advice not to appoint a poor or indebted man as wall guard or gatekeeper since he might be tempted to betray his city or to incite revolt. Even closer to Plato is Aeneas' suggestion to secure the loyalty of the "mass of citizens" by the cancellation of interest or even principal since, as Aeneas puts it, of all potential internal enemies, debtors are the most "fearsome."[62] An inscription from the city of Ephesus in Asia Minor, set up around 300 BCE, provides evidence for such a moratorium of interest payments in time of war (see below), and similar measures were taken in various places in Hellenistic times.[63] Aeneas' advice was not a theoretical exercise.

The Absence of Debt Crises in the Classical Period

And yet, upon closer inspection, the evidence for the idea that debt crises regularly sparked civil wars crumbles. Let us start with Plato. Like all political thinkers of his time, he restricts his discussion of debt and poverty to the citizenry (i.e., a privileged minority of adult males). One of the reasons Plato stresses (relative) economic equality as a necessary condition for sociopolitical stability is the need to preserve the cohesion of an exclusive ruling group. What exactly did Plato have in mind when he suggested abolishing enforceability? Did he want to realign profit and risk re-establishing the trust-based credit ties that businessmen like Kephalos maintained? Or did he want to realign power and status to enable upper-class citizens to disregard their obligations vis-à-vis lower-class creditors who could easily be denounced as petty usurers? Plato's recommendation of a law protecting artisans from fraud points toward the first interpretation. His utopia of a stratified society with static social orders points toward the second interpretation.

Besides Plato's intentions, the accuracy of his explanation of social conflict may be questioned. His own pupil Aristotle criticized it as too materialistic.[64] Aristotle adds another factor, honor. People start civil strife "because of material gain *and* honour" (διὰ κέρδος γὰρ καὶ διὰ τιμήν). They do not just fight to get these things for themselves but also when they see others "unjustly acquire an excessive amount of them." Material equality will not end civil strife: The "noble" (οἱ χαρίεντες) consider themselves "more worthy" (ἄξιοι) and will not bear equal rank.[65] People will as likely start a revolution to become equal as they will start a revolution to become unequal.[66]

Aristotle cites many historical examples of civil strife (*stasis*) that can be dated to the sixth, fifth, and fourth centuries. In only one case—Rhodes in 391, the one example Graeber cites—debts triggered a revolt. It was not the pauperized mass who started civil war in Rhodes but a group of rich men who plotted to overthrow democracy to escape the burden of public expenditure.[67] The episode is similar to the events in Mytilene and Argos. In the three cases, the "upper class" was not just an economic class but a status group distinguished by power and prestige and therefore variously called "the eminent" or "the powerful." In all three cases, it was the elite, or part of it, that initiated political turmoil. This is not to say that the common people in Mytilene or Argos might not have been happy to see the rich and powerful fall. Armin Eich has emphasized the socioeconomic dimension of civil strife that too often has been rejected out of hand in reaction to Marxist approaches. Civil strife regularly involved large parts of the local population and was accompanied by redistribution. The property of the defeated party was confiscated and publicly sold, debts were cancelled (at least partially), sometimes even slaves were freed.[68] As we have seen, the ancient authors took it for granted that material gain was an important motivation to participate in civil strife. What the evidence does not prove is that debt crises were a primary cause for rebellions or that the *dēmos* started them in the hope of achieving general debt cancellation.

Aeneas Tacticus and Thucydides think of individual impoverishment rather than collective pauperization. Indebted men are a security risk because they are tempted to exploit situations of war or internal strife. The typical man to start a revolution is not a poor man pushed into utter destitution but a disgruntled member of the elite, threatened by downward mobility or marginalized by democratic inclusiveness. These men had the ambition and the means to make their personal misery a cause of public concern. In his critique of Plato's theory of civil strife, Aristotle duly notes that "when some of the leaders (ἡγεμόνες) have lost their properties they stir up innovations, when men of the other classes are ruined nothing fearful happens."[69]

What about the notorious slogans of "debt cancellation" (*chreōn anakopē*, the literal "cutting of debt") and "redistribution of land" (*gēs anadasmos*)? Plato expected a would-be tyrant to promise these measures to seduce the poor citizens. There are two cases from or close to the classical period for tyrants delivering on these promises, but they concern places at the periphery of the Greek world and are passed down to us by post-classical authors.[70] Most attestations of the slogan of debt cancellation stem from even later authors writing in the Roman imperial period or even Byzantine times.[71] These late accounts of turbulent multitudes and evil tyrants relied on earlier biased accounts of elitist writers and are so topical and abbreviated in nature that it is impossible to figure out what had actually happened and what "debt cancellation" meant in each instance.[72]

A more reliable picture of the scope and context of debt relief emerges from the Ephesian inscription from c. 300 BCE already mentioned. The text reproduces a decree that continued measures taken in an earlier decree. The first decree stipulated a moratorium of interest payments during a war. The second established a procedure for debt redemption after the end of a war, which is unfortunately never specified. The careful wording of the decrees suggests that tensions ran high. A considerable number of people stood to lose either the money they had lent or the farmland they had pledged as security. The scenario of indebted farmers ruined by external calamity brings to mind the vicious circle of peasant indebtedness. Yet, the Ephesian case does not exactly fit the model of an agrarian society with a huge divide between landlords and peasants. The loans were secured by hypothecation, and landownership was with few exemptions restricted to citizens. The Ephesian debtors were propertied, then, to some degree; and most of them were probably citizens like their creditors.[73] They were themselves members of the very group that issued the decrees regulating interest and debt redemption. The debtors' civic status seems to be the reason the Ephesians passed laws on their behalf in the first place. It was generally accepted that farmers and men of landed property bore the cost of war most heavily whenever enemy troops invaded a city's territory. Landowners were a prominent group within the citizenry, in both numbers and status, so their well-being could not easily be ignored. The Ephesian decree is evidence for a crisis but not necessarily a testimony to exploitation or impending revolution. It carefully formulates a compromise that was meant to acknowledge, not abrogate, existing laws and contracts.[74] The inscription indicates that indebtedness was a more frequent political problem than our fragmented literary record reveals. It also reveals the reluctance to cancel debts even in times of emergency. A survey of fourth-century references to the slogan of "debt cancellation" confirms this picture. All these statements are general and/ or vague in nature; they are normative, and, with one exception, negative: They decry or outlaw debt cancellation.

The orator Andocides relates that after the Athenians had toppled the oligarchic regime of the "Thirty" in 403, they decreed that only laws passed after the fall of the regime should be valid. Decisions in private suits and arbitrations should still be binding, however, "in order that there shall not arise any cancellation of debts (χρεῶν ἀποκοπαί) or appealing of court decisions."[75] Andocides probably misrepresented the law to serve his own needs as a defendant.[76] The reason he could do so without impunity was the pride Athenians took in their stance against the upheaval of property rights. Fifty years later, the orator Demosthenes could still flatter an Athenian audience by recalling how the restored democracy distanced itself from the arbitrary confiscations of the preceding oligarchy.[77] The *dēmos* made it a point to put his respect for property rights and contractual obligations on display. Thrasybulos, the leader of the democratic exiles that had overthrown the oligarchic regime, reiterated this theme in his speech to the first assembly after the re-establishment of democracy. He addressed the former supporters of the oligarchical regime in the audience: "The commons (δῆμος), though poorer than you, never did you any wrong for the sake of money; while you, though richer than any of them, have done many disgraceful things for the sake of gain."[78] In the same vein, the *dēmos* paid back to the Spartans the considerable loan of one hundred talents (six hundred thousand drachmae), which the oligarchs had borrowed to pay for their military defense against the advancing democratic faction. The pseudo-Aristotelian *Constitution of the Athenians* explains that the *dēmos* did so to restore concord (ὁμόνοια). He adds that this was a remarkable action since elsewhere "the democratic parties" were "in the habit of making a general redistribution of the land."[79] Against the anti-democratic implication of this remark it must be said that a punitive confiscation of property would have been quite appropriate by the standards of Greek public law. Still, the *dēmos* decided to exhibit political prudence and moral superiority and stick to the rule that "one must pay one's debts"—even if that meant paying back money borrowed by a hostile faction to pay for one's own destruction.

In his statement about the Athenian amnesty, Andocides thinks about debt cancellation as a series of individual actions (note the plural *apokopai*). He claims that one of his accusers benefited from the general amnesty, although he was merely a defaulting tax farmer.[80] Since tax farming afforded capital and sureties, this suggests that the ban on "debt cancellations" was not necessarily aimed against a rebellious multitude but rather against individuals who might exploit political upheaval for private profit. This was a general fear. The *Constitution of the Athenians* relates how a couple of "notables" (γνώριμοι) used their knowledge of Solon's upcoming *seisachtheia* to make a profit. They borrowed money and bought a lot of land. When debts were cancelled soon afterward, they refused to pay back the borrowed funds.[81] The story was probably invented to smear the ancestors of prominent men of the fourth century.[82] The fact that it was told shows how in the fourth century a story about debt cancellation as relief to indebted peasants could be reinterpreted as a tale about daring notables who exploited political turmoil.

The Athenians' fear of the abuse of political power or conflict for the sake of private gain was widely shared.[83] According to a Pseudo-Demosthenic speech, when most of the Greek states united under Macedonian hegemony in 338, the treaty they concluded provided that

> there shall be no executions and banishments contrary to the laws established in those states, no confiscation of property, no partition of lands, no cancelling of debts, and no emancipation of slaves for purposes of revolution (ἐπὶ νεωτερισμῷ).[84]

This is the conventional list of evils associated with the subversion of the rule of law. The speaker vaguely hints at constant violation of these terms but fails to specify the circumstances. Instead, he conventionally and sweepingly puts the blame on "the orators." The text of the original treaty did not even specify the evils the way the orator does. It simply included a vow to respect the member states' autonomy and present constitution, regardless of whether it was an oligarchy, a democracy, or the Macedonian monarchy itself.[85] Around the same time, Isocrates employed the same vague and topical language to contrast idealized Sparta with the cities in the rest of Greece. The latter experienced all kinds of "irreparable ills," among them debt cancellation.[86] Isocrates remains unspecific about where and how these calamities happened and the exact role of debt played in them. Even Plato, who had a certain sympathy for economic leveling, has to reach back to mythic prehistory to find a lawgiver who accomplished a redistribution of material wealth. For his own days, Plato records only a negative formula. Any lawgiver attempting such a thing is met with the cry, "do not move what is not-to-be-moved" (μὴ κινεῖν τὰ ἀκίνητα) and "is cursed for introducing redistributions of land and remissions of debts, with the result that every man is rendered powerless."[87] Plato suggests the lawgiver should advance by small changes and to a large degree rely on the voluntary munificence of the elite.[88]

Plato's words echo official oaths sworn by citizens or magistrates. An oath of allegiance, sworn by the citizens of the Cretan city of Itanos at the beginning of the third century, provides a long list of evils to be shunned by all citizens and the magistrates especially and broadly calls for concord, loyalty, and the rule of law.[89] Somewhere in the middle of the text, the oath stipulates "not to undertake either a redistribution of land, or of houses, or of housing-plots."[90] The laborious formulation makes it clear that the stipulation is not particularly aimed at the redistribution of farmland, the primary means of peasant subsistence, but aims at violations of private property rights in general. The same concern is even more pronounced in an inscription from Pistiros in Bulgaria, the site of a Greek emporium in what was ancient Thrace. The inscription records a guarantee of rights and immunities granted to Greek traders around 359, most probably by a Thracian king.[91] The promise not to cancel any debts accumulated by Thracians figures prominently but only as part of an extensive list of privileges that include local autonomy, tax exemption, and various protections of property rights.[92] The Greek traders were specifically concerned not about a looming debt revolt but about the general prospect of a foreign prince preying on them. Deep in inner Thrace, they could not ban such an abuse of power the way they did at home. Like foreign traders in the Middle Ages, the Greek traders in Thrace had to rely on guarantees of legal enforceability to carry on their business.

The best evidence for a debt crisis that induces political reform is an inscribed law from Delphi that probably passed around 400.[93] The law's main concern is to fix the rates of interest within the city's territory.[94] As David Asheri notes, the law carefully distinguishes between conflicts about excessive interest rates and any demagogic call for "land distribution and cancellation of debt"—the latter is anathematized.[95] This and other passages indicate that the law marked the end of a serious conflict about debt.[96] Despite this original context, the Delphic law was more than an emergency measure.[97] It established general rules about credit transactions, including specifications concerning petty loans,[98] loans involving women,[99] and legal procedure.[100] The citizens of Delphi apparently felt a need for the legal regulation of an economic sphere which so far had still been regulated by custom or individual contract. Their perception of debt as a collective problem did not lead to the abolishment of enforceability (the law rules out retroactive action). Instead, it led to a more exact definition of the conditions of enforceability. I add that Phocis, the region surrounding Delphi, was an economic backwater compared to the interconnected cities of the Aegean. That fits the hypothesis that collective indebtedness exploding into revolt is a phenomenon of traditional agrarian economies (see above).[101] Our reports about serious attempts to cancel debts refer to colonial cities at the periphery or rural polities.[102] Debt crises were most absent from the very places where money, credit, and enforceability were most entrenched.

Explaining the Absence of Debt Crises in Classical Greece and the Paradox of Debt

If debt was omnipresent, why were debt crises so absent from classical Greece? Any answer must be hypothetical given our fragmented and biased historical record. It is nonetheless worthwhile to attempt an answer as it helps to explain the apparent paradoxical assessment of debt as both a bond of friendship and a curse of hatred. My discussion has focused on the most urbanized, interconnected, and economically developed regions of Greece, the Aegean region and its adjacent coastlines. This focus seems justified insofar as these areas spawned most of the intellectual discourses that constitute our literary source material. In the more backward and rural parts of Greece, many a peasant rebellion driven by debt and poverty may have gone unnoticed by historical writers.[103] To explain why something similar did not happen in a city like Athens, I propose four factors of varying importance: (1) city-state imperialism, (2) commercialization, (3) civic self-government, and (4) public lending and leasing.

City-state imperialism is often cited to explain the relative welfare of ordinary Greeks (likewise by Graeber).[104] In Athens, elites and commoners formed a partnership to maintain a profitable empire. Elite citizens grudgingly accepted that they needed their poorer fellow citizens as soldiers and sailors to expand their dominion. They received pay as rowers, soldiers, or jury members; and some of them received a plot of land in one of the overseas colonies, called *cleruchies*. State pay was not sufficient to support an Athenian household of four to six people, but it helped to endure periods of economic distress.[105] Imperial traffic and trade generated further income opportunities in the Piraeus and the city itself.[106] The Athenian empire was extraordinary in both extent and duration. Many other cities, however, created smaller hegemonic spheres of control, from which their citizens drew at least some economic benefit.[107]

Urbanism was another cause of comparative liberty and prosperity. Densified cohabitation and a higher degree of social division of labor had two effects, commercial opportunities and civic self-government. Urban environments offered more opportunities to earn an income besides agriculture. The emergence of a diversified economy in the Aegean was driven by an ecology fragmented by geology, climate, and political structure but unified by low-cost maritime transportation, cultural emulation, and the need to balance local shortages and surpluses through trade.[108] In their study of subsistence agriculture, Colin Clark and Margaret Haswell cite a range of preindustrial societies to demonstrate the correlation of urbanization and workers' income. Income for rural workers and small tenants is lowest (near subsistence level) where cultivation has specialized in cash crops and urban centers are few and far off. Competition for labor is low, while rents are high, a combination that widens the power gap between laborer/tenant and landlord. Once urbanization and commercialization increase employment opportunities, rents fall, and wages rise.[109] This finding squares well with the high degree of occupational diversification and high wage rates in the urban centers of classical Greece.[110] Many small households probably did not completely switch from agriculture to handicraft or trade. By diversifying their sources of income, they minimized the risk of subsistence crises and became less dependent on any single employer.[111]

Urbanization favored the lower classes in yet another way. Close cohabitation lowered the cost to organize resistance against exploitation by easing communications and congregation. While this is true for all classes, the comparative advantage is greater for the non-elites who lack horses, messengers, and first-rate weaponry.[112] Attempts to create narrow and exploitative governments could be held in check by spontaneous violence or, later, by laws and procedures institutionally protecting all citizens.[113] Even oligarchical regimes had to accommodate the peculiarities of close civic habitation. Aristotle advises them—as a matter of expediency, not philanthropy—to abstain from exploiting the *dēmos* and to ensure the well-being of the common people, to make them accept political exclusion.[114] Most cities devised some scheme to secure supplies. The success of such measures is a matter of scholarly debate. Either way, an amount of evidence shows that both democratic and oligarchic governments attached importance to feeding the citizenry.[115] The downfall of oligarchical Mytilene is a reminder of the expediency of such a focus.

The economic well-being of Greek citizens had its cost. The development of a monetized urban economy in the Aegean is inseparably connected to the spread of chattel slavery. While chattel slavery was a universal institution in ancient Greece, its economic importance varied. In rural or peripheral regions with an extensive regime of crop farming and stockbreeding, traditional forms of rural dependency and servitude long remained the predominant form of dependent labor. Slave labor, in contrast, was first introduced on a massive scale in the more urbanized parts of the Aegean. The cities in these regions were connected to maritime trade routes, which allowed them to import slaves and export slave-produced goods. Slave labor predominated where it was most profitable: in places where production was market-oriented (to some degree) and intensive in terms of capital input.[116]

As Menander knew, slavery and debt bondage can become quite similar in practice. Like slaves, bondsmen had to be fed by and guarded by their masters. In one regard, bondsmen were even more troublesome than slaves. They were not born into slavery and often stayed in their original community, so they preserved the memory of the freedom they had lost, along with community ties. Chattel slaves, violently uprooted from their native community and isolated through language, customs, and looks, were easier to control.[117] The traditional form of debt bondage lost its economic importance in Athens and elsewhere in part because in the process of commercialization: Masters found chattel slaves more convenient to exploit.

Still, debt bondage had one economic advantage over slavery. While bondsmen worked to redeem their debt, bought slaves lacked personal motivation to dedicate their strength or acumen to the master's profit. To remedy this fact, Greek masters increasingly promised manumission as an incentive to a few privileged slaves. Paying with their labor or, in case of independently working slaves, in cash installments, slaves could "purchase" their freedom—as if redeeming a debt.[118] Turning chattel slavery into a kind of indebtedness took even more direct forms. A freedman (*apeleutheros*) was considered indebted to his master and was obliged to pay him his respects but also provide services or shares of his profits. These customary obligations became more exactly defined by written contracts and law during the fourth century. In Athens, a conditionally freed person who neglected the obligations toward their former master risked a trial for "desertion" (*dike apostasiou*)—the punishment was re-enslavement. Conditional manumission became a general practice all over Greece during Hellenistic times.[119] Two hundred years after Solon had abolished debt slavery and debt bondage went out of use, both institutions were reintroduced, remodeled through the combination of chattel slavery and conditional manumission.

Finally, I turn to the factor most difficult to assess, public lending and leasing. City-states themselves as well as their sanctuaries, cult associations, and parish communities (called *demes* in Attica) handed out money on loan or arable land and workshops for rent.[120] One might assume that these corporate creditors performed a philanthropic function similar to the *Monti di Pietà* set up in Italian cities during the Renaissance age or the Hindu and Buddhist temples and monasteries Graeber describes.[121] The loans were often comparatively small (one hundred to three hundred drachmae), interest rates were fixed, their duration was long, and the treatment of belated debtors was mostly lenient.[122]

Caution is in order, however, when highlighting the benevolent effects of public loans and leases. First, it is difficult to gauge its extent. The steady trickle of newfound inscriptions lends credibility to the view that we simply lack information about what was a widespread practice as even small demes earmarked significant sums for lending.[123] Even so, it remains doubtful whether public lending was bringing much relief for the poor or was ever intended to do so. Most sanctuaries and associations demanded landed security, a requirement that barred the dispossessed and foreigners not entitled to real property. In at least one case, a sanctuary had pledged pieces of real estate seized and duly put on auction.[124] In no case I know of were interest rates as low as the 5% demanded by the Italian *Monti*.[125]

Robin Osborne has stressed that the lessees of public and sacral land were predominantly men of wealth and at least local prominence, and almost all of the Attic lessees were members of the deme that was leasing the land.[126] Two tentative conclusions seem possible. First, even if public loans and leases did help to ease the "credit market" and provided low-risk income, they were not designed to this end. Second, any help that these loans and leans provided was limited to members of the local community. Needy non-citizens were left exposed to the harsh reality of Greek rules of enforceability.

Although the effects of public loans and leases are doubtful in practice, it is interesting to note that Aristotle advocated similar measures to help the needy. In the *Politics*, he suggests providing "the hapless" (ἄποροί) with "lasting prosperity" (εὐπορία χρόνιος) by giving them capital out of public funds to purchase a small estate or to start with trade or husbandry. The Carthaginians and Tarentines did so, Aristotle tells us, to win the goodwill of the *dēmos*.[127] Aristotle's advice seems quite remarkable, even if the measures he proposes look tiny compared to modern economic policies. The limits of Aristotle's vision confirm the epigraphical record. Aristotle advertised such measures because they were *not* generally applied in his day. Like Isocrates, Aristotle "preserves" democracy by nudging it toward oligarchy. The suggested provision of seed money is meant to replace direct redistribution through state pay. His choice of examples is suggestive: Aristotle considered Carthage an aristocracy tipping toward oligarchy[128] and Tarentum a democracy with oligarchical features.[129] Like all learned writers of his time, Aristotle adhered to an elitist ideal of social concord. The elite governs and patronizes needy citizens. These poorer citizens in turn abstain from direct participation in government.[130] Another aspect is so self-evident that Aristotle does not even state it: All measures of economic help are restricted to citizens.

Conclusion

The combined factors of imperialism, commercialization, self-government, and—to a limited degree—public loans and leases worked to protect Greek city-dwellers from the vicious circle of indebtedness so present in other premodern societies. This conclusion must be qualified by two cautionary remarks.

First, most of these factors worked only in favor of citizens. Legal protection against fraud and abuse was usually extended to foreigners and resident aliens. Economic support and privileges granted to citizens were not. Away from their home community, non-citizens could also rely less on the safety net of kinship and inherited friendship. All surviving allusions to debt bondage in Athens refer to non-citizens.[131] Whatever the letter of the law was, when an Athenian audience imagined debt bondage, it imagined it as the fate of foreigners.

Second, the fact that the Aegean offered opportunities to enterprising individuals does not mean that everyone succeeded. Where there is profit, there is risk. The pattern of individual opportunities, however, changed the perception of these risks. The same factors that mitigated the problem of debt inhibited resistance against excessive indebtedness by politically isolating debtors. Since citizenship was a privilege, it promoted the upward solidarity typical of stratified societies. Better to keep what one has than lose it all in revolt. Citizen assemblies outlawed the cancellation of debt in both democratic Athens and oligarchic Delphi. Since opportunities to get rich were seemingly many, everyone struggled for individual success rather than collectively striving for redistribution. Although everyone knew someone who had succumbed to debt and misery, people upheld the notion that "one must pay one's debts" to protect their own reputation and property.[132] In classical Greece, debt was a familiar, but not a shared, experience.[133]

This isolation of the debtor helps to explain the Greek paradox of debt. Greek city-state societies were pervaded by monetary credit. Farmers, artisans, and traders all loaned money or bought and sold on credit to keep their businesses running. Small households took short-term loans to survive another day; big households used credit to meet their sociopolitical commitments. The difference between an interest-free loan granted as a favor and an interest-bearing loan granted as an investment often lay in the eye of the beholder; kin turned business partner, business partners turned friends, bound together by debt. For this reason, everyone accepted the notion that "one must pay one's debts" and considered repaying a debt to be the mark of justice. For the same reason, the specter of debt cancellation lingered in everyone's mind. Where there is profit, there is risk; and in the Greek *polis*, winners and losers lived next door to each other, in full view of one another. If an external attack or internal strife changed expectations about the future, the same bond that had united people in peace now pitched them against each other like a curse of hatred: debt.

5

Debt, Death, and Destruction in Ancient Rome

Lisa Eberle

Points of Departure: Moral Confusion about Debt (in Ancient Rome)

Moral confusion pervades the history of debt. This was one of the starting points for David Graeber's seminal *Debt: The First 5,000 Years*. As he suggested at the beginning of this work, most people in most places have combined a certain readiness to malign people who lend out money at interest with thinking that debts should somehow be repaid.[1] Roman thought about debt would appear to support this idea. Romans in the middle and late Republic—from the third to the first century BCE, that is—were in (at least) two minds about debt. In the second century BCE Cato likened usury to murder. For him, choosing to make a living by lending out money at interest was tantamount to getting by on killing people; in both cases, he implied, your livelihood was predicated on somebody else's death.[2] In the first century BCE Cicero suggested that an insolvent debtor who saw their possessions being auctioned off was actually witnessing their own funeral; this funeral, however, was attended not by their friends but by executioners ready to lacerate the remnants of their life.[3] For Cicero such a person was not only no longer among the living; they were actually below, inferior to, the dead. More specifically, then, people like Cato and Cicero were not only confused about debt. They were extremely confused or, rather, confused in extremes.[4] For them, debt, no matter how they approached it, was intertwined with death and destruction, with the end of life as they knew it.

Cato and Cicero were prominent and controversial politicians in Rome, but their moral confusion about debt—not least what I have called its "extreme"

Lisa Eberle, *Debt, Death, and Destruction in Ancient Rome* In: *Debt in the Ancient Mediterranean and Near East*. Edited by: John Weisweiler, Oxford University Press. © Oxford University Press 2023.
DOI: 10.1093/oso/9780197647172.003.0005

nature, the way in which their thinking about the issue was intertwined with death and destruction—would appear to have had a broader social basis. Among other things, this moral confusion in extremes also found expression in the Roman law of debt at the time. The Romans thought that already the XII Tables, the body of laws they considered the foundation of their legal order, limited interest rates.[5] They imagined that several laws in the fourth century BCE further reduced that limit until the *lex Genucia* in 342 completely outlawed lending at interest.[6] In the early first century BCE such a prohibition was still on the books in Rome, but practice had superseded it.[7] Provisions in 88 and 51 BCE allowed lending at interest again and set annual maximum rates at $8\frac{1}{3}$% (or 10%) and 12%, respectively.[8] In the second century BCE people who exacted interest beyond those varying limits had to pay back four times the amount that they had exacted in contravention of the law; for comparison, thieves were asked to pay back double.[9] Usury, or *usura*, as the Romans called it, was a dangerous matter; as such, it had to be limited, and its excesses had to be punished.

Analogous observations can be made about the law of insolvency. While there is reason to distrust imperial jurists' interpretation of the law of the XII Tables according to which creditors could carve up their insolvent debtors' bodies, the inability to repay one's debt in the middle and late Republic nonetheless meant death and destruction.[10] The Roman *praetor*, the main judicial magistrate in Rome, could give a defaulting debtor to their creditor in temporary servitude (*addictio*), and, as a last resort, he was able to make over all possessions of recalcitrant debtors to their creditors (*missio in bona*), who could then recover the debts by selling the debtors' possessions at auction (*venditio bonorum*).[11] Importantly, insolvent debtors not only suffered economic destruction. Beyond losing all their property, they also suffered social and political death because they became subject to *infamia*, which spelled the loss of political rights as well as differential treatment in law.[12]

In his important 1966 article on debt reforms in the middle of the first century BCE, Martin Frederiksen described these sanctions against defaulting debtors as "unduly harsh," especially because "they hardly reflected the important role that money exchanges were playing in society at the time." This observation can readily be extended to the laws on usury.[13] The intellectual framework that David Graeber articulated in *Debt: The First 5,000 Years* allows us to articulate Frederiksen's puzzlement through a more precise analytical lens. Shouldn't the "extreme" nature of Roman moral confusion about debt give pause for thought in a society that can be seen as one of the most successful and convincing examples of a "military–coinage–slavery complex" in the Axial Age? In a society, that is, in which military conquest, the minting of coins to pay the soldiers doing the conquering, and the increasing enslavement of other people to carry out the old and new tasks that these soldiers could not be made to do contributed to the creation of a (precariously) free peasantry and the emergence of markets and commercial exchange?[14]

Rome began minting and casting coins, both bronze and silver, in the late fourth century BCE. The precise context in which the Romans adopted this social technology remains disputed: Recurring debt crises, major building projects, and the growth of commercial environments very likely all played a role.[15] Throughout the following centuries, as the city's military success made ever more precious metal (and slaves) available, it minted ever larger issues of coinage.[16] While Rome had probably begun paying its soldiers in the late fifth century BCE, possibly by weighing out metal, in the third century BCE the city used the coins it was producing to do so.[17] The city's simultaneous insistence that payments to the state be made in coin probably accelerated the emergence of commercial exchange, including the borrowing and lending of such coins.[18] At the end of the third century BCE, during the Second Punic War, even the Roman polity entered the local credit market.[19] At some earlier moment in the same century the Romans had also introduced a legal procedure called *legis actio per condictionem*, which allowed parties to sue for the delivery of coined money that was owed.[20] Crucially, unlike in earlier procedures such as *sacramentum*, the party in breach incurred no penalties but simply had to repay their debt.[21] *Legis actio per condictionem* was also not limited to specific grounds for owing money. As such, it had an abstract and general nature that seems well suited to encompassing the multiplicity of different situations that might characterize an emerging commercial environment.

By the early second century BCE Roman legal thought had thus gone quite a long way in transforming debt "from a moral obligation into a business deal"—to use David Graeber's words.[22] And yet, while Roman law during this time demonstrably acknowledged and shaped a market environment, it also punished usury and insolvency with economic, social, and political death. The seeming inconsistency in this legal situation becomes even more distinctive once we look at other examples of military–coinage–slavery complexes in the ancient Mediterranean. In classical Athens, for instance, interest rates were not limited by law, and with the exception of debts to the state, insolvency entailed no social or political sanctions.[23] Extreme moral confusion about debt thus emerges as a distinctly Roman phenomenon that demands an explanation specific to the Roman context.[24] Attempting such an explanation is the goal of this chapter.

In short, I will argue that the particular ways in which the Roman elite was confused about debt—that the way in which their thinking about debt was intertwined with death and destruction—resulted from the way in which this elite positioned itself vis-à-vis the emergent sphere of market exchange that accompanied Rome's military–coinage–slavery complex. I begin by considering the distinctive strategy that this elite adopted to set themselves apart from self-interested market exchange: Emphasizing unequal relations of gift-exchange, not least to show that the biggest threat that such exchange posed for them and their social positions—potentially depending on others—did not in fact concern them; by contrast, everyone else was always dependent on them (see the following section, "Rome Joins the Axial Age"). Due to this particular strategy the Roman elite ended up casting monetary debt as part of ongoing relationships of gift-giving, thus mixing up gift and monetary debt in one and the same transaction. The conceptual confusion that followed from this intermingling of what were different forms of debt can help explain the particular Roman attitudes concerning usury and insolvency that were also enshrined in the Roman legal framework for usury and insolvency (see below, "Monetary Debt and Gift Debt in Rome"). In the final part of the chapter I build on these arguments to recontextualize a first-century BCE reform in the Roman law of debt that Theodor Mommsen hailed as the birth of the modern law of bankruptcy (see "Beyond Death and Destruction"). Overall, this chapter partakes in a recent trend in the study of the Roman economy that no longer adopts a purely economistic perspective, which has prevailed for much of the twentieth century, especially in anglophone scholarship, but draws on economic anthropology to take account of the social and moral dimensions of exchange and economic life more generally.[25] Beyond the content of the argument, its contribution consists of harnessing the potential of non-elite sources such as comedies and mimes for this purpose.

Rome Joins the Axial Age: Speculating about the Origins of Patronage in Roman Society

At the end of the fourth century BCE Rome was a relative late-comer to the Axial Age and to the transition from a human to a commercial economy that the coinage–military–slavery complex entailed; they were rather late, that is, to begin using money not just to measure a person's honor and status but also to procure mundane objects and foodstuffs in the marketplace.[26] Still, just as in most other cases, the precise outlines of this transition remain shrouded in darkness as contemporary sources for Roman history only begin (in a very fragmentary state) in the second half of the third century BCE. However, once the curtain goes up on Rome, we see Roman elites struggling with the realignment of circuits of exchange that this transition involved in much the same way as the elites of other Axial-Age societies. The case of Greek elites, who had undergone this very process about two hundred years earlier, would appear to provide an illuminating comparative case.

The cultural consequences of the introduction of coinage in the ancient Greek world have been the subject of much productive research in recent decades.[27] One of the key insights of this research has been to uncover the ways in which the development of coinage and the market exchange accompanying it could threaten existing social hierarchies and the constructions of value on which they were predicated. Above all, metal coinage and market exchange made things commensurable that had not been so before. The worth of a person's life, the fine imposed for hurting or killing them, was now expressed in silver and so was the value of fish in the *agora*. The Greek word *time* could mean both honor and price. Furthermore, market exchange and the dependence on money that it introduced created the situation in which even members of the elite might be dependent on others to get it.[28] Greek elites responded to this new system of value and the threats it posed by setting themselves apart from what they came to see as the sordid marketplace. One strategy in this struggle was their construction of a separate sphere of exchange that worked along opposing logics to market exchange. This aristocratic world of exchange was governed by gifts, generosity, and honor; by contrast, market exchange was all about profit, greed, and deceit—or so the elites would have it. As such, it was not for them. Correspondingly, their own households were ideally all self-sufficient.[29]

At first glance, the responses of Roman elites appear to have been quite similar. Members of the Roman elite also valued their independence from the market.[30] Cato, for example, maintained that a respectable landowner should only be a seller, not a buyer (*Agr.* 2.7). And they, too, constructed a world of gift-exchange separate from and superior to market exchange.[31] In the first century BCE Cicero could state that the exchange of favors (*beneficia*) and the relationships of friendship (*amicitia*) to which they gave rise constituted the paradigmatic way in which men should interact with each other (*Off.* 1.22).[32] However, beyond these similarities we can also detect meaningful difference between the two cases. Above all, Roman elites, unlike Greek elites, were particularly interested in unequal gift-exchange.[33] In what follows, I will suggest that this Roman emphasis on unequal relations can usefully be understood as yet another way of encountering the threat to social hierarchies that coined money and commercial exchange posed.

In cases of unequal gift-exchange the parties gave each other gifts that were unequal in kind. These types of exchange then resulted in a hierarchical relationship between them, which scholars often describe as patronage. To be sure, such patronage relations existed in many societies in which gift-exchange was an important mode of social interaction—even in classical Athens, where it has long been denied.[34] But unlike the inhabitants of ancient Athens, the Romans developed a language that singled out these unequal relationships. *Patrocinium* and *clientela*, *patronus*, and *cliens* were the key categories in this regard. Their application

was a matter of perception, tact, and mutual acknowledgment.[35] Once a relationship had been categorized along these lines, certain duties arose for both parties,
especially the inferior one, the *cliens*. Roman *clientes* were expected to crowd the
courtyards of their *patroni* every morning in a ritual called *salutation*, and they
were expected to accompany the same men throughout the streets of Rome, a
practice known as *adsectatio* that could acquire great importance in the context of
electioneering.[36] These acts of mere presence constituted the gift that those with
nothing else to give were expected to bestow on their *patroni*.

The interest among the Roman elite in unequal gift-exchange is also reflected
in the many passages in which receiving a gift, a *beneficium*, was not experienced
as a privilege but as a burden.[37] At its most extreme, this way of thinking resulted
in the description of *beneficia* as tantamount to chains in which the recipient
was now bound.[38] On one level, these metaphorical chains were a way of talking about the obligation to bestow a *beneficium* in turn. At the same time, they
provided an avenue for thinking about the continuous inequality and obligation
between two parties that ensued when the recipient of the gift was unable to
reciprocate in kind. The most extreme version of this type of exchange consisted
of the gift that could never be repaid. Several relationships in Roman society were
structured around such gifts. They included the gift of freedom, which permanently obliged manumitted slaves to their former masters, as well as the gift of
continued existence, which was part of the ritual of *deditio in fidem* that bound
Rome's defeated enemies to the particular general who had conquered them and
more generally to the city of Rome.[39]

Overall, then, Roman society was pervaded by a keen awareness of the hierarchies that could result from unequal gift-exchange. Members of the Roman elite
were eager to exploit these dynamics of gift-exchange to their advantage, using it
to bind ever more people to themselves. One of their reasons for doing so, I suggest, was to counter the threat of dependence on others that market exchange
posed. In addition to avoiding market exchange altogether—in addition to insisting that they did not need anyone else, that is—they went on the offensive and
used the language and logics of gift-exchange to claim that a great many needed
them, that they were the person on whom men depended. If they received anything from anybody else, they were simply enjoying the fruits of their own generosity.[40] A set of passages from Roman comedies, some of the earliest Latin that
has survived, lend further support to this suggestion.

The Roman comedies in question were performed in the city of Rome in the
late third and early second centuries. While they were all based on Greek origi-
nals, scholars have repeatedly shown them to be deeply concerned with the world
of their Roman audience.[41] These plays commented on contemporary political
events as well as on the changing social makeup of Roman society, especially as

regards the ever-increasing number of enslaved persons who came to Italy and Rome as prisoners of war during the third and second centuries BCE. The performances of these plays attracted large crowds that arguably represented a cross section of Roman society, and the performers involved in composing these comedies very likely were slaves and freedmen themselves.[42] Unsurprisingly, then, some of the jokes on which the plays rely have been shown to articulate the perspective of the lower ranks of society, of slaves and poor people, rather than that of the political elite.[43] Crucially, these plays would appear to have been profoundly interested in the dynamics of unequal gift-giving, which they mainly explored through the relationship between *patroni* and their *clientes*. As such, these plays are a unique body of evidence to explore the social dynamics resulting from the Roman elite's investment in unequal relationships of gift-giving.

The plots of Roman comedies are populated by stock characters. One such character, the free old man, often a father, is prone to worry about being obligated to others, including to Love, *Amor*, but especially to those over whom he is supposed to have power: his sons, his wife, and his slaves (*Trin.* 266–270; *Bacch.* 1195–1197; *Mil.* 745–746). In one such comedy, the *Asinaria*, the audience also saw slaves plotting to oblige and subdue their masters by doing them enormous favors, such as procuring large sums of money at a moment's notice (282–284, 649–653). Some of the humor in these scenes quite likely resulted from the role reversals that they showed. Free men were not supposed to be obligated to anyone, and the type of behavior that the slaves in the *Asinaria* displayed was precisely the sort of behavior in which Roman masters in the audience were known to engage: subjecting others with their generosity, making them their dependents. In other passages the comedies also poked fun at this behavior in a more direct fashion.

In the *Poenulus* Agorastokles, a free citizen, claimed that even Jupiter, the king of the gods, was beholden to him and feared him (1192). Agorastokles was the type of man, the joke went, that tried to subdue just about everyone with his favors, even the gods. When characters in the comedies were at the receiving end of such aggressive gift-giving, they repeatedly insisted that what they had received was not a gift; instead, they had simply engaged in a one-off market exchange. The *Poenulus* provides a good example of such an interaction. Again, the joke focused on Agorastokles as the would-be giver of a subduing gift. In this particular scene he brought some men onto the stage who were to act as his witnesses in a plot against a pimp. Agorastokles called these men his *amici*, his friends (504, 512), which indicates a relationship of reciprocal gift-giving. The men in question had previously been enslaved, and very likely Agorastokles had been their owner. In addition, they were significantly less wealthy than Agorastokles. All of these details together make it rather likely that a Roman audience would have understood Agorastokles and his potential witnesses as a Roman *patronus* with his *clientes* (515–516).[44] When Agorastokles ordered these witnesses to walk more quickly, they replied that while they might be poor, they were not in any way beholden to him: They had bought their freedom with their own money (518–521).

In making this statement, these witnesses expressed the opposite sentiments to those that are commonly associated with the figure of the parasite, which was one of the main characters through which Roman comedies reflected on patronage in Roman society.[45] While the parasite was always on the lookout for an invitation to eat at somebody else's dinner table, to enjoy the *beneficia* that his host might bestow upon him, the witnesses in the *Poenulus* were eager to avoid entering or maintaining relationships of (unequal) gift-exchange. If some characters in Roman comedies articulated the fantasies of slaves, these characters and their behavior might be read as the dreams of Roman freedmen and *clientes* ready to tell their *patroni* that they did not owe them anything. Intriguingly, they did so in the language of the market. When they insisted that they had bought their freedom with their own money, they claimed that this had been a one-off transaction and that, as such, it had terminated the relationship between them and their former master. It would appear, then, that the difference between market and gift-exchange was a matter of interpretation. The answer depended on whom you asked. Wealthy members of Roman society, so the joke went, would always answer that they had given you a gift, preferably one that you could not return in kind, because that meant that you were now obligated to them.

A fragment of Caecilius, a contemporary of Plautus, would appear to reveal an analogous dynamic. There, an unidentified character insisted that just because another character had given him money, he was not obligated to him (Gell. *NA* 6.17.13). Just like the witnesses in the *Poenulus*, this character asserted that the interaction in question belonged to the sphere of market exchange: Things of equal value had been exchanged for each other without giving rise to an ongoing relationship or obligation. Arguably, his fear was that the other party might try to construe their relationship as one of mutual gift-giving, which would give that other party the upper hand. Just as with Agorastokles in the *Poenulus*, a Roman audience might well see here a man trying to counter an overbearing member of the Roman elite looking to make yet another man the recipient of his obliging *beneficia*. Passages such as these seem to reflect on the way in which Roman elites realized their supposed abstention from market exchange: by casting every exchange as an instance of gift-exchange, in which they had the upper hand. Rather than admitting that they needed the services of somebody else and were willing to pay for them, they argued that they had bestowed a great *beneficium* on this person, who was now obligated to them. In short, they needed nobody, and everybody else depended on them.

Overall, then, we might say that Greek elites had construed a sphere of gift-giving in which only they participated; by contrast, Roman elites were inclined to insist that all their interactions, regardless of whom they involved, were part of relations of gift-giving. Gift-exchange was the only mode of interaction they knew. As a result, it marked the construction of their social identities through and through. Lexical features of middle and late republican Latin would seem to testify to this phenomenon most eloquently. Just consider that the *beneficia* that members of this elite bestowed were supposed to engender the *gratia*, the goodwill, of the recipient. But giving a gift also affected *gratia* in another sense: It increased the *gratia*, the social status and influence, of the person giving the gift.[46] The *clientes* assembled in the courtyards of the members of the Roman elite every morning thus physically manifested the *gratia* of the man they visited: They symbolized both the goodwill he inspired as well as the influence he wielded. The people who maintained more equal relationships of gift-giving with the man in question performed much the same function when they accompanied him through the streets of Rome (Cicero, *Comment. pet.* 9.34). Overall, then, it would appear that gift-giving, especially in its unequal version, was a crucial way by which members of the Roman elite construed and explained their status. As a result, it should not come as a surprise that these men were also profoundly invested in the particular ethics of such gift-exchange. As I will argue in the following section, this investment can go a long way in making sense of the Roman law of debt in the middle and late Republic.

Monetary Debt and Gift Debt in Rome: A Story of Collapse and Confusion

From the third to the first century BCE the use of coined money and the commercial exchange that accompanied it developed rapidly in the Italian peninsula, not just in cities but to some extent probably also in the countryside.[47] The borrowing and lending of money played a crucial part in the rise of a commercial environment, with bankers being a fixture at rural and urban markets, ready to lend to both sellers and buyers, especially at auctions.[48] By the first century BCE members of all parts of Roman society were demonstrably in debt.[49] This included social and political elites, who used, borrowed, and lent out money just like their contemporaries. However, just as they did with all other social interactions, they cast borrowing and lending as part of ongoing relationships of gift-giving: The giving and procurement of loans was one of the main *beneficia* that a member of the

Roman elite could bestow on and receive from their partners in gift-exchange.[50] This inclusion of monetary debt in relationships of gift-giving gave rise to considerable confusion about the type of obligation that arose in such exchanges, a confusion that threatened to collapse the social identities that the members of the Roman elite were constructing for themselves through gift-exchange.

"Remembering a gift (*beneficium*) is enough interest (*usura*) to pay for it."[51] Quite likely this was a sentence that characters in mimes, a form of popular comedic theater, uttered throughout Italy in the first century BCE. It is preserved in the book of aphorisms attributed to Publilius Syrus, a former slave and one of the most successful composers and performers of such mimes during this period.[52] Characters in his mimes uttered one-liners like this one, which soon began circulating independently due to Publilius Syrus' reputation for wit and insight about Roman morality.[53] The aphorism in question illustrates that the inclusion of monetary debt in relationships of gift-exchange not only was a practical matter but also had a conceptual dimension. The recipient of a loan and the recipient of a *beneficium* both incurred obligations—that much was clear—but what exactly did they owe? The aphorism proposed one answer to this question: The recipient of a *beneficium* had to remember it; in other words, they owed *gratia*. The fact that Syrus used the concept of *usura*, which stems from the world of monetary debt, to make this point suggests that other answers were possible.[54] Indeed, when a *beneficium* took the shape of a monetary loan, two different obligations arose: the duty to return the money on an agreed-upon day, possibly with interest, and the duty to remember and one day return the favor. This double obligation that resulted from the inclusion of monetary debt in relations of gift-exchange stands at the origin of the different ways in which this inclusion threatened to collapse the world of gift-exchange and its ethics that was central for the social identities of the Roman elite.

One core virtue in these ethics was *liberalitas*, the generosity and lack of self-interest that a person put on display when they bestowed a *beneficium*.[55] Publilius' aphorism possibly reflects a debate among the Roman elite that was motivated by a concern for the appearance of their generosity: the debate about whether to lend out money at interest. Charging interest for a loan went against the principle of generosity as the absence of (self-)interest could no longer be maintained. Indeed, Latin had a separate term for an interest-free loan—*mutuum*—and this type of loan is well documented between Romans who recognized each other as *amici*, as people who bestowed *beneficia* on each other.[56] The *faenerator*, the man who only lent out money at interest, embodied the opposite to this way of lending money.[57] He was clearly and unambiguously associated with self-interested commercial exchange, thus constituting one of the ways in which the Roman elite patrolled the world of gift-exchange. By the first century BCE, however, members of this elite also leant out money at interest.[58] In a rather ingenious argumentative move they maintained that because of the leniency with which they exacted the repayment of these loans plus interest, their *liberalitas* was still intact.[59]

The intermingling of gift debt and monetary debt in Rome also threatened to collapse the world of gift-exchange into self-interested, acquisitive commercial exchange in relation to yet another problem: how to effect repayment. Mariana Ioannatou has shown that a veritable "code d'honneur" designed to maintain the ethics of gift-exchange developed around this problem.[60] Debtors had to take care to not repay too early. Early repayment might give the impression that they were eager to escape their indebtedness, not just on the level of monetary debt but also in relation to gift debt. In other words, early repayment might give the impression that they were eager to end the ongoing relationship of gift-exchange and transform it into a one-off transaction. By contrast, creditors were to be lenient with their debtors, to avoid taking them to court and to consider the reasons they might not be able to pay on time. Concern for their *liberalitas* obligated the creditor to act in this way. But also concern for their creditor's *fides*, the second core virtue in the Roman ethics of gift-exchange, made this course of action a desirable option.

Fides is commonly translated as "trust." In the Roman ethics of gift-exchange it refers to the trust in the recipient of the *beneficium*, that they will one day return the favor. At the same time, the word designates a personal quality of the recipient: their disposition to effect such returns, their trustworthiness.[61] In this sense *fides* was not simply a part of this ethics of gift-exchange; it was the precondition for participating in gift-exchange in the first place. Several aphorisms attributed to Publilius Syrus reflect this indispensable feature of a person's *fides* in the context of gift-exchange. Just consider "He who loses his *fides* has nothing left to lose" (*Sent.* F 1) or "With one's *fides* being lost, what means are there of saving what remains?" (*Sent.* F 14). These lines suggest that once you have lost your *fides*, you have lost everything. From the perspective of the Roman ethics of gift-giving you were unable to form further relationships. Indeed, two further lines from the collection of Publilius' sayings suggest that *fides*, once lost, could never be regained: "Once *fides* has left a mind, it never returns" (F 16) and "Noone ever loses his *fides* unless he has never had it" (F 17). As a result, a person could never not show their *fides*, even in relations with enemies and those who had done wrong.[62] There is a certain logic to this way of thinking. After all, the bestowal of *beneficia* was predicated on the *fides* of the recipient, on the expectation that they were the person who would give gifts in return. If they failed to do so once, there was no way of making sure that they would not do so again.

That being said, in gift-exchange the finality of the loss or lack of *fides* posed rather limited problems in practice, for how could such a loss or lack of *fides* reveal itself? Relations of gift-exchange were construed as ongoing, the way in which *beneficia* should be returned always remained unspecified, and the timing of their return lay with the person who had received the favor. However, once monetary debt was included in such relations, the refusal to repay the monetary debt at the agreed-upon time could be seen as a loss of *fides*, which could then never be recovered. Given this way of thinking, it does not come as a surprise that Cicero could praise a man for having sold off most of his properties so as to be able to repay his debtors (*Sull.* 20.56 and 58). The man in question, a certain Sittius, was a man who met his obligations and thus maintained his *fides*—no matter the cost.

If concern for a debtor's *fides* was supposed to keep individual creditors away from court, this concern arguably also shaped the measures that Romans took in the context of a credit crisis. In the 80s of the first century BCE ever more Romans found themselves unable to repay their debts.[63] The effects of the Social War and the civil wars that followed it were compounded by Mithridates' attack on the province of Asia in 88, during which many Roman creditors lost the money they had loaned out in that province.[64] In 86 Lucius Valerius Flaccus, the suffect consul after Marius' death, introduced a law to address the crisis: Debts were to be repaid at a fourth of their value.[65] Velleius Paterculus, who was critical of the measure, emphasized that creditors were forced to accept a fourth of what was originally owed (2.23.2). By contrast, in Sallust's *Bellum Catilinae* Gaius Manlius, a general in Catiline's army, described the measure as making sure that silver could be paid in bronze (*Cat.* 33.2), thus emphasizing that repayment happened. It is tempting to see the *lex Valeria* and the way in which Sallust had Manlius spin it as an attempt to maintain the debtors' *fides*. In fact, Catiline's agitation around debt and his demands for *novae tabulae*, new account books, are the first attestation of an attempt to cancel debts in Rome completely.[66] Previous measures and demands instead tinkered with what it meant to repay, thus, one might argue, maintaining the *fides* of the debtors; after all, these debtors did on some level pay.[67] Intriguingly, in Sallust's portrayal Gaius Manlius seems to have understood that demanding *novae tabulae* meant abandoning a great Roman virtue; hence, he seized on another one—*libertas*, freedom—to make his case (*Cat.* 33.1 and 4).[68]

Lastly, then, it should not come as a surprise that the crucial role that *fides* played in the Roman ethics of gift-exchange left its traces in the Roman law of debt.[69] A person who failed to meet their obligations could not go unpunished, not just because of this one instance of misconduct but because this one instance cast doubt on their entire character. The social, economic, and political death that the law around *missio in bona* engineered simply put into practice what the Roman ethics of gift-exchange dictated: Once *fides* was lost, it could never be regained. As a result of this way of thinking, Cicero maintained that once a person had been forced to repay their debts, they were below the dead. And this way of thinking also explains why Cato likened the activity of a *faenerator* to murder. People who lent out money with interest were those known to not shy away from taking the debtors to court and from thus demonstrating the latters' lack of *fides*.[70] As such, they were the people who had no compunction about killing the social standing of others. In short, what I have called the extreme nature of the moral confusion about debt in ancient Rome—the highly particular ways in which debt, death, and destruction were intertwined in that particular polity—would appear to have been the result of yet another confusion. It was a consequence of the intermingling of different types of debt within the context of the overbearing and unequal practices of gift-exchange in which the Roman elite liked to engage.

While such structural analyses have their merits, it should also be pointed out that the Roman elite's attitude to debt would appear to have changed over time. Lending out money at interest seems to have been a case in point. In the second and first centuries laws against lending money at interest were still on the books; arguably, though, they were no longer enforced on a regular basis. One might speculate that the elite found the profits to be reaped from interest-bearing loans too attractive to resist. This elite's quasi-legalistic arguments about just what it meant to display *liberalitas* constituted the refinement of the Roman ethics of gift-exchange that made this transformation possible. By contrast, in relation to *fides* no such refinement can be observed. In fact, in the first century BCE *fides* appears to have been a more essential virtue than ever before. Cicero could call it the foundation of human society and justice (*Inv.* 1.47). And yet, toward the end of the century the Roman law on defaulting debtors did become much less punitive. In the fourth and final section of this chapter, I explore the circumstances that made this change possible.

Beyond Death and Destruction: The Political and Moral Economy of Cessio Bonorum

The legal change at issue is the introduction of *cessio bonorum* into Roman law. This new procedure provided an alternative remedy for insolvent debtors, which, unlike *missio in bona*, did not spell the social, political, and economic death of insolvent debtors.[71] As part of *cessio bonorum*, the insolvent debtor declared their bankruptcy before a Roman magistrate, who then gave them permission to hand over their possessions to the creditor. Unlike with *missio in bona*, however, the person was allowed to keep enough property to keep them alive while also not suffering *infamia*. Not just economically, then, but also socially and politically, the insolvent debtor stayed alive. The introduction of the procedure quite likely went back to a *lex Iulia de bonis cedendis*, a law most likely introduced by Caesar.[72] Understanding the passage of this law and the innovation it constituted requires a closer look at the connection between debt and Roman political careers as well as at the semantics of the law itself.

By the late Republic politics in Rome was a thoroughly financialized affair. Beyond the fact that political careers in Rome were only open to men who had enough property to qualify for the highest census class, these men also needed to invest a lot of their wealth, often far more than they had, in order to be able to run for political office: Every campaign for an office in the sequence of ever more exclusive posts that a Roman politician could hope to hold required expenses for anything from games and meals to cash handouts.[73] Conversely, success in this competition for offices also provided opportunities to achieve a return on one's investment: Roman rule abroad played a crucial role in allowing politicians to make back what they had spent on coming into office, whether as governors or as privileged investors, and so did the ever increasing amount of inheritances that successful Roman politicians could expect to receive.[74] Julius Caesar's career illustrates this "return-on-investment" principle of Roman politics rather spectacularly. Caesar was known for running up far more debts than his contemporaries in competing for office early in his career in the mid-60s.[75] When he returned from his command in Gaul in 50, Gallic gold made him the richest man in Rome and many of his friends much richer.[76] This financialization of politics in Rome had two important consequences: Roman politicians were in debt for most of their careers, and losing in the competition for office was an assured way of making creditors doubt that the politician in question would be able to service his debts.[77]

In the first century BCE expenditure on election campaigns seems to have spiraled out of control, which made politics ever more risky, not just for the individual politicians seeking office but also for the system as a whole.[78] In 62, after Cicero had bought his house on the Palatine, he joked that he was in enough debt to join any revolution that was going (*Fam.* 5.6.2). The irony of his remark stemmed from the fact that only a year earlier Lucius Sergius Catilina, who had failed to gain the consulship two years in a row, had done just that. He had made common cause with the less well off to force a cancellation of debts.[79] Uncovering and frustrating Catiline's plan had been Cicero's hour of glory as consul in 63 BCE. Political crises exacerbated the threat that the financialization of politics posed to the political system as a whole. They led to the collapse of credit, and they made money in the form of coins ever more valuable. Such was the case at the beginning of the civil war between Caesar and Pompey in the early 50s.[80] At that time politics in Rome seems to have been dominated by the question of debt.

In 48 and 47 two Roman politicians tried to "do a Catiline" and accomplish a total cancellation of debts and arrears in rents.[81] Caesar was able to frustrate both attempts. But he himself had to engage with the problem of debt. Already in 49 he and his allies had begun instituting a set of measures that allowed repayment in kind and used *aestimationes* to set the value of the properties at prewar levels.[82] These *aestimationes* provide the context in which the *lex Iulia de bonis cedendis* seems to fit so well—because on one level *cessio bonorum* can readily be seen as a perpetuation of the principle that underlay them.

Cessio bonorum, just like the other more informal measures that we know Caesar took in relation to debt in the early 40s, allowed a debtor to manage their obligations by handing over property they owned. As such, they were both meaningful ways of relieving debtors who had assets with which they could service their debt—those, that is, who were reasonably well off to begin with. As such, these measures should be seen not so much as a way to resolve the debt crisis more generally but as a way to eliminate its explosive political potential: by providing a way out for the many members of the sociopolitical elite who were unable to service their debts. Notably, at one point Caesar also addressed the question of rent arrears but only in 48, it seems, after Caelius Rufus, one of the imitators of Catiline, had called for a suspension of a year's rent earlier in the year.[83] In general, Caesar's strategy seems to have been to alleviate the difficulties of those who were well off, especially of the chronically indebted elite, by helping them sidestep the economic, social, and political death that bankruptcy had previously entailed in Roman law. Crucially, he seems to have done so in a way that was compatible with the Roman ethics of reciprocity.

Caesar's *aestimationes* stood in a long tradition of Roman measures concerning debt that redefined what it meant to pay one's debts, what it meant to maintain one's *fides*.[84] *Cessio bonorum* would appear to have sidestepped this tradition only to arrive at the same outcome: the maintenance of the insolvent debtor in the world of gift-exchange. For with *cessio bonorum* the debtor's declaration of their inability to service their debts initiated the procedure. As such, the debtor would appear to publicly acknowledge that they were not able to repay debts and services rendered. However, the magistrate's actions in response to this declaration could be characterized as a *beneficium*, a gift, toward the debtor. The emperor Alexander Severus in 223 adopted this language in a law on *cessio bonorum*, possibly echoing the *lex Iulia* (*Cod. Iust.* 7.71.1); and Cicero quite likely did so too (*Fam.* 11.28.2).[85] While this rhetoric opens the door to a legal debate about when Roman magistrates could and should grant the *beneficium* of insolvency without punishment, its origin in the ethics of reciprocity is much more pertinent here. By casting *cessio bonorum* not as a matter of right but as a *beneficium*, Roman magistrates suggested that the insolvent debtor had not actually lost their *fides*.

Indeed, the precondition for receiving a *beneficium* was *fides*, the expectation that the recipient was the type of person who remembered and repaid favors. As such, *cessio bonorum* not only not led to the economic, political, and social death of an insolvent debtor but also publicly performed the continued existence of such a debtor in the world of gift-exchange. On one level, this attention to the Roman ethics of gift-giving further supports the idea that this law was aimed at the political elite. More importantly, though, it shows that what Mommsen could hail as the modernization and commercialization of the Roman law of debt was carried out through the rhetoric and techniques of gift-exchange.[86] As such, this law built on the willingness of the Roman political elite to see any interaction in which they engaged as gift-exchange—also, as we can see here, when they acted as magistrates. This willingness, so my argument here, stood at the origin of their problems with insolvency (and usury). Demonstrably, however, it also provided them with a solution to these problems.

Epilogues

At the end of this chapter I want to return once more to David Graeber's *Debt: The First 5,000 Years*. In his afterword to the 2014 edition Graeber set out what he had aimed to accomplish in writing the book.[87] His paramount goals included a demonstration of the myriad ways that humans had found to arrange their political and economic lives and an assessment of the kind of historical change that the financial crisis in 2008 and the struggles over debt following it constituted. His ultimate hope, he wrote, was that the book would somehow contribute to a broader moral reassessment of the very idea of debt, work, and "the economy." In light of this hope it seems fitting that this chapter concludes with a historical moment of just such a moral reassessment. While so far I might have highlighted the hard-hitting political calculations that underpinned the *lex Iulia de bonis cedendis*, it did arguably constitute a break in how the Roman elite thought about debts and the inability to repay them. This law ensured that insolvent debtors did not have to be ostracized from society, that they did not have to suffer *infamia* and the symbolical death it constituted, and that they did not have to await a singular political measure for all this to be accomplished. Instead, through the actions of Roman judicial magistrates they could go on living, and not just among or below the dead—as Cicero had still claimed—but alive and well among their friends and peers, continuing to partake in the ongoing exchange of gifts that gave rise to social bonds in Roman society. Partial and elite-driven though this moral reassessment of debt may have been, it nonetheless demonstrates the very real possibility of such reassessments.

In the end, then, there is possibility and hope: the possibility that David Graeber has made thinkable for so many people and the hope that his work continues to inspire in countless others. Such possibility and hope are what remain—for me at least and, I suspect, for many other people. They are gifts of the sort that can never be repaid.

Acknowledgment

I thank the editor John Weisweiler, the participants of the original conference as well as Valentina Arena and Philipp Höhn for their insightful comments and conversations surrounding the issues with which this chapter tries to grapple.

6

The Poetics and Politics of Exchange in Roman Agronomy

Neville Morley

Introduction: Roman Economic Thinking

One of the central themes in David Graeber's *Debt: The First 5,000 Years*—established with his opening anecdote on how the claim "one has to pay one's debts" has become established as a self-evident truth in the modern West, even among those otherwise suspicious of predatory lenders and self-interested institutions—is the way that certain ideas become naturalized and taken for granted.[1] In modernity, he suggested, "value" has become ever more associated with the language of the market, going hand in hand with the assumption that the presuppositions of mainstream economics offer a true and objective description of the world and the only reasonable mode of organization; alternative definitions and modes of thought are crowded out or made to disappear.[2]

This is the reason that history, including the history of classical antiquity, is so important for his argument. Firstly, Graeber aimed to show that modern assumptions about economic behavior and the nature of value are not in fact universal or transhistorical but are at best partial descriptions of the specific conditions of capitalism; this argument echoes the "substantivist" economic anthropology of Karl Polanyi and his followers but without confining the critique of economistic thinking to premodern societies.[3] Secondly, he noted the way that modern accounts of the past play an active role in making such assumptions about human motivation and values appear universal and transhistorical in the present, by representing other societies and their practices in a manner that obscures their differences from our own.[4] "*Bourgeois* relations," Marx had remarked, are established "as the inviolable laws on which society in the abstract is founded. This is more or

Neville Morley, *The Poetics and Politics of Exchange in Roman Agronomy* In: *Debt in the Ancient Mediterranean and Near East*. Edited by: John Weisweiler, Oxford University Press. © Oxford University Press 2023.
DOI: 10.1093/oso/9780197647172.003.0006

less the conscious purpose of the whole proceeding."[5] The sophisticated but significantly non-modern societies of the "Axial Age" and its immediate successors are key case studies for this enterprise, especially the ancient Mediterranean as the supposed point of origin of "the modern West." Thirdly, and most importantly, Graeber sought to explain *how* specific modes of thinking and organization come to dominate in a given society, rather than, as the substantivist school tended to, simply developing incommensurable taxonomies of "economic" thinking for different cultural contexts. The Axial Age was, he argued, the critical phase in the emergence of the market as the organizing and disciplining principle that now rules our own society. The market, and associated institutions like money, had not always existed, certainly not in their now familiar forms, and nor could they be assumed to be the natural reflections of inherent human tendencies or preferences; rather, they were the product of specific historical forces in a given context, namely the "currency–slavery–warfare complex" of classical antiquity and contemporaneous societies.[6]

There is an obvious risk—a paradoxical result for a writer whose original field was cultural anthropology—that this third line of enquiry comes to be understood in a relatively crude materialistic manner; that is to say, the development of distinctive new modes of thinking about human values, motivation, and identity in terms of money and debt is seen as simply a product or reflection of wider economic, political, and technological changes, which comes to be thought of as natural and universal because it matches the new historical reality. On the contrary, we need to pay as much attention to the complex processes whereby certain ideas are made thinkable, the world is represented and hence perceived in new ways, and as a result, new possibilities for action and change are created. Further, we need to pay close attention to the processes of change in different societies, rather than assuming that, once the crucial intellectual and institutional developments had taken place in the Axial Age, an inexorable process of marketization was set in motion. Rome is a striking absentee from Graeber's historical narrative in *Debt*; it is difficult to escape the impression that he simply assumed that the structures of Roman society were a straightforward manifestation of the principles of money, slavery, markets, and state power that had been established in classical Greece, and therefore of little interest.[7] But there is no reason to imagine that the market reflected natural human instincts and desires in Roman Italy any more than it did anywhere else. Market values had to become thinkable and conceived as first an acceptable and then an integral part of society; indeed, not least because coinage was a much later development here than in the eastern Mediterranean, we might see Rome as a crucial case study in the ways that Axial-Age developments had subsequent ripple effects, and/or found echoes, in other societies.

This chapter is focused not on the historical emergence of coinage and monetized exchange in archaic Italy but on the interpretation and negotiation of these developments by later writers as even centuries later elite Roman authors were thinking through the changes and their implications for their own position in society.[8] It develops a case study of key passages and themes in a single text, the *Rerum Rusticarum* (*Of rural things*) written by the retired politician and energetic polymath Marcus Terentius Varro in 37 BCE, one of the classic works of Roman agronomy. Varro's work has in the past been taken by historians as a reliable and straightforward source of evidence for agricultural practices and dismissed by literary scholars as a philosophical joke with no purchase at all on material reality; the ways in which it has been interpreted shed interesting light on the tendency noted above to see premodern economic thinking as either identical with modern assumptions or entirely primitive and alien, rather than seeking to make sense of it in its own terms. But David Graeber's wider thesis should prompt us to consider also how such texts were not just passive reflections of their cultures but also active and self-conscious interventions in contemporary developments, working to create and legitimize new ways of thinking and acting in the world; this was as true of Varro as it was of Graeber's own work.

Rethinking Roman Economic Thought

The tendency to represent premodern economic institutions and practices in modern terms through the choice of vocabulary used to describe them, and thus, perhaps quite inadvertently, to obscure differences from modernity that might otherwise be of interest, is a familiar issue to ancient economic historians. M. I. Finley, inspired partly by the Marxian tradition and partly by the substantivist ideas of his erstwhile colleague Karl Polanyi, made this one of the central themes of his critique of existing approaches to the subject.[9] Finley's substantive account of the ancient economy has been widely criticized, especially since the late 1990s, for its essential negativity and tendency to extrapolate his interpretation of classical Greek conditions to other regions and periods; his methodological point has not been so consistently addressed.

A simple illustration of this practice is the way that the Latin word *fructus*, and related terms, are rendered into English in translations of Varro's *Rerum Rusticarum* and similar works. The verb *fruor*, from which *fructus* derives, means to enjoy a thing; *fructus* can simply refer to enjoyment in the abstract (as in the legal term *usufruct*), but it is more often used for the enjoyment proceeding from a thing or the things that are enjoyed—in concrete terms, the produce of a fruit tree or the offspring of an animal or the product of human labor in the fields or on a farm or the rewards of successful endeavor or the return on a loan.[10] In the context of Roman farming—when, for example, Varro discusses the question of whether the *fructus* of an estate will justify the expense and labor involved in its cultivation (*RR* 2.8) and insists on the need for any estate to be *fructuosus* (1.2)—it might best be translated as "fruitful" or "productive," maintaining a certain ambiguity as to whether this is intended to emphasize the produce of the fields or the eventual financial return from selling that produce. In conventional translations, however, the adjective is invariably rendered as "profitable" and the noun as "profit" or "return," focusing on just one of the possible connotations of the original—and the one that corresponds most closely to a modern, market-orientated rationality.[11] It is not that Varro's choice of vocabulary excluded or was intended to exclude the possibility of evaluating a course of action in terms of financial return, but the translator's choice makes it appear that monetary profit was his only concern, silently erasing any trace of less modern or market-orientated values. Varro is implicitly represented as a modern economic rationalist, thus demonstrating the long tradition of market-orientated rational decision-making in agriculture, or at least its triumph by the late first century BCE.

It is worth noting that Varro's predecessor in the genre of Roman agronomical treatises, Marcus Porcius Cato, whose *De Agri Cultura* was written around 160 BCE, had preferred the adjective *quaestuosus* to describe the returns to be expected from an estate (*De Ag.* 1.6). This term is more directly related to ideas of profit, gain, and wealth than *fructuosus*, to the point that it can be considered as a possible synonym for *lucrosus*, lucrative. In other words, Varro's choice of vocabulary also reveals a more complex situation than would be recognized in either a conventional substantivist interpretation or a simple account of progression in Roman farming from self-sufficiency to production for the market. His account of agriculture is apparently less "modern," in terms of its orientation toward market values, than Cato's was over a century earlier; it is hard, then, to maintain that he must be unconsciously reflecting a traditional, inherited idea of farming as focused primarily on self-sufficiency and hence on the physical products of the land, not least because his text reveals deep familiarity with Cato's work and attitudes. Rather, insofar as Varro's choice of words does indeed evoke the possibility of a less marketized approach to agriculture and the exploitation of one's property, this is surely a studied ambiguity, in contrast to Cato's explicit concern with monetary expenses and returns.

The practice of these translators of Roman agronomical texts echoes wider tendencies in the modern study of what we might term "Roman economic thinking."[12] Some studies take a descriptive approach, focusing on the development of ideas about wealth, labor, and other "economic" themes within a limited range of largely philosophical texts; these have the merits of taking ancient ideas as their focus but at the expense of remaining within the realm of abstraction. When it comes to the study of actual economic behavior and institutions, however, most discussions fall into polarized positions; they either assume the existence of basic economic rationality in modern terms, or they insist on the absolute non-rational, primitive nature of ancient economic behavior.[13] The former approach largely discounts discussions in the ancient sources as being literary and philosophical, with no serious connection to actual practice. For example, the emphasis on "performance" rather than "structure" in the programmatic statements of the *Cambridge Economic History of the Greco-Roman World* serves as a means of discounting ideas or other cultural factors as being part of the "structure," implying instead that the level of economic performance of ancient societies can be taken as a sign of their basically modern and profit-orientated nature, regardless of the "culturalist" arguments of less modernizing historians.[14] The widespread adoption of ideas from New Institutional Economics (often abbreviated as NIE) can be seen in a similar light, as a means of paying lip service to the importance of cultural practices and conceptions and non-economic institutions but then recuperating them for conventional economics—there is an easy slippage from the idea that, for example, religious oaths might play a role in lowering transaction costs to the assumption that their basic function is economic.[15] To some extent, this approach may be understandable, given that the alternative position, based on a wholly literal and often simplistic reading of the sources, is an insistence that the non-modern elements of ancient economic thinking must always have operated as an absolute impediment to any sort of growth or development and that the economic was always subordinated to the political, social, and cultural.

In neither case are ancient economic ideas taken seriously in their own terms or regarded as in any sense complex and sophisticated—which brings the further implication that ancient people were likewise simple and predictable, either consistent utility maximizers or consistent irrational primitives. This is somewhat bizarre, given that one of the most fertile areas of contemporary economic research is behavioral and cultural economics, analyzing the actual behavior of individuals in making decisions—as opposed to the simplifying assumptions of most economic models—and the concepts and beliefs that govern or influence their choices.[16] The "parsimonious micro-foundations" of rational actor theory that a modernizing economic historian like Josh Ober accepts as a taken-for-granted foundation of his analysis are in fact placed in question for modern society, let alone any premodern one.[17] In other words, the fact that the ideas and principles that can be identified in a work like Varro's *Rerum Rusticarum* do not neatly conform to modern expectations (presenting it as a straightforward manual of practical advice based on the rational maximization of utility requires the willful neglect of its many curious, non-modern, and thoroughly literary features) does not mean that they are therefore either irrelevant to actual practice or simply alien and anti-economic. We can read them instead as, in part, a genuine reflection of the complex underlying motives and principles that governed Roman elite management of their landed estates, influenced, if not determined, by wider cultural values and assumptions; for example, we may consider the ideas of "frugality" and "cost management" as rational responses to specific environmental and economic conditions.[18]

Modern accounts of Roman agriculture, like accounts of other aspects of the Roman economy and grand narratives of historical economic development, thus tend to naturalize market behavior as a human universal or, at any rate, take it as a norm of complex, developed societies, against which other societies and their ideas must be measured. This is not simply a problem for our understanding of Roman economic behavior and how Roman agriculture worked in practice and developed over time. It also obscures the extent to which this process of naturalization of market values is not a solely modern phenomenon. The works of the Roman agronomists are full of practical advice and were clearly intended to engage with real-world practices, but they are also complex, highly literary works that are simultaneously engaged with political, moral, and cultural issues; they did not simply embody Roman economic thought and behavior but sought actively to shape it.

The literary form of Varro's work, not a factual treatise or compilation of advice but a series of conversations between elite Romans and other interlocutors that are represented as the author's recollection of real exchanges, should make this unmistakable. His account offers a staging and performance, an *Inszenierung* of crucial contemporary debates and issues, developing its account of correct and advisable villa management through a series of multivocal, historically situated debates rather than a single didactic voice.[19] Varro's text offers evidence not only of how Roman ideas and practices were changing in response to new economic, political, and social conditions but also of the means—above all the literary means—by which such ways of thinking could be changed. If the natural conclusion from reading Varro is that Roman agriculture was in fact for the most part rationalistic, profit-motivated, and market-orientated, then that is at least in part because these were the values and assumptions he sought to promote and legitimize.

Frugality and Profit

One of the most striking examples of the complex interaction of different layers of discourse and rhetorical strategies in Varro's work comes at the beginning of his third book, which is dedicated to the theme of *pastio villatica*, the raising of different sorts of small animals and birds in and around the farmstead.[20] Varro

opens this book with a dedicatory letter to a friend that first establishes the precedence of country over city life through the former's greater antiquity—signaling
that this is a book where questions of tradition and precedence will be of great
importance—and then insists on both the importance of his subject as a legitimate part of agriculture, despite its apparent insignificance and neglect by other
writers, and on his own originality in treating the theme in detail separately both
from agrarian cultivation and from the normal business of raising animals:

> At first, because of their poverty, people practised agriculture, as a rule,
> without distinction, the descendants of the shepherds both planting and
> grazing on the same land; later, as these flocks grew, they made a division,
> with the result that some were called farmers, and others herdsmen. This
> matter of herding has a twofold division (though no writer has made the
> distinction clearly), as the feeding around the steading is one thing, and
> that on the land is another. The latter is well known and highly esteemed,
> being also called *pecuaria*, and wealthy men frequently have ranches
> devoted to it, which they have either leased or bought; while the other,
> that of the steading, as it seems insignificant, has, by some writers, been
> brought under the head of agriculture, though it is a matter of feeding;
> and the subject as a whole has not, so far as I know, been treated as a sepa-
> rate topic by anyone. Hence, as I suggested that there are three divisions of
> rural economy which are instituted for gainful ends—one of agriculture, a
> second of animal husbandry, and a third of the husbandry of the steading
> (*pastio villatica*)—I fixed on three books. (*RR* 3.1.7–9)

We then move to the dialogue proper, set during an election in Rome for the
magistrates known as *aediles*. It takes place between Varro; his friend the
senator Quintus Axius; various Roman aristocrats with "bird" cognomina
(Merula = blackbird, Pavo = peacock, etc.), which provides an opportunity to
introduce the theme of aviaries; and the augur Appius Claudius (one of whose
ancestors had notoriously drowned some sacred chickens). The setting is the
Villa Publica, the central office of the Roman censors and used for other public
business, which gives Appius, characterized as a spokesman for more traditional
Roman values, an opening for a debate with Axius on the true nature of the *villa*:

> Isn't this villa, which our ancestors built, simpler [*frugalior*] and better
> than that elaborate villa of yours at Reate? Do you see anywhere here citrus
> wood or gold, or vermilion or azure, or any coloured or mosaic work? At
> your place everything is just the opposite. Also, while this villa is common
> property of the whole population, that one belongs to you alone. (3.2.3)

Axius counters that the Villa Publica is not only lavishly decorated with paintings and sculptures, rather than being truly plain and undecorated, but more importantly has never seen any sort of productive activity and is therefore not at all a traditional "villa":

> What has your villa got that is like that villa which your grandfather and great-grandfather had? For it has never, as that one did, seen a cured hay harvest in the loft, or a vintage in the cellar, or a grain-harvest in the bins. For the fact that a building is outside the city no more makes it a villa than the same fact makes villas of the houses of those who live outside the Porta Flumentana or in the Aemiliana. (3.2.6)

Appius' response is that, if it is not the presence or absence of decoration that is decisive, nor the location, then neither is the presence or absence of a particular form of productive activity:

> "Why," he replied, "if your place in the Rosea is to be commended for its pasturage, and is rightly called a villa because cattle are fed and stabled there, for a like reason that also should have the name in which a large revenue is derived from pasturing. For if you get a revenue from flocks, what does it matter whether they are flocks of sheep or of birds? Why, is the revenue sweeter on your place from oxen which give birth to bees than it is from the bees which are busy at their task in the hives of Seius's villa?" (*RR* 3.2.10–11)

He goes on to discuss the levels of financial return—explicitly presented in terms of market prices—that can be obtained from such activities, to Axius' growing amazement and excitement; Varro himself then joins the conversation, with mention of the estate of his maternal aunt, twenty-four miles to the northeast of Rome:

> "Well, from the aviary alone which is in that villa, I happen to know that there were sold 5,000 fieldfares, for three denarii apiece, so that that department of the villa in that year brought in sixty thousand sesterces—twice as much as your farm of 200 *iugera* at Reate brings in." "What? Sixty?" exclaimed Axius, "Sixty? Sixty? You are joking!" "Sixty," I repeated. "But to reach such a haul as that you will need a public banquet or somebody's triumph, such as that of Metellus Scipio at that time, or the club dinners which are now so countless that they make the price of provisions go soaring. If you can't look for this sum in all other years, your aviary, I hope, will

not go bankrupt on you; and if fashions continue as they now are, it will happen only rarely that you miss your reckoning. For how rarely is there a year in which you do not see a banquet or a triumph, or when the clubs do not feast?" "Why," said he, "in this time of luxury it may fairly be said that there is a banquet every day within the gates of Rome." (3.2.15–16)

The scene is thus set for a discussion of all the different aspects of *pastio villatica* as Axius is determined to find out more about such a lucrative activity. As is customary in Varro's approach to discussing agricultural matters, the first step (given to Merula) is to establish the divisions and ordering of the subject—since "the owner ought to have so clear an idea of those creatures which can be reared or fed in the villa and around it that they may afford him both profit and pleasure" (3.3.1)—distinguishing between the raising of birds, animals, and fish.

> Each of these three classes has two stages: the earlier, which the frugality of the ancients [*frugalitas antiqua*] observed, and the latter, which modern luxury added. For example, first came the ancient stage of our ancestors, in which there were simply two aviaries: the barn-yard on the ground in which the hens fed—and their returns [*fructus*] were eggs and chickens—and the other above ground, in which were the pigeons, either in cotes or on the roof of the villa. On the other hand, in these days, the aviaries have changed their name and have become *ornithones*; and those which the dainty palate of the owner has constructed have larger buildings for the sheltering of fieldfares and peafowl than whole villas used to have in those days. (3.3.6)

The literary aspects of these passages are unmistakable, not just the punning names (Varro does something similar in his other two books) and the paratextual letter of dedication but above all the choice of the dialogue form. Varro's work is conventionally read by modern scholars as if all the characters are equally his voice and equally reliable, but they are clearly distinguished in the text, at least insofar as they are given different areas of expertise. This establishes a particular form of authorial authority; rather than risking the appearance of talking down to his audience on a subject with which Roman aristocrats would be expected to be familiar, Varro appears as the mere compiler of the views of various experts, ostensibly for the benefit of his wife (noted in the dedicatory letter at 1.1.1–4), while the male elite reader can imagine himself as a silent participant in a conversation between equals. More importantly, especially in this third book, the speakers' characters are delineated in a way that clearly indicates we should not treat them with equal respect; Axius in particular displays excessive and barely concealed greed, and it seems entirely appropriate when he turns out to be an expert on fishponds, which were regularly associated with the worst sorts of excess and extravagance.[21]

In her reading of different classical texts on agriculture, Kronenberg argues that such rhetorical elements clearly mark out the work as a satire on philosophical debate, with the rural subject matter merely a vehicle for this critique.[22] However, Varro's account seems remarkably concrete, with its emphasis on specific historical settings and evocation of Roman political institutions as well as the practical advice offered; it makes more sense to follow Nelsestuen in seeing it as a deliberate engagement with contemporary moral and political questions and the reality of first-century Italian society and economy.[23] The *Rerum Rusticarum* represents, he argues, an attempt at rationalizing how Rome was changing as a result of imperial success and the consequent influx of wealth—a theme that is clearly identified in the historical overview quoted above that sees the "luxurious" *pastio villatica* as a recent development in response to changing habits of consumption in the city of Rome.[24] This is why the question of the definition of a "villa" is so important; agriculture was central to Roman elite identity as (in theory) the only respectable way to make a living, so debates over what activities should count as proper agriculture, whether everything that is done on the land should be regarded as equally virtuous, and whether everything that appears to be "luxurious" is necessarily to be condemned, went to the heart of Roman values and hence political activity.[25] Further, insofar as wealth—or at least the confidence on the part of one's creditors that one would eventually repay debts—was a vital prerequisite for participation in Roman politics, the interplay of the twin themes of the appearance of wealth that was actually unproductive (the luxurious villa) and the appearance of poverty that disguised genuine resources (the tiny estate that yielded a fortune from honey) could not help but be political.[26]

Recognizing the literary and political aspects of Varro's presentation does not imply that it therefore has no purchase at all on the realities of Roman economic thought and behavior; on the contrary, his account of *pastio villatica* does contain substantive practical advice and reveals some of the underlying principles that governed the economic decision-making of the Roman elite. Identifying some forms of activity as potentially less desirable or reputable than others can be seen as an expression of preferences, albeit not fully substitutable or even necessarily consistent. For the Roman elite, not all profit was considered to be identical; they evaluated different courses of action in terms of excess and moderation, and non-economic prestige and social capital, as much as monetary profit. Further, the importance of managing costs, in relation to risks and potential gains—the sort of *parsimonia* found in Cato's insistence on controlling expenditure (e.g., *Agr.* 1.6, 2.7), rather than the elaborate *frugalitas* discussed and arguably invented by

Cicero (e.g., *Tusc.* 3.16–17)—can be seen as perfectly rational means for managing risk and uncertainty within an uncertain environment, rather than dismissing it as a non-rational preference for moral values over economic return.[27] Varro's interlocutors in Book 3 do not insist on making a clear-cut decision between ancient frugality and modern profit; on the contrary, they present them as always interwoven so that any decision about estate management involves choosing where to strike the balance—somewhere on the scale between Appius and Axius.

At the same time, we need to pay attention to what Varro chose *not* to raise in his staged discussion. These debates over what kinds of activity are acceptable and advisable take for granted the idea that profitability, in financial terms, is a key criterion of evaluation. As discussed above, it is the presence of productive, profitable activities involving the rearing of "flocks," naturalized by using terms like *pastio*, that defines the line between a "proper" villa and other things that share the same name—whether the non-profitable institutions of the Roman state or the private indulgences of the very rich. *Pastio villatica* has, as Varro suggested in 3.1.7, always been a part of Roman farming, even if not always distinguished as a separate activity or highly regarded. The fact that it is now prominent enough not only to be identified as an important theme by a commentator like himself but even to sustain an entire landholding on its own, rather than being a mere adjunct to more mainstream activity, is a sign of the changing times and the new wealth of Rome—but he presents this as a natural development from those more humble origins, rather than an abrupt change in economic practice as the simple, small-scale domestic chicken-rearing of the self-sufficient farmstead becomes a lucrative free-standing enterprise.

This is part of the power of Varro's chosen dialogue form; the reader is pushed to focus on the issues which the different speakers present as worthy of debate, clearly identifying the different perspectives on display and the assumptions that underpin them—while accepting at face value the ideas that all the characters seem to take for granted. If Varro had developed in his own voice an argument that all estate management is based on the pursuit of gain, understood in monetary terms, readers ancient and modern might have been more inclined to question whether his assumptions are wholly representative; but when we are apparently presented with a group of Romans, who express divergent views on certain issues but accept without question that agriculture is profit-orientated and market-driven, then we may take this for granted as something to be taken for granted. Kronenberg identifies the way that new forms of economic activity are granted by Varro's characters the same legitimacy and moral worth as traditional practices, and the elevation of profit into a gauge of ethical value, as deliberate contradictions intended to satirize philosophical arguments.[28] Rather, the revaluation of Roman values was precisely the aim of the exercise, shifting the terms in which Romans thought about farming by presenting these new profit-focused ideas as something that has always been the case and therefore should occasion no anxiety or suspicion.

Money and Markets

We can see similar discursive and ideological moves if we look back at the opening of Book 2, where Varro focuses on more traditional and large-scale forms of herding and pastoralism. The dialogue is set this time in Epirus, during Pompey's campaign against the pirates in the eastern Mediterranean in 67 BCE, where Varro claims to have been commanding the Greek fleets (bolstering his credentials as a traditional Roman aristocrat) (*RR* 2 preface). Once again, this episode is presented as a conversation where everyone is already familiar with the subject—which does not prevent them from reviewing basic material anyway—but each participant has some special expertise to contribute. Varro opens the discussion with a historical overview:

> As it is a necessity of nature that people and flocks have always existed . . . it is a necessity that from the remotest antiquity of human life they have come down, as Dicaearchus teaches, step by step to our age, and that the most distant stage was that state of nature in which man lived on those products which the virgin earth brought forth of her own accord; they descended from this stage into the second, the pastoral, in which they gathered for their use acorns, arbutus berries, mulberries, and other fruits by plucking them from wild and uncultivated trees and bushes, and likewise caught, shut up, and tamed such wild animals as they could for the like advantage. There is good reason to suppose that, of these, sheep were first taken, both because they are useful and because they are tractable; for these are naturally most placid and most adapted to the life of man. For to his food they brought milk and cheese, and to his body wool and skins for clothing. Then by a third stage man came from the pastoral life to that of the tiller of the soil; in this they retained much of the former two stages, and after reaching it they went far before reaching our stage. (2.1.3–5)

Hunting and gathering, then pastoralism, then farming; Varro offers a conventional account of different modes of production as progressive developmental stages, in which each builds on the previous one and retains its advantages. There is no suggestion here that these different stages might relate to different ecological contexts; rather, all take place within the same geographical space, and more significantly all are driven by the same underlying forces of utility maximization (the search for advantage) and rational calculation (sheep being domesticated first, it is assumed, because of their utility and tractability).[29] The different regions and traditions of Italy and the Mediterranean are combined into a single unified tradition—much as the Roman Empire under Augustus claimed to have done.

Although one of the ostensible aims of the dialogue is to present the claims to expertise in cattle-rearing of the men of Epirus, Varro is concerned to claim a special relationship between Romans, Italians, and stock-rearing:

> And, finally, is not Italy named from *vituli* (bullocks), as Piso states? Further, does not everyone agree that the Roman people is sprung from shepherds? Is there anyone who does not know that Faustulus, the foster-father who reared Romulus and Remus, was a shepherd? Will not the fact that they chose exactly the Parilia as the time to found a city demonstrate that they were themselves shepherds? Is not the same thing proved by the following facts: that up to this day a fine is assessed after the ancient fashion in oxen and sheep; that the oldest copper coins are marked with cattle; that when the city was founded the position of walls and gates was marked out by a bull and a cow; that when the Roman people is purified by the *suovetaurilia*, a boar, a ram, and a bull are driven around; that many of our family names are derived from both classes of domestic animals, the larger and the smaller? (2.1.9–10)

History, myth, and etymology establish the inherent character and traditional way of life of the Romans and their allies—but they also project contemporary values and assumptions back into the past, by locating the origins of wealth and money back at the very beginning of Roman society. The idea is immediately repeated when Varro hands over the discussion to his friend Scrofa, who had already featured as an expert on agrarian cultivation in the first book:

> "It remains to speak of the science of animal husbandry, and our friend, Scrofa, to whom this generation presents the palm in all agricultural matters, and who is therefore better fitted, will discuss it." When the eyes of all were turned on him Scrofa began: "Well, there is a science of assembling and feeding cattle in such fashion as to secure the greatest returns from them; the very word for money is derived from them, for cattle are the basis of all wealth." (2.1.11)

Pecunia, money or wealth, derives from *pecus*, flock. In his etymological work *De Lingua Latina*, Varro had argued that "it was among keepers of flocks that these words originated" (5.92), but Scrofa makes the point more explicit: Money comes from cattle because cattle *are* money, even before the invention of coinage, as seen a little earlier in the way that fines were once levied in oxen and sheep and the earliest coin carried an image of cattle to indicate its function and value.[30] In other words, from an early stage, if not from the very beginning, cattle had more than use value; exchange and money existed in Rome's distant, pre-agrarian past, and thus the acquisitive drive is established as a long-standing, if not inherent, human trait, in a variant on the myth of original barter that Graeber discussed.[31] Roman moral discourse of the late Republic regularly establishes a contrast between the simple, self-sufficient, and more communal customs and practices of the ancestors and the luxuriousness and focus on profit of the present; Varro's schematic account of development subtly undermines this contrast, implying that even the virtuous men of the early Republic were perfectly familiar with such things, hence naturalizing money and the pursuit of profit.[32]

The widespread ancient perception that pastoralism was a more "primitive" way of life, and hence antecedent to agriculture, meant that this section of his work was the logical place for Varro to develop such claims; but it was also more straightforward since arguably flocks are more easily imagined as objects of exchange, fully alienable and portable, than land. The *fructus* of animals consists not only of the milk, cheese, meat, fleece, and hides that their owners can use but also of successive generations of animals which in turn can be milked, shorn, slaughtered, sold, or multiplied. *Pecunia* breeds more *pecunia*, not only replenishing the owner's wealth but expanding it, whereas farming produces more or less the same amount of value every year without the possibility of easy expansion. The best hope for substantial accumulation for the landowner—and clearly this is something that is well beyond the capabilities of the average peasant farmer, although the advice of Varro's characters is ostensibly offered to anyone with a farm—is to increase the value of the land itself, in order to sell the estate at a profit. It is in this context that the two goals of farming that Varro established early in his first book are almost immediately collapsed back into one, reinforcing the message that everything is and always has been about profit:

> Equipped with this knowledge, farmers should aim at two goals, at utility and pleasure [*ad utilitatem et voluptatem*]. Utility aims at a return [*fructum*], pleasure at enjoyment; that which is useful takes priority over that which is pleasurable. And yet those methods of cultivation which improve the appearance of the land, not only make it more fruitful, as in the cultivation of fruit trees or olive trees in rows, but also more saleable, and add to the value of the farm. For any man would rather pay a high sum for a piece of land that is attractive than for one which is fruitful but unsightly. Still more useful is a piece of land which is healthier than others, because

there the return is certain; on the other hand, in a farm that is pestilential, however fertile it is, calamity prevents the farmer from making a profit. For where the calculation is with death, not only is the return uncertain, but also the life of the farmers. Where there is no healthfulness, farming is nothing other than a roll of the die for the life and property of the owner. (1.4.1–2)

Pleasure usually serves utility and hence profit, whether the harvest gathered from the land or the proceeds of the sale of that land; the link is broken only in the case of some of the most extravagant and unacceptable forms of *pastio villatica* discussed and condemned in the third book. The two goals of farming therefore appear more like a single goal, to be achieved by several different means; a country estate that is solely a place of pleasure, with no form of productive or profitable activity, ceases to be a "true" villa (but might still be sold for a profit to someone equally uninterested in a proper return).

It is clear throughout Varro's first book that the *fructus* of the agrarian enterprise is intended primarily for conversion into monetary *fructus* through the marketing of the produce, rather than simply being consumed by the owner, his family, and the laborers. It is therefore curious, on the face of it, that the topic of the market and the sale of produce is not so much passed over as quite deliberately evaded in his discussion. Earlier in the dialogue, marketing had been identified as one of the six key components of agriculture, the final stage of the farming year:

> "There is," said Stolo, "a second, a sixfold division of seasons which may be said to bear a relation to the sun and moon, because almost every product [*fructus*] comes to perfection in five stages and reaches jar and basket in the farmstead, and from these is brought forth for use in the sixth. The first stage is the preparation, the second the planting, the third the cultivation, the fourth the harvesting, the fifth the storing, the sixth the marketing [*promendum*]." (1.37.4)

We should note the way that the "utilization" of the produce at the sixth stage (*prodit ad usum*) is rapidly restricted to being a matter of sale rather than consumption. The same emphasis is seen at the end of the book, at the conclusion of the discussion of storage, which is presented as not just a matter of convenience (ensuring food supply for the whole year) but a source of increased financial returns: "for often products which have been stored quite a long time will not only pay interest on the storage but even double the yield if they are marketed at the right time" (1.69.1). This is then the moment for discussion of the final stage of the process, the marketing—but it never takes place.

While he was speaking the priest's freedman runs up to us with tears in his eyes and begs us to pardon him for the delay, and asks us to go to a funeral for him the next day. We spring to our feet and cry out in chorus: "What? To a funeral? What funeral? What has happened?" Bursting into tears, he tells us that his master had been stabbed by someone, and fallen to the ground; in the crowd he could not tell who it was, but had only heard a voice saying that a mistake had been made. As he had carried his old master home and sent the servants to find a surgeon and bring him with all speed, he hoped he might be pardoned for attending to his duty rather than coming to us; and though he had not been able to keep him from breathing his last a few moments later, he thought that he had acted rightly. We had no fault to find with him, and walking down from the temple we went our several ways, rather blaming the mischances of life than being surprised that such a thing had occurred in Rome. (1.69.2–3)

This dramatic conclusion emphasizes the political setting of the dialogue and the issues at stake in any discussion of agriculture and traditional Roman values, but it also neatly evades the whole topic of marketing, despite having earlier identified this as a crucial stage in the farmer's year and hence the ultimate source of the farm's *fructus*.[33] How should we understand this fundamental inconsistency in Varro's presentation of profit-orientated agriculture? One obvious response is to juxtapose it with Cicero's often-cited account of respectable occupations for a member of the elite (*Off.* 1.150–151), which is explicitly suspicious of anything connected to trade (especially on a small scale) and Cato's description of traders as energetic risk-takers subject to disaster (*Agr.* Preface): Markets, and the skills involved in deriving profit from marketing, may be essential to elite exploitation of their own estates, but they are associated with excessive risk and social disrepute. We can see a similar suspicion of markets in the intermittent emphasis in the agronomists' texts on self-sufficiency, supplying the needs of the farm laborers from their own production rather than buying in supplies; this can be seen as a rational response to uncertainty (both climate and prices), rather than a primitive mentality, but it certainly has an ideological component.[34] Similarly, in the passage cited above from Book 3.2.15–16 on the opportunities for profit represented by *pastio villatica*, we can detect some anxiety as well as excitement: the realization that such gains depend on constant banquets and dinners in the city of Rome, which is fine—so long as current fashions persist and this time of luxury continues.

Agriculture may be a traditional, and traditionally secure, way of making a living; but, at least in the form promoted by Varro and his characters, it is vulnerable to the insecurity and unpredictability of market forces and changing fashions.

The market is a source of economic power for the elite that can be converted into political and social power and is thus an essential basis of their continued dominance; but, unlike in the political and social spheres, where their control is largely uncontested—the fiercest struggle here is between different members of the elite—market involvement necessitates competition with other players, who may be more skilled and/or more willing to take risks.[35] The market thus becomes a threat as well as an opportunity. The elites' practical response, arguably, was a preference for selling their produce through private auctions and other personalized arrangements, where their superior status might give them an edge, rather than full participation in anonymous markets.[36] The ideological response was a deliberate evasiveness as too much explicit discussion would reveal the tensions and contradictions within elite economic activity and thought.

Conclusion

As recent research has shown, Varro's work is complex and multilayered, bringing together economic, political, philosophical, and cultural discourses in a sophisticated rhetorical and literary structure. It is engaged with changing political and economic realities in first-century BCE Italy; the interaction of imperialism, economic integration, and globalization; and the institutions of power and their consequences for the landowning elite.[37] It offers a sense of the complexity of Roman economic thinking, the different and often competing principles and assumptions involved in decisions about the management of estates—and, in particular, the non-economic rationalities that influenced such decisions, alongside the hard-headed pursuit of profit. It echoes, at several centuries' remove, the wider changes of the "Axial Age" discussed by Jaspers and Graeber, the nexus of money, military power, and rationalizing thought that characterized separate regions during the same critical period.[38] The rise of the impersonal market, integrated (however imperfectly) into wider regional and transregional networks and driven by the expansion of the Roman Empire, goes hand in hand with the rise of instrumental and profit-orientated thinking—but the transformation of more traditional ways of thinking is never complete.

Varro's dialogues are not just a reflection of changing times and ideas; he actively sought to shape the discourse, to change people's manner of thinking. The process of "radical simplification" of conceptions of human motivation, so that it comes to be possible to think of people acting solely according to ideas of profit and advantage, is not something that happens naturally or spontaneously in response to material conditions and the habits of thought they inculcate; it also takes hard and deliberate intellectual labor.[39] Varro's deployment of different speakers and of the appearance of a debate works to reconcile apparent contradictions between traditional conceptions and practices in agriculture and the supposedly traditional values of the Roman elite and the new realities and opportunities presented by the influx of the spoils of violence into Italy. His text sets about naturalizing money and the pursuit of profit—indeed, not only naturalizing them as having been central to Roman agriculture from the beginning but at the same time conveying the excitement of new opportunities and techniques. In modern terms, he sought to shift the Overton window of Roman economic thinking by changing not just what could be thought but what was taken for granted without question—transforming traditional moral discourse by making honor and social standing a matter of good profit and rational business management, opposed to dubious luxuriousness and extravagance.[40] This is arguably a significant step in ideological development from the genuinely self-sufficient household or community to the market-orientated enterprise, not least by making it appear, to contemporaries and to modern historians alike, as a natural development based on inherent human tendencies and motives. Far from a potential opposition between Roman moral values and the values of the market, Varro's text works to identify morality and virtue with the rational pursuit of profit.

7

Monetization, Marketization, and State Formation

THE LATER ROMAN EMPIRE AS AN AXIAL-AGE ECONOMY

John Weisweiler

SOMETIME IN THE year 427 or 428, Augustine, the Bishop of Hippo (Annaba in modern Algeria), sent a confidential letter to Eustochius, a high-ranking official in the Roman administration.[1] As bishop, Augustine not only fulfilled spiritual functions but also served as arbitrator in disputes among his flock.[2] In the letter, he asked for Eustochius' advice in a delicate matter of law. He was interested in the status of *coloni*, tenant farmers who were formally free but legally prohibited to leave the estate on which they worked. Roman law maintained a firm boundary between freedom and slavery; legal experts unanimously agreed that outside of warfare, a freeborn person could never be turned into a slave. Yet Augustine's letter shows that in the North African countryside of the early fifth century applying this principle was not straightforward. Rural workers were deeply enmeshed in webs of indebtedness and patronage to local landowners. The force of these obligations frequently undercut the protections theoretically granted to them by imperial legislation.[3]

For example, there was a long-standing loophole according to which indebted persons were allowed to rent out the labor services of their children for long periods of time (usually twenty-five years).[4] Augustine enquired whether such agreements remained in force after the father who had leased out his children had died:[5]

John Weisweiler, *Monetization, Marketization, and State Formation* In: *Debt in the Ancient Mediterranean and Near East*. Edited by: John Weisweiler, Oxford University Press. © Oxford University Press 2023. DOI: 10.1093/oso/9780197647172.003.0007

My question is whether after the death of the fathers who have sold them they should still be forced to serve for the same number of years. Or are they freed by the death of those who have sold them, or rather rented them out, because they no longer stand under the legal power of their fathers?

Significantly, Augustine was unsure how to describe these transactions correctly: Had the children been "sold" (*uenditio*) or "rented out" (*locati*) by their father? Either way, in practice, their status closely approximated slavery. Moreover, Augustine also took it for granted that some parents sold their children outright into unfreedom:

I also ask whether free fathers can sell their children into perpetual slavery and whether mothers can also sell the labor services of their children. Finally, I also enquire whether if a *colonus* sells his child (in whatever manner the child is sold by his father), the buyer has more rights over the person who has been sold than the owner of the property, from where the *colonus* comes, and whether a property-owner can turn his *coloni* or the children of their *coloni* into slaves.

It is unclear whether the practices Augustine describes here were legal. Maybe he alludes to a custom, sanctioned by the emperor Constantine, according to which babies in the period immediately after birth (before they had been recognized by their fathers) could legally be sold off.[6] In any case, Augustine wanted to hear from Eustochius who had ownership rights over such persons: their parents, the bosses of their parents, or their buyers? All in all, the letter reveals that many of the practices which David Graeber associates with the "Axial Age" remained in place in early fifth-century North Africa. The world in which Augustine lived was a violent and highly unequal society in which debt was one of the major institutions of exploitation.

At first sight, the letter to Eustochius seems to corroborate long-standing views that the status of the rural population drastically declined in the later Roman state (roughly the period from the late third to the late fifth centuries CE). According to scholars such as Max Weber (who in 1908 published a groundbreaking monograph on the agrarian history of antiquity) and the founding father of ancient social history, Mikhail Rostovtzeff (whose *Social and Economy History of the Roman Empire* came out in 1926), the power of the free peasantry was broken in the warfare of the third century.[7] In their view, in order to defend the empire against barbarian invasions, late-Roman emperors created a highly bureaucratic state which narrowly regulated economic life. Rural workers were tied to their land. The commercial bourgeoisies on which the wealth of ancient city-states had allegedly been founded were destroyed.[8] The imperial economy reverted to barter and gift-giving. Private trade largely ended, and land came to be concentrated in the hands of large aristocratic households, which operated with increasing autarky from the outside world.[9] On this reading, when in the later fifth century the superstructure of the Roman state collapsed under the weight of barbarian invasions, this made little difference for the great majority of its inhabitants. They had already much earlier declined to the status of serfs, who no longer owned their own lands but were compelled to perform labor services on aristocratic estates, which they were legally prohibited from leaving.[10]

However, there are problems with this view of the later Roman Empire as a proto-feudal economy. As the last two generations of late-antique scholarship have shown, it simply does not fit the evidence. New excavations and surveys continue to demonstrate that late antiquity did not witness a decline of inter-regional trade networks. On the contrary, in the fourth and fifth centuries, the mobility of material goods and human beings increased. On the one hand, the redistributive systems of the Roman state provided an environment that was highly conducive for commerce between major regions of the empire; the security and infrastructure provided by public institutions opened up manifold opportunities for private trade. The fact that late-Roman emperors enlarged the size of the imperial administration and the imperial army may have increased levels of economic integration of the Mediterranean and western Europe.[11] On the other hand, international trade expanded too. Roman elites had always imported luxury goods, slaves, and soldiers from the regions beyond the imperial frontier in central Europe, Africa, and western Asia.[12] But the formation in the late second, third, and fourth centuries of complex political structures in the Sahara and in the Steppe increased the strength of these pan-Eurasian and pan-African circuits of long-distance commerce.[13]

Also, the view of large estates as autarkic households can no longer be defended. As scholars such as Dominic Rathbone, Jairus Banaji, Peter Sarris, and others have pointed out, Egyptian papyri clearly show that late-antique large estates were not self-sufficient production units but profit-oriented enterprises which calculated their revenues in cash and produced for the market.[14] We are also no longer certain that the fourth century witnessed a decline in the legal status of the peasantry. As Jean-Michel Carrié demonstrated in 1983 in a pioneering study and as Cam Grey and Paolo Tedesco have recently reasserted, the legislation prohibiting *coloni* from changing their place of residence was inspired by tax purposes. By barring agricultural workers from leaving their workplaces, emperors did not formally reduce the legal status of peasants or subject them to the judicial authority of large landowners.[15] On the contrary, there are signs that the restoration of a robust imperial state in the late third and fourth centuries led to an economic boom in the countryside. While northwestern Europe probably no longer reached quite the same level of prosperity as it had enjoyed in the early Roman period, in most other regions of the empire site density increased.[16] North Africa in particular was doing better than in any previous period of Mediterranean history. At the time of Augustine's writing, it was home to a vibrant urban culture and a highly profitable agroindustry whose products were consumed all across the Roman world.[17] Surprisingly, also the Vandal conquest of North Africa would not end what has been called "the African boom." Until the sixth century, Mediterranean consumer culture penetrated the most remote areas of the region, and the grain and olive produced in North Africa were exported to all major markets in the former empire.[18]

For all of these reasons, recent scholarship has abandoned the view that the Mediterranean economy in the fourth and fifth centuries CE was in a state of regression. Instead, it is now widely agreed that the later Roman state was marked by high levels of prosperity and vibrant inter-regional markets. This new consensus on late-antique economic history has led to a reassessment of the reasons for the disintegration of the Roman state. It has become clear that until shortly before the breakup of the western half of the Roman Empire in the second half of the fifth century, the Mediterranean economy was *at least as* integrated and the institutions of the imperial state functioned with *at least as much* efficiency as in earlier periods of Roman history. To be sure, the late-antique administration appropriated perceptibly higher taxes from its subjects than the imperial government in the early Roman Empire. However, this expansion of state power did not necessarily weaken the Mediterranean economy as early twentieth-century liberals such as Weber and Rostovtzeff had thought. Rather, in the view of recent scholarship, the late-antique strengthening of state institutions may have served as a kind of "Keynesian stimulus." As Chris Wickham pointed out, the extractive institutions of the Roman state created a stable public demand from which private enterprise also profited.[19] As a result, in the view of historians such as Bryan Ward-Perkin and Peter Heather, the fall of the Roman Empire was not the inevitable product of internal weaknesses but a "catastrophe flip," the unforeseeable product of a concatenation of political and military misjudgments.[20]

No doubt, the new consensus view of the later Roman economy as a success story marks a great advance over traditional interpretations. It fits the evidence of rural wealth revealed by archaeological fieldwork and the editing of new papyri much better than the traditional interpretation of late antiquity as a proto-feudal economy. However, there are at least two blots in the joyful picture of prosperity painted by new orthodoxy. Firstly, it seems unlikely that state institutions and the elite landowners played as large a role as drivers of inter-regional exchange as the now predominant "Keynesian" interpretation of the late-antique economy suggests. Tax rates in the late-antique Mediterranean remained quite low by comparative standards; they were hardly ever higher than 10%.[21] Moreover, as Walter Scheidel and Steven Friesen have argued on theoretical grounds and as is corroborated by a fourth-century tax register from the city of Hermopolis in Egypt, most of the national product of the Roman Empire was controlled not by ultra-rich trans-regional landowners who could draw on the infrastructure of the Roman state to distribute their produce but by medium- and small-scale proprietors, who were less integrated into imperial exchange networks. This suggests that the expansion of state institutions was not quite as important a driver of the late-antique boom as the new "Keynesian" consensus suggests.[22]

Secondly, the new optimistic interpretation fits oddly with the quick collapse of Roman social and economic structures in the wake of the dissolution of the western half of the empire in the fifth century. To be sure, in the eastern Mediterranean, the late-Roman "strong state" as reconfigured by the reforms of the emperors Diocletian and Constantine survived at least until the later sixth century. Also, North Africa under Vandal rule and Italy under Ostrogothic kings remained prosperous and highly monetized societies that were deeply integrated into inter-regional trade networks. Yet in large parts of northwestern Europe, especially in northern France and Britain, Roman social and economic structures unraveled remarkably swiftly after the imperial army lost control.[23] If imperial institutions functioned as smoothly and efficiently as is now generally believed and if the late-Roman countryside was as prosperous as recent archaeology has shown, why were the ruling groups of these regions unable to recreate the Roman model of a tax-raising "strong state"? The speed of change suggests that some groups within these societies deliberately rejected the imperial model. This in turn implies that the benefits of empire were not quite as widely shared as the most optimistic cheerleaders of the Roman economic miracle assume.

In this chapter, I will suggest that David Graeber's theory of the functioning of what he calls "Axial-Age" economies offers an explanatory framework to make sense of these paradoxes. To my mind, one feature of his theory is particularly useful for late-antique historians: Graeber's book offers a more compelling explanation of the relationship between markets and state institutions than recent interpretations of late-antique economic history. Graeber encourages us to see ancient Mediterranean states not as opponents of private enterprise (as traditional models do) or merely as stabilizers of private demand (as Keynesians argue) but rather as creators and energetic defenders of ancient market societies. I will propose that this view of an inextricable link between markets and states illuminates features of the late-antique economy which have remained underexposed in traditional accounts. It explains how the later Roman state could reconcile economic dynamism with high levels of inequality. And it is suggestive of the reasons why in some parts of the former empire the imperial system dissolved with surprising speed after Roman armies had left, despite the enormous material benefits landowning elites reaped from that system.

An Axial-Age Empire

If I argue that Graeber's theory is helpful for late-antique historians, I do not mean to endorse his interpretation of late-antique history. In the few sections of his book in which Graeber discusses the final centuries of the Roman Empire, he follows the outdated view of the later Roman Empire as a proto-feudal economy: "By the end of the empire, most people in the countryside who weren't outright slaves had become, effectively, debt peons to some rich landlord, a situation in the end legally formalized by imperial decrees binding peasants to the land."[24] The later Roman Empire here appears as the predecessor of the Middle Ages, in which most economic exchange was (supposedly) conducted not through the market but through rents and labor services agricultural workers owed to their lords. We have already seen that this view is no longer tenable in view of the archaeological and papyrological evidence. But I am not sure whether we can take this as a decisive refutation of his broader theory of how ancient economies functioned.

What we have to recognize is that the later Roman Empire was (in Graeber's terms) not a "medieval" but an "Axial-Age" economy. In Graeber's retelling, the "Axial Age" was a period which extends from around the beginning of monetization in the Mediterranean in the seventh century BCE until the dissolution of the Roman and Iranian Empires in late antiquity. Politically and economically, it was marked by the emergence of fiscally intensive trans-regional states, which financed their warfare through metal currencies and whose economic systems were based on market exchange and large-scale slavery: Drawing on the work of Geoffrey Ingram, Graeber calls this the "military–coinage–slavery complex."[25] Once this is recognized, the conceptual framework developed in his book turns out to be quite helpful for understanding the distinctive shape of the Mediterranean economy in late antiquity. I would like to suggest that the later Roman state represents the dynamics of Graeber's "Axial Age" in exceptionally pure form.

Like all "Axial-Age" economies, the later Roman state was born out of warfare. Its distinctive features were formed in an existential military crisis. Since the 230s, central European groups crossed the Rhine and Danube and Iranian armies the Euphrates frontier. Mainland Greece was invaded and Athens captured by the Goths and Heruli;[26] Antioch, the third-largest city in the empire, plundered by the Iranian "kings of kings"; and in 259, the Roman emperor Valerian fell into

Iranian captivity.[27] In the wake of this catastrophe, the Roman state began to disintegrate. Valerian's son Gallienus only maintained control over the core territories of the empire; western Europe and the eastern Mediterranean were ruled by independent imperial regimes with their own armies. Yet the empire survived. In the final decades of the third century, a series of military emperors from officer families in the Balkans managed to defeat foreign invaders and competing rulers.[28] In order to bring about this turnaround, they employed similar methods as Axial-Age rulers in other regions of Eurasia. Three such tactics may be singled out.

First, emperors sought to appropriate a larger share of the surplus generated by their subjects. Initially, they frequently relied on ad hoc exactions to finance their armies; but in time, they developed more sophisticated methods to extract wealth from their subjects. In 287 CE, the emperor Diocletian and his co-rulers introduced a new taxation system. Immunities enjoyed by inhabitants of Italy and local elites were removed. All lands across the empire were assessed on the basis of an accounting unit, the *caput siue iugum*. New tax registers were created, and for the first time imperial officials created an empire-wide budget. The creation of this new centralized fiscal system had two effects. On the one hand, the tax burden was more equitably distributed. On the other hand, the detailed knowledge acquired by emperors over the resources of their subjects enabled them to increase overall revenues.[29]

Of course, setting up fiscal registers was a complex process. Diocletian's reforms were only possible because during the permanent warfare of the third century his predecessors had begun to strengthen state capacity. This is the second package of reforms typical of Axial-Age rulers. All across Eurasia, new trans-regional states run by powerful bureaucracies emerged. The Romans were comparative latecomers in this process. As Walter Scheidel has pointed out, in the first centuries CE, the Roman imperial administration was much smaller and less effective than its Chinese counterpart. However, during the military crises of the third century, emperors caught up. They created a much-enlarged imperial bureaucracy which enabled them to discipline local power networks. While the state did not penetrate society quite as deeply as in China, the formation of a centralized and salaried imperial administration markedly increased the capacity of emperors to impose their wishes on subject populations: "Driven by the internal logic of traditional empire, the two systems had become about as similar as their discrepant starting conditions permitted them to be."[30]

Also in a third respect, the later Roman Empire conforms to Graeber's model. In his book, Axial-Age economies are defined by a distinct monetary system: the use of metal currency. In Graeber's telling, the militarized ruling classes of Axial-Age states preferred this impersonal method of payment because it is ideally suited for highly mobile mercenary armies: "Bullion predominates, above all, in periods of generalized violence."[31] This theory cannot fully explain the invention of coinage in the first millennium BCE Mediterranean; after all, Greek city-states (and not the territorial empires of Persia and Carthage) were the most enthusiastic early adopters of coinage.[32] However, the idea of a close link between monetization and militarization provides a useful vantage point from which to consider the role played by coinage in Roman history. It is likely that the intensification of imperial warfare was one of the reasons for the introduction of bronze coinage in the third century BCE (though a growing interest by some members of the ruling elite in new forms of market production played an important role too).[33] Similarly, the exigencies of warfare explain the shape of the late-Roman monetary system. During the military crises of the third century, the metal content of silver and bronze currencies declined. Faced with the urgent need to pay their soldiers but lacking ready access to new sources of silver, emperors debased their currency. As recent scholarship has demonstrated, this did not inevitably have detrimental economic effects. Prices long remained stable, despite the loss in metal content. The Roman currency effectively became fiat money.[34]

Nor is it clear when in the 260s and 270s finally inflation set in, this development equally affected all inhabitants of the empire. To be sure, civic foundations and other collective institutions whose income depended on stable interest payments suffered heavily. As Carrié suggested, the disappearance of many of these bodies may have been an effect of inflation.[35] But, of course, a "clean slate" was not in the interest of the cash-hungry emperors, who needed bullion to pay their armies. In the late third and early fourth centuries, rulers experimented with new currency structures. Only one had lasting success. In the late 310s (possibly helped by the discovery of new metal deposits in the Balkans), Constantine created a new monetary system based on a new gold currency, the *solidus*, literally the "hard" coin.[36] Henceforth, the metal content of the *solidus* currency remained stable. All fiscal dues to the imperial state were calculated in this new "hard" currency; the value of bronze and silver coins no longer was defined by the state but was determined by the market. For those who had access to gold, this decision ended inflation. The introduction of the *solidus* enabled the state to precisely calculate future taxes, landowners to precisely calculate future rents, and creditors to precisely calculate future interest payments.

Like the creation of a more efficient fiscal system and the establishment of a more robust imperial administration, so also the development of a new inflation-proof gold currency was a key precondition for the economic resurgence of the fourth century. The formation of a strong state and of a highly monetized market economy across the empire offered ideal conditions for wealth accumulation by landowning classes in the Mediterranean and western Europe. On this reading, the later Roman state marked not the end but the culmination of the patterns of accumulation typical of the "Axial Age."

Marketization and State Formation

Graeber's theory of a link between monetarization, militarization, and state power not only fits well with current understandings of late-antique history. It may also help explain features of the late-Roman political economy that have remained underexplored in recent scholarship. One among them is the link between state formation and the subjection of new fields of human life to the logic of the market. A long historiographical tradition conceives of state power and private enterprise as opposing forces. For this reason, the strong state of the later Roman Empire has long been seen as a destroyer of the commercial civilization of antiquity. As we have seen, more recent scholarship has abandoned such views. But it may be possible to go further. I should like to suggest that the late-antique expansion of state power promoted an expansion of markets. In at least three ways, the reforms undertaken by emperors of the late third and fourth centuries subjected new fields of life to an economic logic.

First, levels of monetization significantly increased. The reduction in the metal content of silver and bronze currencies from the later third century onward enabled the state to greatly expand the supply of coinage. For example, in a recent study, Ludovic Trommenschlager and Gaël Brkojewtisch trace the date of issue of coins found in seven villas in Lorrain in northeastern France; 88% come from the period after 260.[37] The same pattern occurs in sites all across the empire. For example, according to Richard Reece's classic study of the coins found in Britannia, 84% come from the late third and fourth centuries and 16% from the early Empire;[38] and in the North African evidence recently examined by Leslie Dossey, late-antique coins outnumber early imperial ones by a factor of ten or more.[39] Crucially, the same pattern occurs not only in excavations and surface surveys but also in hoards. This shows that the predominance of late-antique coins was not a product of uneven survival of the evidence but reflects a real increase in the money supply. To be sure, in principle, the flood of new coinage does not necessarily mean that more transactions were carried out through market mechanisms than before. As Luuk de Ligt has shown, even in the early Roman Empire, in the countryside prices were often expressed in monetary terms, even if in practice transactions were usually carried out in kind or through credit systems.[40] This shows that already in the first two centuries CE, the imposition of Roman rule had set into motion a process by which older credit systems were being replaced by market exchange. Nevertheless, the late-antique expansion of the money supply turbocharged this process. It further reduced the importance of local systems of redistribution and hierarchy and made it easier for non-elites (and especially the rural population) to participate in regional and imperial networks of market exchange.

Second, since the fourth century, government posts and services were officially sold. Fees paid by litigants in imperial court were carefully advertised in public inscriptions, and law codes laid down in detail the sums bureaucrats needed to pay to their future colleagues and supervisors to win a job in the Roman administration. Like in the early modern period, the official sale of government posts and services offered rulers a cost-effective way to quickly expand the size of the central administration. In this sense, as Christopher Kelly points out, the new system reflected a strengthening of state power.[41] At the same time, the new fees-for-services model of government was a product of monetization in at least two ways. Most obviously, it could only work if prospective buyers had sufficient cash (or cash-like commodities) at hand to purchase state services or state offices. More subtly, the new model presupposed a market mentality. It implied that a user of state services understood them no longer as public goods, which should ideally be provided for free by the leaders of one's own face-to-face community, but as commodities, which could be bought and sold and were best supplied by independent outsiders.

A third field in which market relations seem to have played an increasing role in late antiquity is in agricultural labor. As recent scholarship has shown, far from being serfs whose obligations toward their landlords chiefly consisted of labor services and who largely operated outside the cash economy, late-antique estate owners predominantly relied on wage-labor to pay their workers.[42] These salaries were denominated in the new gold currency created by Constantine (although in practice payment often worked through various forms of credit). In general, this was an adaptive response by landowners to local labor markets. In regions where population density was high, relying on salaried workers (who just had to be paid during harvest seasons) was cheaper than carrying out the same work through slaves or tenants (who had to be fed in the winter as well).[43] More specifically, the growing importance of wage-labor was a result of the late-antique changes in monetary and fiscal systems. The spread of coinage made it easier to pay day laborers in cash; at the same time, the fact that the imperial administration assessed all lands in the empire according to accounting units whose monetary equivalent was defined each year by its officials put pressure on landowners to calculate the obligations of their tenants also in the new gold currency. In this way, the state set in motion a process by which traditional relationships of dependence and exploitation were redefined in strictly quantitative terms: Not only the taxes owed to the imperial state but also the obligations owed to the landlord were expressed in cash. Significantly, when late-Roman authors talk about the value of an individual estate, they usually record not its purchasing price but the yearly revenues derived from it in *solidi*.[44] And when they discuss the wealth controlled by large landowners, they no longer record their net worth (as was customary in previous periods of Roman history) but the annual revenues derived from their estates in gold currency.[45]

All of this evidence is suggestive of the ways in which the monetary and fiscal reforms undertaken by late-Roman emperors promoted an expansion of quantitative logics to new fields of life. The increase in levels of monetization, the official sale of government services, and the expansion of wage-labor created a situation in which services that previously had normally been discharged without money changing hands now increasingly obtained a price and became precisely calculable. In the later Roman state, the expansion of state power and the subjection of new fields of life to market forces were synergetic processes that mutually reinforced each other.

Winners and Losers of Marketization

It is easy to underestimate the benefits inhabitants of the Roman Empire derived from the formation of this more marketized state. The spread of economic logics to new fields of life not only reduced the scope of traditional practices of redistribution and solidarity but also undermined long-standing forms of hierarchy and exploitation. In a recent study, Stephen Collins-Elliott has traced the impact of monetization on the late-antique countryside through a case study on the region of Cinigiano in south-central Tuscany, excavated by the Roman Peasant project. He shows that in the fourth century (just as coins come to be more widely used by rural populations) also evidence of craft production is found in a larger number of sites. He plausibly reads this as a symptom that many peasants had obtained greater independence; they no longer needed to rely exclusively on credit systems and networks of mutual obligation to fulfill their needs but could satisfy them directly on the market: "the inhabitants of each site were able to see to their own needs independently, rather than to rely on networks which made them dependent upon one another for meeting their demands."[46] Similar developments are paralleled in other regions of the empire. The process has been studied in detail by Dossey in her important study on the North African peasantry. She shows that the fourth century witnessed a notable increase in rural production; most notably, all across the countryside, new ceramic factories were constructed. Also, consumption increased. The widespread use of bathhouses, glass, and high-quality pottery shows that forms of luxury which previously had been the exclusive preserve of city-dwellers were now also accessible to some sectors of the rural population.[47] Similar processes have been observed in recent work on other regions of the empire, such as Iberia, Greece, Britannia, and Anatolia.[48]

Yet not all benefited from this more marketized economy. As mentioned above, the introduction of a new hard currency by Constantine ended inflation only for those who had access to gold coins. While landowning elites, soldiers, and imperial officials were henceforth protected from further devaluations, lower strata of the population (who relied on silver and bronze currencies for their daily payments) were not. As Jairus Banaji has shown, throughout the fourth and fifth centuries, the exchange of metal coinage vis-à-vis gold fell. Since rents, taxes, and increasingly debts were denominated in gold currency, it would seem that the late-antique monetary system exerted constant downward pressure on non-elite incomes.[49] The fragmentary evidence from Egyptian papyri, compiled by Kyle Harper in a recent study, appears to bear out this hypothesis. Wage levels seem to gradually decline in late antiquity, while land prices increase.[50] The widespread evidence of prosperity should thus not be taken to imply that the fruits of the late-antique boom were shared equally. While monetization opened up new opportunities for the top stratum of the rural population, others may have found it more difficult to participate in this new gold-based economy.

Other developments contributed to reduce the bargaining power of agricultural workers vis-à-vis landowners. As mentioned earlier, from the fourth century onward, in a growing number of regions, emperors began to prohibit tenant farmers, so-called *coloni*, from leaving the estates on which they were registered. In this way, the imperial administration sought to ensure that tax registers from which the payment of the poll tax was determined remained up to date. While this policy advanced the interest of the imperial state (interested in the maximization of taxes) and of proprietors (interested in the maximization of profits), it weakened the ability of tenants to negotiate good deals with their landlords. To be sure, this may not have been the original purpose of the legislation. Still, as large landowners began to play an important role in the collection of revenues from tenants, the profitability of private estates "became a concern of the imperial administration.[51] Notably, the body of laws regarding *coloni* formed part of a larger trend. As the interests of private landowners and the imperial fisc became increasingly aligned, emperors began to defend the interests of landowners in energetic ways that are unparalleled in earlier periods of Roman history. In a law passed in 382, the imperial administration granted landowners the formal right to abduct homeless persons in Rome and deploy them as laborers on their own landholdings.[52] And as Sebastian Schmidt-Hofner has shown, the settlement of barbarians on Roman soil was partly motivated by anxieties about agrarian labor shortages; notably, many of the new migrants who arrived in the Roman Empire in the fourth and early fifth centuries ended up as workers on large estates.[53] Of course, the Roman government had always had an open ear to the concerns of its landowning classes. Nevertheless, the imperial state had never before interfered quite so directly into agrarian relations or defended the interests of their largest taxpayers in quite so energetic and imaginative ways.

We would expect that the late-antique expansion of markets disadvantaged rural workers also in another way. The comparative evidence suggests that monetization and marketization tend to promote an increase in rural debt and tend to enmesh peasants in new webs of dependence and exploitation.[54] Papyri from late-antique Egypt, analyzed by Papaconstantinou in her contribution to this volume, enable us to trace this process.[55] It is tempting to read the abuses mentioned by Augustine in his letter to Eustochius (discussed in the opening section of this chapter) as evidence for similar developments. On this reading, the sale of children into forced labor would have been the result of rising levels of indebtedness among North African peasants. But we have to be careful. It is important to note that the practices attested in Augustine's letter are not new. Already in earlier centuries of Roman history, legal prohibitions on the sale of freeborn persons had been regularly evaded.[56] As Ville Vuolanto has pointed out, if we hear more often about such practices in late antiquity, this may well be due to a change in the nature of our sources: "the rise of Christianity . . . made every-day life an issue of discussion more than before."[57]

Nevertheless, in at least one way, the later Roman state relaxed previous prohibitions on the sale of freeborn persons. As Harper has shown, while in several laws the emperor Constantine reiterated the rule that freeborn humans beings could not be sold, he also introduced some interesting exceptions to this general principle. According to a law issued in 331, children abandoned immediately after their birth—"still covered with blood" (*a sanguine*, as was the technical term)—could be legally retained by their purchaser.[58] Already in the year 329, Constantine had issued an edict to the inhabitants of Italy in which he protected the property rights of persons who had bought children in this way:

> According to the statutes of former Emperors, if any person should lawfully purchase a child covered with blood in any manner and should suppose that he ought to rear such a child, he shall have the right to hold it in the condition of slavery; and if after a series of years any person should bring an action to restore the child to freedom or should defend his right to it as his slave, such claimant shall provide another of the same kind or shall pay a price which can be adequate. For when a person has executed a written instrument and has paid an adequate price, his possession of the slave shall be so valid that he shall have unrestricted power to sell him also

for his own debt. Those persons who attempt to contravene this law shall be subject to punishment.

In the opening sentence of the edict, Constantine claims that he restates the "statutes of former emperors." But extant imperial legislation does not preserve any such rule. Whether or not there was an earlier emperor who had issued such a law, the text provides striking testimony of the extent to which the marketization of social relations had progressed in the later Roman Empire. In Rome, since the fourth century BCE, it had been considered a hallmark of civilization that free persons could not be sold. Now this principle was relaxed. Constantine ruled that persons who had purchased a freeborn child could only be forced to abandon their property rights if the parents of the child offered appropriate compensation, either the equivalent amount in cash or another human being: "such claimant shall provide another of the same kind or shall pay a price which can be adequate."[59]

Of course, we should not overstate the difference this legislation made in reality. Slaves had long played an important role in the Roman labor supply, and a significant amount of that supply must always come from the sale of children into slavery.[60] As Harper points out, by legalizing this practice, the legislation we just considered merely validated long-standing social realities: "The Roman slave system was ferociously addicted to the internal consumption of slaves, and Constantine was one of the only emperors who tried to confront the tensions between the law of status and the practices of enslavement directly."[61] Still, the fact that the imperial government legalized the trade in the bodies of freeborn children expresses a far-reaching shift in Roman ideas of value. Like the sale of government offices and the growing importance played by cash payments in the management of agricultural labor, the new commitment by the imperial state to shore up property rights over citizen children who had been sold into slavery highlights how far the quantification of fields of human life which previously had been shielded from the logic of the market had progressed in late antiquity.

Resistance

If this analysis is correct, this raises a final question. Unlike the unequal exchange of services in a hierarchical relationship, market sales imply an idea of equality between buyer and seller. The same goes for debt. As Graeber points out, a credit contract is (at least in theory) an agreement freely entered between equal parties: "it is premised on an assumption of equality."[62] This line of reasoning would suggest that the application of the radically simplifying logic of the market to new fields of life not only generated new forms of inequality but also offered subordinate groups a new language to contest long-standing forms of exploitation. Can such a process be observed in late antiquity?

Unfortunately, we generally lack the sources to trace the ways in which subordinate groups made sense of the economic transformations of the fourth century. The legal dossier compiled by Optatus, the bishop of Milev (modern Mila in northeastern Algeria), against an opposing faction of the African church, the so-called Donatists, is maybe the best evidence for the emergence of an oppositional discourse among rural populations. The bishop notes that when in 349 a group of imperial officials arrived in his town to carry out grain distributions financed by the provincial administration, they were attacked by angry demonstrators. Led by two agitators, Axido and Fasir, peasants went after the rural rich (*Contra Parmenianum Donatistam* 3.4):[63]

> Nobody was secure on his own properties; the records of debts had lost their force, no creditor at that time had the freedom to enforce payment, all were terrified by the letters of those who boasted that they were the generals of the saints; and if there was any delay in obeying their commands, an angry mob suddenly came to their help, and, as terror went before them, besieged the creditors with dangers, so that those who should have been entreated on account of their loans were forced into groveling prayers through fear of death. Each one hastened to write off even his greatest debts, and considered it a profit if he escaped injury at their hands. Even the roads were not safe, because masters, thrown out of their vehicles, ran in the manner of slaves before their own retainers, who were sitting in their masters' place. By the verdict and bidding of those men the conditions of master and slave were reversed.

The provincial administration no doubt expected that the inhabitants of Milev would be grateful for the distribution of grain. Similarly, creditors thought that the rural poor would use this communal event to entreat them to reduce their debts. But they were disappointed. Far from entreating creditors to reduce the amount owed, they demanded an outright cancellation of debts: "those who deserved to be begged for their own gifts, were compelled by fear of death to entreat, humiliated."

At first sight, this passage might seem to confirm the disruptive effects of the subjection of rural populations to market forces in the Roman Empire. As peasants transformed from loyal retainers into contract partners, they no longer were ready to put up with long-standing forms of exploitation. But upon closer inspection, it is not clear to what extent this highly rhetorical account can be taken as an accurate representation of realities on the ground. As Shaw has observed, church officials like Optatus were well aware that the imperial administration was normally reluctant to interfere in a purely sectarian conflict. By claiming that Axido and Fasir abolished debts and brought about a full-scale reversal of social hierarchies, Optatus hoped to convince the imperial administration to mobilize the state apparatus to crush his ecclesiastical opponents. Whether their objectives were really quite as socially revolutionary as Optatus asserts is open to question.[64]

This is not to deny that the economic order of the later Roman state was regularly criticized. Most obviously, the Christian scriptures, deeply shaped by the Near Eastern social thought of the early Axial Age (analyzed by Reinhard Pirngruber in his contribution to this volume), offered a language through which the stark inequalities of Roman society were repeatedly denounced.[65] Holy men and holy women through spectacular acts of renunciation proved that it was possible to escape from the necessity to give away one's labor power to the reproduction of Roman society.[66] Indeed, several Christian intellectuals insisted on the unavoidably sinful nature of earthly wealth. Ultimately, however, leaders of the church were able to reconcile the moral demands of the gospels with an accommodation to the status quo.[67] Also, pagan intellectuals recurrently condemned the subjection of new fields of life to the logic of the market. Most famously, in his *De Rebus Bellicis*, a treatise addressed to an unknown emperor, an anonymous author asserted that the introduction of a gold currency by Constantine had not only sharpened inequality but also undermined the moral fiber of Roman society:[68]

In the age of Constantine extravagant public spending prescribed gold for petty transactions instead of bronze, which previously had been highly valued; and the origin of this display of greed is believed to have sprung from the following cause. When the gold and silver and the enormous quantity of previous stones which had been hoarded up many years ago in the temples reached the public, it inflamed everyone's desires to spend and possess. And although the spending of bronze itself (which, as I have said, had been stamped with the portraits of kings) could already be seen to be excessive and difficult to control, nevertheless, as a result of some blindness or other, there came about an increasingly widespread insistence on spending gold, which is understood to be more valuable. The private mansions of the powerful, filled from this flood of gold, were turned into more signal instruments for the oppression of the poor; the less-well-off, obviously, being held down by brutal means. But the suffering poor, driven to attempt various acts of wickedness, and having before their eyes no respect for the law nor feelings of loyalty, entrusted their revenge to the criminal arts. For frequently they inflicted extremely serious damage on the empire by laying the countryside waste, by persistently disturbing the peace with acts of brigandage, by stirring up hatreds.

But it is important to note that this critique did not lead the author to put forward an alternative vision of a just social order. The only solution he can envisage is the introduction of a program of thrift and austerity by a new ruler: "Your prudence, most excellent emperor, will therefore take steps to hold down public spending, and thereby both look to the interests of the taxpayer and extend to ages to come the splendor of your name."[69] It turns out that in the view of the anonymous author, the root cause of the current crisis is not structural but individual—the moral depravity of Constantine and his associates. By hoping for a period of moral reform under the reign of an ethically superior ruler, *De Rebus Bellicis* reasserts the inevitability of the current social order. This is typical. There was a long tradition in Roman literature according to which the invention of private property and the rise of imperial warfare had corrupted human society and ended a bygone golden age. Ultimately, however, this insistence that we live in a society which has irretrievably lost its innocence served to justify a coercive state as the only bulwark against a return to a state of nature and a war of all against all.[70]

At the same time, the lack of a revolutionary discourse does not necessarily mean that that the late-Roman economic system enjoyed widespread support. Indeed, it is striking how quickly key features of the imperial order dissolved when in the early fifth century the western imperial government suffered a series of unexpected defeats against central European invaders. Only in North Africa, Italy, and (to some extent) Mediterranean Iberia were new ruling classes able to rebuild Roman-style fiscally intensive strong states (albeit on a smaller scale). In other regions of western Europe, Roman administrative systems and material culture evaporated very quickly.[71] Chris Wickham has suggested that the disappearance of the accoutrements of classical civilization in these regions might be read as a happy story. As large landowners whose power was backed by the coercive machinery of the Roman state disappeared, peasants were able to keep a larger part of the surplus: "elaborate productive patterns and large-scale bulk exchange are above all signs of exploitation and of the resultant hierarchies of wealth."[72] If Wickham is right, this would explain why Roman material culture disappeared so quickly. After the departure of the imperial administration, there was no longer sufficient local support to maintain the property rights of large landowners.

This argument has been criticized as underplaying the benefits broader social strata derived from the Roman system: For Bryan Ward-Perkins, "what is most striking about the Roman economy is precisely the fact that it was not solely an elite phenomenon."[73] Yet new evidence may make it more difficult to dismiss Wickham's assessment. Advances in biological anthropology enable us to measure the health of ancient populations with increasing precision. In particular, body height has long been recognized as a proxy for physical well-being.[74] By measuring the length of skeletal remains, especially the upper and lower leg bones, it is possible to trace the ways in which food insecurity and other health stresses affected past populations. Willem Jongman, Jan Jacobs, and Geertje Klein Goldewijk have created the most exhaustive database of Roman-period skeletal data assembled so far. It is based on the bones of around 10,000 individuals, found in all major areas of the empire.

In his earlier work, Jongman emphasized the remarkable scale of Roman prosperity.[75] All the more surprising are the skeletal data. This body of evidence clearly shows that the Roman period witnessed a significant decline in average height, indicating a decline in overall health of the population at large. By contrast, the disintegration of the Roman Empire in the west was accompanied by an increase in well-being: Cohorts born after the year 400 CE were markedly taller than earlier generations. Interestingly, too, in the eastern Mediterranean, where the Roman state endured, no such development seems to have taken place; the skeletons examined by Jongman, Jacobs, and Klein show a remarkable amount of stability from the Hellenistic period until the sixth century CE.[76] To be sure, it is important to keep in mind the limits of this analysis; for earlier periods of Roman history, when cremation was the predominant method of interment, and for most individual parts of the empire, the number of skeletons is still too low to allow for robust inferences. Yet it is notable that the best regional analyses reach the same conclusions as this empire-wide study; in both Britain and Italy, leg bones from the Roman era are significantly shorter than those of the Iron Age and the medieval period.[77] All of these data suggest that the end of empire led to an increase in human well-being.

Jongman, Jacobs, and Klein Goldewijk ascribe the ill health of the majority of inhabitants of the Roman Empire to the high incidence of pathogens in an economy that integrated the entire Mediterranean world and western Europe.[78] At first sight, this argument seems plausible. The increase in mobility made possible by imperial communication systems provided an ideal environment for the spread of infectious diseases.[79] Yet it is notable that the major pandemics that took place under Roman rule—the Antonine plague in the 160s and the Justinian plague in the 540s—leave no traces in the data assembled by Jongman, Jacobs, and Klein Goldewijk. This raises the question whether the osteological data are really incompatible with the evidence on Roman prosperity Jongman has compiled in his earlier work. We should at least consider the possibility that the economic boom spawned by the Roman imperial project made the majority of inhabitants of the empire less well off.[80] On the face of it, this evidence would seem to suggest that Wickham and Graeber were not entirely wrong when arguing that the collapse of the dynamic market societies that characterized the Mediterranean Axial Age was a happy event.

8

Zoroastrian Materialism

RELIGION, EMPIRE, AND THEIR CRITICS IN
GRAEBER'S LATE AXIAL AGE

Richard Payne

THE PANORAMIC PERSPECTIVE of David Graeber's *Debt: The First 5,000 Years* productively disorients the historian of late antiquity geographically, chronologically, and methodologically. He locates the rise of Christianity and Islam—whose uniquely transformative effects and entwined co-development have been a primary concern of ancient historical scholarship since the 1960s—not only in a pan-Eurasian geographical context but also within a wider chronological frame, giving the periodization of the Axial Age, c. 800 BCE–500 CE, priority over the prevailing, more parochial schemata of premodern historians. He also dismisses the division of the spiritual and the material realms propagated by the architects of the new religions of the first millennium BCE and CE that historians so often wittingly or unwittingly reproduce in their own narratives. The "Axial Age of spirituality," he argues, was "built on a bedrock of materialism."[1] It was the interdependency of what are commonly known as "world religions" and the regimes of extractive imperialism in which they flourished that the disparate civilizational centers of Eurasia shared, albeit at different chronological junctures. The self-abnegation, charity, and apparently immaterial concerns of the quintessentially axial religions such as Buddhism, Jainism, and Christianity should be understood in a dialogic, even dialectical relationship with the self-aggrandizement, greed, and overwhelmingly material concerns of an age in which military elites dominated the great bulk of the Eurasian population, consumed its surplus, and consolidated imperial regimes so formidable that, all agreed, they were both eternal and universal. In Graeber's account, religious specialists were no less materialistic

Richard Payne, *Zoroastrian Materialism* In: *Debt in the Ancient Mediterranean and Near East*. Edited by: John Weisweiler, Oxford University Press. © Oxford University Press 2023. DOI: 10.1093/oso/9780197647172.003.0008 than their militaristic counterparts, even if they sought to transmute worldly commodities into supernatural ones. The monuments of the age demonstrate as much: the Bamiyan Buddhas encased in gold, sprawling Christian monastic complexes whose landholdings could encompass entire regions, or Hagia Sophia at the heart of the Roman Empire, with its mosaiced rulers on display.[2] They elide the distinction between the worldly and the otherworldly, between monks and the warriors, merchants, and rulers who funded their asceticism. And as scholars of late antiquity are aware, monks were often aged warriors or merchants, in blissful retirement from the brutalities of the Axial Age.

In providing a novel vantage point for regarding the religious history of late antiquity, Graeber supplies new, useful tools for tackling the most fundamental, and urgent, question of the period: How did novel ideological systems oriented toward the supernatural reinforce the most worldly of powers? The Axial-Age periodization, in Graeber's retooling, suggests that the dizzying scale of violence, expropriation, and exploitation should serve as the common starting point for analyzing the origins, development, and diffusion of the spiritual systems that coevolved with empire, whether under the Achaemenids, the Mauryas, or the Romans. What the geographically, culturally, and chronologically disparate states of the Eurasian Axial Age shared were intensive fiscal systems based on coinage, the widespread use of subordinated human dependents—slave, servile, or semi-servile—as a source of labor, and extensive commercial markets, created by and for state elites. Graeber's Axial Age differs from other versions in its unambiguously materialist rather than spiritual or philosophical foundations.[3] Coins are the primary drivers of its characteristic changes rather than philosophers or prophets, in contrast with the accounts of Karl Jaspers and his acolytes in which cultural phenomena enjoyed greater autonomy even as they were linked with imperial projects. The religious movements definitional of Jaspers' Axial Age responded, Graeber argues, to the "military–coinage–slavery complex" not only with accounts of meta-human realities that transcended and redeemed the circumstances of ever-increasing debasement in which most humans found themselves but also with moral frameworks disciplining the exploitative possibilities that the combination of empire and rationalist, self-interested thinking had unleashed. They did so with thought systems focused squarely on the quotidian materialities of the age: Characteristically, the question of how to use money morally, through charity, figured prominently in Axial-Age systems, as did questions of corporeal consumption. Such systems served, in the main, to sustain the imperial projects that gave rise to them. The separation of material and spiritual spheres—state/market/worldly power, on the one hand, asceticism/moral economy/spiritual power, on the other—characteristic of Axial-Age ideologies enabled the dominant to legitimate their actions through patronage of, or membership in, institutions that in no way impinged on the autonomy of the political–economic domain, as long as the boundary between the material and the spiritual remained firm.[4] But as the need for such a boundary implies, the co-development of Axial-Age empires and religions precluded neither contradictions nor conflicts, and their trajectories frequently diverged. Graeber goes further than most historians in recognizing liberatory potential—for imagining alternative futures, providing charity, abolishing slavery, and, above all, rejecting exploitative credit arrangements as usurious—in Axial-Age religious systems.[5] It is the tension between sanctioning the imperial orders on which they depended and creating an alternative and transcendent domain, theoretically if not practically autonomous of the coinage–military complex, that would consistently repay the attention of historians of the Axial Age, in particular in its final centuries, late antiquity.

The materialist definition of the Axial Age requires a revision of its chronology. Graeber extends the era by almost a millennium, from the third century BCE in Jaspers' original account to the fifth century CE. Such is a period defined by fiscally intensive, imperial states, at least in East and West Asia, though the chronological horizons of the Axial Age will, of course, vary according to region. Without becoming embroiled in a critique of the details of the book, a task well outside the purview of the present essay, the dissatisfaction that the proposed fifth century conclusion of the age elicits requires discussion. If the dissolution of the Roman Empire in the West presumably provided its inspiration, no such dismantling of the coinage–military complex took place in the political–economic core of West Asia, the Fertile Crescent. Not only did the eastern Roman and Iranian Empires arguably develop the most intensive fiscal systems of the ancient world in the fifth through early seventh centuries but their early Islamic heirs combined their institutions within a geographical expanse that dwarfed earlier empires in a paradigmatically axial state, in Graeber's terms, until the beginning of the breakup of the Abbasid caliphate in the ninth century. To speak meaningfully of Graeber's Axial Age, we need to extend the chronology further forward: 800 BCE–800 CE in place of 800 BCE–500 CE. It is both unlikely and inadvisable that historians adopt the term "Axial Age" outside of sympathetic engagements with the work of its exponents, such as this book and chapter. It resonates too strongly with historical sociology, a discipline from which historians learn a great deal while distancing themselves from its tendencies toward universalizing, generalizing, and teleology. The chronology, however, has more to recommend itself to practitioners, for precisely the reasons Graeber has identified. The redefined Axial-Age periodization fits well with recent moves toward placing empire, rather than the "classical world," at the center of ancient historical scholarship, from the Assyrians to the Abbasids. The new ancient imperial historiography has largely proceeded comparatively as specialists on East Asian, Middle Eastern, and Mediterranean empires explore convergences and divergences in their respective administrative structures, infrastructural development, and political cultures.[6] Implicit in such studies is an alternative periodization for West Asian history in terms of an age of empire. Its successive period, the Middle Ages, could be defined in terms of the absence of empire. But *Debt* does not simply join ranks with such works in framing West Asian history in terms of empire and its absence but also suggests that ancient historians do more to link the synchronous development of empires and their religions across Eurasia more directly than comparative studies have done.[7] By making the institutions of the military–coinage complex that were disseminated widely across cultural and geographical frontiers in the first millennium BCE the primary drivers of change, Graeber invites us to view empires as the outcome of institutional possibilities shared across Eurasia. Robust networks of exchange across the central Eurasian steppes ensured that few technological innovations relevant to state formation failed to find their way across the continent, and the roughly contemporaneous appearance—that is, within centuries—of both the practice of minting and the idea of empire in West and East Asia was hardly accidental. Even if historians remain rooted in their respective regions, periods, and literary traditions, the pan-Eurasian perspective of an Axial Age of imperial religions, of materialist spiritual systems, can produce the kind of productive, disruptive disorientation through which scholars re-evaluate the potential of their evidence and its connections with other fields.

Such a perspective proves highly revealing for the study of what has long been considered the inaugural Axial-Age religion and the one most intimately connected with militaristic, imperial projects.[8] From circa 1000 BCE, Zoroastrianism generated a number of the definitional features of so-called spiritual religions, in the literal sense of religions oriented around the liberation of the spirit from the body (whether by means of exit or reconstitution): ethical action, as the means of safeguarding the spirit from worldly corruption; an ethical dualism distinguishing good and evil humans; differential experiences of the afterlife, as heaven or hell; and the ultimate redemption of the world.[9] It was also unambiguously materialistic. All material things, animate or inanimate, possessed agency in Zoroastrian cosmology, to act on behalf of good or evil deities. The aim of Zoroastrian ethics and ritual was the management of the material world, with the goal of achieving the ultimate cosmic restoration—the sooner materiality was ordered in accordance with Zoroastrian principles, the sooner the world would regain primordial paradise. The two most important ethical tasks of Zoroastrians were straightforwardly materialist: the cultivation of plants and sexual reproduction. The seven divine spirits that cooperated with the beneficent creator god Ahura Mazda in the cosmic struggle against the evil deity, the so-called Amesha

Spentas (Middle Persian *amahraspandān*), manifested themselves materially in the world through particular elements, specifically humans, cattle, fire, metals, earth, water, and plants. Herman Lommel drew attention to the central role of spiritualized materials in Zoroastrianism in order to argue that its religious specialists had preserved an archaic perception of the world in which the spiritual and material were indistinguishable from one another. If his emphasis on the materiality of Zoroastrian religion was salutary, the political–economic circumstances of the early Axial Age make better sense of the interdependency and the interpenetration of the spiritual and the material. As Lori Khatchadourian has recently argued, the manifestation of the divinity Šahrewar ("Sovereignty") in metals reflected its association with rulership, "a project in which metals, whether bronze or iron, silver or gold, were by the time of these writings without question the most effective partners."[10] The silver coins in which taxes were denominated, the iron swords with which war was made, and the gold adorning elite bodies were the agents, or presences, of a divinity.

It is unsurprising that a religion that spiritualized metals and made agrarian and biological production its overriding priorities proved so effective an ancillary of empire across a millennium. The entwining of Zoroastrianism with the Achaemenid imperial project that features in so many accounts of the Axial Age has come under sustained questioning in recent scholarship. But if the religious landscape in which the Achaemenid Empire and the culture of its ruling elite took shape has emerged as far more diverse, defined as much by traditional Elamite as by Zoroastrian cults, the cosmological framework embodied in the ritual texts attributed to Zoroaster continues to play a leading role in animating the ideal and practice of imperialism in most accounts of Achaemenid history.[11] As the scholarship of Bruce Lincoln demonstrates, Zoroastrian cosmology enabled rulers to frame violence and exploitation as cosmically beneficent actions of bringing "happiness for mankind," embodied in the paradises constructed to prefigure the cosmic restoration that empire would bring.[12] The Hellenistic and Parthian kingdoms that succeeded the Achaemenids never granted the religion so signal a role in their ideological frameworks, although Zoroastrian cultic centers continued to operate on the Iranian plateau and in central Asia and to preserve memories and myths evocative of the Achaemenid imperial project.[13] It was only in late antiquity, however, that the religion came to provide the foundations—ideological and infrastructural—for an empire that endured longer than any of its Axial-Age predecessors in the Middle East.

Its unique and unprecedented name signaled the central importance of the Zoroastrian religion to its organization. The mid-third-century Sasanian "kings of kings" incorporated formally Parthian territories, from eastern Arabia to Bactria, into an empire they called "Iranian." The name *ērānšahr* evoked the mythical–historical ruling class of the Avesta—the Iranians, or *ērān* in Middle Persian, who had supported the prophet Zoroaster—and the designation already implied the interpenetration of religious and aristocratic powers, in what would prove an enduring institutional complex.[14] The great Parthian aristocratic houses could adopt the label "Iranian" for themselves without forgoing their pre-existing lineage and land-based affiliations. In so doing, they embraced an explicitly and exclusively Zoroastrian religious identity, as only adherents of the so-called Good Religion could call themselves *ēr*.[15] They also gained access to the services of Zoroastrian religious specialists who were empowered as judges presiding over a juridical architecture designed to augment the sources of aristocratic power. The early Sasanians elevated the Zoroastrian priest-scholars, who had previously occupied politically marginal positions, as the exclusively state-sanctioned jurists with a monopoly on juridical authority.[16] The decisions of the *mowbedān mowbed*, the highest-ranking priest-scholar, were regarded as infallible. The Zoroastrian priest-scholars of the Iranian court dedicated themselves—through their rituals, their theorizing, and, above all, their juridical activities—to reinforcing the powers of the aristocracy and the ruling Sasanian house simultaneously. Apart from such ideological and institutional incentives to participation in empire, which developed gradually from the mid-third century onward, the early Sasanians immediately offered a more conventional reward in exchange for loyalty and military service, one whose persuasive power was self-evident: silver coinage of unprecedented purity and stability. The silver drachm the first Sasanian, Ardashir I, introduced not only were beautifully and consistently minted across the empire but also possessed a silver content of upward of 90%, a dramatic improvement on irregularly minted late Parthian coinage typically of no more than 70% purity.[17] The third-century wars against the Romans, moreover, resulted in the large-scale importation of captives as a source of labor in both urban and rural contexts, and their ranks were not infrequently replenished during the successive three centuries of Iranian rule.[18] The Iranian Empire thus conforms, broadly speaking, with Graeber's model of Axial-Age states predicated on a military–coinage–slavery complex, with the important qualification that the "slavery" in question more often took the shape of semi-servile dependent labor rather than formal slavery.[19] It is nevertheless the materialist tendencies of its religious elite that are of greatest interest for the comparative study of Axial-Age imperial dynamics.

Zoroastrian religious specialists developed a system of jurisprudence that guaranteed the gradual, intergenerational enhancement of aristocratic fortunes. They did so primarily in two ways. Firstly, the jurists innovated forms of marriage that secured the transmission of each individual aristocratic house across generations.[20] Temporary marriages not only maximized elite access to female reproductive capacities but also enabled men to produce legitimate male heirs for other men. Through the novel institution of *stūrīh*, substitute-successorship, elites could have marriages arranged on their behalf, before or after death, to produce truly legitimate heirs, even if not biologically related to the paterfamilias. Every Zoroastrian house continued, theoretically, until the eschaton. Secondly, the law of endowments, forerunner of Islamic *waqf*, allowed aristocratic houses to invest their property in fire temples, without forfeiting control or the ability to profit from their lands.[21] The house retained a share, often the great bulk, of the produce of endowed lands as even the maintenance of an aristocratic house could be considered a religious, charitable function. Fire temple properties had the advantage of permanency: They could never be expropriated, not even for political reasons. Iranian jurisprudence did not simply safeguard but ensured the positive, long-term growth of patrilineages and patrimonies, the two pillars of aristocratic power, over the entire course of four Sasanian centuries. Profoundly material concerns animated the activity of jurists who regarded their work as wholly cosmological in purpose. As jurists, Zoroastrian priest-scholars worked to realize the religious ideology's vision of a society in which an ontologically superior class of Iranians ruled over the mass of agricultural laborers. The empire was their possession.

Debt played a crucial role in creating and maintaining so stratified a social order, even if its workings remain obscure in the absence of the kind of extensive documentary available in cuneiform to scholars of the Achaemenid Empire. In Middle Iranian languages, the term for debt, *abām*, designated moral guilt as well as a payment owed, like German *Schuld*. In Zoroastrian ritual discourse, the relationship between humans and the divine was framed in terms of a debt that can never be repaid, and the Middle Persian translations of Avestan texts presented rituals as the means of repaying debts, *abām*, using the same terminology encountered in juridical discourse.[22] In their capacity as jurists, Zoroastrian priests demanded the repayment of debts, according to the same moral logic evident in the rituals. After marriage and inheritance, credit and debt appear as the other major domain of Iranian jurisprudence, far more important than what we would call criminal law. While restricting interest exacted on credit to more than the original value alone, the imperative of repayment could result even in the enslavement of the debtor. The transfer of the bodies of debtors into the hands of creditors appears commonplace in the *Thousand Judgments*, an early seventh-century compendium of case law that constitutes our primary source for Iranian jurisprudence.[23] The editor of the text, Maria Macuch, argues that debt bondage seems to have been the most common route into slavery alongside captivity in warfare.[24] Apart from policing credit arrangements in favor of the moneyed, Zoroastrian jurists also transformed their fire temples into storehouses of credit: Debts to the fires carried a particularly heavy moral burden and, according to the jurists, had to be paid under all circumstances.[25]

What gave this institutional complex its integrity was its framing in a discourse of reciprocity, namely the claims made and remade, at the level of royal pronouncement and representation as well as in quotidian transactions, that the superior position of the aristocracy enhanced the material well-being of its subordinate population. The sixth-century Iranian court articulated such claims through its literary productions in an era of heightened social conflict and disequilibria. In the *Letter of Tansar* and the *Testament of Ardashir*, both evocations of a legendary golden age of third-century kingship, the political order was presented as the mutually beneficial relationship between four social classes: the warriors; the cavalry-based landowning aristocracy; the priests, whose ranks also include judges; the scribes and literary specialists; and the laboring population of agricultural workers, artisans, and merchants.[26] The boundaries between the classes were supposed to have been impassable, and social location was inherited. But these texts equally stressed that, in establishing and maintaining a quadripartite order, the court simultaneously ensured the respective prosperity and well-being of each. As a fiction, the narrative of the four orders occluded the hierarchical binary that defined Iranian society: between landowners and the landless, semi-servile laboring population. The distinction between warriors and religious specialists was a mystification: They were both members of the same aristocratic landowning class. The inclusion of merchants among the agrarian laborers distorted the social order no less profoundly as the former were unbound, often moneyed inhabitants of cities, while the latter remained bound labor. The overall aim of such narratives was to underpin elite claims to benevolence vis-à-vis their inferiors. The aristocracy was reimagined not as extracting rents from but as providing security on behalf of the agrarian population. Laboring persons were reimagined as the worthy poor, *driyōšān*, deserving of elite magnanimity, in contrast with the unworthy destitute, *škōhān*, at the same time as the category of the poor as a socially distinct group began to become prominent in late Roman Christian discourse.[27]

Such claims were no more baseless than those of the Christian Roman elite to provide charity for their poor. In their capacity as judges, Zoroastrian priests bore the title *driyōšān jādaggōw*, "advocates of the poor"; and the claim to serve as caretakers of the landless was therefore asserted even in mundane juridical transactions.[28] And as judges, Zoroastrian priests made the physical abuse of dependents—laborers, slaves, and women—a criminal offense, punishable by fines, making the violence so conventional a feature of the ancient experience of dependency an aberration, if not unknown.[29] But dependent laborers will have experienced aristocratic benevolence far more directly. Thanks to the recent publication of the first archive of an aristocratic estate, a collection of leather documents from the region of Qom dating to the late sixth through seventh centuries, we can now trace the practical application of the Zoroastrian theory of sustenance. According to cosmological texts, it was the responsibility of the powerful to provide the nourishment and garments their inferiors required to fulfill their appropriate social functions, whether agricultural or artisanal labor. The term employed in the theoretical texts is *rōzīg*, literally "the daily," as in daily ration.[30] The same term is ubiquitous in the documentary texts, used to describe disbursements ranging from small quantities of barley—a daily ration in the literal sense—to several head of cattle, whether for higher-status beneficiaries or for the enjoyment of a larger group. To fail to provide nourishment for one's dependents, even for one's sheepdog, constituted a criminal offense in Iranian jurisprudence known as *adwadād*.[31]

The late Sasanian court that articulated, and to some degree enjoined the practice of, the ideal of reciprocity between ruling and dependent classes witnessed the appearance of major fissures not only in its social order but also in its ideology. The priest-scholars who specialized in the cosmological texts and rituals on which the imperial ideology was based were hardly unanimous in their understanding of the relationship between religion and empire, nor were their views as unchanging as the surviving compendia of Zoroastrian literature often seem to suggest. In the first half of the sixth century, an alternative vision of the social and political order emerged in the scholarly circles of the *hērbedestān*, the Zoroastrian priestly school. A priest-scholar known as Mazdak espoused the doctrine of an earlier, third-century thinker known as Zoroaster of Fasa that offered a vision of cosmo-political order starkly opposed to what the Iranians had established as normative, in Zoroastrian terms, in the preceding three centuries.[32] Mazdak's cosmological teaching constituted an inversion of Iranian Zoroastrianism. Landed property was to be extracted from aristocratic hands and held in common, with equal access for all to the productive capacities of agricultural land and irrigation systems, a system Patricia Crone called "Zoroastrian communism."[33] The reproductive capacities of women were distributed across the male population in a similarly communist fashion. If the sharing of women was perhaps not unusual to elites accustomed to practices such as temporary marriage, allowing commoners access to aristocratic female bodies was unthinkable. What is more, Mazdak replaced Iranian patriliny with a matrilineal conception of personal identity.[34] The institutionalized wife-sharing he and his followers introduced presumed the uncoupling of the link between sons, fathers, and father's fathers on which Iranian order had been predicated.

The communal sharing of land and women entailed nothing less than a dismantling of the foundations of the Iranian ethno-class, and the propagation of the doctrine took place in the context of a rebellion against Iranian rule in the 520s.[35] The court responded to the movement with a violence that impressed historiographers across the Middle East and the Mediterranean—and continued to do so for several centuries. Accounts of the tens of thousands of Mazdakite rebels and priests who the king of kings Husraw I slaughtered in the early 530s were among the most commonly recurring historiographical vignettes from the pre-Islamic Iranian world in early Islamic literature. The tendentious narratives of uniformly anti-Mazdakite authors make the scale of the so-called rebellion impossible to measure, but the overriding concern of late Sasanian texts with defending the highly stratified social order against implied critics of its inequalities suggests that the Mazdakite movement represented the most extreme end of a spectrum of criticisms against aristocratic domination. The movement would, moreover, have a long afterlife, with rebellions in early Islamic Iran frequently invoking the sharing of land and, especially, women as the basis for alternative, anti-imperial forms of social and economic organization—and as a way of appealing to dependent laborers to join rebel armies.[36] It is paradoxical that the Axial-Age religion seemingly best suited to supporting an imperial project gave rise to one of the most radical critiques of imperial order known from late antiquity. It is all the more remarkable that the advocates and critics of Iran drew on common sources within Zoroastrian thought and jurisprudence for their arguments. What they shared were materialist concerns. On the one hand, the priest-scholars and jurists of the normative Zoroastrianism known from the literary traditions their successors transmitted in the Middle Ages regarded the enhancement of the sources of aristocratic power—patrimonies, patrilineal houses, and credit arrangements—as the means through which to facilitate the cosmic restoration. On the other hand, the priest-scholars and jurists marginalized in the tradition as Mazdakite pursued the same goal by means of a destratified, matrilineal social order in which the natural resources of fertility—agrarian and human—were distributed equally. If Iran in late antiquity brought Axial-Age trends toward imperial expansion to a culmination, its final century also portended the decline of the military–coinage–slavery–debt complex.

Graeber's claim that Axial-Age religions were materialist in their concerns, however spiritual their rituals or theories, helps to account for the co-development of empire and Zoroastrianism, especially in late antiquity. What its proponents called the Good Religion directly addressed the political–economic circumstances of the age: staggering stratification, dependent labor reduced to semiservile status, and the proliferation of debts denominated in high-value coinage available almost exclusively to elites. Political regimes fostering such conditions across massive distances and differences, which limited the coercive capacities of the state, derived their viability from shared cosmological frameworks that rendered their exploitative institutions ethical, even eschatological in function. Zoroastrian cosmology made the hierarchical differentiation of humans, especially between ontologically superior aristocrats of Iranian lineage and their inferiors, an ethical imperative. So, too, was the repayment of debts to creditors. In demanding labor from a villager, whether juridically a slave or not, an aristocrat could frame the action as cosmically beneficent, even if its exploitative nature was unambiguous to labor and landowners alike. A priest-scholar could similarly represent the enslavement of a guarantor for a debt to a fire temple. In this respect, Zoroastrian rites and juridical practices facilitated the exploitative practices integral to the imperial projects of the late Axial Age. But the expectation of ethical, cosmologically grounded political action not only created openings for the critique of empire but also tempered its characteristic cruelty. The restriction on violence against laboring dependents and women and the obligation to nourish human and animal dependents arose in Zoroastrian cosmological thought quite as organically as its theories of human hierarchy and debt. The Zoroastrian evidence supports Graeber's suggestion that Axial-Age religious responses to empire went beyond mere escapism—"promising the victims . . . liberation in the next world as a way of letting them accept their lot in this one"—to bring about incremental change and, in turn, ultimately to inspire the dialectical response of medieval religious movements.[37]

Early Islamic elites defined their political, economic, and social order partly in opposition to its Iranian predecessor. While maintaining the key Axial-Age institutions of a military remunerated in coinage, a monetized fiscal system, and a dependent labor force, early Muslims rejected, at least symbolically, the stratification that had become so characteristic of imperial rule in the Middle East. Their habitus constituted a deliberate disavowal of the objects and acts through which Iranians had performed their ontological superiority vis-à-vis their inferiors.[38] In place of the silken, gilded riding coats that made aristocratic bodies appear incommensurably finer than other humans, early Muslims donned simple white linen or cotton, regardless of their social class. Their rejection of wine and silver vessels similarly dismissed the Iranian culture of the banquet, perhaps the most important institution of sociability and deliberation in Iranian aristocratic politics. The preference for industrious, mercantile activity over patrimonial landholding evident in early Islamic literary and legal traditions upended the Iranian tripartite, or quadripartite, division of the social order. As Graeber suggests, the most consequential of political–economic changes the early Muslims introduced was the condemnation of interest as usurious, a principle that should be regarded in relation to the preceding political–economic order predicated on an understanding of interest-bearing debts as fundamental ethical obligations. As current research begins to recover the influence of Iran and its political culture on pre-Islamic Arabia, the possibility of regarding early Islam as in dialectical conversation with the Zoroastrianism of an empire its adherents would displace in the middle of the seventh century is emerging.[39] In imagining the egalitarian convening of the Muslim community in shared submission to a single god, dressed in simple linen or cotton, undivided by patrilineage or patrimony, we should recall what was implicitly rejected: one particular solution to the contradictions of the Iron Age, in favor of a radical alternative. The argument that we shift our focus to the materialist concerns of religions in late antiquity proves productive in revealing not only their roles supporting or critiquing the political economies of empire but also their sometimes dialectical patterns of interaction. Some Muslims came to borrow as much of the Zoroastrian, Iranian order as they rejected, when early Islamic egalitarian aspirations encountered the familiar stratifying effects of empire, especially from the middle of the eighth century onward. Iranian ideas and institutions, reinvented as "Persian" and evacuated of their Zoroastrian religious significance, became enduringly influential to medieval Muslims seeking hierarchically to organize their societies, far more influential than the radical alternative of Mazdak.[40]

9

Debt, Debt Bondage, and the Early Islamic Economy

Michael Bonner

READERS OF *DEBT: The First 5,000 Years* know that the premodern Islamic world had a central role in a series of global developments in the economic sphere. They also have an idea of the Islamic world's capacity and creativity, for instance, in technological advances that included sophisticated financial instruments and in sustaining fiscal bureaucracies that rivaled those of the Chinese (Graeber 2014: 271–305). But what role did Islam itself have in all this? By this I refer, of course, to the religion of Islam but also to political, juridical, and cultural frameworks and institutions that we are accustomed to calling "Islamic" even when they are not, strictly speaking, religious.[1] How did the coming of Islam change things in places such as Egypt, Syria, Iraq, and Iran that already had millennia of experience of bureaucratized administration and were utterly familiar with markets and merchants? What "value added" did Islam actually bring to the Near Eastern economy in a broad sense?

For some time now, a number of writers have portrayed the arrival of Islam as an economic liberation for the entire region. According to this view, Islam freed marketplaces from the stifling embrace of imperial governments and encouraged a flourishing of trade and production such as the world had rarely, if ever, seen (Lombard [1971] 2014). Taking things further, some scholars have described the commercial economy of early Islam as a precursor of the capitalist one of early modern Europe.[2] It has now become relatively commonplace to say not only that Muhammad was a merchant, as everyone knows, but that he became a kind of prophetical CEO, running his state enterprise according to sound business principles (Koehler 2014) and, more broadly, that Islam is utterly pro-business and

Michael Bonner, *Debt, Debt Bondage, and the Early Islamic Economy* In: *Debt in the Ancient Mediterranean and Near East*. Edited by: John Weisweiler, Oxford University Press. © Oxford University Press 2023.
DOI: 10.1093/oso/9780197647172.003.0009

pro-market, without all the woes of inequality and instability that result from the secular discourses and practices exerting global hegemony nowadays. These and similar views have led to difficulties for some modern Muslim intellectuals (Tripp 2006). But for now we may simply note that the early Islamic economy is a consequential topic for our time.

Here, I propose to examine certain aspects of debt, including debt bondage, in the Near East during the rise and early expansion of Islam (the seventh and eighth centuries of the Common Era, the first two of the Hijra), for while historians have largely neglected this topic, I think it can improve our understanding of the broad issues just outlined. However, I propose to set aside questions, however timely, over Islam's "modern" elements and its possible role as a harbinger of modernity and to concentrate instead, to the extent possible, on circumstances and events of the early Islamic period itself.

We begin with a brief outline of the source materials available to us for the first two centuries of Islamic history. These materials fall, broadly speaking, into two main categories. The first consists of objects that originated in those times and places, including coins, inscriptions, and documents written on papyrus and other materials. In Chapter 10 of this volume, Arietta Papaconstantinou shows how much we can learn about debt from these documents, the papyri in particular. At the same time, they mostly refer to local circumstances, especially in Egypt, which at that time did not yet have a political and cultural role commensurate with its economic and fiscal importance. This is more of an advantage than a disadvantage, but a comprehensive picture remains difficult to achieve.

Our other main body of evidence consists of texts that have come down through a process of literary transmission. These convey information about the early period, and plenty of it. The texts themselves, however, at least the Arabic ones, date from later times as we have little manuscript evidence for them until the late eighth century CE at best. Of course, there are exceptions, including manuscripts of the Qur'ān; but in most areas, including the Arabic historiographical and juridical literature, the gap remains.

Since the juridical literature is important for what follows, we may briefly consider its characteristics. Early Islamic juridical source materials are mainly "literary" and "non-documentary," in that they do not literally and physically originate from the times and places in question. They fall into a wide range of genres including treatises on methodology and jurisprudence, systematic and monographic presentations of substantive law, and ethical manuals for judges. Especially useful for modern researchers are biographical compendia that provide information on thousands of relevant individuals.

The juridical literature also includes a genre that is peculiar to Islamic civilization and learning, namely the *ḥadīth*. This term literally means "conversation, discourse." In modern scholarly parlance it refers to a large body of narratives, most of them rather short, relating sayings and deeds of the Prophet Muhammad and of other people who lived during his time or soon afterward. The term can also refer to a single one of these narratives. European languages often use "tradition" as an equivalent to *ḥadīth* in both senses. These narratives were transmitted orally at first but over time were also written down so that by the mid-ninth century the *ḥadīth* already constituted a massive genre of Arabic literature. From a jurisprudential point of view, the *ḥadīth* is the primary vehicle for knowledge of the *sunna*, or Example of the Prophet, and is thus especially important for Muslims, particularly those of the Sunnī persuasion. At the same time, the genre extends beyond traditions of the Prophet. Especially in some of the earlier extant *ḥadīth* collections, we find materials that go back not only to the Prophet and his Companions but also to jurists, judges, and political figures of later generations, known as Successors. In recent decades, some scholars have treated materials of this kind as, in effect, lawbooks providing access to the teachings and controversies of the early phases of Islamic jurisprudence.

The *ḥadīth* has long been the focus of controversies, both in Muslim scholarship and in Western scholarship on Islam (Berg 2000; Brown 2009). Within early Islamic studies, these controversies have had a central and valuable role. At the same time, however, the focus on the *ḥadīth* itself—its authenticity (see next paragraph), its literary and rhetorical characteristics, and so forth—has had the unfortunate side effect of muting or even drowning out substantive historical arguments, this present topic of debt and debt bondage being a case in point.

The central term in debates—both Muslim and Western—over the *ḥadīth* has been its "authenticity." This often refers to whether a particular narrative tradition corresponds to events that took place in the world. If a tradition tells us that Muhammad did or said a certain thing on a certain occasion, did this actually happen or not? However, other approaches have also been proposed. In the West, Ignaz Goldziher in the late nineteenth century maintained that the *ḥadīth* emerged in the urban Islamic world during what we might now call the "long eighth century" and, as such, constitutes an excellent source for the political, social, and intellectual history of that environment; its value for seventh-century Arabia, however, would be limited at best (Goldziher 1971). Others have rejected this approach, arguing that the *ḥadīth*, or at least a portion of it, does provide reliable information about the earliest Islam. Other positions have evolved; one of these argues that a tradition's "authenticity" relates first and foremost to the networks within which it was recorded and taught and that we can reconstruct these networks through detailed and extensive analysis of the *ḥadīth* itself.

The Modern Argument over Early Islamic Debt Bondage

This topic has received little attention in the modern scholarly literature, for reasons that may soon become clear. The major exception has been a book by Irene Schneider with the provocative title *Kinderverkauf und Schuldknechtschaft* (Schneider 1999). Here, I begin with a brief summary of its most important arguments.

In a methodological section, Schneider establishes the following rough chronology. What she calls the "pre-literary" era of Islamic law extends from the beginning of Islam in the early seventh century until the flourishing of ʿAbbāsid rule in the later eighth. At more or less the same time as the onset of the following "literary" era, around the year 800, we have the beginning of what Schneider calls the "pre-classical" era of Islamic law, from which we have works by early masters such as Mālik, Abū Yūsuf, al-Shaybānī, and al-Shāfiʿī. This "literary" era then continues into the "classical" era of Islamic law, which begins in the later ninth century and then, over time, reaches maturity, assuming the characteristics familiar to us now.

With regard to the juridical literature, the *ḥadīth* in particular, Schneider adopts a modified version of the theories set out in Joseph Schacht's *The Origins of Muhammadan Jurisprudence* (Schacht 1950). Schacht's approach had elements in common with Goldziher's but focused on the early development of Islamic law rather than the overall cultural and political environment. For Schneider the relevant points include the following.

Schacht maintained, generally and roughly speaking, that individual narrative traditions that have as their earliest source a "successor" (i.e., a juridical authority from the generations right after Muhammad) are most likely to be "authentic" (i.e., most likely to correspond to what that person actually said and taught). (Traditions of this kind, however, have low status within the hierarchy established by mature Islamic scholarship.) Traditions that go back to a Companion (i.e., a contemporary of Muhammad) are less likely to be "authentic" in this sense, and traditions going back to Muhammad himself are least likely of all.[3] Schacht also maintained that Islamic law took form in several distinct environments, which he called the "ancient schools," of which the most important were in Arabia (Medina) and Iraq (Kufa and Basra). While these schools had elements in common, including the Qurʾān, they differed in their jurisprudential method and substantive law, all still at a formative stage (Schacht 1950: 6–10 passim). These counterintuitive positions of Schacht's won wide, though not universal, acceptance, though over time they have lost some ground.

Using a largely Schachtian approach, Schneider arrives at the following conclusions. Mature Islamic law, as expressed in the "classical" period onward, had a negative consensus about debt bondage, although it expressed this more by downplaying or ignoring the phenomenon than through outright condemnation. Like late antique legal systems, it did permit the imprisonment of insolvent debtors (Schneider 2000: 108–109). For the earlier periods of Islamic law, however, especially the "pre-literary" one, the situation is different. Here we cannot identify a prevailing consensus among the jurists. The Qur'ān does not address the matter, at least directly. Some early jurists pronounce in favor of debt servitude of various kinds, others against it. Interestingly, the advocates of debt servitude or bondage include several *qāḍīs*, or judges in the employ of the state. They also include no less a personage than the caliph 'Umar II (r. 717–720), admired for his piety and good judgment.

The *ḥadīth* literature mostly ignores these matters—which is remarkable, considering that it deals with such a vast array of topics. This seems consistent with the attitude of mature Islamic law, which, as we have seen, condemns debt bondage but as much by ignoring it as by confronting it. However, one relevant narrative does occur a number of times in the *ḥadīth*, though not in the most prestigious collections. This is a story about a certain Surraq, which means "brazen thief" (*dreister Dieb*), a nickname he received from the Prophet himself. The story has several variants, which in Schneider's analysis boil down to the following. This man came to Medina during the Prophet's residence there (622–632 CE). According to some accounts, he coaxed some people into lending him money, which he then proceeded to squander. According to other accounts, he agreed to buy some fabric or (more likely) camels from a Bedouin, took the camels while promising to pay for them, and absconded. Either way, he found himself hauled before the Prophet, who assigned him his nickname and ordered him to restore what he had taken, to which Surraq replied that he could not since he owned nothing whatsoever. Here, in just about all versions, the Prophet tells Surraq's victim or victims to sell him on the market, to recover their losses. Then comes a conversation between the prospective seller(s) and buyers; these decide to let Surraq go free, so as to achieve religious merit for themselves, and there the matter ends. Meanwhile, however, the Prophet has pronounced in favor of selling a debtor—and not for a limited time to work off his debt, but into outright slavery, apparently against Qur'ān 2:280 (see later in this section) as well as the consensus of "mature" Islamic law.

Still applying a modified Schachtian method, Schneider finds that this Surraq story cannot be taken as "authentic" in the sense of being an accurate report of events in seventh-century Medina, though it can be proved that the tradition was related there at some later time. She also finds that many variants of the story show links to Egypt, both through the affiliations of the story's transmitters and through its setting, since Surraq usually tells his story as an old man in Egypt, having migrated there long before. Schneider also adduces a letter attributed to 'Umar II, sent to a *qāḍī* in Egypt, confirming a sentence of bondage imposed on a destitute debtor.[4] All of this leads Schneider to propose that Islamic debt bondage, at least in this instance, had its origins in Byzantine Egypt.

Here, Schneider takes another cue from Schacht, who maintained that much of the material of the earliest Islamic law was taken over from pre-existing systems including Arabian customary; Roman, Sasanian, and Jewish law; as well as the (partly hypothetical) "Roman provincial law" (Crone 1987a). Here, Schneider finds no reference to an older Egyptian practice or norm that would have carried over into early Islam. At the same time, she finds that early Islamic Medina—the Prophet's home and the capital of the earliest Islamic state—did *not* condone servitude or bondage for debtors. She also adduces a biblical text, Exodus 21:37, imposing bondage on debtors, from which she surmises that Jewish converts in Alexandria may have been the conduit for this practice into early Islam (Schneider 1999: 345). However, there is no other evidence to support this assertion.

To summarize, in Schneider's view debt bondage or servitude did not exist in Arabia, or at any rate was not condoned there, in particular in Medina during the days of the Prophet. After the Muslim conquest of Egypt in the early 640s, however, some governors, judges, and jurists in that province adopted it from local practice or custom. Seeking to justify this position, some of them circulated this narrative about Surraq, perhaps after fabricating it out of whole cloth. In this way the story eventually found its way back to Medina and elsewhere. However, this position in favor of debt bondage constituted only one among several others regarding the practice, all tending in different directions, for at this time the edifice of Islamic law was still under construction, as judges and governors throughout the caliphate looked about for rationales and precedents for deciding the cases that came their way. Gradually, over time, the consensus moved toward condemning or, as we have seen, downplaying debt bondage. Accordingly, the practice receives little mention in mature Islamic law, and references to it for the early, "pre-literary" period amount to odd, chance survivals. However, the very facts of their survival and their "going against the grain" speak in favor of their historicity. It accordingly appears that debt bondage did exist during the "pre-literary" period and that it was applied and enforced in some instances but not others. In any case, it was not an Arabian inheritance.

This book immediately came under challenge from Harald Motzki, well-known then (as now) for his *Die Anfänge der islamischen Jurisprudenz* (Motzki 1991, 2002), which from its very title offers a challenge to Schacht's earlier *Origins of Muhammadan Jurisprudence*. As we have seen, while Schacht's theories have exerted considerable influence, opposition to them has grown over time; this work by Motzki constitutes, inter alia, one of the most important refutations of Schacht.[5]

It is impossible to give a balanced account of Motzki's method in a short space, beyond noting its considerable power of persuasion; but a few points deserve mention. This method involves close analysis of the text (*matn*) of a tradition together with its "support" (*isnād*), that is, the chain of authorities who have transmitted it. Although Motzki sets out, at least in part, to refute Schacht's *Origins*, he does not propose a comprehensive theory of early Islamic law to take its place. Unlike Schacht, he is interested mainly in the traditions themselves, especially their dating—relatively and even, within limits, absolutely—and their authenticity. The latter concept, a key to Motzki's enterprise, hovers between two senses already noted here: on the one hand, accurate representation of events that took place in seventh-century Arabia and, on the other hand, reconstruction of the environments in which traditions were handed down over the generations. So, for instance, when Schacht declared that no *ḥadīth* going back to before the year 100 of the Hijra (717–718 CE) may be considered reliable or authentic (Schacht 1950: 4–5), he was proceeding deductively from a broad, schematic view of the development of early Islamic law. Motzki, by contrast, who claims to be able to prove that at least certain traditions date from earlier than 100 AH, works inductively, arguing that different instances of transmission of traditions probably happened in markedly different ways.

Motzki's method includes a statistical element. If we take a single tradition which relates a narrative through a single strand of transmission (from one transmitter to the next, over the generations) and examine it on its own, we cannot say much about its historicity or authenticity. But if we examine large numbers of traditions with similar, comparable characteristics, we may get significant results. For example, we know that a Meccan scholar named Ibn Jurayj, who died in 150/767, transmitted traditions from his teacher "Aṭā," who also lived in Mecca and who died in 115/733. Many of these are available now in *ḥadīth* collections that include material from Successors. Motzki performs a minute analysis of these traditions, including their formal characteristics (*dicta* and *responsa* of a Successor, sayings and deeds of the Prophet, etc.), content, and message. He also compares them with other, similar bodies of material. In this particular instance he concludes that the traditions ascribed to Ibn Jurayj by way of "Aṭā" are authentic, in the sense that they accurately represent the juridical environment of Mecca at that time and, at least to some extent, the views of those two individuals.[6] If we want to investigate the history of these or other traditions in earlier or later generations, we need to perform a similar operation all over again.

The debate over *Kinderverkauf und Schuldknechtschaft* (Schneider 1999, 2000, 2007; Motzki 2000, 2001, 2010) astonished some observers because of its intensity and detail, even though Schneider brought it to an end fairly quickly. By going back to it now, however, we may find things that prove helpful as we take a fresh look at these matters.

Motzki finds that the Surraq narrative had its origins in Medina rather than Egypt. In fact, he assigns it to the time of the Prophet himself, thus declaring it literally "authentic." No one denies that narratives about Surraq also circulated in Egypt, through multiple lines of transmission; but according to Motzki, these represented views and doctrines that went back ultimately to Medina. This choice between early seventh-century Arabia and late seventh-century and eighth-century Egypt pervades the debate between Motzki and Schneider.

To go back for a moment, Schacht maintained (again, counterintuitively) that the Qur'ān did not have much direct presence in the earliest Islamic legislation, beyond providing general ethical principles and the like; only at a later stage would it have achieved its status as the primary source of the law (Schacht 1950: 224–227). Not surprisingly, Schacht's critics have disputed this notion. In this case the critics seem to have been right, in the sense that the Qur'ān appears here not only as a source of Islamic law but also as a participant in a peculiarly Arabian argument, which we can trace only with difficulty.

At issue, first of all, is the term *ribā*. This means literally "increase" and is usually understood as "usury" and "lending at interest," forbidden in mature Islamic law. In the Qur'ān these translations are no doubt accurate much of the time. At other times, however, the Qur'ānic *ribā* seems to involve some kind of gift: "The *ribā* that you give, so that it may increase the wealth of the people, does not increase with God. But the *zakāt* (alms) that you give out of a desire for the countenance of God: those are the ones whose [wealth] is doubled" (30:39). This verse, like several others, contrasts some kind of bad circulation, *ribā*, with some kind of good circulation, *zakāt*. The medieval exegetes were nearly united in saying that *ribā* here means a gift that a man gives to another man, in the hope of receiving a greater gift in return. Some of them identified this, rather persuasively, with a practice current in Arabia before Islam (Bonner 2005: 397).

Again, here the Qur'ān takes part in an utterly Arabian conversation, for Arabia was a place where an archaic morality of the desert prevailed, even as it maintained familiarity with towns, markets, merchants, and so forth. Arabia wasn't unique in this combination by any means, but its inner conflicts had a different character from those in the more densely populated (though not necessarily more civilized) countries nearby.

The Qur'ānic *locus classicus* for *ribā*, debt, and treatment of insolvent debtors occurs in a series of verses in Sūrat al-Baqara (2:270–283). Here, the Qur'ān differentiates between capital (*ru'ūs amwāl*) and *ribā*, whatever that may mean here. One verse in particular (2:280) recommends (or prescribes) that we go easy on a debtor in difficulty and instead "practice charity" (*wa-in taṣaddaqtum khayrun lakum*), which apparently means renouncing the debt in whole or in part. The Qur'ān thus calls for donations and alms for the needy, in the context of (partial) forgiveness of debts, while at the same time permitting debts to be contracted in the first place (2:282). Motzki argues that here the call for deferral of payment refers to the capital of the loan and that what is at issue is the interest connected to it. Several early juridical authorities from around 700 CE do indeed say that *ribā* here refers to an increase in the amount of a debt if this has not been paid on time—or, in other words, compound interest, associated with "oppression" (*ẓulm*) at 2:279. Motzki concludes that a pre-Islamic Hijazi creditor, facing an insolvent debtor, had two options: He could require the debtor to offer himself, his wife, or his children to work off the debt; or he could sell the debtor into outright slavery, with or without his family (Motzki 2000: 58–59, 2010: 184–185). Motzki maintains that Qur'ān 2:280 militates against both options, and he finds support for this in exegetical tradition. In the end, however, as Schneider maintains, it is difficult to prove conclusively that here the Qur'ān specifically addresses debt slavery or bondage, rather than the treatment of insolvent debtors in a more general way.

Motzki presents other evidence (though not much of it) that forced service for debt, over a limited time, was common in the Hijaz. Especially interesting is the story of al-ʿĀṣ b. Hishām b. Mughīra, who after becoming indebted to Abū Lahab, offered himself to work off the debt. In the event this took the form of military service in Abū Lahab's place, and al-ʿĀṣ died at the battle of Badr. Again, it is impossible to determine the literal historicity of any of this, but it does appear that debt servitude in some form, or indebtedness itself, was at least an issue in Arabia at the time. This does not mean that Irene Schneider was necessarily wrong in suggesting that it entered the Islamic system from outside Arabia. But the situation in Arabia needs a closer look.

The debate between Schneider and Motzki had other aspects, including fascinating arguments over the exegesis of the Qur'ānic verses just mentioned. However, since space is limited, I would point to the debate's focus on the best methods for dating traditions. Schneider, as we have seen, deployed a Schachtian approach, largely deductive in character. She provided a detailed thematic analysis of the Surraq traditions, focusing on textual content (*matn*) as well as on techniques of transmission (*isnād*). She also looked to the late antique context of this early Islamic debate. Motzki, however, insisted on considering the transmission history of these traditions *before* any thematic analysis; accordingly, for him the late-antique context was not of primary importance. But while we may complain that underlying historical issues have gone neglected in this argument, the fact remains that *ḥadīth*, in some broad sense, remains our primary source of information for debt bondage in early Islam. As we try to re-enter this territory, Irene Schneider's work, and her debate with Harald Motzki, still provide the starting point.

Markets and Trade in Arabia before Islam

While the modern argument over early Islamic debt bondage has focused on the dating and authenticity of the sources, it has also produced opposing positions on an underlying historical issue. Irene Schneider maintained that debt bondage was foreign to pre-Islamic Arabia and may have entered Islamic doctrine and practice as a borrowing from Byzantine Egypt. Harald Motzki, by contrast, claimed that debt bondage did exist in pre-Islamic Arabia; accordingly, to the extent that it existed afterward under Islam, it would have been an Arabian inheritance. Either way, it is interesting that references to debt (*dayn*) as such do not occur often in our sources for pre-Islamic Arabia. Equally striking is our lack of knowledge about the general phenomenon of slavery in that environment: While relevant terms (*qinn*, etc.) occur here and there, we know little about the conditions of enslavement, the legal status of slaves, and so forth. Mecca and Medina during Muhammad's career as a prophet constitute an exception,[7] but here we are dealing with a body of narrative literature (*sīra, maghāzī*) that stands apart in some ways from other literature relating to pre-Islamic Arabia.

What our literary sources do tell us about constantly is generosity, gift-giving, and hospitality, those thematic mainstays of the pre-Islamic Arabic poetry (Nana 1994). Especially in the long, formal odes (*qaṣāʾid*), the protagonist will typically boast of his achievements in this domain, together with (and weighted equally with) his derring-do in battles and raids. He protects and shelters the needy, sometimes at considerable risk to himself; he parts with his wealth quickly and heedlessly; and he regularly treats his guests to feasts of roast camel, washed down whenever possible with large quantities of wine.

Not surprisingly, generosity is a heavy, crushing obligation. The poet-narrator-host must find the resources that will allow him to continue in his self-destructive path. He must endure the complaints of his own womenfolk, described as "chiders" (*ʿawātib*) worried about sustaining the household. And in times of hardship the steady influx of needy supplicants can turn quickly into a flood. A lifelong practice of generosity accordingly requires stoic fortitude. We see this when, in a moment of crisis, the Prophet Muhammad's wife, Khadīja, praises his ability to withstand "the vicissitudes of the claim" (and/or the "right," *nawāʾib al-ḥaqq* [Kister 1965]).

While later Arabic literary tradition liked to portray pre-Islamic Arabian society this way, we cannot say that obligation and dependency were created and expressed there entirely through acts of generosity, gratitude, and reciprocity, rather than through contracts, loans, and so forth. As we have noted already, markets and merchants had been familiar fixtures in Arabia for ages. As in many (or even all) historical environments, these modes of exchange and interaction coexisted and overlapped, as David Graeber has shown; understanding just how they did so is an important part of the task before us.

To a much greater extent than generosity and gifts, merchants and markets have prevailed in modern arguments about the Arabian background to the rise of Islam, as we have already seen. In the twentieth century, scholarly consensus formed around the idea that when Islam first emerged in the Hijaz (west central Arabia), it was so market- and merchant-friendly as to instill commercial habits and ideals into its followers, for once and for all. How did this happen? Long before Muhammad's time, we are told, his tribe, the Quraysh of Mecca, were great traders who established commercial networks so successfully as to become the peninsula's dominant economic actors. And even though most of Quraysh opposed Muhammad and his teachings, they all, including Muhammad himself, shared these ways of thinking and behaving. According to one theory, the rapid accumulation of wealth in Mecca created inequalities and dislocations so that the tribal system for maintaining loyalty and security came unraveled. The result was a crisis, at once social, economic, and spiritual, to which Muhammad's teachings and the Qur'ān provided a response and a cure (Watt 1953).

This view of the matter received a challenge in Patricia Crone's *Meccan Trade* (Crone 1987b). Crone argued that Mecca, with its barren, off-track location, never was the favorable location for trade that modern scholars have made it out to be. Mecca never dominated Arabia's commerce with other countries and failed even to attract any notice from those countries. Meccan trade, if it existed, must have consisted of local distribution of leather, cheap cloth, livestock, and other such things. Crone based this demolition work on an ongoing, devastating critique of the Arabic literary, narrative sources for pre-Islamic Arabia.

While some responses to *Meccan Trade* consisted of outraged rejection of the entire thing (Serjeant 1990), other arguments were piecemeal, in the sense that they sought to overturn parts of the argument but not all (Lecker 2003). As a result, it has seemed for some time that the argument over Meccan trade is over and done with, even though it never came to resolution. If you accept Crone's argument, you may agree that the edifice of Meccan and Arabian history, as constructed by twentieth-century scholars, has collapsed, with nothing available to replace it. On the other hand, if you don't agree with Crone, you may maintain that Quraysh extended their commercial networks to the point where Mecca came to resemble the medieval and early modern Italian merchant republics (Lammens 1910); that being shrewd businessmen, they grew rich; that this accumulation of wealth, together with increasingly individualistic behavior, led to a social and spiritual crisis in Mecca; and finally, that the triumph of commercial values and free markets in early Islam emerged from this sequence of events or something like it. And while there have been contributions to the problem of Meccan trade since 1987 (Heck 2003, 2006; Crone 2007), in larger terms there has not been much progress.

The debate over Meccan trade, which has (correctly) presented pre-Islamic Arabia as contested territory, focuses on such questions as whether Quraysh sought and achieved commercial dominance throughout Arabia. For those who think they did, Quraysh's political preeminence seems a logical (if not often explicitly stated) corollary. For those who, following Crone, think they did not, pre-Islamic Arabian tribal politics remain something of a puzzle. Either way, arguments over the veracity of the literary sources have received the lion's share of attention. As with the Schneider–Motzki controversy, these debates have inhibited thinking about historical events and processes.

While seeking an alternative approach, I have written about an Arabic narrative tradition about "the markets of the Arabs before Islam" (Bonner 2010, 2011, 2012). This tradition describes an annual series of markets or fairs that would have extended throughout the Arabian peninsula according to a fixed schedule. The series began in north-central Arabia at Dūmat al-Jandal. It then moved across the eastern coast and Oman and on to Ḥaḍramawt and Yemen, before reaching its culminating point, the annual fair of 'Ukāẓ. Mecca and Medina did not belong to the sequence; in spatial terms, the closest they came to it was at 'Ukāẓ, located not far from Mecca but still distinct from it.

With regard to the tradition's veracity, it has value for much the same reason that statements in early Islam in favor of debt bondage have value: They go against the prevailing view, while maintaining inner consistency. To take this a little further, while something like this sequence of markets may well have taken place and some people may have visited them in the prescribed order, at the same time others must have gone in different directions and visited other markets that did not belong to the sequence at all. Accordingly, while the sequence describes concrete reality to some extent, it also describes an idealized movement in space and time.

Since the annual series of markets recurs in a fixed order, it seems reasonable to describe it as a cycle. When viewed on a map, however, it takes the form of an inwardly directed, accelerating spiral, concluding in Arabia's geographical heart. This spiral describes a moral trajectory which begins at a low point, Dūmat al-Jandal, where the local ruler enjoys a proprietary role in the market, levying taxes and selling his goods before anyone else, thus fixing prices. Even worse, the market at Dūma specializes in prostitution and slavery, both considered here to be negative things. The tradition associates slavery with the local tribal confederation of Kalb, who "practiced slavery more than any of the Arabs"; and it may be significant that the Kalb were described elsewhere as *musta'riba*, Arabs assimilated to non-Arab culture or vice versa (Blachère [1952] 1980: 237–241). Again, we know little about slavery in general in pre-Islamic Arabia. But for now we can confirm that in the tradition on the markets, slavery and prostitution occur at Dūmat al-Jandal, on the southern fringe of the Byzantine and Sasanian Empires, and then do not reappear. The sequence thus begins at a moral low point consisting of total commodification. Instead of good deeds requited or benefits reciprocated, we find persons deprived of their social status and the use of their own bodies. Even for free participants, exchanges are constrained by the selfish activity of a ruler who is, in turn, hampered in his sovereignty and autonomy.

The following points in the sequence come under the partial control or protectorate of the Sasanian Empire. Here, local Arab rulers enjoy the same privileges as the ruler of Dūma. Afterward, in Ḥaḍramawt, we find the absence of any sovereignty whatsoever, together with the necessity for visitors of finding "protection," another kind of forced payment. By contrast, the tradition expresses admiration for the markets at 'Adan and Ṣanʿāʾ, in Yemen. Here, the rulers do not exact taxes and refrain from any activity at all: "they never bought or sold in their markets and were all admirable in their character and deportment" (al-Marzūqī 1914: 164).

At 'Ukāẓ the sequence reaches its moral high point. Here, the negative aspects of the earlier markets are absent: 'Ukāẓ imposed "neither tithes nor protection" (al-Marzūqī 1914: 165), with neither greedy "kings" nor extorting tribal chiefs. And so, whereas everything had been a commodity at Dūmat al-Jandal, at 'Ukāẓ the situation was entirely different. This does not mean that there weren't commodities at 'Ukāẓ. Indeed, all sorts of things were sold there, including luxury goods and everyday items such as "leather of 'Ukāẓ" (Crone 1987b: 83, 2007). However, the medieval sources devote little attention to these goods. Instead, they single out 'Ukāẓ in terms such as these: "The tribes of the Arabs used to congregate at 'Ukāẓ every year and used to hold their boasting contests there (*wa-yatafākharūna fīhā*). Their poets would attend [the market] and would vie with one another with their most recent compositions. Then they would disperse" (al-Bakrī 1998: 3:218; Yāqūt al-Rūmī 1957–1958: 4:142). All sorts of gifts were given and received, chief among them being a camel for slaughter or a feast of camel meat (Bonner 2011: 33–34).

While we may doubt the literal historicity of these anecdotes, they consistently associate the fair of 'Ukāẓ with the twin themes of generosity and competitiveness. 'Ukāẓ was also a place where questions of leadership were decided, even though—or precisely because—it lay under the control of no one. In former times, the kings of Yemen used to send agents to 'Ukāẓ to find out who was "the most valiant of the Arabs" and then "to cultivate him and offer him presents" (al-Marzūqī 1914: 165). Meanwhile other "kings" gave presents and "shares of the profits" to the "nobles." *Ribḥ*, the usual Arabic for "profit," is tied here to the evaluation of nobility and the constant competition among "nobles" for prestige, recognition, and royal gifts. The effect of 'Ukāẓ, and ultimately of the market sequence as a whole, was thus to transform the proceeds from commerce and taxation into prestige-enhancing gifts (Bonner 2010).

The world described in this tradition on the "markets of the Arabs" differs starkly from the world of early Islam in its ethics (boastful self-aggrandizement, wine-drinking) and politics (highly limited and fragmented sovereignty). But it also has things in common with that world. To begin with, the sequence of markets features such activities as transporting and selling goods. Its participants include full-time merchants, some of them foreigners from overseas. It shows reticence about rough-and-tumble marketplace behavior, imposing decorous silence in some circumstances (Bonner 2010). But in the end it brings together international maritime trade, desert-crossing caravans, and local production and traffic, all within a single grand sequence. At the same time, the tradition favors an archaic morality, exalting gift-giving and competition for "noble" status over what we have been referring to here as commoditization and market exchange.

We can find a similar contrast (or contradiction?) in fundamental texts of early Islam. The Qur'ān and Sunna regulate behavior in the marketplace, laying down principles that we can, without much exaggeration, interpret as favoring the "free market," for instance, by insisting on complete transparency in transactions and by protecting weaker actors from stronger, tendentially predatory ones. But at the same time, these texts prescribe a morality based on notions of generosity and reciprocity. As we have already seen, in what are usually considered to be the earliest parts of the Qur'ān, we begin with the fact of God's generosity to us: Not only our sustenance but existence and life themselves are gifts that we cannot reciprocate. What we can and must do, therefore, is follow God's lead by practicing generosity toward the weak and the poor. From this derives the constant, overpowering claim or right (*ḥaqq*) that the poor exert over us, much like the claim they previously exerted, under different conditions, in pre-Islamic Arabia. The Qur'ān uses lots of commercial metaphor, as is well known; but this does *not* mean that it imposes a morality based on what we moderns consider "free-market principles" (Rippin 1996). These similarities between the tradition on the markets and the fundamental texts of early Islam may indicate tension between competing ideologies within the Arabian "contested space" (Bonner 2011: 40–44). Or, alternatively, perhaps it is better to view the market sequence as a harbinger of the new order. Either way, we find ourselves in a (to us) largely unfamiliar Arabian environment, historiographically broader and more promising than the impasse of "Meccan trade."

Conclusions

Here, I may repeat once again that our focus on method in *ḥadīth* studies has had a net negative effect on historical research. Perhaps "method" has been too narrowly conceived, for even in the most broad-minded discussions, the argument usually returns to the *ḥadīth* and its authenticity, again, not necessarily asking whether its narratives correspond literally to events in seventh-century Arabia but focusing all the same on the dating of traditions and their literary and rhetorical characteristics. Yet the *ḥadīth* ought to be available as a tool for historians—even if, inevitably, a slippery and unwieldy tool. In this particular case, the matter of *Schuldknechtschaft* merits consideration over and beyond the dating and authenticity of the relevant *ḥadīth*.

I would also propose that while our sources for early Islam always present challenges, at times it may be useful if we do *not* follow the procedure of first isolating these problems with the sources; then confronting them head-on; after which, having developed an approach and a method, we proceed to set the sources to work, so to speak, in the solution of historical problems. Instead of this procedure, we may do better to view these difficulties within the sources, their inner conflicts above all, as heuristically valuable elements.[8] For example, interesting results may emerge from contrasting the view of pre-Islamic Arabian commerce that we find in the tradition on the "markets of the Arabs" with the more familiar view of these matters that we find in the *sīra* and *maghāzī* literature and other, more "mainstream" historical sources. Doing this requires, of course, a detailed confrontation with the sources for the tradition on the markets, including their transmission history (Bonner 2012).

The question of debt bondage has also brought us to the perplexing matter of slavery in pre-Islamic Arabia. Here, we may conclude, if only tentatively, that slaves, at least in some "proper" sense, were usually foreign and non-Arab, as in early seventh-century Mecca and Medina (Ghada 2005), and that slavery in itself was considered a tainting, non-Arab (or only marginally Arab) practice for all concerned, as at Dūmat al-Jandal in the tradition on the markets. Meanwhile, when the early Islamic texts, especially the Qur'ān, discuss *ribā*, they are referring to a current social problem, even if we cannot pinpoint it precisely. Perhaps certain debt-related practices had entered Arabia recently from the neighboring empires? If so, it seems that the problem quickly became "native," expressed in Arabic and Arabian terms.

Most modern observers, though not all (Kuran 2005: 798–799) agree that the early Islamic economy achieved considerable success, at least by the later eighth century. Of course, this success must be measured by the standards of the time, whereby growth could never be achieved at the rates at which we think we can achieve it nowadays. Accordingly, if we return to the questions asked at the beginning of this chapter—where did all this come from? what did Islam itself have to offer?—we may reply that the early Islamic economy owed a considerable portion of its success to an "Arabian value-added" element. However, we must *not* identify this "Arabian value-added" simply with the arrival throughout the Near East of a new, rigorously monotheist message, emphasizing care for the poor and straight dealing in commerce, for messages of this kind were already available, in great abundance, throughout the region.

David Graeber has pointed out that some debt-related phenomena of the "Axial Age" lost much of their harshness during the medieval era, with the Islamic world taking the lead. This may seem strange since the Islamic world continued to practice slavery until well into the modern era. But Islamic law, once it reached maturity, had no use for debt bondage, as we have seen, while the Muslim jurists declared from early on that freedom is the fundamental condition of humanity (*al-aṣl huwa l-ḥurriyya* [Motzki 2000: 1, 2013: 125; Schneider 2007: 355–357). So while the early Islamic world featured bustling markets and trade, including large-scale traffic in persons, it also set clear limits on the commodification of persons. The historical context and ethical vocabulary for these limits derived in part from an "Arabian value-added" element which contributed to the success of the early caliphate and eventually of the entire Islamic world, in the economic sphere and beyond.

Debt's Fourth Millennium Seen from Below

HOW PAPYRI MODIFY THE PICTURE

Arietta Papaconstantinou

*For most of us, "Medieval" remains a synonym for superstition,
intolerance, and oppression.*[1]

TO PUT THIS on paper in 2011 is to ask for trouble, at least with medievalists. The profession has been trying to shed that image for almost half a century—largely successfully, it thought.[2] Yet, as David Graeber's brief sentence shows, this may well be an illusion: the long rehabilitation of the Middle Ages in scholarship since the 1970s seems to have escaped even a book with the breadth of erudition of *Debt*. "According to the *conventional wisdom*," Graeber continues, "with the collapse of the empire, the cities were largely abandoned and the economy 'reverted to barter,' taking at least five centuries to recover."[3] His intention was to deconstruct that narrative, with the now well-known argument that the lack of coins was not a lack of money. The mistake of "conventional wisdom" is that it takes for barter what is actually virtual money, the prevalence of which was a defining feature of the Middle Ages. As Alice Rio shows in this volume (Chapter 11), the demonetization of the Middle Ages is greatly overstated by Graeber, even if the coinage system was not as central politically as it had been under the early Roman Empire. Graeber has here followed much earlier scholarship on the period than was available in the late 2010s—but even in those earlier works, one would be hard-pressed to find the expression "reverted to barter."[4] It is, for example, curious that Graeber did not make use of Chris Wickham's *Framing the Early Middle Ages*,[5] which had appeared six years earlier and offered a systematic and wide-ranging attempt by a specialist to analyze the structural and economic transformations that took place between 400 and 800. It would have provided a convenient and up-to-date point of departure for Chapter 10, and so

Arietta Papaconstantinou, *Debt's Fourth Millennium Seen from Below* In: *Debt in the Ancient Mediterranean and Near East*. Edited by: John Weisweiler, Oxford University Press. © Oxford University Press 2023.
DOI: 10.1093/oso/9780197647172.003.0010

would much of the work done since the 1970s on late antiquity, "long" or not,[6] which has contested the idea that it represented a steady decline into some sort of barter-based "dark age."[7]

Yet even though Graeber draws out the "Axial Age" in the Mediterranean area until at least the sixth century and, like Pirenne, sees the rise of Islam as a harbinger of the Middle Ages, this remains a boundary of principle. In practice, *Debt* describes and compares, on the one hand, the classical world—imperial Athens, the Roman Republic, and the Principate—and, on the other, the later Abbasid caliphate and the European high Middle Ages. The centuries in between are neither here nor there—an ambiguity well illustrated, for instance, by the use of the "Church Fathers"[8] as examples both of the "Axial Age" situation (lenders were ruthless) and of the ideological framework of the Middle Ages (denunciation of usurious lending).

This lack of engagement with the process of historical change and the pitfalls of chronological boundaries is perhaps the greatest drawback of the diachronic paradigm of *Debt*. It adopts a periodization that is culturally constructed to suit the West's image of its own past, as has been repeatedly argued,[9] and transforms it into a heuristic device that, ultimately and despite significant efforts to achieve the contrary, applies Western interpretive categories to a global grand narrative. This leads to a reification of canonical "periods," which come into existence with no transition: There is little—if any—discussion of the evolution that led from the "collapse" of the ancient empires to the "Middle Ages" several centuries later.

Arguably, however, such critique misses the point. If one considers the overall organization of the argument in *Debt*, it becomes clear that the approach feeds into a rhetorical strategy adopted by Graeber in order to build up a counternarrative of sorts—one in which the West's traditionally glorious periods are cast as negative and its "decadent" or "dark" ones as positive and where the Near East becomes the "Near West," signaling the adoption of a non-Western point of view and underpinning the—entirely justified—statement that "for most of the middle ages, Islam was . . . the core of Western civilisation" if seen from a world-historical perspective.[10] The historiographical shortcuts mentioned above are, in fact, part and parcel of that strategy: they serve to mark clear oppositions between set periods, which are assessed by Graeber in a way that runs against common conceptions. The contrast appears all the more clear-cut when the transitional centuries are left out of the picture.

Therefore, as Miranda Joseph has pointed out in a long review, one should judge Graeber not as a historian but as a prophet.[11] Indeed, in *Debt*, world history is conceptualized metaphorically as a pendulum going from one pole to another, one bad, the other less so; and the aim of the book is, ultimately, to presage an unavoidable swing of the pendulum in the near future. Because of this implied cyclical repetition, the historical narrative is above all a tool that serves to establish the unavoidability of that swing, and therefore the Middle Ages have to be not only different from the Axial Age but at the opposite end. This is built up through a series of binary oppositions, most of which work in parallel with the central couple, empire (or state) versus community. The former is abstract and depersonalized, the latter personal; the former creates "commercial economies," through abstract and exploitative "markets," while the latter fosters "human economies." Overall, the choice of terms to describe the opposites leaves little doubt as to the moral value the respective periods are given in the book.

Yet even if *Debt* is not a work of history, it uses history to make an argument. In that sense, the historical evidence presented to back up that argument functions like an anthropologist's fieldwork notes: Even though they are necessarily selective and based on the questions asked, they also have to reflect with some precision the situation on the ground. This is especially true with regard to the opposition between "Axial" and "Middle" Age as it is central in establishing the historical possibility of a social alternative to imperialistic, overmonetized, oppressive, and exploitative states based on slaves, armies, and markets—which, hardly caricatured and to a large extent justified, is Graeber's view of classical antiquity. It is this premise, central to his entire argument, that I would like to discuss here, with reference to the transition—and by extension the opposition—between his "Axial Age" and his "Middle Ages." Was it really so radical? Was that "middle" period so immune and resistant to the aspects of human nature that made the great ancient empires? Instead of focusing, like Graeber, on the legal and intellectual framework of the period and the overall macrostructures, I shall instead apply a microhistorical lens to several village communities to observe how debt was handled in practice and explore what that can tell us about the broader model. To do this I shall rely on the information supplied by Egyptian and Palestinian documentary papyri, a source that allows us to zoom into the rural communities of the eastern Mediterranean like no other and covers equally the entire time span from the early Roman Empire to the caliphate. I shall attempt here to treat the entire period thematically without preconceived points of rupture, to offer as far as possible a bottom-up view of actual practice.

Using Debt and Credit

The first thing that becomes evident to anyone perusing papyrological documents is that microcredit pervaded rural life and that its forms hardly differed at the local level throughout the Greco-Roman and post-Roman periods, even if it corresponded to constantly changing modes of fiscal administration and labor organization. In the Egyptian countryside, loans and debts were on the whole treated as socioeconomic tools by all parties involved in a variety of ways, reveal-ing a versatile use of borrowing and of the sorts of relations it creates and sustains.

Throughout the period under consideration, most rural loans were taken out for agricultural investment of different sorts, often simply the acquisition of seed but also of irrigation devices, tools, or cattle. Repair of infrastructure and transport were other costs that could be covered by small loans, almost always short-term agreements to be repaid after harvest. Many of these could bypass coins altogether, as it was possible, for example, to borrow seed and repay directly in produce. This system is very common for preindustrial rural credit and has been abundantly studied for late medieval and early modern Europe, where the documentation is very rich.[12] It is also a system that tends to function in parallel with highly monetized economies: Monetized cities and market towns coexisted with a much less monetized countryside. There were numerous contact points between the two, of course, the most obvious one being the tax system. When the central authority demanded taxes predominantly in coin, the necessity to borrow cash increased, while in periods when taxes could be collected partly in kind one could function to a much larger extent on virtual money.

During the almost seven Roman centuries taxation was far from stable. Even though eventually the taxes paid at the provincial level were in coin, they were not always collected in coin locally: Local collections changed several hands before arriving at their destination and could be in kind at the point of collection and transformed into coin in the process.[13] In the specific case of Egypt, this was compounded by the levy of the *annona*, which was a large, province-wide tax in grain intended for the imperial capital, measured in volume and only (if at all) converted to a monetary value at a later stage in the process.[14]

Under the Umayyad and early Abbasid caliphates, on the other hand, taxes were invariably demanded in gold even at the village level. Combined with the introduction of a poll tax, which extended taxation to those who did not own land, this demand for gold increased the dependence of rural inhabitants on individuals who could lend them the necessary cash or pay the tax for them in exchange for labor or services.[15] Examples of such transactions show that they could be much less straightforward than they sound. In 667 or 682, in the Palestinian village of Nessana, George, son of Patrikios, the scion of a local fam-ily that had been lending money for at least a century, paid the tax for Sergios, son of Menas, one of his fellow villagers, directly to the tax collectors and had Sergios sign a debt acknowledgment to him for the same sum, 4⅓ *solidi*.[16] Two years later, George again advanced the tax for Sergios but at 12 *solidi* this time, six for the poll tax and six for the land tax.[17] Even though he borrowed money to pay his taxes, Sergios was evidently not a man in dire need. His land tax indi-cates that he owned land of some size and that over the two years for which we have information on him, his land tax, and therefore presumably his holdings, increased. The second time he was also paying the poll tax, in addition to himself, for five other males over 14 years of age—either members of his household or dependents for whom he paid the tax in an arrangement similar to his own transaction with George. Borrowing for the tax, in this case, may well have been a way of maintaining his role as patron of his client network at a time when he was short on cash; alternatively, it could have been a way of freeing his own cash for investment on his land. This highlights the complexity of local credit arrangements and of the power relations that they imply. Was Sergios paying the poll tax for other villagers who would later repay him (or George) in kind or service? Or did he simply have a large family? As there is no mention of interest in either document, can we assume that George was helping out a fellow member of the local elite with a free loan? Or was there some unrecorded return for the favor? Did he see Sergios as a social climber it would be advisable to help, or did he reckon that with the burden of a large male family he would eventually default on his debts so that he, George, could take his land?

Like today, loans were used in many different ways and were the foundation of a number of local transactions. They allowed several individuals to remain in circulation economically who, without the possibility of borrowing, would have slipped into the margins of the system. It is no surprise, therefore, that so much late-antique Christian literature and even many documents make a connection between lending and charity. Unsurprisingly, this is a well-studied aspect of the credit economy, and I will not go into it further. What is less studied is the importance of the credit economy as a tool for women. Their ready access to objects with exchange value, largely through dowry and their own textile production, allowed them to obtain quick cash through the practice of pawning. Among women lenders, a higher proportion were pawnbrokers than simple moneylenders; and among women borrowers, pawning domestic objects, generally jewels, metal plate, or textiles, was the preferred procedure.[18] This was a constant feature of the Egyptian credit market from the Roman period until at least the eighth century.[19] In less affluent circles, it gave women some financial autonomy, while in wealthier ones it allowed them to conduct business or engage in conspicuous consumption.[20] In some cases, when women got married, they gave a sum to their husband that provided him with a form of working capital, and in the marriage contract this was framed as a loan rather than as dowry and had a repayment date. The arrangement gave the wife more control over the sum as well as over the husband and was accordingly popular in the Roman period.[21]

Another common credit relation was to make advance payments for services or labor, something that preexisted the Roman conquest but was formalized under Rome in the practice known as *paramone*.[22] This was, in effect, a loan given in exchange for time-limited bound labor, the quantity of which was defined in advance. The labor in question could be supplied by the debtors, who would sign a contract binding themselves for a specific period of work in exchange for the advance of a sum. It could also be provided by one of the debtor's dependents: In particular, there are several extant cases of parents contracting out their children in exchange for cash advances.[23] All such contracts also contain a clause stipulating that if the laborer wishes to leave, it is possible on condition of the full repayment of the loan/advance payment: The laborer is therefore only bound as long as part of the debt subsists. Among other things, the arrangement provided another way for women to obtain quick cash, and it is sometimes found for wet-nurse contracts.[24] In a contract from the second half of the third century, for instance, a woman receives in loan from another woman a sum with which to pay off a debt incurred by her father; in lieu of interest, she binds herself to do weaving work for the lender until the debt is repaid. This could be a woman whose father died leaving her with a debt, which made it necessary for her to borrow; or if the father was still alive when the document was drawn up, it could be a concealed case of ceded labor, where the father effectively used his daughter's labor as a way to pay off his interest—on a loan contracted to pay off another loan.[25] The same arrangement can be found in documents from the early Islamic period, both in Egypt and in Nessana.[26]

This leads me to another common practice, namely what one might call serial borrowing.[27] Indeed, it is clear that at all levels individuals took loans to pay off other loans or even took loans to lend to others. A variant of this is the borrowing agreement made with a third person as guarantor instead of a collateral security: In case of default or simply at the end of the agreed period, the guarantor paid the creditor and then signed a new agreement with the debtor, possibly with yet another guarantor.[28] This was a way of refinancing ad infinitum and did not involve providing services or losing land or other property. As it involved a complex network of patrons, however, it was only accessible to those with the necessary social capital, while at the same time tying them into several concurrent relations of dependence and clientage. Presumably, over time the sum owed grew with the interest, but this hardly mattered—until, for instance, one's wife or daughter inherited the loan and did not have the same social means to continue moving ahead heedlessly. This practice was also common at all levels: We see it with small loans between villagers and with much larger ones involving official figures. One very interesting case is a bilingual declaration in Coptic and Arabic from the first half of the eighth century, in which Antony, son of Herakleides, the headman of How in Middle Egypt and a deacon, agrees that he has no further claims on Severos, son of Bane, who had borrowed forty gold pieces from him, because the sum had been paid on behalf of Severos by Muslim b. Bashshār, an inhabitant of Shmun (the area's big city). The reason there is an Arabic version of the declaration is that it served as a security for Muslim and as proof that Severos now owed *him* the forty gold pieces.[29] This document is interesting because it shows not only the extent to which such practices continued at the local level throughout the period but also how quickly the Muslim newcomers tuned into the prevailing system of patronage. The same form of "refinancing" was also practiced in aristocratic circles: In the sixth century, for instance, we see the very wealthy Fl. Christodote start an action against an Alexandrian banker who did not pay her a sum on behalf of her brother, from whom she borrowed to repay another creditor. The sum in question, sixty-one pounds of gold, is enormous for the time and was no doubt secured by mortgaging her vast landholdings. It also gives an indication of the levels of conspicuous consumption practiced by aristocratic circles in late antiquity, which fueled a thriving credit economy among the elites.[30]

There is enough evidence for this well-practiced system of networking to show how borrowers could surf their way out of default by transferring their debt from creditor to creditor. Most individuals in rural areas had networks of both patrons and dependents, even if only their children, and could use them to engage in different forms of transactions that balanced debt and credit in a way that gave them more agency than allowed by narratives of total dispossession. Those who owned land or houses could also use them to secure their loans. But the majority of rural loans were too small for such valuable counterparts, and we see them secured against movables, generally objects but also cattle or camels, and in some cases short spells of labor (one loan is given against the one-off sowing of the creditor's field[31]). These securities were sometimes returned and sometimes lost; both scenarios gave rise to contracts stipulating the transfer of the property. Even allowing for a higher degree of documentary invisibility, very few individuals were only on the bottom side of everyday transactions: Most rural inhabitants functioned as both debtors and creditors or mobilized other resources to resist loss of status.

Abusing Debt and Credit

The many social uses of credit account for its success and pervasive presence, despite the risk taken on both sides. The risk taken by the creditor has been at the center of countless studies by economists, not to mention ongoing protective legislation. Yet it was nothing, experience shows, compared to the risk taken by the debtor. The ruthlessness of lenders mentioned by Ambrose of Milan and Basil of Caesarea, whom Graeber cites as representative of the church fathers,[32] was above all a morality tale that they used in heavily allegorical works about Christian behavior. Yet they did tap into a bleak social reality: Documents indeed show that their metaphors were embedded in everyday life and therefore resonated with their audience. Some documents indeed offer textbook cases of exploitation of peasants by the inhabitants of towns or cities. A telling example comes from the eighth-century Herakleopolite nome. An inhabitant of the village of Thelbo had initiated proceedings against an official of the city "on account of some objects of mine which I left as a pledge some days ago." The official had claimed that the objects had been bought, not deposited as a pledge. The standard procedure of taking an oath in the church was followed, and the oath of the official was taken as proof that his claim was true. The villager had to renounce the ownership of the objects and pay a fine for accusing the official wrongly.[33] Other documents show powerful local elites behaving similarly, often, after the fourth century, with the complicity of the church. In the southern town of Jeme, the early eighth-century archive of the pawnbroker Koloje, whose family had been in the lending business for at least three generations, contains several transfers of pledges after default. One document indicates that she did not hesitate to take her debtors to court and another that at least one debtor suspected her of tampering with his pledges: Again, the affair was settled by an oath which she took in a church, and apparently her word was proof enough that she was not guilty.[34]

Other cases highlight gendered forms of abuse. Male lenders evidently found women without male protectors easy prey: A number of documents are pleas by women for help against such abuse. Again in the region of Jeme, several seventh- and eighth-century letters from women formulate requests for help with debt issues they might not have experienced if they had not been acting alone. A widowed woman from the Theban area, for example, wrote to a well-known local monk requesting his help with two priests who had borrowed grain from her late husband and were now, after his death, refusing to pay it back.[35] Another woman of the area, who also appears to have been acting alone, wrote to two priests asking them to intervene with a man who was holding her captive on account of a loan for which she seems to have pledged her house.[36] The letter does not go into detail as the recipients evidently know the affair, which therefore remains unclear to us. It does, however, bear witness to a practice we know was very common, namely the seizure and detainment of a debtor as a means of pressure to proceed with repayment. This form of imprisonment was purely private and predicated on a local consensus that the creditor had the power and authority to carry it out. From this letter, as from other cases of such confinement, it is clear that no official authority was involved in the process.

Even in cases of such gender-related abuse, social status played a role, as another case makes clear. A letter sent by a local woman to the well-known seventh-century bishop Pisenthios of Koptos contains a description of her plight: Her husband died, and her son had to flee because of the Persian invasion, which also resulted in the loss of part of her cattle; her letter to the bishop is a request for him to intervene with the authorities so that "the moneylender," who had already taken the rest of her cattle, would not also take her house.[37] She had clearly been a woman of some means since she owned a house, a field, and cattle; and even though the circumstances had made her vulnerable, she had no doubt been on the exploiting side of the barrier some years earlier. The fact that her social status was higher than her economic position at the time of writing allowed her to hope that she could escape the seizure of her house for what must have been a relatively large loan for the region, through the intervention of an important figure of authority to whom she had direct access.

As the examples above show, abusive credit/debt relations did not need the state to thrive: Social norms, group consensus, and the latent violence present in hierarchy and dependence were more than enough to sustain them. Imperial legislation, even though it secured the property rights of lenders and by implication their right to enforce repayment, also attempted to control that enforcement and limit the more extreme forms of abuse. In the sixth century, ostensibly for reasons to do with Christian principles, the emperor Justinian not only halved the official interest rates but also took measures against lenders who accepted land as security for loans and did not return it after the loan was repaid; in addition, land under cultivation could not be seized in case of default, transferring land as a result of default was regulated and made more difficult, and detaining a debtor's children as security for loans was prohibited.[38] Coming after earlier attempts to regulate credit practices, Justinian's legislation was concerned not only with the protection of the lenders but also with that of the borrowers. This does not necessarily show Justinian's concern for the weak: It can be understood as an attempt to curb the rising power of local aristocracies by limiting their sources of income.

Disputes related to debt are prominent in the late-antique documentation. This is possibly—at least partly—an effect of the rise of private arbitration, a procedure that produced several documents locally, in places where papyri have been found. But one should not underestimate the role played by the decline of some of the earlier centralized institutions, which resulted in the reinforcement of the power of local worthies. Most of the abuse we see in the documentation actually comes from individuals in the same villages or districts who deemed themselves more powerful than the borrower—sometimes, as shown above, simply because they happened to be men dealing with women.

In some cases, protecting the lenders was not an idle pursuit, especially in the case of transactions among relatively well-to-do individuals. Borrowers mortgaging their land, for example, often seem to have been so confident that they would not lose it that they mortgaged the same piece of land for different loans from different lenders. This was common enough to warrant the introduction in the second century of a new registry office by the Romans where all claims on land, houses, and slaves were registered and archived.[39] This sparked a rise in the credit market, with generally higher loans in coin than had previously been the case. The institution slowly changed nature, however, and disappeared from the documentation after the 320s. The practice of allowing competing claims to accumulate on the same land resurfaced, and one of the most famous cases is a dispute settlement from the sixth century featuring none other than the ex-consul Apion. One of the longest Greek document on papyrus published to date, it recounts a litigation between a monastery in the area of Oxyrhynchos and the Apion estate, both of which had lent money to the same man, secured on the same land. The case might never have come to light had the borrower not died without repaying either lender.[40] Others would sell land that was mortgaged without letting the buyer know.[41] We only know of such cases when unexpected circumstances gave rise to contestation or conflict, which are by nature document-producing situations. No doubt the practice was much more common than what is reflected in the documentary record.

Debtors, Creditors, and Imperial Institutions

It was common for individuals to borrow within their own social group, setting up a relation of trust that was one of equals—what Roman businessmen would have called "friendship."[42] This is reflected in the minimal information given on some debt acknowledgments, which presupposes another level of relations between the two parties. Others were forced to borrow from usurious or exploitative lenders who built their fortunes from the seizure of collaterals without much personal involvement. Most credit relations, however, were between a patron and a client, or at least between a socially powerful local creditor and a socially weak debtor. That weakness did not necessarily imply insolvency, but it transformed the loan into an obligation that went beyond its monetary value because it was usually framed as a favor or, as some documents call it, a "charity."[43] This sort of relation also resulted in domination and exploitation but not always in complete dispossession: It was the fear of dispossession that maintained the relation of domination, which was arguably more useful to local elites in building their authority and power base than the accumulation of pledged objects.

In this conundrum of exploitative relations, state institutions often appeared to act as regulators. Even though legislation created a framework of rules and principles that permitted—or made possible—forms of coercion used by creditors against debtors, in principle at least recourse was available to all when the rules were broken. The fact that the legal tools offered were more easily manipulated by the rich and powerful is not entirely surprising. It is clear, however, from the number of petitions made to the authorities, that the imperial administration was perceived as a way to circumvent the local powerful and raised hopes of obtaining justice in the face of abuse.

In the seventh century, when the reach of state authority was at its weakest in remote areas because of the Persian and Arab conquests, this possibility broke down. Other figures of authority, like members of the clergy or "great men" (elders?) in a village, were called upon by the weaker party to mediate in cases of conflict. One almost mechanical consequence of the lack of state authority was that the interest rates, which had been lowered by Justinian to between 4% and 6% for private loans, soared to 16.67% in the seventh century. After the Arab conquest, the hands-off attitude of the new rulers reinforced the power of the local elites. The principle of the caliphate that gave autonomy to the "people of the book" to govern their own people allowed village and town elites to control wealth, justice, and forms of coercion all at the same time, with no recourse for weaker group members. The imperial legal frame of reference remained, but it was both interpreted and applied by the same local elites: There was no longer a central instance to control its implementation. The only form of recourse against abuse was to enter a relation of patronage with another member of the elite.

Very soon it became again possible to appeal beyond the local worthies to the Arab governor or to the qadi of the province. Several papyri show debt litigations having taken that route. Mostly these were creditors who had not been repaid, and the cases concern relatively large amounts of money.[44] Often, such litigations were complex cases that defy binary oppositions such as creditor/oppressor versus debtor/oppressed. For instance, in 786–787, a case was brought before the governor of Egypt, ʿAli b. Sylaymān al-Hāshimi al-ʿAbbāsi, by a man whose father had died while he was a child. The father had lent four dinars to a certain Ilyās, who for a number of years used part of that money for the subsistence of the orphan but then had left, taking the rest with him. This left the orphan without means of subsistence, even though he was officially the creditor.[45]

The early caliphal regime was still a strongly military one, with the soldiers in the provincial capital living—and seasonally raiding their Byzantine neighbors— off the extractive revenue from taxation and extraordinary requisitions.[46] It was very evidently inspired by the Roman model and in that respect did not at all herald a transition to virtual money and a "human economy." Taxes were demanded in gold coins, which would even be sent back if they were not of the right alloy with an injunction to send the right amount.[47] The reach of the apparatus of control set up by the state was very broad, and we see, much more systematically than under Rome, a carceral organization run by the caliphal administration alongside the private initiatives that were common locally. By the late eighth or early ninth century there was in Fusṭāṭ a prison for debtors, and the reasons for their imprisonment were duly recorded in the archive of the qadi, who had sent them there.[48] Those prisons were administered by the governor, who had political and military authority, rather than the qadi, even though the latter could imprison individuals in them.[49] This seems to have been the case not only in the capital but also in towns and cities along the Nile Valley, such as al-Ushmūnayn, at least by the tenth century.[50]

* * *

This quick overview covering the Roman and early Islamic periods shows that, on the ground, credit and debt practices varied little from the establishment of Roman rule down to the early Fatimid period. There was, in that respect, no opposition between Rome and the successive early caliphates but rather a strong continuity of approach and of administrative culture, despite the constant evolution of ideologies of power at the center and the variety of geopolitical situations in which Egypt and Palestine found themselves embroiled over that millennium. Throughout, the central administration—call it "the state"—appears from below as a remote rule-setter and arbiter. Made to benefit the most powerful, its rules were also protective of the weak, who could—and did—use them as a form of recourse. This was essential if the rules were to have any legitimacy in the eyes of the population.

As in most large territorial polities, resource extraction was devolved to local administrators, which was what one might call a high-risk, high-gain approach, at once counting on their greed and hoping it would not spin out of control. Much of the abuse usually associated with such extraction was carried out locally: not by impersonal agents of an impersonal center but by the man down the street, acting as the last link in a hierarchical chain of individuals who all sought to turn the imperial system to their advantage. This created a triangulation between the central authorities, the local powerful, and the weaker and otherwise defenseless inhabitants, which gave the latter a degree of leverage, something that was especially effective in periods when the state felt threatened by provincial elites. In both empires, such power dynamics meant that there was constantly a latent conflict between local elites and the imperial center, resulting in attempts from the latter to restrain abusers by "protecting" the peasants.[51]

It is also important to note that papyri provide ample evidence that violence perceived as legitimate was not—far from it—a state monopoly throughout the period. The local powerful—often within a single village—clearly considered it was their right to detain debtors or seize their goods or family members, without any due process. One could interpret the constant efforts at centralization and increased control mechanisms on the part of imperial regimes as an ongoing effort to claim that monopoly, and this was precisely what offered a break to those who suffered from the local manifestations of oppressive violence. At the same time, central authorities could benefit from community discipline and local mechanisms of inclusion and exclusion and harness to their advantage those aspects of community life that correspond least to the "human economies" of *Debt*: coercion, dependence, and exploitation of anyone perceived as weak or unprotected, even—if not especially—of people one met "face to face"—indeed, sometimes of one's own children.

The evidence from Egypt comes, in its way, to corroborate the sustained critique of *Debt* by Miranda Joseph, for whom Graeber's very welcome debunking of a number of myths (barter and primordial debt) goes hand in hand with the reaffirmation of another myth, based on what she calls the romantic discourse of community. In that narrative, "communities" function on relations of interpersonal trust, which are displaced by the abstracted and depersonalized "arithmetic" and calculation that come with the non-communal.[52] Because of their local and often rural origin, papyri bring to light the degree of intracommunal exploitation and the development and establishment of hierarchies that all rely on the latent violence of debt and obligation—which, in most cases, are not as differentiated as they are in *Debt*'s main argument. In that world, the existence of formal, impersonal institutions is seen as positive, and the state, not *despite* but *because* of its distance, is understood as a delocalized potential protector.

The case of the seventh century is instructive in that respect. It saw the Persians conquer the country and then retreat, only to be followed by the Arabs some twelve years later, whose internal problems for another quarter century prevented stability and long-term organization. When the organization came, it initially left a large degree of autonomy to local communities on internal economic and social matters. During that period of weak centralization, we see the levels of local oppressive behavior rise and with them the requests for the intervention of patrons. Where the Romans had maintained interest rates at official levels, moneylenders in the autonomous Christian communities of the caliphate did not hesitate to overburden their fellow villagers.[53]

To come back to Joseph's critique, I would argue that it is not only the myth of the community as a human economy that needs to be nuanced but also that of the Middle Ages as a society based on such communities. These were territorial, non-voluntary communities that were coercive, exploitative, abusive, and exclusionary. They did not, at least in the period treated here, offer a safe haven against an oppressive state: Where individuals and their debts were concerned, they often even represented the opposite. The main way of escaping exploitation within the community was through local networks of patronage, which in turn involved various forms of dependence. The more patrons one had, the more likely one was to avoid dispossession—but that was at the expense of more dependence: One was able to pay off one debt by contracting another. Patrons gave their help but in a system of reciprocity that typically upheld the existing hierarchy so that the system could hardly fit the model of "baseline communism," even at its simplest. In such cases, which certainly did exist, the intracommunal assistance could be framed more usefully in terms of "the instrumentality of sociability" and "the sociability of instrumentality," as Alena Ledeneva has put it.[54]

Because debt situations were so much a mix of both local and supra-local, of legal and human, of sets of rules and of networks aimed at circumventing them, of patronage and social competition, all at the same time, the role of money throughout the period does not appear to have had the function of quantification alone. Its convertibility was constant, into objects, produce, and/or services of perceived equivalent value; and the loans themselves were sometimes in a mix of two or more of those. Nor was this less exploitative than pure coin loans. Local communities did not function on credit money as opposed to imperial coin money: Rather, they provided micro-clusters of credit money economies that subsumed coin money into their broader exchange system and were embedded within a macroeconomic system of coin money. The point of contact and conversion between the two was taxation: If taxes were demanded in coin at the base of the supply chain, the need for coins touched every inhabitant and resulted in loans from local grandees that helped protect individuals vis-à-vis the fiscal administration but at the same time were virtually impossible to repay, at least in coin.

Thus, the effect of state policies and coin use on intracommunal debt seems to have been indirect. The leverage given (or not) to local elites and communal leaders was essential in determining the fate of the rural population, and the extractive weight put on local societies made competition within them more or less acute. Unsurprisingly, imperial authorities varied their approaches over time according to their needs, and the consequences on the ground varied accordingly. This did not, however, map neatly onto our modern reified constructions of ancient and medieval empires or onto our equally reified historical periods: It changed more than once within each of these empires and periods so that many "Axial Age" characteristics were prominent from the Umayyad to the Fatimid caliphate, and many "medieval" characteristics were just as prominent in the Roman Empire. Ultimately, the development of binary oppositions based on received categories requires from the narrator of a story a clarity in assigning characters to one or the other that appears artificial when tested on the ground.

Acknowledgments

This chapter is part of a broader project on debt and dependence in late-antique Egypt and Palestine, which has been generously funded by a Forschungsstipendium and a supplementary small grant from the Gerda Henkel Stiftung, to which I am most grateful. It was written before David Graeber's untimely death in September 2020, in a spirit of friendly debate and with the intention of pushing him further in his reflection, much as he pushed me in mine. His work will have helped transform the book that is the ultimate goal of this research into something very different from what I first imagined.

11

After the Axial Age

DEBT AND OBLIGATION IN THE EUROPEAN EARLY MIDDLE AGES

Alice Rio

IT IS A great gift to any historian when a brilliant scholar from another discipline takes the time to think deeply and sympathetically about one's area of interest—above all, perhaps, because it restores a feeling of unsettling unfamiliarity to the period one is supposed to know most about. This is certainly how I experienced reading David Graeber's *Debt: The First 5,000 Years* as a historian of early medieval Europe. Most of what makes Graeber's Middle Ages so full of productive strangeness is that they are framed in a genuinely innovative way and in a global context. The point of this chapter, then, is not to write a "nit-picker's guide to *Debt*" or to assess whether Graeber gets the detail right for the European early Middle Ages, since he is not after all concerned with them for their own sake and in fact deals with them very little in the book. Graeber's thesis is anyway not of the kind that can be verified or invalidated from the perspective of a single narrow area of specialism. My starting point is that it is useful to think with for historians. My aim is to try to see what the period looks like when it is asked the questions drawn from Graeber's model—as well as, perhaps, what questions it might have to ask of the model in return.

From Axial Slaves to Serfs in Late Antiquity: Old and New Narratives

The Middle Ages matter a great deal within the book because they are a crucial phase of Graeber's historical cycles of credit. They are in fact the historical

Alice Rio, *After the Axial Age* In: *Debt in the Ancient Mediterranean and Near East.* Edited by: John Weisweiler,
Oxford University Press. © Oxford University Press 2023. DOI: 10.1093/oso/9780197647172.003.0011

moment that establishes the process as cyclical in the first place: the only period of letup in the debt crises and commodification of human beings characteristic of the earlier Axial Age and of later early modern and modern empire-building. Without the medieval period, the story would be one not of cycles but of continual intensification. All of this makes the moment of transition away from the Axial Age into the medieval period, and the mechanisms by which it took place, particularly important.[1]

Graeber's account of the transition from the Roman to the post-Roman world involves the following narrative: While in the classical period Roman Gaul had been an "endless succession of slave plantations" (p. 252), "[b]y the waning days of the empire, most people in the countryside who weren't outright slaves had become, effectively, debt peons to some rich landlord, a situation in the end formalized by imperial decrees binding peasants to the land" (p. 232). Late Roman society began looking more and more like feudal Europe, "with magnates on their great estates surrounded by dependent peasants, debt servants, and an endless variety of slaves. . . . The barbarian invasions that overthrew the empire merely formalized the situation, largely eliminating chattel slavery, but at the same time introducing the notion that the noble classes were really descendants of the Germanic conquerors, and that the common people were inherently subservient" (pp. 204–205). Thus "[f]ormer debt peons were gradually transformed into serfs or vassals" (p. 286). The overall dynamic presented here is one in which the enslavement of debtors, promoted and enforced by the late-antique state, took on so much momentum that it eventually culminated in the establishment of a much more formal and fixed hierarchy, so securely established as to survive the demise of the state that had originally underpinned it. This completed the transition from an Axial system, in which debt was the key mechanism that justified inequality, into a medieval one where inequality was simply a permanent, self-justifying fixture explicitly structuring society.

This outline is rooted in a traditional and now essentially discarded narrative positing a direct line of descent between the forms of oppression of the late Roman era and those of the "feudal" era. It is now well established that Roman Gaul was not a succession of slave plantations. Despite receiving a disproportionate level of attention in classical-era agricultural treatises, latifundia were in fact very rare in the Roman empire in general, except in Italy and perhaps North Africa in the first and second centuries CE.[2] The late-antique poor becoming debt peons to rich landlords is strongly reminiscent of a passage by Salvian, a fifth-century Christian polemicist, which describes poor men unable to pay their taxes having to cede their own property to great landlords and becoming their *coloni* (tenants of free status but in theory bound to remain on the same estate). Salvian likens this to Circe turning men into pigs.[3] This is a much-quoted passage and provides a vivid illustration of the oppressive nature of the late-antique state as well as of great landlords. The idea of a direct line of continuity between these late-antique *coloni*, as described by Salvian, and medieval serfs goes back to the late nineteenth century and specifically to Fustel de Coulanges.[4] There has since then been an extraordinarily long-lasting debate over the nature of the late-antique colonate, regarding such issues as how far it may have reflected, and then in turn helped to forge, a new reality on the ground; whether it was meaningful essentially for purposes of tax assessment; or how far it may have been intended to further the interests of landlords as well as those of the state.[5] Either way, it is not now thought to have led directly to medieval serfdom.[6] While the late-antique colonate probably, and central medieval serfdom certainly, each in their different ways represent an intensification of control over rural tenants, they seem to have corresponded to two quite distinct and unrelated moments, without a clear trajectory from one to the other.[7] The period in between (the early Middle Ages), by contrast, has been characterized as much less consistently oppressive: without a Roman state but as yet without the sort of totalizing, all-encompassing, and permanent hierarchy that lords, churchmen, and kings started to wish into existence, with some degree of success, from the twelfth century onward.

While all this does mean that Graeber's narrative is some way off the current state of the field, it is not necessarily bad news for his overall argument. If anything, it could help to smooth out some inconsistencies and make the European version of the Middle Ages look less like the odd one out.

How Medieval were The Early Middle Ages?

The very idea of Europe as an "odd one out" may require some explanation, since the Middle Ages are at heart such a deeply European-centric historiographical construct: Only modernity is more so and not by much. The desire to include the centuries before 1500 within the scope of global history has recently led to an intense drive to unmoor the concept of the Middle Ages from western European narratives and imperialist historical trajectories, but this project is still very much in its infancy. It was even more so when *Debt* came out.[8] Graeber came up with an unusually challenging version of what the Eurasian Middle Ages might be about, which turns everything upside down by removing Europe's status as paradigmatic template of historical development and replacing it with that of a marginal and tardy misfit:

"the Middle Ages proper are best seen as having begun not in Europe but in India and China, between 400 and 600 AD, and then sweeping across much of the western half of Eurasia with the advent of Islam. They only really reached Europe four hundred years later."[9]

This puts the beginning of the "medieval" period at around 1000 in Europe. The chronology indicates that Graeber is here subscribing to the much-disputed "feudal revolution" model, which places the key moment of change from ancient to feudal societies just around then, through a "mutation of the year 1000."[10] The obvious inference is that Graeber thinks Europe before then was still more Roman, or Axial, than it was medieval. But it is difficult to know for sure how he would characterize this pre-1000 period because he does not really discuss early medieval Europe in its own right in the chapter on the Middle Ages— understandably enough since his periodization places them outside the "medieval" period proper.

Graeber does, however, discuss one early medieval society at some length, and that is early medieval Ireland. He discusses it not in his chapter on the medieval period, though, but in a chapter otherwise concerned with much earlier societies, as part of what he refers to as the "heroic" age—implying it had more in common with the world of the *Iliad* than with the other medieval societies featured in the book. Graeber situates Ireland in the historical cycle as "*still* a human economy, in which money was used for social purposes," not commercial ones (p. 176, my italics). It is not that he considers early medieval Ireland as a never-never land, lying outside of time, where everyone did things differently from the rest of Europe, as it has sometimes been treated. Indeed, he goes out of his way to note that the system of compensation for injury on which he concentrates his discussion existed in every other region of Europe at the time (p. 172). This, then, puts early medieval Europe as a whole somehow a little outside of time or, at the very least, out of step with the cyclical schema developed in the later, chronological chapters. It is therefore not quite clear whether Graeber considers the early Middle Ages to be too Roman or too much of a throwback to even earlier, pre-Axial societies to count as truly "medieval." Either way, they seem behind the curve.

Graeber's Global Middle Ages

How, then, does Graeber define the "medieval" globally? Graeber characterizes the medieval period as marked by "the decline of empire, armies, and cash economy, [and] the rise of religious authorities, independent of the state, who win much of their popular legitimacy through their ability to regulate emerging credit systems" (p. 258). The state, its size, and the intensity of its violence feature in the book as the key variables affecting the meanings and consequences of debt. For Graeber, cash-based conquer-and-spend state tactics led to an emphasis on bullion over virtual credit. This was the ultimate source of the strictures of the Axial Age, when cash intensified both economic inequality and problems of debt. At the same time, cash was also used to some extent to mitigate its own worst effects through a combination of handouts to citizens and reliance on chattel slavery as a source of labor, both of which were also enabled by the imperial conquest that was driving the whole process in the first place. The state was thus ultimately responsible for the most anti-social uses of money during the Axial Age, rooted in conflict and expansionist policies.[11] The decline of the state and, consequently, of its warlike activities during the medieval period resulted in fundamentally more benign consequences for debt, once more essentially involving "virtual" money within networks of trust.

Graeber, broadly speaking, ascribes to religious institutions a much less oppressive character than the state, as well as much less socially harmful uses for money.[12] There is, indeed, a sense of ongoing tension throughout the book between state and religion, starting with the initial opposition at the beginning of the Axial Age between, on the one hand, early city-states and, on the other, major world religions emerging in hostile reaction to them among marginalized patriarchal pastoralists hard-pressed to protect their households. These world religions, according to Graeber, then contributed to forging the new and more benign character of "medieval" societies as they became dominant. Axial-Age states had spread coinage and sponsored markets, and thereby laid down the conditions for debt spirals, largely as a means of supplying their own needs and collecting revenue. By contrast, control of bullion by religious institutions, which Graeber sees as characteristic of the medieval period, resulted in thesaurization. This then allowed these institutions to act as controls and guarantors in a context of increased reliance on virtual money and trust-based credit arrangements throughout rural society: "real gold and silver ended up largely in churches, monasteries, and temples, money became virtual again, and at the same time, the tendency everywhere was to set up overarching moral institutions meant to regulate the process and, in particular, to establish certain protections for debtors" (p. 268). This enabled the emergence of quite complex virtual credit arrangements and financial instruments, which are also counted by Graeber as a feature of the Middle Ages and the one most conspicuously lacking in Europe before the twelfth century.

In practice, this basic outline of what the "medieval" consists in finds extremely diverse applications in the different societies described by Graeber (India, China, the Islamic world, and western Europe). India provides the initial type, in some ways the truest to the model and probably the one that will seem most familiar to a European early medievalist, with small states, no cities, and little coinage. There, social asymmetry became rooted no longer in debt relationships but instead in a much more permanent form of hierarchy (castes).

Graeber sees the "hierarchical" moral rationale for economic relations as dominant in medieval India as well as in medieval Europe (pp. 109–112). Unlike

Graeber's other two possible rationales ("communism" and "exchange," his chapter 5), hierarchy is not grounded in reciprocity. It is in fact the opposite of reciprocity: That is, it is inherently disposed to making obligations permanent rather than based on a tit-for-tat dialectic. While these obligations may be occasionally justified in reciprocal terms in principle, for instance, with protection from lords given in exchange for food renders from peasants, this is never understood in terms of x amount of protection for y amount of food renders: Instead, dues are based on tradition and existing power relationships. This makes the hierarchical mode the least conducive to the logic of debt since entering into a credit–debt relationship rests on the idea of temporariness (since the relationship is in principle destined to expire on repayment) as well as of putative equality between the parties. This sense of putative equality, of an initially even and fair starting point, is what had led to the horrors of the Axial Age, by removing all sense of moderation from the punitive demands made of defaulting debtors, seen not as inherently inferior but as equal, free, and responsible agents brought low through their own moral failings. By contrast, much more robust and explicit hierarchies, such as those found in the Middle Ages, paradoxically resulted in less devastating effects for debt, involving as they did permanent relationships of dependence and protection, less apt to turn people into commodities. Graeber thus sees more stable and permanent hierarchies as standing in contrast with chattel, commercial, and/or debt slavery. He notes a simultaneous disappearance of chattel slavery around 600 CE in India, China, and Europe, which he associates with a dramatic cutting down in size of the commercial cash economy and its replacement with trust-based credit systems (pp. 212–213). The change to a more hierarchical society, Graeber argues, left no real place for slavery in medieval India, where debtors were typically no longer enslaved (pp. 256–257); for Europe, he notes that serfdom was an "extraordinary improvement over the terrors of the Axial Age" (p. 251) and that, "[h]owever oppressed medieval serfs might have been, their plight was nothing compared with that of their Axial Age equivalents" (p. 252).

China and the Islamic world present very different case scenarios, in particular through the persistence of many Axial-Age features, not least the state. What really matters in defining "medieval" societies for Graeber, though, is not necessarily the *absence* of a state, coinage, a standing army, or slavery but the breakdown in the nexus connecting all these things with markets and debt. The significance of each element was fundamentally altered by the breaking of the nexus: Without it, empire and conquest, usury, debt peonage, and the commodification of human beings conducive to chattel slavery were largely robbed of the centrality they had had during the Axial Age. For instance, in China the state eventually joined and enabled the use of virtual paper money as opposed to cash and took on many features elsewhere typical of religious institutions, such as attempting to limit usury. In the Islamic world, Graeber sees the state as fundamentally divorced from wider society, forcing the military–coinage–slavery complex into a much shorter loop (one notable shortcut being the use of slaves *in* the military).[13] This privileging of the whole chain or nexus over any particular element of it is what allows his concept of the "medieval" to be so elastic and to bring together societies that initially seem like very unlikely bedfellows. Each certainly presents major exceptions to the parameters he sets out: India in not becoming dominated by a religion sprung in reaction to the brutalities of the Axial Age; China in continuing to have a state; the Islamic world in continuing to have states *and* slavery; and Europe in the comparatively late arrival of more sophisticated forms of credit money, as well as in its conjunction of virtual money with war and military expansion.

Money, Human Value, and Commodities

Within Graeber's model, then, early medieval Europe could count as medieval insofar as it witnessed a collapse of widespread coinage, a decline of state control, a concentration of resources into the hands of religious institutions, and the disappearance of slavery (pp. 250, 252, 282–283). What might count *against* it being medieval, or make it not quite *yet* medieval by Graeber's definition, is the absence of any very complex credit arrangements or abstract financial instruments, such as tallies, promissory notes, or things like insurance or corporations, which would only turn up later—and, perhaps, the relative absence of a strong discourse against usury or of meaningful attempts by religious institutions to regulate it. Graeber gives no examples of an anti-usury discourse between the patristic era—when it first arose, after the manner of much Axial-Age religious thought, in hostile reaction to contemporary practice, in this case "the ancient world's last debt crisis" (p. 283)—and scholasticism in the twelfth century.

Coinage, clearly, was a key area of change. There was certainly much less of it about than there had been in the Roman world and no longer in the low denominations necessary for routine use. As we just saw, Graeber classifies Ireland, his main case study, as a "heroic," more than a "medieval," society. The main difference between heroic societies and European medieval societies in the central and later Middle Ages, for Graeber, seems to be that in heroic societies status was much less secure and life more like a competition of every moment. Another main difference is that money was not really to do with economic life and more about quantifying the value of people rather than the value of commodities— above all through the concept of honor price (or, elsewhere, *wergeld*). Graeber takes it as highly significant that the main symbolic currency used to calculate honor price in Irish law codes was not money but slave women, even when the slave women in question had become, as they had by the early Middle Ages, only an abstract unit of account rather than corresponding to actual flesh-and-blood people, as suggested by the occasional reference to paying "half" a *cumal*, or slave woman. This symbolism still underlines that, in societies of this kind, honor price was indexed ultimately not on material goods but on other people so that the value of human beings could only be calculated using other human beings as a point of reference: a king's honor expressed as multiple slave women, a woman's honor as a fraction of her husband's.

For Graeber, this point in fact applies whether or not the unit of account was women or money. Ireland is obviously an extreme case in having no coined money at all until very late in the early medieval period and no Axial past to change from since it had never been part of the Roman Empire. It did use bullion: Even though law codes continued to use traditional units of account such as cows and slave women, by the time they were being produced in writing, using gold, silver, or bronze had become an important marker of elite status.[14] This, however, does not affect Graeber's analysis, provided bullion itself functioned essentially as a prestige item rather than a commercial currency. Even when money existed as a point of reference (as it did in contemporary continental law codes, p. 172), it was not a vehicle for commodity exchange: It expressed human value, not the value of goods. If, Graeber says, Irish lawyers were able to put an "exact monetary price on human dignity," it was because the price of honor was not in fact in the same category as more prosaic understandings of price: "for us, the notion that the sanctity of a priest or the majesty of a king could be held equivalent to a million fried eggs or a hundred thousand haircuts is simply bizarre.... If medieval Irish jurists felt otherwise, it was because people at that time did not use money to acquire eggs or haircuts" (p. 176). In heroic societies, "the value of money was, ultimately, the value of the power to turn others into money": Slavery and slave-taking were ways of gaining honor, not commercial ventures. In other words, while these practices in heroic societies did correspond to an instrumentalization and objectification of other human beings, this did not amount to their commodification or fungibility, as in Axial-Age societies.

Graeber's picture of early medieval Europe as a society either with no coinage at all or where coinage was used essentially for gift-giving or other prestige activities at the elite level—a world where money fulfilled an exclusively social rather than a properly economic function—derives from Philip Grierson.[15] Grierson's work, foundational though it remains for early medieval numismatists, is now regarded as much too extreme in its assessment. Coinage is now thought to have been much more widespread. Graeber refers, for instance, to Carolingian *denarii* as "imaginary money," something "purely conceptual" (p. 282). This is clearly a significant overstatement. For the Carolingian era at least, that is, before *denarii* began to function as a unit of exchange for local currencies, they were absolutely not imaginary but firmly material objects; and it is equally clear that a commercial, market economy did exist, even if it was not necessarily the most important motor force behind the circulation of goods.[16]

It is certainly true that actual cash was generally used in the least trust-based relationships—those involving strangers or those carried out between members of different social groups—while virtual money almost certainly remained dominant in most other contexts.[17] The relative lack of impact of the availability of bullion and the size of the currency on the price of goods over time suggests that a large proportion of exchanges expressed in terms of money were not dependent on the use of actual cash. Nonetheless, it seems such exchanges could always translate back into cash, and there was a stable expectation that cash and virtual money could be converted into each other.[18]

The emerging consensus among historians and numismatists, then, is that most people would have been at least occasionally drawn into the orbit of coin use, in order to deal with at least some aspects of their lives. This does not invalidate Graeber's (or Grierson's) general point that coinage use was much more restricted than it had been under the Roman Empire, but it does have implications for how coinage was seen and understood, for instance, when it was referred to in law codes. It means, notably, that a system of monetary compensation for injury or death was indeed compatible with a context in which the very same kind of currency was also used to express the value of commodities. Strange as it may seem, people really were evaluating their honor using the same currency that would be used to buy goods: admittedly, not fried eggs or haircuts but certainly wheat or wine or olive oil. Although, then, cash was not very widespread at all compared to the Axial Age, enough of it existed, and it was in use through enough of society, to bring about the key possibility of equivalence between honor or life and an anonymous, impersonal quantity of bullion and, therefore, between humans and commodities. In that sense, the early Middle Ages still represent very much a post-Axial world, more than a return to a prelapsarian "heroic age."

Debt and Debt Bondage

All of this is obviously pertinent to issues of debt. It was once doubted whether any credit systems could really be said to have existed in the early Middle Ages since this seemed far too complex for the economy of the period before the eleventh and twelfth centuries. François Bougard, reviewing a wide range of archival sources, has convincingly demonstrated that credit, on the contrary, was everywhere.[19] This will come as no surprise to readers of Graeber, who shows so well that debt exists everywhere all the time, regardless of the degree of complexity or monetization of the economy. The kind of debt he associates with the Middle Ages, as we saw, involves virtual money, not cash, and less predatory circumstances, within networks of trust. This fits the early medieval picture only partially. Bougard shows that credit was often motivated by the desire or need specifically to obtain liquidities, most often smallish sums, of a few *solidi* or tens of *solidi*.[20] The fact that this was a period when cash might be hard to come by could then, paradoxically, have brought about a situation where credit was *more* cash-centered, not less, and when its relative scarcity could also make repayment difficult. On the other hand, interest itself was hardly ever monetary, which makes a difference.[21] Most of the documentation involves mortgages—that is, loans made against land, in which the land itself functioned as the security and its produce as the interest. While non-repayment of debt in these cases could, then, lead to loss of property, it was not of the kind that could spiral out of control beyond that point.

Credit arrangements were certainly very much embedded in existing social networks, and they were typically one element within a more complex and nuanced relationship, rather than its be-all and end-all. But they did not always remain so: Although assets given as security could not normally be transferred to a third party, the credit note might well be, so there was always a possibility that a debt would be transferred to a new creditor with whom the debtor had no preexisting social relationship.[22] This did not alter the terms of the original agreement, but it is hard to imagine that the less formal expectations which debtor and creditor might have had of one another would not have been upended in the process. For instance, the theoretical connection between "virtual" money and hard cash may well have resumed very sharply in such circumstances, to the detriment of borrowers.

Bougard's conclusion is that credit in this period was not chiefly an emergency measure and was not particularly associated with either rampant pauperization or concentration of wealth.[23] Admittedly, the surviving source base is unlikely to feature the very poorest since it is naturally skewed toward credit arrangements involving land as security. Poorer people are much more likely to feature in loan agreements made not against land but against labor and service. Agreements of this kind are much less likely to have been kept in archives over the very long term and so survive mostly through formularies (documents gathered as models for future use).[24] These contain many instances of what appears to be debt bondage. It is not always easy to be sure since unrepaid debt was commonly treated as a theft, so that the penalty was presented as penal enslavement rather than debt bondage. In practice it made little difference since penal enslavement expressed a debt too: the compensation owed to someone for having wronged them, when the culprit could not afford to pay it. Alternatively, debt bondage could also, in another set of symbolic associations altogether, be expressed as a self-sale or self-gift in which the self-seller or giver supposedly handed themselves over "of their own free will," as the documents nearly always stipulate.[25]

These different ways of expressing debt bondage, as a gift, a sale, or compulsory enslavement for debt or crime, operated on a continuum reflecting different kinds of wrangling and situations: My own favorite is the case of a man who negotiated to hand over just half of his freedom, with part-time service and part-time liability to corporal punishment, in exchange for a loan.[26] All this can make the language of debt difficult to interpret. This is of course true in all periods because it is always such a charged issue, but it was perhaps especially so in this one. It is hard to know, for instance, how many debts specified in these agreements were ever intended to be repaid. It may well be that some of these credit notes were just a way of expressing the creation of an intentionally much more lasting hierarchical relationship, in which case the use of the more egalitarian language of debt would only represent a documentary form, a sort of Axial-Age aftertaste. This would not be surprising for this period, and sometimes this may well have been the case. But there is no reason to choose one way or the other: The language of debt was evidently used to do many different things. Sometimes it really was about cash—this much is clear when, for instance, debtors tried to add unusual clauses and to guard against long-term consequences—and sometimes default may well have been expected and the debt only a way of entering a permanent power relationship or fine-tuning a preexisting one. Either way, it is difficult to see a stabilizing of debt into a definitive hierarchical order taking place during this period.

On the face of it, then, the interchangeability of human beings with material goods seems to have stuck remarkably tenaciously as a possibility throughout the early Middle Ages. If anything, it seems to have become easier than it had been in the Axial Age, and people seem to have become much more matter of fact about it. Unlike the many Christian voices raised against usury in the patristic era, examples of religious objections to debt bondage from the sixth century onward are few and far between. The Christian discourse against the oppression of the poor by the rich and powerful certainly remained, but it went through many shifts and changes in emphasis. Salvian, writing around the middle of the fifth century, had accused the rich of taking advantage of poor people's poverty in order to drive them into slavery and had criticized them severely for their lack of Christian compassion and charity.[27] By the time Charles the Bald, king of West Francia, issued his Edict of Pîtres (864), it had become possible to talk of buying poor people during times of famine as a religious and moral duty—something that reflected well on the buyer.[28]

The effects of debt bondage might sometimes be mitigated. Although there was usually nothing to distinguish them in law or in vocabulary, in many places in early medieval Europe there seems to have been a growing tendency, both in principle and in practice, to distinguish people who had become unfree within their own community through some fault or accident from those who had been born so or who had been captured through war or raiding. Penal slaves, for instance, seem to have been freed at their owner's death preferentially in Anglo-Saxon England (which alone did have a different word, *witetheow*, for those enslaved as a result of legal action). In Francia penal enslavement over debt seems to have been understood increasingly as a temporary pledge rather than a definitive loss of status. A few laws explicitly tried to prevent sale, and especially sale abroad, for debt peons so that they would not be permanently severed from their social network. On the other hand, this may reflect less any fundamental aversion to community members becoming enslaved in a full sense than the relatively privileged negotiating position, compared to those captured in war, of those who could still rely on such networks. When networks of support were withdrawn or non-existent, it is clear that sale was also a possibility for debtors. Venantius Fortunatus wrote a poem about a girl who had been enslaved and sold for theft.[29] A capitulary of Charlemagne ruled that "those who have thrown themselves on the emperor's mercy and sought his intervention are not to be bound, enslaved or sold"—showing an expectation that violent demands could be made of defaulting debtors.[30] Wulfstan of York, a major religious and political figure of late Anglo-Saxon England, bemoaned the sale of poor people and their children abroad in his apocalyptic *Sermon of the Wolf to the English*.[31]

Of course, self-sale and penal enslavement had happened during the Roman era too, but ideologically this had been very much frowned upon—indeed, had to be swept under the carpet. It was, after all, the Roman world that had produced such legal maxims as "a free man is not to be valued at any price."[32] By the early medieval period, by contrast, it seems most people, including Christian commentators, had managed to make their peace with the fact that, when someone owed money and could not pay it back, the normal solution was for them simply to become their creditor's unfree dependent.

Chattel Slavery

All this is not to say that the early Middle Ages were in the grip of a perennial debt crisis. There is no way to quantify these agreements or guess how many people might have been involved. The point is qualitative rather than quantitative, but it is nevertheless suggestive of a change in attitudes which did not go the way of more benign consequences for debt or of increasing irrelevance for debt slavery and peonage—if anything, the opposite. In this case at least, therefore, a less monetized, less market-driven economy, governed by much less powerful states, in which debt was perhaps less pervasive and certainly less apt to spiral out of control through interest rates, seems—paradoxically within Graeber's scheme—to have led to a situation in which the consequences of default were, if anything, held less in check than they had been during the Axial Age. The social embeddedness of debt could lead to much more humane outcomes for defaulting debtors but also to considerably worse ones, when social networks either failed or became activated by creditors in more aggressive ways.

A parallel point, again qualitative rather than quantitative, might be made regarding chattel slavery. Graeber proposes 600 CE as the end point for commercial, chattel slavery across China, India, and Europe but not, crucially, the Islamic world. This matters because the demand for slaves in the Islamic world was partly met from Europe: through direct raiding in Spain, southern France, and Italy; via the extensive Viking trading networks which developed from this time throughout northern and eastern Europe; and via Venice, which seems to have become an important middleman in the sale of Slavic slaves. In eastern Europe, the scale of the trade and its economic impact seem to have been enormous, judging from finds of Islamic coin hoards there—perhaps even to the point of fostering state-building in Slavic lands.[33] More generally, regions on the so-called periphery of Europe (highly politically fragmented, with little or no state, and where short-range raiding for movable goods was still an important and normal part of elite political and economic behavior), rather than the bigger political formations such as the Carolingian empire, seem to have been the ones best placed to take advantage of Muslim demand when it emerged from the mid-eighth century onward.[34]

The situation could be likened to that of Africa during the Atlantic trade, a parallel Graeber makes in connection with Ireland: "a human economy perched uncomfortably on the fringe of an expanding commercial one."[35] It is true that during the early Middle Ages this trade seems to have fed only minimally into the labor supply within Europe itself: Long-distance, commercial chattel slavery seems to have been concentrated on trading routes and elite households, partly because of the very large expense which imported slaves represented. At the same time, there is some evidence for it from everywhere in Europe, albeit in small numbers compared to those who went toward the Viking "Northern Arc" or the Islamic world. Slave-raiding and slave-trading in northern Europe did eventually come to be seen as something that barbarians, pagans, or bad Christians typically did to other pagan barbarians; but in southern Europe, in Italy, and in the Iberian peninsula, which had more mixed and diverse religious communities, the distinction between insiders and outsiders was made on a more individual basis so that the purchase and sale of at least *some* people always remained entirely acceptable and unproblematic. This is what allowed chattel slavery, dealing in Muslims, pagans, and sometimes Orthodox Christians, to take off again in a big way in these areas during the later Middle Ages and the Renaissance.[36] It anyway took a long time for the ranks of the legitimately enslavable to become definitively restricted to non-Christians: Genoese and southern Italian documents show Christians being sold by other Christians as chattels well into the twelfth century.[37] All of this suggests that social, political, and economic changes in the early Middle Ages did not in fact result in the kind of blanket popular rejection of slavery which Graeber associates with medieval Europe and which he regards as a grassroots movement (pp. 211–212; 432, n. 3).

Conclusion

How much does all this matter for Graeber's argument? Eventually, of course, things did settle into a situation conforming slightly more to his definition of the "medieval"; and since the European early Middle Ages had not been meant to be covered by this definition in the first place, the preceding observations do not even require any change in periodization. But it may pose some useful questions regarding what mechanisms should be envisaged when considering a change from "Axial" to "medieval," in particular the role of the state within it.

The role of the state did change very significantly during the early Middle Ages compared to the Axial Age. The Roman state had been in principle profoundly opposed to the enslavement of citizens through self-sale, and it kept a theoretically strong distinction between penal convicts and slaves, though in practice, as Graeber argues, it had functioned as a promoter and enforcer of spiraling debts through its continual demand for taxation, encouragement of markets, and insistence on cash use.[38] The barbarian successor states, by contrast, took self-sale and penal enslavement as a fact of life in their legislation and had much less of a problem with it—something that is not really surprising in view of the fact that they no longer really had any ambition to regulate the status of individuals.[39] On the other hand, by then it is also hard to see the state (such as it was during this period) as a key driving force behind either markets, the use of cash, or widespread debt. Although the use of coinage in the early Middle Ages was somewhat greater than Graeber allows for, it was not primarily driven by any late-antique-style tax-and-spend policies nor, in general, by the needs of the state (though it could enjoy some side benefits).

This means there was without doubt a breaking of the nexus between state, coinage, a standing army, slavery, and markets and debt. These things all existed but were no longer connected to each other in the same integrated sequence. Clearly, then, this was no longer an Axial world. But it equally clearly took an

extremely long time for this changed situation to bring about the key consequences which Graeber associates with a society with such a small state, tiny cash
economy, and pervasive religious authority—that is, a lessening of the tendency
to make a direct equivalence between people, on the one hand, and cash or material goods, on the other. There was still considerable scope for the commodification of human beings. Money was sometimes less virtual than Graeber allows for,
and there were still plenty of debt peons. Nor, unlike in the Axial Age, was there
any real concern to offer minimal protections against the worst consequences of
debt to a citizen body. Co-religionists and neighbors, when they were socially
weak enough, were for centuries included in the category of the enslavable and of
the human-as-commodity.

As Arietta Papaconstantinou also finds in her own contribution to this volume on Egypt under the early caliphate (Chapter 10), harder-edged, deeply
exploitative forms of credit persisted for a long time into the medieval period,
including in contexts involving virtual credit within communities. Admittedly,
Egypt's microcredit networks, even when they dealt in "virtual" currency, were
still "embedded within a macroeconomic system of coin money" and affected by
the needs of an extractive imperial power, in a way that early medieval European
communities were not. Nonetheless, similar traits apply to Europe as well: Both
cases suggest that non-predominantly state-driven, virtual money too could
be turned to profoundly anti-social uses. Once the values and habits of a coin-
centric credit framework had taken root, it might be sustained through the logic
of practice even in the absence of very deep continuity in terms of sociopolitical
structures. The genie was hard to put back in the bottle.

What a rereading of the earlier medieval evidence in light of Graeber's model
might emphasize, then, is that the disappearance of state institutions and mechanisms of enforcement does not necessarily yield more benign results. The early
medieval example shows that the mere memory of a strong state could sometimes
give elites the ability to make some of its tools and instruments of domination survive, even in spite of a near-total absence of strong institutional backing. Indeed,
they could even make these instruments go further. It took a very long time for
the sort of mellowing described by Graeber to come into being—certainly much,
much longer than it took for the state to float up away from its Axial underpin-
nings into a much airier structure or for coinage to flow into much more niche
uses—and so much so as to make it difficult to think of the breaking of the nexus
as a sufficient direct cause of such mellowing. The centuries-long European gap
between the Axial and the "medieval," then, may point to a need to fill out in
more detail the causes of the disappearance of the one and the appearance of
the other—including, perhaps, in other Eurasian case studies. This is all to the
good: No really interesting book can ever be the final word on anything, even on

its own terms. None of this, therefore, is to take away from Graeber's wonderful gift to medievalists everywhere—of turning "our" Middle Ages once again into a foreign country.

Acknowledgment

I warmly thank Rory Naismith for commenting on a draft version of this chapter.

12

Afterword

Keith Hart

THE IDEA OF modernity rests on believing that we have escaped from everything that went before. Its basis is the evidence of wholesale social change in the
two centuries since the Industrial Revolution. But this belief is a groundless fantasy. The founders of modern social theory, especially Karl Marx, saw the two-
sided character of societies built on capitalism. He understood that the shift
from peasant agriculture to urban manufacturing massively increased the scope
for production and accumulation; but, by calling the latter "surplus value," he
drew attention to parallels with extraction of surplus labor in agrarian civilizations whose development rested on intensifying labor inputs with diminishing
returns—working harder for less. Capitalism, in other words, was feudalism in
drag, resting as it did on private property that could never organize complex societies, thereby opening the door for the state in these societies.

Workers in the eighteenth century's two most advanced regions, western
Europe and China, lived permanently under the threat of starvation and death.
This prompted Robert Malthus, whose *Essay on the Principle of Population* was
published in 1798, to argue that improving their food supplies would only lead
to population growth, land scarcity, and more starvation. It is unsurprising that
millions of European peasants in the next century voted with their feet for
urban wages, however miserable the conditions, over that. I argue here that early
twenty-first-century world society increasingly resembles the old regime of agrarian civilizations. This gives *Debt in the Ancient Mediterranean and Near East* a
salience that goes beyond what its authors claim for it.

Inspired by the work of anthropologist David Graeber's 2011 book *Debt: The
First 5,000 Years*, its case studies examine the rise, fall, and aftermath of large
empires in "western Eurasia," taking in much of the first millennium BCE and the

Keith Hart, *Afterword* In: *Debt in the Ancient Mediterranean and Near East*. Edited by: John Weisweiler,
Oxford University Press. © Oxford University Press 2023. DOI: 10.1093/oso/9780197647172.003.0012

first millennium CE. The unifying focus is the role of debt in a shared form of political economy defined by precious metal coins, slavery, warfare, and long-distance trade. They included the Persian Empire, the Greek city-states, Alexander's conquests, and Rome after defeating Carthage, then the empire's expansion, decline, and fall. The chapters discuss early Greece compared with India, Greece in its classical period, the Roman Republic, the late Roman Empire, Sasanian Iran, early Islam, Egypt after the Islamic conquest, and early medieval Europe. A lucid editorial introduction and a general assessment of the period's relevance for political economy today bookend these chapters.

The world as a whole now resembles the advanced centers of agrarian civilization more than the bourgeois revolutions that thought they had swept them away. Three centuries of political struggle and economic development have left our world in a condition very similar to the arbitrary regimes that provoked Rousseau's discourse on inequality, published in 1754. How else can one describe a world where a socially exclusive minority ("White men in suits") holds so much power over an impoverished mass whose powerlessness is now measured by how little money they have to spend? The latest wave of mechanical invention has granted a few men control of the global information industry, while billions of people lack material essentials. The project of documenting national communities, largely by means of statistics, is 150 years old. Since the Second World War, it has become normal to collect statistics on the global population; but thinking about world society as a single entity has not yet taken hold. It is about time that it did, for our moment in history, the last half century, is when it was first formed in a meaningful sense. Yet the fragmentation of perspective produced by national consciousness prevents us from imagining the human community as a whole.

There are two main features of our world: An explosion of markets, transport, and communications has led to an unprecedented integration of society as a single interactive network; and a neoliberal counter-revolution against postwar developmental states has restored the polarization of rich and poor within countries and between regions, evoking the gilded age of the 1890s more than any phase of the last century. Becoming closer and more unequal at the same time is a dangerous combination—another feature that we share with the first millennium BCE.

The West spends billions a year on pet food, perfumes, and cosmetics ("let them eat dog food"), a sum equal to the estimated additional cost of providing basic education, health, nutrition, water, and sanitation for those deprived of them. The rate of car ownership in rich countries is 40% but 2% in most developing countries. The rich pollute the world fifty times more than the poor, but the latter are more likely to die from the pollution. The 2009 Copenhagen climate change conference failed because the West would accept only small reductions in carbon emissions. The Chinese and Brazilian presidents both made the same joke: Obama was like a rich man who dines on luxuries alone, invites the neighbors in for coffee, and then asks them to split the bill. This did not prevent Western propaganda from blaming the BRICS countries (Brazil, Russia, India, China, and South Africa) for the failure.

Solutions to the obscene inequality and ecological risks facing world society require us to focus on the global picture first. As a thought experiment, we might conceive of humanity as being stratified by wealth, race, age, and gender. Women everywhere are struggling with patriarchy. The world's poor, however, are concentrated in the Global South. The young are to be found predominantly in Africa, where the median age is under twenty years. For the first time world projections are falling because populations everywhere else are aging. This can be summarized as a two-class model. A rich, mainly White, aging minority (North America, Europe, and Japan) is surrounded by a majority who on average are a lot poorer, darker in color, and much younger. A stagnant Western elite is about to be replaced by others from whom it is separated by cultural arrogance and ingrained practices of social exclusion. United Nations' projections for world population in 2100 have Africa and Asia with 82%. Europe, which had 25% in 1900, will have shrunk to 6%.

Likewise, in agrarian civilizations, small urban elites sought to maintain control over rural masses condemned to drudgery and political impotence. The main difference is that modern world society is supposed to be organized by an ideology of human freedom and equality. This is the legacy of democratic revolutions begun in the seventeenth and eighteenth centuries that aimed to install rule by the people as the only legitimate form of government. The Industrial Revolution, which closely followed its political counterpart, made it possible for humanity to be released from material as well as social constraints on our development. But global inequality today shows that this emancipatory rhetoric is an illusion.

World society is at base as rotten as the aristocratic regimes that preceded the modern age. Power has been concentrated into forms held against the people, first as big money (capital) and then in a revived and strengthened state apparatus. In the second half of the nineteenth century, no major thinker thought that fixed political centers could control the restless energies of industrial/commercial society. Yet in the last century, the rule of elites has been restored: State bureaucracy is absolute, and world society is divided into national fragments. There is no popular government anywhere. The widespread use of democratic rhetoric cloaks the purposes of the few who jealously guard their monopoly powers. Western states are no more liberal than the Soviet Union was Marxist. At least the old regime of agrarian civilization called itself what it was—rule by the best, aristocracy. The vast majority of intellectuals and educational systems generally are complicit in the lies needed to sustain all this. Behind a smokescreen of progressive slogans, bureaucracy relies on impersonal institutions to maintain grotesquely unfair levels of inequality.

A world society polarized between a remote elite and the undifferentiated masses is unsustainable. Most people alive are exposed to conditions of poverty and violence that are humanly unacceptable, while a few enjoy the benefits of wealth in forms that were unimaginable before the Industrial Revolution. As Rousseau put it long ago (1984: 137), "It is manifestly contrary to the law of nature, however defined ... that a handful of people should gorge themselves with superfluities while the hungry multitude goes in want of necessities." Moreover, a society so cruel and indifferent to human interests is heading for economic, military, or ecological disaster, probably all three. Ours is a corrupt ancien régime that must soon find a new democratic revolution, if human intervention in the life of this planet is not to end in catastrophe.

The form of society underpinning this universal crisis is national capitalism, the attempt to manage markets and money through nation-states whose progenitor was G. W. F. Hegel in *The Philosophy of Right*, published in 1821. We know that agrarian civilizations ruled the Old World for five thousand years before the machine revolution. Since then, the world's population has multiplied seven or eight times, the proportion living in cities has gone from under 3% to one half, and energy production has grown at twice the rate of the people. As a result, many now consume more, work less, and live longer; but the benefits of machines are distributed most unevenly, with Americans consuming on average four hundred times more energy than Ugandans, for example. A third of humanity still work in agriculture with their hands; the rest live in modern cities or an urbanized countryside.

We live in a world that only appears to have made a decisive break with the past. Governments now claim to rest on science and democracy, the twin foundations of modernity and the lasting legacy of the eighteenth-century revolutions. This modern religion is similar in many ways to older claims made by world religions on behalf of God and with the same level of plausibility: If society is omniscient and good, how can there be so much suffering in the world? We are less emancipated from the past than we imagine and further from a desirable future than we would like.

The breakout from agrarian civilization was led by urban middle-class elements in a few European places beginning with the Italian Renaissance. This was not the first time: For a thousand years BCE, class coalitions based, respectively, on property in land and money slugged it out for control of Mediterranean society, before the Romans made the world safe for landed aristocracy. Fustel de Coulanges' neglected classic *The Ancient City*, which appeared in 1863, tells this story in compelling detail. The bourgeois revolution seemed to be home and dry when mechanization was married to capital accumulation. But, fearful of the proletarian monster they had made, the middle classes shrank back and embraced an alliance with the traditional specialists in crowd control, the military landlord class. Society was reconceived as homogeneous nations whose origins were shrouded in a mythical rural past, and the counter-revolution took off with a vengeance. Marx was right to rely on a feudal metaphor for the new wage-labor system since everywhere old forms of property and power were harnessed to the task of holding the workers down.

Even so, as the nineteenth century drew to a close, the issue was in the balance. The world had been drawn together by a revolution in transport and communications (steamships, railways, the telegraph) and by European empires' control of 80% of the land mass and population. The workers were concentrated in smokestack industries. Could they seize power from the owners and their political allies? The issue was settled by the First World War, when governments discovered that they now possessed unprecedented powers of social mobilization and control. Society was centralized at the top, and twentieth-century national capitalism was inaugurated. Since then, until recently, when another revolution in transport and communications has begun to undermine territorial states, the question was not whether the people or their rulers would win out but to which form of state people would be subjected all over the world. The middle classes abandoned their previous commitment to commerce and conquest in order to sup copiously at the trough of national bureaucracy, relying on their university diplomas for a lifetime of privilege as experts in social reproduction.

The institutions of agrarian civilization, developed over five millennia to extract wealth from an unfree rural workforce, are, in form if not in content, our institutions today: territorial states, landed property, warfare, racism, varieties of slavery, embattled cities, money as currency and credit, long-distance trade, an emphasis on work, world religion, and the nuclear family—all of this to preserve gross inequality.

The middle-class revolution with which the modern age began has stalled, even regressed, first allying itself with landed power and then assuming the form of rule traditional for agrarian civilization. Despite the intellectuals' original rejection of the state form as a suitable straitjacket for urban commerce, most people today are conditioned to think that no other form of society is imaginable. Consider what happened to all the wealth siphoned off by Western industrial states after the Second World War, until then the largest concentrations of money in the history of humanity. It went on subsidizing food supplies and armaments, the priorities of the bully through the ages, certainly not those of the urban consumers who paid the taxes. Then the creditor class took over, and we are back to the gilded age. No, we have never been modern, as Bruno Latour (1993) says. We are just primitives who stumbled recently into a machine revolution and cannot yet think what to do with it, beyond repeating the inhumanity of a society built unequally on agriculture.

Humanity is caught between the machine revolution and agrarian institutions, and the combination is potentially lethal. Its most striking pathology is the polarization of rich and poor at every level of society. Nothing less than a world revolution, with war as its catalyst, will redress this situation. The hangover from agrarian civilization (Gordon Childe's "urban revolution") stands in its way and cannot be discarded overnight. Preindustrial agriculture as a mode of production relied on intensification of labor inputs, making people work harder for less; and the institutions we still live by were formed by small urban elites bent on controlling populations tied to the land.

The second explanation for global inequality lies in capitalism itself. The system of money-making favors those who already have lots of it. Left unchecked, the rich will always get richer, and the poor will stay poor. Modern capitalism at first flourished when linked to machine production. These machines have hitherto been assembled in huge, centralized complexes so that power went to those capable of launching large enterprises—corporations and states. Mechanization too requires cultural and social institutions (science, education, work discipline, finance, property law) that are unevenly spread between and within societies.

As a result, world labor markets take on a dualistic character: two streams of workers, one highly paid in jobs using sophisticated machinery, the other performing tasks of little skill for low wages and in poor working conditions, often no better than in traditional agriculture. Marx identified these trends as "relative and absolute surplus value." Although squeezing profit out of sweatshop workers is a naked form of exploitation, he considered that mechanization allowed workers to be paid an even smaller share of the value of their production, despite their nominally higher wages. This, after all, was why capitalists invested in machines. The migration streams of fifty million Europeans and the same number of Asians that ushered in the last century had to be separated because the former earned nine times as much for the same work. This division entrenched labor market dualism at the global level (Lewis 1978). Now national and international institutions were devised to maintain it in the interests of the rich and powerful. Their chief function is to justify inequality and to keep the poor in their place by controlling any movement that might undermine the separation of rich and poor— in other words, the globalization of *apartheid*.

Long-distance trade in information services requires a substantial technical infrastructure. The internet has its origins in scientific collaboration between America and Europe during the Cold War, another link with the military–agrarian complex. Its main language is English. The countries that pioneered the Industrial Revolution in its first and second phases are well placed to take the lead in this third wave. Every stage of the machine revolution has been initially concentrated in a narrow enclave of world society, and this one is no different. But diffusion of the new techniques has been rapid and decentralized. Mobile phones have brought telecommunications to people's pockets and purses. Some processing and service tasks have been outsourced to where educated labor is cheaper; equally, the destruction of old manufacturing industries in the West has often been brutal. Many poor regions have become even more marginal in this latest round of uneven development; others have joined them. But global networks sustained by digital technologies do open up cracks in top-down society. The most probable outcome, further proof of the age of ancient empires' relevance to us, is world war.

This brings us back to the contemporary importance of this book's contents. The editor's introduction provides an admirable summary of the individual contributions as a set. I will restrict these remarks to a slightly fuller account of David Graeber's *Debt: The First 5,000 Years* (2011) which inspired this volume. The very word "debt" speaks of unequal power. What is it? We might be indebted to God, the sovereign, or our parents for the gift of life; but Graeber rightly insists that the social logic of debt is revealed most clearly when money is involved. Debt is an obligation with a figure attached and hence is inseparable from money. Both the French and the Germans conceive of money as debt, whereas the English speakers prefer to think of it as credit, as something for nothing, at least for now.

He devotes a lot of attention to where money comes from and what it does. States and markets each play a role in its creation, but money's dominant form has fluctuated historically between virtual credit and metal currency. Much of the contemporary world revolves round the claims we make on each other and on things: ownership, obligations, contracts, and payment of taxes, wages, rents, fees, etc. David Graeber aims to illuminate these claims through a focus on debt seen in very wide historical perspective. It is, of course, a central issue in global politics today, at all levels of society. Every day sees another example of the class struggle between debtors and creditors to shape the distribution of costs after a long credit boom went dramatically bust in 2008.

His book also feeds off popular movements, which is not surprising given how much time he spent as an anarchist outside the classroom and his study. His analytical framework is spelled out in great detail. Two chapters tackle the origins of money in barter and "primordial debt," respectively. He shows, forcefully and elegantly, how implausible the standard liberal origin myth of money as a medium of exchange is; but he also rejects as a nationalist myth the main opposing theory that traces money's origins as a means of payment and unit of account to state power.

Two more chapters introduce what is for me a principal idea of the book, the contrast between "human economies" and those dominated by money and markets (Graeber prefers to call these "commercial economies" and sometimes "capitalism"). He identifies the main characteristics of human economies and then shows what happens when they are forcefully incorporated into the economic orbit of larger "civilizations," including our own (the Atlantic slave trade). This is to some extent a great divide theory of history. In a sense, "human economies" are a world we have lost but might recover after the revolution. Graeber (2011: 130) points out that these societies are not necessarily more humane, just that "they are economic systems primarily concerned not with the accumulation of wealth, but with the creation, destruction, and rearranging of human beings." They use money but mainly as "social currencies" whose aim is to maintain relations between people rather than to purchase things. An extended reflection on slavery and freedom—a pair he sees as being driven by a culture of honor and indebtedness—culminates in the ultimate contradiction underpinning modern liberal economics, a worldview that conceives of individuals as being socially isolated in ways that could only be prepared for by a long history of enslaving conquered peoples.

So far, Graeber has relied heavily on anthropological material, especially from African societies, to illustrate the world that the West transformed, although his account of money's origins draws quite heavily on the example of ancient Mesopotamia. Now he formalizes his theory of money to organize a compendious review of world history in four stages: the era from c. 3000 BCE that saw the first urban civilizations; the "Axial Age," which he, rather unusually, dates from 800 BCE to 600 CE; the Middle Ages (600–1450); and the age of "the great capitalist empires," from 1450 to the US dollar's rupture with the gold standard in 1971, which is indeed the pivotal moment in contemporary economic history. This periodization relies heavily on long historical swings between broad types of money. Graeber calls these "credit" and "bullion," that is, money as a virtual measure of personal relations, like IOUs, and as currency or impersonal things made from precious metals for circulation. The first and third eras mainly used credit money, he thinks, and phases 2 and 4, bullion. The present book examines phase 2, with some leakage into 3.

Money started out as a unit of account, administered by institutions such as Mesopotamia's temples and banks, as well as states, largely as a way of measuring debt relations between people that were often occasioned by producers' unmet needs before they harvested their crops. Coinage was introduced in the first millennium as part of a complex linking warfare, mercenary soldiers, slavery, looting, mines, trade in exports, and provisioning of large armies on the move. The period from 1971 is obviously transitional, but Georg Simmel, in *The Philosophy of Money* (1900), identified money's material form and the community of users as sources for its credibility. The recent rise of virtual credit money as a result of the digital revolution has undermined both. Ours could become a multi-polar world, more like the Middle Ages than the last two centuries. It could offer more scope for "human economies" or at least "social currencies." The debt crisis might provoke revolutions and then, who knows, debt cancellation along the lines of the ancient *jubilee*. Perhaps the whole institutional complex based on states and capitalism will be replaced by forms of society more directly responsive to ordinary people and their capacity for "everyday communism."

Graeber argues that economic life everywhere is based on a plural combination of moral principles that take on a different complexion when organized by dominant forms. Thus, helping each other as equals is essential to capitalist societies, but capitalism distorts and marginalizes this human propensity. Yet he appears to expect a radical rupture with capitalist states fairly soon, and this is reflected in his "stage" theory of history. Inevitably in a book like David Graeber's the fact checkers will catch him out sometimes. But it is a work of immense erudition and insight and deserves to be celebrated as such, as our authors do here.

Notes

CHAPTER I

1. For Jaspers 1949 and Eisenstadt 1986, the Axial Age ends around 200 BCE. Graeber deliberately extends these chronological boundaries to include the period until the dissolution of the agrarian empires of antiquity. Wittrock 2015 usefully summarizes recent debates on the Axial Age.

2. Graeber 2011: 223–250; for the "military–coinage–slavery complex," see 229 and index. On the "military–coinage complex," see Ingham 2004: 99–100.

3. Graeber 2011: 251–306.

4. Graeber 2001, 2004, 2007.

5. Graeber 2009b.

6. Graeber 2009a.

7. Graeber 2011: 21–42.

8. The classic analysis of barter (on which Graeber draws) is Humphrey 1985. For a collection of anthropological studies on the subject, see Humphrey and Hugh-Jones 1992.

9. Graeber 2011: 89–126. Cf. 2009a: 112–117.

10. Polanyi 1944. For an engagement of Graeber with Polanyi, see Graeber 2009a.

11. The concept of "human economy" is developed by Hart, Laville, and Cattani 2010 and Graeber 2011: 127–164. The differences between Graeber's and Hart's conceptions are laid out in Hart 2013.

12. Graeber 2011: 223–250, quoted at 227.

13. North 1981 and 1990 succinctly summarizes the chief tenets of neo-institutional economics.

14. North and Thomas 1973 and Acemoğlu and Robinson 2012 sketch neo-institutional theories of world economic history.

15. Boldizzoni 2011, especially 18–86, highlights the methodological limitations of this approach.

16. Milanovic 2019 assesses the logic of the Chinese model of political capitalism. Weber 2021 maps the intellectual foundations of this model. Piketty, Yang, and Zucman 2019, especially 2481–2483, highlight the size of Chinese public wealth.

17. Hobson 2014 examines the implications for ancient historians of the links between NIE and neoliberalism.

18. Manning and Morris 2005. This vision of an ancient Mediterranean deeply interconnected with Near Eastern economic systems is further developed by Manning 2018.

19. See especially Jursa 2010, 2014.

20. See the volumes in the Oxford Studies in the Roman Economy series, currently ranging from Bowman and Wilson 2009 to Erdkamp 2020.

21. The most influential contributions are Scheidel and Friesen 2009; Monson and Scheidel 2015; Scheidel 2017, 2019, 2020. For a wide-ranging critique of macroeconomic modeling in ancient history, see Bowes 2021.

22. Bresson 2016.

23. Scheidel, Saller, and Morris 2007: quoted at 11–12.

24. Temin 2013, Kron 2014, and Ober 2015 put forward the most sophisticated optimistic assessments of the structure of Greek and Roman economies.

25. On inequality, see Scheidel 2017. On human well-being, see Scheidel 2012, 2019.

26. Bresson 2016, especially 221–222, highlights the role played by the exploitation of slaves in Greek prosperity. For Jursa 2014, especially 30 and 38, imperial domination is a key driving force behind Babylonian economic growth.

27. See Chapter 6.

28. Von Reden 1995, Kurke 1999, Seaford 2004.

29. Purcell 2012.

30. Shaw 2008, 2013, 2020.

31. Van Oyen 2016 and 2020.

32. Van der Spek et al. 2018, Bernard 2018, and Elliott 2020 exemplify some of these exciting new approaches to monetary history.

33. See also the useful collection of specialist studies on credit in different ancient Mediterranean societies edited by Campagno, Gallego, and García Mac Gaw 2017 and Démare-Lafont 2019.

34. On monetization in Mesopotamia, see the literature cited in n. 51 below.

35. See Chapter 2.

36. See Chapter 3.

37. See Chapter 4.

38. Publilius, *Sententiae* S. 41, quoted by Eberle (see Chapter 5).

39. See Chapter 5.

40. See Chapter 6.

41. Payne 2016: 519–520 examines the sociobiological effects of that unequal social order.
42. See Chapter 8.
43. See Chapter 9.
44. See Chapter 10.
45. Especially Joseph 2002, 2013.
46. See Chapter 11.
47. Of the vast literature on the spread of coinage in the Aegean, I found especially helpful Bresson 2001; Schaps 2004; Von Reden 2012: 35–41; Mooring, Van Leeuwen, and Van der Spek 2018: 132–138.
48. See the osteological evidence harnessed by Jongman, Jacobs, and Klein Goldewijk 2019, discussed in Chapter 7.
49. Jursa 2010, 2014; Pirngruber 2017; Van der Spek et al. 2018; Bresson 2020.
50. Von Reden 2015: 41–44.
51. On the concept of "deep" monetization, see Jursa in Van der Spek et al. 2018: 135; on "deep" monetization in the Mediterranean, see Verboven 2016: 364.
52. Graeber 2011: 212–214, quoted at 213.
53. On warfare and state formation, see Scheidel 2009. On slavery and empire, see Scheidel 1997. On empire, slavery, and epistemicide, see Peralta 2020.
54. On economic dynamism in the Near East, see Jursa 2014.
55. Von Reden 2007, 2012: 41–47.
56. See Chapter 6.

CHAPTER 2

1. On markets in first-millennium Babylonia, see, for example, Jursa 2010 and 2014 (on the former of which this introductory section mainly draws); the pertinent essays in Van der Spek, van Leeuwen, and van Zanden 2015 and Pirngruber 2017. On the crucial watershed of 484 BCE, see Waerzeggers 2003–2004 and the contributions in Waerzeggers and Seire 2018.
2. Jursa 2014: 33.
3. Jursa 2011.
4. Nam 2019: 160, reviewing Pirngruber 2017.
5. Van de Mieroop (1999: 121 passim). See also the essays gathered in Clancier et al. 2005 for an appreciation of Polanyi's pervasive influence in ancient Near Eastern studies.
6. Liverani 1990 is a brilliant analysis of the Late Bronze Age based on the Polanyian concepts of reciprocity and redistribution.
7. Bresson 2016: 103–104.
8. Graeber 2011: 89–126. In his own words, "all human interaction are not forms of exchange" (Graeber 2011: 122). See also Graeber 2009, tellingly an essay in a volume

dedicated to Polanyi's central work *The Great Transformation*, for a rough sketch of this scheme, as well as the remarks of Weisweiler in the introduction to this volume.

9. Graeber 2009: 114.

10. Graeber 2011: 110: "Whenever the lines of superiority and inferiority are clearly drawn and accepted by all parties as the framework of a relationship, and relations are sufficiently ongoing that we are no longer simply dealing with arbitrary force, then relations will be seen as being regulated by a web of habit and custom."

11. Graeber 2009: 125.

12. Graeber 2011: 103.

13. Graeber 2011: 46–52.

14. Graeber 2011: 120–122.

15. Graeber 2011: 239.

16. The quote is from literary historian Stephen Greenblatt, one of the most influential proponents of the New Historicism School focusing on the historical, cultural, and social context of literary texts; quoted after Baßler 2005: 14, n. 41. See also 30–36 on the lasting impact of Clifford Geertz' oeuvre. See also the sensitive appreciation of literary sources in Eberle's discussion of debt and obligations in Rome in Chapter 5 of this volume.

17. Jiménez 2017: 39–54. For the text, see Lambert 1960: 186–209 as well as the editions of new fragments in Jiménez 2017: 377–395.

18. Jiménez 2017: 47–50.

19. SAA 3 51, line rev 1; see also Jiménez 2017: 385–386, who translates the line with poetic license thus: "you would sue your friend over a penny." For rendering *šiqla muṭṭû* as "demand payment" *vel sim.*, see Postgate 1976: 153; on the basis of i.a. the legal record SAA 14 171, which is roughly contemporary with our text). The shekel (of silver), in spite of its actual value, is not infrequently used to designate a petty amount, see CAD Š/III: 98a s.v. *šiqlu*.

20. Jiménez 2017: 377–380.

21. In the course of the first millennium BCE, rations in Babylonia became increasingly standardized (and sometimes even replaced by silver payments) and are better conceived of as "salaries in kind," see Jursa 2008.

22. *šumma awīlum harrānam itbima surdû ištu šumēl awīlim ana imitti ītiqma ana kutallišu itūr awīlum šū ašar illak zittam ikkal libbi ṭāb.*

23. CAD M/1 385b-387a s.v. *mašrû*.

24. Lambert 1960: 139–149. The passage quoted in extenso corresponds to lines 62–69 in Lambert's counting.

25. The literature on these decrees (also known as *mīšarum* decrees) is vast; see, for example, Charpin 2000 and the introductory essay of Hudson there as well as van de Mieroop 2002. They are also mentioned in Graeber 2011: 216–217.

26. Jursa 2010: 241 and, in general, 240–245.

27. Brinkman 1984.

28. On economic activities of private entrepreneurs during the "long sixth century BCE," see the extensive survey in Jursa 2010: 153–315.

29. Skaist 1984: 41–51; quote from 51. For *qīptu* during the Old Babylonian period, see also Stol 2004: 884.

30. For the "happy heart" (*ṭub libbi*) denoting both physical and spiritual well-being, see Steinert 2012: 232–233, n. 6.

31. Diakonoff 1975: 130 considers the village community "as a mechanism of self-defence and co-operation of the free and more especially the free rural population outside of the state sector," a stance which was recently popularized by Scott 2017. See Liverani 2016: 142–148 for an intellectual genealogy.

32. Graeber 2011: 251.

33. Lambert 1960: 225–233; all translations are taken from his masterful edition.

34. Lambert 1960: 230 (sub ii 19–20) translates "Who is *miserly*? Who is opulent? For whom shall I reserve my vulva?" but notes that the word, which he translates, following B. Meissner's edition, as *miserly* (his italics), *gitrunu*, primarily signifies accumulation of wealth.

35. Lambert 1960: 239–250, line v 39–40. The Akkadian text uses the expression *kaspam šaqālum*, which is the regular term for payments in silver.

36. Alster 1997: 31, no. 1.153, and the parallel 261 (no. 22 col. I). Another saying with a similar worldview regarding the role of the family is "Marrying is human, getting children is divine" (p. 219, no. 14.39, iii 3).

37. Alster 1997: 33 and 92, nos. 1.165 and 3.64. Note, similarly to no. 1.165, 92, and 266, nos. 3.65 and 266, vi (24), the former reading "The merchant—how small he made the amount of silver! How small he made the amount of oil and barley!"

38. Alster 1997: 8, no. 1.8.

39. Alster 1997: 244, no. 9, sec. B4; paralleled by 273, no. 24.3.

40. Alster 1997: 101, no. 3.123; for his translation of the Sumerian word *kadri* as "bribe," see p. 389, s.v. SP 3.123. The binary opposition left/right is discussed by De Zorzi 2014: 127.

41. Lambert 1960: 277–278.

42. Alster 1997: 83, no. 3.17, and Lambert 1960: 258–259; the latter translates rather misleadingly "Friendship lasts for a day, business connexions last forever."

43. Hackl, Jursa, and Schmidl 2014: no. 114.

44. CAD Š III:197b–198b, s.v. *šugarrû*.

45. On the nature of this and other, similar payments and the difficulty of equating them with our contemporary term "bribe," see M. Jursa 2021, to which I refer for further examples.

46. Hackl, Jursa, and Schmidl 2014: no. 103.

47. Pirngruber 2017: 31–33, with references.

48. Jursa in Hackl, Jursa, and Schmidl 2014: 104–105.

49. Steinert 2012: 427–428, 469–473, and 479–503. On the dichotomy of honor and shame in Mediterranean societies, see the influential Campbell 1964. According to a well-known passage in a letter dating to the Neo-Babylonian period, a husband urges his wife to send him ten shekels of silver as "out of shame" (*ina bultu)* he does not want to ask anyone from among his peers (Hackl, Jursa, and Schmidl 2014: no. 71).

50. The seminal work on this archive is Stolper 1985; see also, for example, Van Driel 1989 and Pirngruber 2017: 47–70.

51. The term is discussed in Jursa 2010: 492–496, who discards the earlier interpretation by A. Leo Oppenheim of *nišhu* as an exchange rate for various commodities (which had found its way into the CAD). Alternatively, it may simply act as an umbrella term for the stipulations that follow, namely modalities and place of repayment.

52. It is well established that most promissory notes dealing with tax obligations in the Murašû archive used dates as the unit of account, rather than as the actual medium of transaction. Hence, the Murašûs provided cultivators with silver to discharge their tax obligation, but the latter were able to acquit their debt in kind with their own produce, while the Murašû took it upon themselves to monetize the agricultural output. Yet, the quantities in these standard promissory notes (which usually contain a pledge of agricultural land on the part of the debtors) are significantly higher compared to the short-term consumption loans discussed here: Whereas about 75% of all tax-related debts fall in the range between ten and sixty *kurrus* of dates per debtor (and the remainder exceeding these quantities), the barley loans fall in the range between two and ten *kurrus* for each debtor. See Jursa 2010: 408–413 on the promissory notes, and compare the quantities in his tables 40 (debts stipulated in dates) and 51 (debts in barley, to be repaid according to the *nišhu*), also Pirngruber 2017, 56–59 and table 3.2.

53. For example, Graeber 2011: 86–87, 121.

54. Steinkeller 2017: 197.

CHAPTER 3

1. Berger 1967: 20, 25.

2. Athenian debt bondage is discussed by Moritz Hinsch in this volume (see Chapter 4).

3. Even if (as some suggest) the poetry was not in fact by Solon himself, it is an excellent early witness to a communal viewpoint.

4. Frr. 4c, 16. The cosmic projection of limit has a productive future in Greek philosophy (especially Pythagoreanism and Plato).

5. Seaford 2004: 92–93.

6. Seaford 2004: 199.

7. Anaximander may well have lived from about 610 BCE to about 540 BCE.

8. B1. References to Presocratic fragments are in Diels and Kranz 1951.

9. For the controversies surrounding this issue, see Seaford 2004: 190–192.

10. Seaford 2004: 205–207.

11. Seaford 2004: for Anaximander, see 190–209; accepted by Graeber 2011: 244–247, 430, n. 73.

12. Seaford 2004: 193–198.

13. Seaford 2004: 231.

14. Seaford 2004: 233, n. 12.

15. For example, Pindar *Isthm.* 1.68–70; Aeschylus. *Ag.* 437–441, Psychostasia; Euripides *Suppl.* 775–777, *Med.* 968, *Pho.* 1228; Isocr. 6.109; Xen. *Cyr* 3.1.36; *Anth. Gr.* 7.622.6.

16. Pindar Ol. 2.56–58. For this interpretation of the passage (and against others), see Edmunds 2009: 667–669.

17. This is controversial but argued in detail in Seaford 1986, especially 4–9.

18. Graf and Iles Johnston 2007: 6–7. Another (Graf and Iles Johnston 2007: 4, fourth century BCE), contains—along with very obscure mentions of cosmological elements—ἀνταμοιβή ("exchange"), used by Herakleitos in B90 (see above).

19. Graf and Iles Johnston 2007: 28, from Pherai.

20. A fourth-century BCE gold leaf (Graf and Iles Johnston 2007: 5) contains the mystic formula "I have flown out of the painful circle (κύκλος) of heavy grief." This is generally regarded as meaning the cycle of reincarnations: Graf and Iles Johnston 2007: 127).

21. For example, Euripides. *Alc.* 419, 782, *Andr.* 1272; Plato *Tim.* 942e–43a; *Anth. Pal.* 10.105.

22. True, money can seem to change in value (if what it buys falls or rises in value), but an assumption of its stability is a precondition for using money.

23. See also B1, B50, B89, B113.

24. Sotion ap. Diogenes Laertius 9.21.

25. B1.3, 27, 30; B6.4.

26. *Phaedo* 100b–e; *Republic* 505a; also *Republic* 508a–e, 532b1; *Laws* 965b–966b.

27. *Phaedo* 114bc; cf. *Timaios* 42bc; *Phaedo* 80d–84b; *Phaedr.* 248c–249d.

28. I take a compelling example from each major tragedian: Aesch. *Suppl.* 472 (see Fraenkel on *Ag.* 1275); Soph. *OT* 156 (see Dawe ad loc.); Eur. *Andr.* 337 (see Stevens ad loc.).

29. Aesch. *Ag.* 85; cf. Eur. *HF* 530, fr. 1011.

30. At Aristoph. *Acharn.* 454 the "χρέος for a wicker basket" is parody (of the tragic *Telephos*) and so perhaps designed to sound absurd. At Bion fr. 5.2 the Doric genitive ἄλλω is a conjecture for ἄλλο, which could equally be restored as ἄλλῳ.

31. It is sometimes translated as "necessity." The only scholar I know of to translate it correctly is Mourelatos 2008: 151.

32. Seaford 2004: 165–169, 277–283; 2012: 291–294, 299.

33. B8.12, 28.

34. Mourelatos 2008: 153.

35. More detail in Seaford 2004, especially 245–249. Parmenides was "of illustrious family and wealth" (Sotion ap. Diog.Laert. 9.21).

36. *De Gen. corr.* 325a19.

37. *ṛṇam* = debt, obligation, debt of money, transgression, guilt, fugitive; from root *ṛṇ*, "to move," "to go."

38. *níṣkṛṇīte*, middle voice with *ātmanam* = redeem oneself from, ransom oneself from, buy oneself off (the verb *krī-* means simply "to buy").

39. 3.6.2.16; cf. 1.7.2.1–2.

40. Lévi 1898: 87–90, 130–131; Biardeau and Malamoud 1976: 190–195; Tull 1989: 113–115; Collins 1982: 47–48; Gonda 1966.

41. Biardeau and Malamoud 1976: 194 (my translation from the French).

42. Krishan 1997: 4–5, 33; Halbfass 2000: 59; Biardeau and Malamoud 1976: 165; Keith 1925: 250, 409, 478.

43. Krishan 1997: 5.

44. For example, Gombrich 1996: 31; 2006: 46.

45. Gonda 1966: 125ff.

46. For example, *Taittirīya Brāhmaṇa* 3.11.8; Bodewitz 1996.

47. Similarly *Atharvaveda* 6.117.3.

48. For the Upanishads I use the translation of Olivelle 1996.

49. Not (as in the BU version) being eaten by the gods (in CU it is the moon that the gods eat). Olivelle notes that *sampāta* generally refers to the residue of sacrifice but (unusually) takes it here to mean the residue of the moon being eaten. But this would imply the total disappearance of the moon, which is unlikely (and cf. "Decrease! Increase!" in BU 6.2.16). And there is no reason why *sampāta* cannot mean what it normally does: It is (failed) offerings, sacrifices, and *iṣṭāpūrta* that distinguishes these people from those who escape the cycle.

50. Killingley 1997 shows how it is put together from earlier Vedic conceptions.

51. Gombrich 2006: 48.

52. This is shown by Obeyesekere 2002.

53. I have shown this in my monograph of 2020.

54. B2, B50, B118.

55. B64, B66.

56. Hclt.: B36 (cf. B31), B117, B118.

57. On animal sacrifice, see Seaford 2004: 41, 49; on mystic initiation, see Seaford 2012: 44–46, 275.

58. Herakleitos, Parmenides, and Plato do use the vocabulary and structure of the Greek cosmic rite of passage (mystic initiation) but without mentioning its practice (other than to *reject* it: Herakleitos B14): Seaford 2016.

59. Even the royal consecration (*rajasuya*) "is not concerned with society or polity but exclusively with the metaphysical fate of the single sacrificer as a private individual": Heesterman 1993: 69.
60. Biardeau and Malamoud 1976: 157–158.
61. On this interiorization and its relation to monetization, see Seaford 2016.
62. Diog. Laert. 3.41–3.
63. Plato, *Republic* 416de.
64. Another way of avoiding being bound to karma is *niskāma karma*, action done without desire for the fruits of karma, propounded especially in the *Bhagavad Gītā*.
65. See, for instance, Gombrich 2006: 68–69.

CHAPTER 4

1. Literature on the Solonian debt crisis abounds; for some recent non-standard interpretations, see Harris 1997, Welwei 2005, van Wees 2006, Meier 2012.
2. Graeber 2011: 228, cf. 390: "continual debt crises."
3. On debt bondage, see Finley [1965] 1981, de Ste. Croix 1981: 136f, Harris 2002.
4. Bogaert 1968, Millett 1991, Cohen 1992, Shipton 2000.
5. My ideas about debt in ancient Greece were conceived independently from Cecchet 2018, an article that discusses some of the problems and sources discussed here.
6. Millett 1991: 5–9; cf. Shipton 2000: 7–14, on credit transactions as a sign of growing monetization.
7. For a wealthy man going to court about debt, see Aristophanes' *Clouds*, staged in 423 BCE. There are titles of lost plays like *The Usurer* (*Tokistēs*) (Millett 1991: 186) and *The Deposit* (*Parakatathēkē*) (Ehrhardt 1958: 83) that point to similar plot lines. For the everyday lending of poorer households, see Millett 1991: 139–148 and Gallant 1991: 155–158.
8. Isager and Hansen 1975, Millett 1983, Cohen 1992: 136–189.
9. Finley 1951: 82–87 has claimed a general prevalence of such non-productive loans.
10. Millett 1991: 6f. On money and debt as conceptual metaphors in Greek philosophical thought, see Seaford (2004) and his contribution to this volume (Chapter 3).
11. *Laws* 4, 717b–c. Adapt., transl. R. G. Bury; cf. Millett 1991: 132f.
12. For Greek laws regarding multiple creditors, see Finley 1951: 107–117, Walser 2008: 122–152, Harris 2015: 128–131.
13. *Nicomachean Ethics* 8.14, 1163 b 13–18. Transl. W. D. Ross. Cf. Millett 1991: 133f.
14. 267a.
15. *Physics* 2.4, 196 a 1–197 a 19.
16. See Graeber 2011: 237–249 on materialism in the Axial Age. I am skeptical of synchronic generalizations such as "If the Axial Age was the age of materialism, the Middle Ages were above all else the age of transcendence" (p. 297). Ancient Greeks, too, were concerned about divine retribution for illegitimate acquisition, like the old moneymaker Kephalos depicted in Plato's *Republic* (1, 330d–c). For empirical

arguments against contrasting the "Axial Age" too sharply with the preceding and successive period, see also the contributions of Pirngruber, Papaconstantinou, and Rio in this volume (Chapters 2, 10, and 11, respectively).

17. Graeber 2011: 251–305.

18. Cf. Osborne 1987: 93f, Gallant 1991: 115–169, Halstead [1987] 2002: 68f. Note that all of these scholars draw heavily on the anthropological literature on peasant societies to build hypotheses for ancient Greece.

19. *Republic* 1, 331c–d: οὗτος ὅρος ἐστὶν δικαιοσύνης, ἀληθῆ τε λέγειν καὶ ἃ ἂν λάβῃ τις ἀποδιδόναι.

20. Graeber 2011: 195–197, here 195.

21. Plato, *Republic* 1, 330a–331b.

22. For the family and estate of Kephalos, see Davies 1971: 587–590.

23. Graeber 2011: 271–282.

24. Plato, *Republic* 1, 331d–333b: When asked for what kind of "peaceful use" or "acquisition" justice is useful, Polemarkhos answers "contracts," specifically "partnerships" (κοινωνήματα), entered for "the use of money." Pace Graeber 2011: 196, Polemarkhos understands "paying a debt" as literally as does his father. See Lycos 1987: 26–39 for a detailed analysis of the differences between Kephalos' and Polemarkhos' positions and Plato's judgment on both.

25. Plato, *Republic* 1, 333c; for returning deposits as a mark of friendship, see Ps-Aristotle, *Problems*, 29.3, 950 a 28–b 4; cf. Ehrhardt 1958, Millett 1991: 204f.

26. For example, a decree from Genoa (1369 CE) translated in Lopez and Raymond 1955: 276f and a Medici partnership contract from Florence (1455 CE) (pp. 206–211).

27. On the interdependence of power and credit in early medieval Egypt, see also the contribution of Papaconstantinou (Chapter 10).

28. Graeber 2011: 193–195 discusses a different episode of Apollodoros' many court feuds.

29. For Pasion and his family, see Davies 1971: 427–442 and Trevett 1992.

30. Ps.-Demosthenes, *Against Timotheus*.

31. *Against Timotheus* 68. Transl. A. T. Murray.

32. Cf. Millett 1991: 1–4 and Cohen 1992: 36f.

33. Ps.-Demosthenes, *Against Dionysodorus*, 48–50. Transl. N. J. DeWitt. A decree from Genoa (cited above, n. 26) states an almost identical motivation for banning recourse to canon law. See Lane 1973: 109, 201, 271–273 for Venice's reputation for impartial justice, echoed in Shakespeare's *Merchant of Venice*.

34. See Ps.-Demosthenes, *Against Phormio* 51f for a similar plea; cf. Xenophon's *Ways and Means* 3.3 for the idea that efficient courts promote commercial prosperity.

35. For such an approach in general, see, for example, Morris and Manning 2005: 34–39, Frier and Kehoe 2007, Harris 2015, Ober 2015: xvi–xx and passim, Bresson 2016, all drawing on North 1990.

36. Cf. Weber's most extensive treatments of the Greco-Roman city-states in his *Agrarverhältnisse* ([1909] 2006) and the essay *Die Stadt* ([1921] 1999). In contrast to the institutional economists of today, Weber stressed the economic significance of medieval civic law in *contrast* to ancient law.

37. Plato, *Laws* 11, 921c–d.

38. Fr. 7, 1–2 (Diels-Kranz). Adapt., transl. A. Laks and G. W. Most.

39. A roughly similar statement survives among the fragments from the fifth-century BCE philosopher Democritus of Abdera; cf. fragment B 255 (Diels-Kranz) (= Stobaeus, 4.1, 46).

40. *Areopagiticus*, 29–34, with 32–34 quoted here. Adapt., transl. G. Norlin.

41. Cf. the passage preceding the one discussed here, Isocrates, *Areopagiticus* 20–28.

42. For agricultural risks and the strategies to cope with them, see Osborne 1987: 36–46, Garnsey 1988: 43–68, Gallant 1991: 94–169, Halstead [1987] 2002: 53–70; for risk management as an element of household economy, see Hinsch 2021: 519–523; for the pronounced fluctuation in prices and opportunities and the ensuing wide margins of loss and profit, see Davies 1981: 73–87 and Eich 2006: 175–256.

43. Cf. Eich 2006: 375–380 for the risks Greek traders faced and their weak position vis-à-vis their lenders.

44. *Plataicus* 48, written c. 373–371.

45. Lysias, *Against Eratosthenes* 96–98.

46. Menander, *Hero* 20–40.

47. de Ste. Croix 1981: 163.

48. Harris 2002.

49. Cf. the literature cited in n. 42 above.

50. Cf. the pseudo-Aristotelian *Oeconomica* 1.6, 1344 b 31–33, on the "attic way of household management" practiced in "small household economies" (ταῖς μικροτέραις οἰκονομίαις).

51. Thucydides, 3, 2–5, 18, 26f, 50, 1; cf. Gillis 1971, Gehrke 1985: 117–120.

52. Diodorus, 15.57, 3–58, 4, is our main source. Isocrates (*Letter to Philipp* 52, written in 346) makes it look like the Argives killed their "most eminent and richest citizens" unprovoked; but in the likely case that Aeneas Tacticus (*How to Survive under Siege*, 11, 7–19) refers to the same events, the "party of the rich" had provoked retribution by instigating a violent revolution with the help of foreign mercenaries; cf. Gehrke 1985: 31–33.

53. On Plato's view on civil strife and its causes, see Fuks 1984: 80–114, 126–171 and Bertrand 1999.

54. *Republic* 8, 551d–e; cf. Gillis 1971: 44, pointing out the parallel.

55. *Republic* 8, 555d–556a. Transl. P. Shorey.

56. *Republic* 8, 557a and 564a–569c.

57. *Republic* 8, 556b.

58. *Laws* 9, 915d–e. Transl. R. G. Bury.

59. Aristotle refers to "some places" where laws banned suits arising out of voluntary contracts but specifies neither place nor date, *Nicomachean Ethics* 9.1, 1164 b 12–15.

60. The historian Megasthenes, a younger contemporary of Aristotle, contrasted India to Greece by alleging that the Indians did *not* litigate over securities and deposits, *Fragmente der Griechischen Historiker 715* fr. 32.

61. Thucydides, 3, 81, 4. For modern accounts, see Bruce 1971 and Gehrke 1985: 88–93.

62. Aeneas Tacticus, 5, 1f and 14, 1.

63. *Inschriften von Ephesos* 4a, extensively analyzed by Walser 2008. Cf. Asheri 1969: 42–46. For measures to ease the burden of debt in Hellenistic times, see Cecchet 2018: 134–137.

64. *Politics* 2.7, 1266 a 37–1267 b 21.

65. *Politics* 5.3, 1302 a 38–b 2; cf. 2.7, 1266 b 37–1267 a 8; 2.7, 1267 a 37–41; 5.12, 1316 b 21 f.

66. See the interpretation of Winterling 1993: 197–204.

67. *Politics* 5.5, 1304 a 27–30, quoted by Graeber 2011: 229. Cf. Gehrke 1985: 137–139.

68. Eich 2006: 543–555.

69. *Politics* 5.12, 1316 b 10–20. Cf. 2.7, 1266 b 10–14, singling out "rich men gone poor" as most liable to start a revolution. Cf. the situation in Republican Rome discussed by Eberle in her contribution (Chapter 5).

70. Dionysius of Halicarnassus reports this for the tyrant Aristodemos, who seized power in Cumae in southern Italy in 504 BCE (*Roman Antiquities* 7.8, 1), and Pompeius Trogus (preserved through the epitome of Justinus) for Clearchus, who seized power in Heraclea at Pontus in 364/3 (16.5, 1–4). On these events, see Asheri 1966: 83f, 93f; 1969: 17f, 27f. Plutarch reports that at Megara the poor citizens rebelliously forced a payback of interest, called *palintokia*, on their rich creditors. Unfortunately, Plutarch's report is clouded by anti-democratic rhetoric; for an attempt at historical interpretation, see Forsdyke 2012: 117–143. On all these episodes, compare Cecchet 2018: 129–131.

71. This is the result of a search in the *Thesaurus Linguae Graecae*. Late antique and Byzantine lexicographers state that *chreōn apokopai* meant "an exemption of what had been owed (literally: taken) by the poor." This explanation seems to derive directly from Pseudo-Aristotle's and Plutarch's accounts of Solon's debt reform.

72. Cf. the reports of Dionysius of Halicarnassus and Pompeius Trogus cited above, n. 70.

73. Walser 2008: 158–180 is reluctant to decide on the group's identity but makes clear most of them were likely citizens.

74. Asheri 1969: 46, Walser 2008: 286–289.

75. *On the Mysteries*, 87 f.

76. Despite what Andocides wants us to believe, this is true only for private cases tried *before* the regime of the Thirty; private judgments during the time of the Thirty were indeed invalidated retrospectively, cf. Demosthenes, *Against Timocrates* 56.

77. *Against Timocrates* 56–60. Demosthenes alludes to the general amnesty that allowed everyone to return "to his own possessions" except for the most culpable oligarchs, cf. Xenophon, *Hellenica* 2.4, 39, and Ps.-Aristotle, *Constitutions of the Athenians* 39.

78. *Hellenica*, 2.4, 40. Transl. C. L. Brownson.

79. *Constitution of the Athenians* 40, 2 f.

80. *On the Mysteries* 92 f.

81. *Constitution of the Athenians* 6, 2.

82. This is suggested by the narratives in the *Constitution* and Plutarch's *Life of Solon*, 15.6 f.

83. For the Athenian stance, compare *Constitution of the Athenians* 56, 2. I have not discussed the text of the so-called Heliastic Oath inserted in Demosthenes' speech *Against Timocractes* (149–151) since Canevaro 2013: 77–80, 173–180 has compellingly challenged its authenticity. Cecchet 2018: 128–131 argues that its ban on supporting debt cancellation nonetheless echoes authentic Athenian oaths and reflects the Athenian anxiety about the violation of property rights.

84. Pseudo-Demosthenes, *On the Treaty with Alexander*, 15. Transl. C. A. Vince.

85. Cf. Urban 1981, citing *Inscriptiones Graecae* II², 236, and *On the Treaty with Alexander*, 10.

86. *Panathenaicus*, 258f.

87. *Laws* 3, 684d–e.

88. *Laws* 5, 736c–d.

89. *Inscriptiones Creticae*, vol. III, iv 8; cf. Asheri 1966: 114f. See ll. 24–38.

90. Ll. 9–23.

91. See Chankowski and Domaradzka 1999 for the text; cf. Loukopoulou 1999 for interpretation and context.

92. Ll. 7–37.

93. *Fouilles de Delphes*, vol. III, fasc. 1, 294, published and discussed in Homolle 1926.

94. Ll. 6–7; see Asheri 1969: 23, against Homolle 1926, 26f.

95. Col. 7, 1, ll. 5 f: κ' αἴ τις [τὰν γᾶν ἀνα]δαστὸν ποιοῖ ἢ χρ[εῶν] | [ἀπο]κοπάν.

96. Cf. Asheri 1969: 23–25 for fuller discussion.

97. Pace Homolle 1926: 105.

98. Col. 1, ll. 19 f., following Asheri 1969: 23.

99. Col. 3, ll. 5–9.

100. Asheri 1969: 23f, referring to the mutilated lines of col. 7, 6ff.

101. See Homolle 1926: 101–103 on economic conditions in fourth-century Delphi; a remark by the historian Timaeus (*Fragmente der Griechischen Historiker 566*, fr. 11a) supports the view that a traditional agrarian labor regime prevailed in the Phocis.

102. See Asheri 1966: 60–121 and 1969 and Gehrke 1985: 323–328 for extensive collections of the evidence on revolts involving debt cancellations and redistribution of land; cf. Cecchet 2018 for a recent discussion.

103. Note Aristotle's remark (*Politics* 2.9, 1269 a 36–39, cf. 2.5, 1264 a 32–36) about the frequency of insurrections by the Helots in Laconia and the Penestai in Thessaly; on the status and economic role of dependent rural populations in ancient Greece, see de Ste. Croix 1981: 147–162, Jameson 1992: 136–139, Burford 1993: 193–207, Eich 2006: 260–274, Welwei 2008. Lewis 2018: 125–165 has recently argued against the idea that the Helots of Laconia and similar rural dependents in Crete should be considered serfs.

104. Graeber 2011: 231.

105. Finley 1985: 172f and Todd 1990: 167–169. Cecchet 2018: 130 likewise identifies public pay as a factor mitigating the problem of debt.

106. Meiggs 1972: 255–272 and Eich 2006: 150–173.

107. The evidence is compiled in Gschnitzer 1958, Bresson 1993: 201–214, and Eich 2006: 136–149.

108. Ehrenberg 1964: 3–9, Horden and Purcell 2000: 54–172, Ober 2015: 21–44 passim.

109. Clark and Haswell 1966: 88–105.

110. See Loomis 1998 for wage rates in classical Athens. The high wages rates per day must be balanced against the volatile nature of employment.

111. Garlan 1980: 9, Burford 1993: 188–192.

112. See Aristotle's remarks in *Politics* 6.7, 1321 a 14–21, on the advantages in civil war of light infantry, recruited from the poor; cf. Xenophon's account (*Hellenica* 2, 4) of the street fighting in Athens' civil war in 403.

113. Finley [1965] 1981: 165f, Ober (2015: xvi–xx and passim).

114. *Politics* 5.8, 1308 b 32–1309 a 15; 6.5, 1320 a 32–b 11; 6.7, 1321 a 35–42.

115. For a rather pessimistic assessment, see Garnsey 1988: 69–86; cf. Whitby 1998 and Bresson 2016: 393–414.

116. For the economic role of slave labor and the geographic pattern of its use, see Jameson 1992: 139–146, Morris and Papadopoulos 2005, Eich 2006: 274–342, Hinsch 2021: 416–440.

117. Cf. Plato's notorious recommendation (*Laws* 7, 777c–d) to apply slaves of different ethnic origins, repeated by Aristotle (*Politics* 7.10, 1330 a 25–27) and Pseudo-Aristotle (*Oeconomica* 1.5, 1344 b 18; cf. Millett 2007: 197f).

118. Compare the pseudo-Aristotelian *Oeconomica* (1.5, 1344 15–17) for a blunt statement of the economic rationale of manumission; see Cohen 1998, Zelnick-Abramovitz 2005, Millett 2007: 202–208, and Fisher 2008 for privileged slaves and freedmen.

119. On conditional manumission, see Hopkins and Roscoe 1978 and Zelnick-Abramovitz 2005 and 2018.

120. For leases, see Osborne 1988 and Eich 2006: 412–433; Pernin 2014 provides a complete compilation of the epigraphical evidence. For monetary loans, see Bogaert 1968: 279–304, Whitehead 1986: 152–160, Davies 2001, Gabrielsen 2005: 140–156.

121. See Partner 1979: 101f and Goldthwaite 2009: 470–483 for the setting up of the *Monti* in the second half of the fifteenth century, cf. Graeber 2011: 252–270 for monasteries and temples in eastern Asia.

122. Thus Bogaert 1968: 292–294, who speaks of a "tendance humanitaire" of at least some loans; Andreev 1974 presents an optimistic evaluation of the social effects of public leases.

123. Bogaert 1968: 302–304 notes the limited volume of transactions of sanctuaries compared to the private bank of Pasion at its prime; Millett 1991: 171–178, following Finley 1951: 96–100, presents what is probably the most skeptical view of corporate lending and leasing. Whitehead 1986: 152–160 and Ismard 2010: 281–294 come to a different conclusion about deme loans.

124. *Sylloge Inscriptionum Graecarum*[3] 46 (Halicarnassus, c. 420–350), newly edited by Blümel 1993. Cf. Gabrielsen 2005: 139f for the conservative lending policies of sanctuaries.

125. Bogaert 1968,: 302–304 and Millett 1991: 173f; cf. Gabrielsen 2005,: 143–156 for borrowers in Hellenistic times. One Athenian deme expressly demanded that money should be lent on the highest interest rate possible, *Inscriptiones Graecae*, vol. I[3] 258, ll. 18–20 (c. 425–413). For the interest rates of the Italian *Monti*, see above, n. 121.

126. Osborne 1988: 289–292, 303f. Cf. Whitehead 1986: 157f and Pernin 2014: 516. Osborne's interpretation has been challenged, unconvincingly to my mind, by Shipton 2000: 39–49; Shipton's approach ignores several difficulties in interpreting the prosopographic evidence, cf. Pernin 2014: 515 and Osborne 1988: 289, n. 26.

127. *Politics* 6.5, 1320 a 17–1320 b 1.

128. Cf.*Politics* 2, 1273 a 21–30; 4, 1293 b 14f; 5, 1316 b 5f, with the commentary of Schütrumpf and Gehrke 1996: 611, 647.

129. 4, 1291 22 f.; 6, 1320 b 11–14.

130. Tellingly, Aristotle (6, 1320 b 4–11) expects such public measures might not be taken, in which case he appeals to the "notables" to be "good willed and thoughtful" and support the needy with private capital; cf. Schütrumpf and Gehrke 1996: 647, who add the example of the Rhodians, for whom Strabo (XIV, 2,5) reports a similar scheme of paternal welfare.

131. In Harris' collection of references to debt bondage (2002) only one concerns an Athenian citizen; Harris argues that when Strepsiades, the lead character of Aristophanes' *Clouds*, exclaims "I am tossed and torn, my possessions are forfeit" (l. 241: ἄγομαι φέρομαι, τὰ χρήματ᾽ ἐνεχυράζομαι) *agomai* means "being led into debt bondage" (for corroboration, Harris points to the meaning of *agomai* in the

Code of Gortyn). Two aspects speak against this interpretation: first, Strepsiades'
exclamation would form an odd anticlimax in his list of sanctions, with debt
bondage coming first and seizure of possessions last; second, as the *Liddell-Scott-
Jones Greek-English Lexicon* reveals (II., 3) the coupling of *agein* and *pherein* is a
common poetic expression of distress—as in Hecuba's lament of the Troian's fate
(l. 1310: ἀγόμεθα φερόμεθ') in Euripides' *Trojan Women* (staged in Aristophanes'
time, 415). Aristophanes' phrase is not an allusion to legal procedure but the kind
of parody of tragedy he so often employs.

132. Cf. Eberle in this volume (Chapter 5), for the anxiety about losing one's credit-
worthiness (*fides*) in Republican Rome.

133. All historical differences notwithstanding, this reminds me of Werner Sombart's
1906 explanation as to why there is no socialism in the United States despite pronounced economic inequality and plight.

CHAPTER 5

1. Graeber 2011: 8–9.

2. Cic. *De Off.* 2.89.

3. Cic. *Quinct.* 15.49–50.

4. For the possibility of an additional layer to this confusion, see Plut. *Cat. Mai.* 21.7,
which raises the possibility that Cato himself might have engaged in certain types
of lending at interest.

5. Tac. *Ann.* 6.16. The precise value of the maximum rate, which Tacitus calls *fenus
unciarium*, remains debated, with theories ranging from 1% p.a. to 100% p.a. On
this debate, as well as on the history of interest rate legislation in Rome more
generally, see Billeter 1898: 115–177, Barlow 1978, Zehnacker 1980, Zimmermann
1990: 166–170, Andreau 1999: 90–92. Gabrielli 2003: 107–177 provides a helpful
summary of the evidence for all legislation related to debt into the second century BCE.

6. Livy 7.42; Tac. *Ann.* 6.16. Laws in the second century BCE possibly reiterated this
prohibition. Candidates include a *lex Marcia* (Gai. *Inst.* 4.23) and a *lex Iunia de
feneratione* (Festus, s.v. "prorsus"). In 193 BCE the *lex Sempronia de pecunia credita*
tried to fix loopholes that allowed creditors to circumvent the legal limits on lending at interest in Rome (Livy 35.7; Plaut. *Curc.* 508–511).

7. App. *B Civ.* 1.54.

8. Festus, s.v. "uncuaria" with Rotondi 1912: 344 and Andreau 1999: 91–92; Cic. *Ad
Att.* 5.21.13.

9. Cato, *Agr.* 1 (*praefatio*).

10. For the text of the relevant section of the XII Table,s see Gell. *NA* 20.1.49. On
imperial jurists' and philosophers' interpretations, see Gell. *NA* 20.1.19 and 42–49
as well as Gai. *Inst.* 3.78. For recent overviews of the long debate on the interpretation of this passage, see Crawford 1996: 629 and Dondorp 2011: 134–136.

11. On *addictio*, see Cic. *Flacc.* 48–49, Sall. *Cat.* 33, Val. Max. 7.16.1b, and Gell. *NA* 20.1.45. On *missio in bona* and *venditio bonorum*, see Cic. *Quinct.* 30 with Jolowicz 1961: 223 and 236–238, Kaser and Hackl 1996: 388–401, and Ioannatou 2006a: 430–475.

12. *RS* I, ll. 115–117 with Greenidge 1977: 135–138 and Kaser 1956: 235–254.

13. Frederiksen 1966: 130.

14. Graeber 2011: 223–250.

15. Burnett 2012: 298–308 gives a helpful summary of the history of Roman coinage in the fourth and third centuries and a bibliographical introduction to the questions that remain unresolved. On the contexts of early coinage in Rome, see, most recently, Bernard 2016, 2018a, 2018b: 148–153, 175–181. Burnett 1989 provides a cultural and geopolitical account of the origins of Roman coinage.

16. For these later developments, see Kay 2014.

17. Diod. Sic. 14.6.5 and Livy 4.59–60 with Crawford 1985: 22–23. Andreau 1997: 261 discusses the use of silver coins to make payments to soldiers, which were still being calculated on the old, pre-coinage bronze standard.

18. Howgego 1992: 10–11 discusses the exceptional cases in which taxes and fines could be paid in bullion. For the earliest bankers in Rome, contemporaries of the earliest issues of Roman coinage, see Livy 9.40.16 with Andreau 1999: 337–340.

19. Bransbourg 2015a, especially 149–153.

20. Gai. *Inst.* 4.19. For an overview of the procedure and speculation about its date, see Jolowicz 1961: 197–200, 295–298 and Kaser and Hackl 1996: 111–113. Prichard 1969 and Tomulescu 1969 attempt to reconstruct how the procedure was instituted.

21. The creation of consensual contracts, probably in the early second century, constitutes another way in which Roman law recognized and shaped an emerging commercial environment cf. Aubert 2014: 171–172.

22. Graeber 2011: 13.

23. Harrison 1971: 185–190 and Millet 1991: 40–44. The Athenian situation also makes the idea that the harsh treatment of defaulting debtors in Rome, especially *missio in bona*, was adopted from the procedure for state debtors, for which see Jolowicz 1961: 223, n. 8, less of an explanation and more of a delay thereof.

24. In an attempt to provide such an explanation, Verboven 2002: 177 pointed to the lasting connections between honor and debt that exist in many societies—a suggestion that would seem to fall short of accounting for the specific nature of the Roman connection.

25. Examples include Aarts 2005, Coffee 2017, and Bernard 2018b. For the fascinating Italian tradition of economic anthropology in relation to the Roman world, see, for example, Lentano 2005 and Viglietti 2011. For a recent law-and-economics approach to the Roman law of debt and its effects on ancient credit markets, see Herz 2015.

26. Graeber 2011: 165–210.

27. von Reden 1995, Kurke 1999, and Seaford 2004 are the main contributions that all build on each other.
28. Graeber 2011: 189–190 develops this idea most eloquently.
29. Xenophon's *Oeconomicus* is crucial for the ideal of household self-sufficiency.
30. On the idea of Roman self-sufficiency, see Finley 1999: 36 and 109, Andreau 2004, and Morley 2012. But see also Cic. *Off.* 1.151, who maintains that the buying and selling of goods at a large scale could be a respectable activity to pursue.
31. Key works on gift-exchange in Roman society include Saller 1982, Wallace-Hadrill 1989, Dixon 1993, Deniaux 1994, Purcell 1994, Damon 1997, Konstan 1997, Eilers 2002, Verboven 2002, Griffin 2003, Lentano 2005, Morley 2006, Burton 2011, Lavan 2013, Satlow 2013, Carlà and Gori 2014, Ganter 2015, and Rollinger 2014.
32. Coffee 2017 outlines various others strategies by which Roman elites sought to pry apart the world of gift and gain in the first three centuries BCE.
33. In a key work on such unequal relationships of gift-exchange, Richard Saller asserts that relations of unequal gift-exchange were more prominent in Rome than in other ancient societies (1982: 84).
34. Maehle 2018 gathers the evidence for such unequal gift-exchange in classical Athens for the first time.
35. Saller 2000: 838–839, Verboven 2011: 413, Lavan 2013: 183–186.
36. Rouland 1979: 484–488, 515–516; Dixon 1993: 453–454; Rollinger 2014: 134–139.
37. Lentano 2005: 130–135.
38. Raccanelli 1998: 35, Lavan 2013: 160.
39. On the obligations of manumitted slaves in Rome, see Waldstein 1986. For the structure of a *deditio in fidem*, see Dahlheim 1968: 1–109. Richardson 1989: 199–201 translates and discusses the ancient text of such a *deditio*.
40. For ancient accounts of the origin of patronage in Rome, see Dion. Hal. *Ant. Rom.* 2.9–11, Plut. *Rom.* 13.2–9, and Cic. *Rep.* 2.16. For modern accounts of its origin, a subject that was mainly of interest to nineteenth-century scholars, see Becker and Marquardt 1844: 125 and von Premerstein 1900: 24–25, which mainly build on these ancient accounts. Ganter 2015 dismisses these ancient accounts (pp. 75–85) and persuasively criticizes the prevailing idea that *patrocinium* and *clientela* are age-old institutions already in existence at the time of the XII Tables (pp. 101–106). Even if that were the case, the fact that the relationship was seemingly actionable in law (IX.21) would make it qualitatively different from what we observe in the middle and late Republic.
41. Gruen 1996, Damon 1997, Burton 2004, Leigh 2004, Ganter 2015: 86–97.
42. Plaut. *Poen.* 17–43 with Duckworth 1952: 272. Richlin 2017 makes most of the social identities of the performers.
43. Stewart 2008, Richlin 2014 and 2017.
44. Lowe 1990 discusses the possibility of Plautine innovation in relation to the part of these witnesses in the play more generally.

45. On the parasite in Roman comedy, see Damon 1997: 37–104.

46. Saller 1982: 21; Lavan 2013: 160.

47. On the monetization of the Italian countryside, see de Ligt 1990: 33–42, Howgego 1992: 20–22, Hollander 2007: 122–135, *contra* Crawford 2017, as well as Weisweiler in this volume (Chapter 7).

48. On bankers and their social position in Rome more generally, see Andreau 1987 and more recently Kay 2014: 113–127. On their presence at different markets, see Andreau 1997: 75–98 and 157–88. For the more abstract debate about the contribution of lending to the Roman money supply, see Harris 2006 and 2008 and Kay 2014: 107–130.

49. Ioannatou 2006a: 20–49.

50. Rouland 1979: 271–274 and 303, Verboven 2002: 116–182 and 333–336, Ioannatou 2006a: 227–308, Rollinger 2014: 315–335.

51. Pub. Sent. S,41: *Sat magna usura est pro beneficio memoria.*

52. On the life of Publilius Syrus, see Giancotti 1967: 129–165 and Leppin 1992: 283. On his work in the context of the history of Roman mime, see Jory 1988.

53. On the creation of the collection of his sayings, see Giancotti 1967: 305–338 and Beckby 1969: 9–10; on Seneca's frequent use of his moralizing sayings, see Diouron 2009; and for the idea that they represented "traditional values," see Haltenhoff 2003.

54. Cf. Pub. Sent. O,9: *Optime positum est beneficium, ubi meminit qui accipit. Positum est, just like usura*, was part of the language of monetary debt.

55. On *liberalitas* as a core virtue in the Roman ethics of gift-exchange, see Verboven 2002: 35–37, Ioannatou 2006a: 104–106, and Rollinger 2014: 64–66. On the history of the concept in this position see Coffee 2017, especially 70–115.

56. Verboven 2002: 120–125, Ioannatou 2006a: 230–309 and 2006b; Rollinger 2014: 317–320.

57. Andreau 1997: 3–46, Verboven 2002: 126–132.

58. Verboven 2002: 171–174 and 334–335.

59. Verboven 2002: 335. These two possible interpretations of *liberalitas* in relation to monetary debt also undergird Crassus' insistence that he lent out no money at interest but was strict in when he exacted repayment (Plut. *Crass.* 1.3): He chose between two ways of showing his generosity.

60. Ioannatou 2001, 2006a: 359–369. Blanton 2013 suggests that rules about how to behave in relations of gift were a function of the economic situation in which the different parties found themselves. Ioannatou's "code d'honneur" belongs to the wealthiest members of society.

61. Verboven 2002: 39–41 and 2011: 409, Rollinger 2014: 108–115. For a semantic approach to *fides* beyond its role in the Roman ethics of gift-exchange, see Hellegarc'h 1963: 23–40, Freyburger 1986, Burton 2011: 40–47. On its role in Roman diplomacy and international law see Nörr 1991 and Hölkeskamp 2000.

62. Pub. Sent. E,2: *Etiam in peccato recte praestatur fides*; Pub. Sent. E,15: *Etiam hosti est aequus, qui habet in consilio fidem.*

63. Kay 2014: 245–242. The main evidence for the credit crisis is the different measures designed to alleviate it. These include the actions of Aulus Sempronius Asellio as praetor in 89 (Liv. *Per.* 74; App. *B. Civ.* 1.54; Val. Max. 9.7.4), the *lex Cornelia Pompeia unciaria* in 88 (Festus, v. *unciaria*, 375M), the *lex Valeria de aere alieno* in 86 (Vell. Pat. 2.23.2; Sall. *Cat.* 33.2; Cic. *Font.* 1 and *Quinct.* 4.17), the actions of Marcus Marius Gratidianus at some point later in the decade (Cic. *Off.* 3.20.80), and an obscure *lex Popillia* in 81 (Varro, *Ling.* 7.105).

64. On the effect of the Mithridatic War in Italy, see Cic. *Leg. Man.* 19.

65. Cic. *Font.* 1 and *Quinct.* 17.

66. On the slogan of *novae tabulae* and its history, see Ioannatou 2006a: 72–94.

67. Examples include the *lex Cornelia Pompeia unciaria* in 88 and the *lex Licinia de aere alieno* and the *lex de Vviris mensariis creandis* as Livy describes them in the first century. Intriguingly, Dionysius of Halicarnassus describes this last measure as an attempt to preserve the *pistis* (Greek for *fides*) of the people (*Ant. Rom.* 5.69).

68. On this ideal and its various interpretations in Roman politics, see Arena 2013.

69. Arena 2019 discusses the ways in which this role of *fides* shaped the Roman concept of *libertas*, especially regarding its economic dimension.

70. See Sall. *Cat.* 33 for the association between *faeneratores* and *praetores*, Roman judicial magistrates, in the complaints of insolvent debtors.

71. For a bibliography on *cessio bonorum*, see Frederiksen 1966: 135, n. 54, to which should be added Guiffrè 1984, Pakter 1991 and 1994.

72. For an overview of the earliest evidence mentioning *cessio bonorum*, which is all Augustan, see Pakter 1991. I follow Frederiksen 1966: 135–141 in his attribution of the law to Caesar on the grounds of historical context.

73. The contributions by Déniaux, Jehne, and Rosillo-Lopez in Beck, Jehne, and Serrati 2016 discuss the various expenditures required for a successful political career.

74. Blösel 2011 and 2016 cast doubt on the long-held view that provincial governorships were the only way in which Roman politicians recovered their investments. Jehne 2016: 199–200 discusses the evidence for inheritances; Pina-Polo 2016 discusses the evidence for such an accumulation of inheritances as a return on a successful political career in the case of Cicero.

75. Suet. *Iul.* 13; Plut. *Caes.* 7.3 and *Mor.* 206 A.

76. Cic. *Att.* 7.7.6; *Fam.* 7.13.1, 7.16.3; *Q fr.* 2.13.3.

77. A lot of the loans were extended through networks of amicitial; for the idea that Roman politicians, especially in the early stages of their careers, at times also borrowed from *faeneratores*, from professional money lenders, see Verboven 2002: 334.

78. On the increasing costs of the political careers in the first century, see Lintott 1990: 8, Yakobson 1999: 141–147, and Jehne 2016: 204.

79. Cic. *Cat.* 2.18, Sall. *Cat.* 35.3, Plut. *Sull.* 56. On the central role that debt played in Sallust's conception of roman history after Sulla, see Shaw 1975.

80. Frederiksen 1966: 132–133 and Kay 2014: 260–261 discuss the concrete circumstances contributing to this crisis. Ioannatou 2006a: 56–72 analyzes what the Romans called *caritas nummorum* more generally.

81. Caes. *BC* 3.20–2, Dio 42.22–3 and 29.1, Cic. *Att.* 11.23.3, Livy *Per.* 113. For a discussion of Marcus Caelius Rufus and Publius Cornelius Dolabella and their respective attempts at debt cancellation as imitations of Catiline's project, see Ioannatou 2006a: 76–79.

82. Frederiksen 1966: 133–135 lays out the sources for the existence of this system of *aestimationes* between 49 and 46.

83. Cass. Dio 42.51.1, with Frederiksen 1966: 133–134.

84. Cf. the examples cited at n. 67 above. Livy's description of the actions of the *quinquiviri mensarii* at Liv. 7.21.5–8 might be added to this list.

85. For the idea that the *lex Iulia* that Cicero mentions here is the *lex Iulia de bonis cedendis*, see Frederiksen 1966: 138.

86. Mommsen 1889: 536. For a more recent iteration of the same idea, see Pakter 1994: 323.

87. Graeber 2014: 392–400.

CHAPTER 6

1. Graeber 2011 passim; 89 on the pervasive language of the marketplace.

2. A line of thought already being developed in Graeber 2001 (e.g., 9): "In the end, most economic theory relies on trying to make anything that smacks of 'society' disappear."

3. Graeber 2001: 9–12 on the formalist-substantivist debate and its limitations.

4. Generally, on Graeber's alternative narratives of modern economic ideas, Morley 2012. On reading the ancient economy in terms of modernity, Morley 2009: 21–47.

5. Marx 1973: 87.

6. Graeber 2011: 223–250, and see Weisweiler in Chapter 1 of this volume.

7. Noted in Morley 2012, with the suggestion that this was perhaps the result of Graeber failing to find any specialist historical scholarship on Rome that was as intellectually congenial to his approach as the work of, for example, Richard Seaford or Leslie Kurke on Greece.

8. On the historical development of money in archaic Italy, see Burnett 1989, Viglietti 2011: 225–300, Bernard 2018.

9. On Finley and Polanyi, Nafissi 2005 and Launaro 2016.

10. Lewis and Short, *A Latin Dictionary*, entries for *fruor* and *fructus*, and Varro, *De Lingua Latina* 5.34–35.

11. Nelsestuen 2015: 48 on *fructus*, 43–44 on Varro's idea of the purpose of farming.

12. Vivenza 2012 offers a brief introduction.

13. General discussions of these polarized perspectives in Cartledge 2002, Bang 2008: 17–60.

14. Scheidel, Morris, and Saller 2007: 1–6.

15. Bang 2009; for a more positive account of New Institutional Economics in a Greek context see Ober 2015 and Bresson 2016.

16. See, for example, Akerloff and Shiller 2009, Kahneman 2011, Sedlacek 2011. Lewis 2018 develops some preliminary ideas on these lines, focused on classical Greece.

17. Ober 2015: xvi–xvii; he does note that these microfoundations are "in principle testable" but takes this no further.

18. See, for example, Morley 2019.

19. Diederich 2007: 172–209. Nelsestuen 2015 engages with similar themes.

20. As opposed to normal *pastio*, which is the raising of sheep, cattle, pigs, horses, and the like. On Varro's third book, see Brown's 2019 thought-provoking reading, which I read only when doing the final revisions of this chapter.

21. On the practice of Roman aquaculture, Marzano 2013: 199–233; on their luxuriousness, Bannon 2014.

22. Kronenberg 2009, especially 73–90. Her analysis focused mainly on Book 1, but Book 3 seems in many respects still more fertile terrain for such an argument.

23. Nelsestuen 2015, especially 11, 43–44, 192–196.

24. But see also Brown 2019, who places greater emphasis on the idea that *pastio villatica* was regarded as too humble an activity for elite Romans and suggests that Varro was taking a deliberately populist approach in advocating it.

25. Cf. the discussion in Edwards 1993.

26. On debt and the importance of *fides* in late Republican politics, see the remarks by Eberle in Chapter 5 of this volume.

27. On Cicero's invention of *frugalitas*, see Gildenhard 2020.

28. Kronenberg 2009: 105. Diederich 2007: 352–364 offers a similar argument.

29. Contrast modern ecological and environmental approaches to narratives of economic development, such as Radkau 2008, Barbier 2011.

30. Note that there is no mention of one modern hypothesis for the use of cattle as the original measure of value, that they were what one gave to the gods; cf. Graeber 2011: 59. On *De Lingua Latina*, compare the thesis of Spencer 2019 (e.g., 184–185), that Varro's etymologies work to construct Roman community through grammar.

31. Graeber 2011: 21–41. On the historical and mythical origins of Roman money and the idea of *pecunia*, Nicolet 1984, Hollander 2007: 5–7, Jiménez 2019; more broadly, on the embedding contexts of Roman money and modern accounts of it, Elliott 2020: 20–50.

32. Cf. Seaford 2004 and von Reden 2010 on the history and myths of the origins of money in Greece. On late Republican ideas of frugality and virtue, Gildenhard and Viglietti 2020.

33. On the political dimensions of this episode, Padilla Peralta 2017; Brown 2019: 342–347 contrasts it with the ending of Book 3.

34. On self-sufficiency as a rational strategy to limit risk under conditions of uncertainty, Morley 1996: 75–76.

35. Cf. Mann 1986 on different forms of power and the relative ease of converting one to another.

36. As argued in Morley 2000.

37. Cf. Roselaar 2019 on these transformations, and Eberle in Chapter 5 of this volume on elite "moral confusion" in this period around ideas of debt, exchange, and social relations.

38. Graeber 2011: 226–250.

39. Cf. Graeber 2011: 239.

40. Cf. Graeber 2011: 248 on attempts in the Axial Age to base morality on the new intellectual tools provided by the impersonal market.

CHAPTER 7

1. Augustine, *Epistula* 24*. Lepelley 1983 is the pioneering social historical study of that text. Elm 2017 examines the links between the economic and theological issues debated in the letter.

2. On the "pragmatic" roles fulfilled by bishops in late antiquity, see Rapp 2005: 23–35.

3. The tension between the law and reality of slavery was exposed by Veyne and Ramin 1981.

4. The meaning of this practice, also discussed in Augustine, *Ep.* 10.2*, is examined by Vuolanto 2003 and Harper 2011: 412–413.

5. Augustine, *Ep.* 24.1*.

6. Harper 2011: 392–398. See further discussion below.

7. Weber 1976 and Rostovtzeff 1957.

8. This traditional view of the decline of urban elites has most recently been reasserted by Liebeschuetz 2001. It is convincingly refuted by Laniado 2002 and Schmidt-Hofner 2014.

9. The last and most sophisticated restatement of that theory is Whittaker 1983. It can no longer be maintained in view of the archaeological evidence, discussed in n. 11–14 below.

10. Meier 2003 and Ando 2008 review the debate on the later Roman state. The volume edited by Ando and Formisano 2021 offers intellectual biographies of various participants in that discussion.

11. Classic overviews include McCormick 2001; Wickham 2005, especially 708–720; and Lavan 2015.

12. Scheidel 1997, Lenski 2011, Harper 2011: 91–99 explore the international slave trade in the Roman Empire and late antiquity.

13. For recent overviews of these rapidly developing fields, see Mattingly et al. 2017 and Di Cosmo and Maas 2018. For a wide-ranging survey of the development of ancient global commerce in the longue durée, see Von Reden 2015.
14. Vera 1983, Rathbone 1991, Sarris 2006, Banaji 2007.
15. Carrié 1983, Grey 2007, Tedesco 2013 explore the fiscal purposes of the legislation on the colonate. Sirks 2008 offers a sophisticated restatement of the traditional view.
16. Bowden, Lavan, and Machado 2004; Wickham 2005; Decker 2009.
17. Urban culture: Lepelley 1979, Leone 2007, Scheding 2019. Agriculture: Hobson 2015.
18. Vandal Africa: Merrills and Miles 2010: 141–176. "African boom" is part of the title of Hobson 2015.
19. Wickham 2005.
20. Ward-Perkins 2005, Heather 2006. Wickham 2005: 13 coined the expression.
21. Wickham 2005: 62–66 discusses tax rates. Bransbourg 2015b lucidly surveys the functioning of the fiscal system as a whole.
22. Scheidel and Friesen 2009 model the distribution of income in the Roman Empire; Bagnall 1992 analyzes the Hermopolis register.
23. The stark divergence in regional development from the fifth century onward is a recurrent theme in recent accounts of late Roman history, such as Wickham 2009, Sarris 2011, Esmonde Cleary 2013.
24. Graeber 2011: 232.
25. Graeber 2011: 223–250 and Ingham 2004: 99–100. See further my remarks in Chapter 1 of this volume.
26. Mallan and Davenport 2015 establish a new chronology of events.
27. Dodgeon and Lieu 1991: 42–58 collect the sources.
28. Carrié and Rousselle 1999, Drinkwater 2005, Ando 2012: 146–175 survey the political history of the period.
29. Carrié 1994, Bransbourg 2015b, Clark 2017 trace the impact of the Diocletianic fiscal reforms.
30. Scheidel 2019: 224–227, cited at 227.
31. Graeber 2011: 213.
32. For recent overviews of the debate, see Bresson 2016: 260–285, Manning 2018: 195–202, and the discussion in Chapter 1 of this volume.
33. On the links between warfare and the creation of a Roman currency, see Crawford 1985, Von Reden 2012: 47–55, Bransbourg 2015a. The relationship between marketization and early Roman coinage is exposed by Bernard 2018.
34. Rathbone 1996.
35. Carrié 2003.
36. Bransbourg 2015b: 264–266 surveys the Constantinian monetary system.
37. Trommenschlager and Brkojewtisch 2016.
38. Reece 1991 and 1993: 865.

39. Dossey 2010: 100–105.

40. De Ligt 1990: 33–43.

41. Kelly 2004.

42. Banaji 2007: 180–189, Sarris 2006: 50–70, Shaw 2013: 80–84.

43. Vera 1986 examines the diversity of labor regimes across the empire. Harper 2011: 144–200 models the shape of the Roman labor market; on population density and estate organization, see 176–179.

44. See the sources collected by Vera 1999: 1021–1025 and Banaji 2007: 226–230, tables 6 and 7.

45. Compare Olympiodorus, Fr. 44 (Müller-Dinsdorf); 41.2 (Blockley) and *Vita Melaniae* 15 with the early imperial sources collected by Duncan-Jones 1982: 343–344.

46. Collins-Elliott 2018, especially 171–174, quoted at 174.

47. Dossey 2010, especially 62–100; cf. Kosso 2003.

48. Iberia: Fernández 2017: 55–56; Greece: Kosso 2003; Britannia: Allen et al. 2017; Anatolia: Izdebski 2013.

49. Mazzarino 1951 broke new ground in exposing the social consequences of the introduction of gold currency. Banaji 2007: 224–225, table 3, traces changes in exchange rates over time.

50. Harper 2016: figures 7–10.

51. See n. 15 above.

52. CTh 14.8.1 with Grey and Parkin 2003.

53. Schmidt-Hofner 2017.

54. On this process, see the remarks by Hinsch in Chapter 4 (section "Must One Pay One's Debts? A Question of Trust and Power").

55. See Chapter 10.

56. Veyne and Ramin 1981.

57. Vuolanto 2003, quoted at 204.

58. CTh 5.9.1 with Harper 2011: 406–407.

59. CTh 5.10.1 with the outstanding discussion by Harper 2011: 404–409.

60. Scheidel 1997.

61. Harper 2011: 391–423, cited at 409.

62. Graeber 2011: 85–87, quoted at 86.

63. The translation is a modified version of Edwards 1997: 69.

64. Shaw 2011, especially 675–720 and 771–806.

65. On ancient Near Eastern conceptions of a just economic order, see Chapter 2. On ideologies of poverty in Christian discourse, see Brown 2002.

66. Brown 2016 investigates the ways in which different ascetic movements made sense of their relationship to the economy and physical labor.

67. Brown 2012 is the classic study of the relationship of Christianity with earthly wealth.

68. *De Rebus Bellicis* 2.1–5 in the translation of Thompson 1952: 26. The date of this text is debated. Mazzarino 1951 influentially argued for a date in the mid-fourth century. Cameron 1979 suggests a date in the reign of Valentinian I. Brandt 1988 proposes that the text was written in the second quarter of the fifth century.

69. *De Rebus Bellicis* 2.7, in the translation of Thompson 1952: 26. Brandt 1988: 163–178 well brings out the conventional nature of the author's moral universe.

70. Wallace-Hadrill 1982 exposes the role played by ideas of a lost golden age in legitimizing the imperial order.

71. Ward-Perkins 2005: 87–122 effectively exposes the scale of simplification.

72. Wickham 2005: 707.

73. Ward-Perkins 2005: 146.

74. Gowland and Walther 2018 excellently survey recent research in this field.

75. Jongman 2014 offers a synthesis.

76. Jongman, Jacobs, and Klein Goldewijk 2019: 145.

77. Giannecchini and Moggi-Cecchi 2008 and Gowland and Walther 2018: 183–184.

78. Jongman, Jacobs, and Klein Goldewijk 2019.

79. A theme repeatedly explored by Harper 2017.

80. Scheidel 2012 also argues that post-Roman populations were taller partly because the decline in inequality gave them access to better diets.

CHAPTER 8

1. Graeber 2011: 244.

2. Janes 1999 foregrounds the paradox of ecclesiastical wealth in late antiquity. The complex, evolving relationship between material and immaterial economies in late Roman Christian contexts has been the subject of a number of remarkably revealing recent studies: Déroche 1995; Caner 2006; Brown 2012, 2015. On the materialist tendencies of early Buddhism, see the work of Gregory Schopen, notably Schopen 2004.

3. Recent work revisiting the Axial Age focuses almost exclusively on its cultural aspects: Bellah 2005; Arnason 2005, 2012; Wittrock 2005; Fromherz 2016.

4. Graeber 2011: 249. For a magisterial account of the negotiation of worldly and spiritual spheres in a Byzantine Empire that never allowed its ruler to become fully, if not partly, priestly, see Dagron 1996.

5. The Middle Ages emerges as an era of improved living conditions, the opposite of its usual historiographical role, in part thanks to the hostility of Christianity and Islam to usury: Graeber 2011: 250–305.

6. Morris and Scheidel 2008; Scheidel 2009, 2015; Lavan, Payne, and Weisweiler 2016.

7. Lavan, Payne, and Weisweiler 2016 argue for an integrative approach to West Asian empires that foregrounds interaction between empires—both contemporaneously across frontiers and diachronically across time—and institutional cross-pollination.

8. For a survey of Zoroastrian origins skeptical of the central role occupied by Zoroaster in Axial-Age accounts, see Shaked 2005.

9. Shaked 1994 provides a simultaneously concise and complex account of Zoroastrian cosmology and its ethical dualism.

10. Khatchadourian 2016: 14, following Lommel 1970: 395.

11. Lincoln 2012; Kellens 2017. But see Henkelman 2008 for a masterful unveiling of the range of religious practices of the Achaemenid elite that the historiographical framework of Zoroastrianism tends to obscure.

12. Lincoln 2012.

13. On Zoroastrianism in the Parthian period, see de Jong 2013; and on the endurance of memories of empire, see Canepa 2010; Shayegan 2011, 2012.

14. Gnoli 1989; Daryaee 2005.

15. Macuch 2010. Christian aristocrats could nevertheless share lineages, mythical–historical connections, and regional identities with their Zoroastrian superiors: Payne 2015: 59–78, 136–157.

16. Macuch 1981: 13–20; Shaked 1990; Jany 2006, 2007.

17. Alram and Gyselen 2003: 167.

18. Morony 2004, Payne 2015: 64–68.

19. Pigulevskaya 1958, Banaji 2009: 78–86. Slaves—*bandag* and *anšahrīg* in Middle Persian—are ubiquitous in the sources, but their prevalence as a source of labor is difficult to discern. For slavery in Middle Persian literary and juridical texts, see Colditz 2000: 123–134 and Macuch 2002.

20. Macuch 1995, 2006, 2010; Payne 2016.

21. Macuch 1994, 2004; Jany 2004. On the archaeology of fire temples, see Huff 1995, Canepa 2013, Callieri 2014: 73–102.

22. Skjaervø 2008.

23. For the Iranian law of suretyship, *pāyēndārīh*, including so-called *pad tan* loans in which the human body served as the guarantee, see Macuch 1981: 225–227, 1993: 401–403, Macuch 2016.

24. Macuch 2009.

25. Macuch 1993: 362. Such principles likely contributed to the prominence of slave labor on the estates of fire temples: Macuch 2002.

26. Marlow 1997: 71–77.

27. Sundermann 1976, Colditz 2000. For the development of the sociological category of the poor in late Roman imperial discourse and practice, see Patlagean 1977, Brown 2002.

28. Garsoïan 1981, Macuch 1993: 600–601, Gyselen 2007.

29. Macuch 1993: 31–33. Contrast practices in the contemporary Roman world: Dossey 2008.

30. Macuch 1990, Weber 2008: xxix–xxxi.

31. Macuch 2012.

32. Crone 1991: 21–23. Typically labeled a Zoroastrian "heretic" in the scholarly litera-
    ture, more recent works placed the priest-scholar within a continuum of possibili-
    ties within Zoroastrian thought: Rezakhani 2015, Macuch 2015.
33. Crone 1994.
34. Macuch 2015.
35. Crone 1991: 30–34.
36. Crone 2012.
37. Graeber 2011: 250.
38. On the rejection of silk and other Iranian luxury commodities and its implications
    for the development of early Islamic economy and society, see Bulliet 2009. See
    also Marlow 1997: 15, for the express early Islamic rejection of Iranian elite culture.
39. Toral-Niehoff 2014, Miller 2016.
40. Marlow 1997: 66–90. For the creation of the category of "Persian" as a means of
    making Iranian culture secular and safe for Muslim consumption, see Savant 2013.

CHAPTER 9

1. As already in Becker 1924: 54, "[E]s sollen die Grundtatsachen, die in der
   Weltanschauung und Lehre des Islam liegen, einmal auf ihre Wirkung auf das
   Wirtschaftsleben hin durchgesprochen werden."
2. Rodinson 1967, Goitein 1968, Heck 2006, dissenting view in Bonner 2001.
3. Although this principle has been drawn from Schacht's *Origins*, it doesn't occur
   there in this stark form, see Schneider 1999: 72–73, 2007: 359; Motzki 2000: 5f,
   2010: 129f. However, it can be derived from, for instance, Schacht 1950: 4–5, 40–
   57, 149–52, 169f.
4. Schneider 1999: 377, 2007: 365, the debtor must work off the debt, but the creditor
   may not mistreat or sell the debtor (al-Kindī 1912: 336f).
5. The others include Azami 1986 and Hallaq 2005.
6. For a recent critique of these theories and procedures, see Gledhill 2012 and the
   response in Motzki 2012.
7. See Ghada 2005, which, however, discusses only slaves of non-Arab origin.
   Schneider has little to say about pre-Islamic Arabian slavery in general (Schneider
   1999: 302, 332).
8. As in Goldziher 1971 and, to a considerable extent, in Schneider 1999, 2000, 2007.

CHAPTER 10

1. Graeber 2011: 251.
2. See already Pernoud 1977; more specifically for the early Middle Ages, Brown
   1971, Marrou 1977, and, more recently, Fouracre 2008 (especially the introduction
   by Paul Fouracre). Graeber's "conventional wisdom" does admittedly resurface

regularly, usually in works addressed to a wider readership; see, for instance, Nixey 2017, to be read with Cameron 2017.

3. Graeber 2011: 251–252, my emphasis.

4. On monetization, see primarily Banaji 2007 and Carrié 2003; more recent work is Naismith 2014a and 2014b and Howgego 2013, contextualizing Roman monetization. On the convertibility of monetary obligations in the Middle Ages, see Feller 2009 and the discussion by Rio in this volume (Chapter 11).

5. Not only is Wickham 2005 is absent from the bibliography but the entire strand of research it represents, and to a large extent epitomizes, is ignored in *Debt*'s account of the Middle Ages. This is all the more surprising as it offers a much more historiographically informed version of the same basic dynamics, namely the demise of imperial state structures in favor of localized aristocratic power.

6. The phrase "long late antiquity" usually refers to the inclusion within the period of the Umayyad dynasty, stretching late antiquity to c. 750, a practice that has left several specialists of the period unconvinced; see Cameron 2002.

7. Starting with Brown 1971, 1978; Marrou 1977, some general reflections on the field in 2008 can be found in the first issue of the *Journal of Late Antiquity*, especially Ando 2008; James 2008; Marcone 2008; more recently, Humphries 2017.

8. The unqualified use of the fundamentally Western Christian emic expression "Church Fathers" is quite surprising in a self-professed anti-establishment narrative.

9. A thorough overview of earlier discussions in Green 1992 (but see already, in a European framework, Gerhard 1956); more recently, see Davis and Puett 2015; Jussen 2016, 2017.

10. Graeber 2011: 272.

11. Joseph 2013: 661–663.

12. Among many examples, see Briggs 2008, 2009; Dermineur 2015, 2018.

13. See especially van Minnen 2008, who shows that the credit economy was one of the main vectors of the transformation of payments in kind or in local currency into the imperial coins that were eventually collected by the central administration. For other areas of the empire, see, for instance, Catsari 2008.

14. On this process, see the detailed analysis in Bransbourg 2016.

15. See also the discussion of this point for early medieval Europe by Rio (Chapter 11), based on Bougard 2010.

16. *P.Ness.* III 55 (April 11, 667 or 682); see Papaconstantinou 2011: 635; 2012: 411–412.

17. *P.Ness.* III 59 (October 669 or 684).

18. Papaconstantinou 2016b; see also Wilfong 1990, 2002; Papaconstantinou 2016a.

19. Lerouxel 2006; examples of loans against pawns from the early empire are *P.Coll. Youtie* II 96 (192), a receipt for pawned gold earrings, and *P.Oxy* I 114 (second or third century), with a list of objects very similar to a dowry list.

20. Samellas 2017 has an illuminating discussion of conspicuous consumption in late-antique elite circles.

21. See, for example, *PSI* I 64 (Oxyrhynchos, first century BCE); *P.Oxy.* II 267 (37 CE), both from Oxyrhynchos.

22. See Westermann 1948; Samuel 1965; Hengstl 1972; Hopkins 1978, chap. 3; and the discussion in Harper 2011: 373–376. This practice is very similar to the one described by Michael Bonner in this volume (Chapter 9).

23. See Vuolanto 2015, Yiftach-Firanko 2010b.

24. For example, *BGU* IV 1058 (31 BCE), which could be an even more complicated arrangement involving a mother and her son for whom the wet nurse is to work; *P.Köln* II 102 (418), contract between a village woman and an inhabitant of the city for two *solidi*.

25. *SB* IV 7358 (Karanis, 277–282).

26. Boud'hors and Calament 2015: 46–53, no. 4; *P.Ness.* III 56 (Nessana, January 18, 687).

27. See the discussion by Rio in Chapter 11, referring to Bougard 2010.

28. Papaconstantinou 2016a: 626–629.

29. *P.Ryl.Copt.* 214 (Hermopolite, first half of the eighth century).

30. PSI I 76 (Oxyrhynchos, 573); see Keenan 1978. On conspicuous consumption and credit in late antiquity, see Samellas 2017.

31. *P.KRU* 59 (Jēme, 733 or 748): in exchange for 1.5 *solidus*, the borrower undertakes to sow one *aroura* (c. 237.5 m^2) with flax on the borrower's land and to irrigate it three times until it is ripe.

32. Graeber 2011: 283–286. A thorough overview of the position of the church fathers on lending can be found in Samellas 2017.

33. *SPP* III 343 (Herakleopolis, eighth century).

34. *O.Medin.HabuCopt.* 93 (Jēme, seventh/eighth century); transl. in Wilfong 2002: 123.

35. *O.Mon.Epiph.* 300; transl. Bagnall and Cribiore 2006: 249; no. 128 of the digital edition.

36. *O.Crum* 133; transl. Bagnall and Cribiore 2006: 309; no. 187 of the digital edition.

37. *SBKopt.* I 295; transl. Bagnall and Cribiore 2006: 242; no. 116 of the digital edition; see also the ed. pr. in Drescher 1944 and the discussion in Papaconstantinou 2020.

38. Respectively, CJ 4.32.26.2, Nov. 32, 33, 34a; CJ 8.26.11; CJ 8.17.8; CJ 1.5.22, Nov. 134.7.

39. Jördens 2010a; 2010b; Yiftach-Firanko 2010a; Lerouxel 2012, 2016: 145–192.

40. *P.Oxy.* LXIII 4397 (545); on this document, see Urbanik 2009.

41. *P.Vat.Aphrod.* 10, 1–24.

42. See Veyne 2000: 1187. The categories of credit relations described by Veyne for Rome in the early empire are hardly different from those of the early Islamic period in Egypt.

43. *O.CrumVC* 71 (Hermonthite nome, eighth century?).

44. Tillier 2015, 2017, especially 62–64 passim.

45. *P.World* p. 186; see Tillier 2017: 107–108.

46. See the overview in Sijpesteijn 2013; on the financing of the military, see Kennedy 2002; and on the logistics of this system in early eighth-century Egypt, see Papaconstantinou 2015.

47. *SB* XX 15102 (Aphrodito, February 19, 709).

48. Tillier and Vanthiegem 2018.

49. Tillier 2008.

50. *P.Ryl.Arab.* 15; see Tillier 2017: 137; for Jerusalem and Cairo in the Fatimid period, see Rustow 2008, 162–164.

51. See Graeber 2011: 265 on just such a triangulation in sixth-century China when the state was worried about the power and wealth of Buddhist monasteries.

52. See especially Joseph 2013 and 2014, which are direct replies to Graeber; both are based on an earlier argument made in Joseph 2002.

53. This is not unlike the mechanism at the heart of the contemporary Indian agricultural crisis, where the withdrawal of the state and of formal credit institutions— which, however profit-oriented, were bound by rules—left the most destitute peasants at the hands of local loan sharks at an unprecedented scale: Sadanandan 2014; see also Mishra 2007.

54. Ledeneva 2018: 31–32, and chaps. 1 and 2.

CHAPTER II

1. Readers of the book, and of this volume, will of course be aware that Graeber extends Jasper's original term "Axial Age" to include the times of Jesus and Muhammad: Graeber 2014: 224.

2. Finley 1998; Whittaker 1987. On this and the issue of transition from the ancient to the medieval world, Wickham 2005: 262.

3. Salvian, *De gubernatione Dei* V, 45.

4. Fustel de Coulanges 1889.

5. Carrié 1982 is at the most extreme level of skepticism regarding its social impact or representativeness, reading it as a method of calculating tax liability, and thus entirely devoted to the needs of the state. But see Sirks 1993; Sarris 2004.

6. Though see Sarris 2004, arguing for its survival at least as an available practice of economic exploitation in some areas in the West. The idea of continuity between late-antique *coloni* and serfs was initially refuted from the medieval side by Marc Bloch, who argued that serfs were descended from late-antique slaves, not late-antique tied tenants: Bloch 1928: 241.

7. As argued most powerfully by Wickham 2005: 521–527. See Banaji 2011 for a more oppressive take on the early Middle Ages.

8. See notably Holmes and Standen 2018.

9. Graeber 2014: 252. And, elsewhere: "the most characteristic medieval institutions and ideas arrived so late in Europe that we tend to mistake them for the first stirrings of modernity" (p. 296).

10. Duby 1968 is certainly in Graeber's bibliography.

11. "While credit systems tend to dominate in periods of relative social peace, or across networks of trust . . . in periods characterized by widespread war and plunder, they tend to be replaced by precious metal" (p. 213).

12. With some exceptions: In China, for instance, Graeber sees the state as curbing the "potential ruination" of rural society wrought by loan-shark Buddhist monasteries (p. 265). Loan-shark monasteries may provoke some twinge of recognition for the Western medievalist.

13. Crone 1980.

14. Breatnach 2014.

15. Grierson 1959.

16. On the Carolingian economy in general, see Verhulst 2002; on Carolingian coinage: Coupland 2007, 2014.

17. Naismith 2014: 36.

18. Naismith 2014: 11–12, 24, 38.

19. Bougard 2010: 442, see also Feller 2008.

20. Bougard 2010: 464, 473 on the size of sums.

21. Bougard 2010: 451–453; he lists one example where the interest was in cash, but this is a rare case from Salerno, one of the most monetized and commercially plugged-in areas in western Europe.

22. Bougard 2010: 453–454. Formularies involving loans seem to assume the transferability of the credit note: for example, *Formulae Andecavenses* nos. 38 and 60 or *Formulae Marculfi* II, 25 (translated in Rio 2008a).

23. Bougard 2010: 477.

24. Bougard 2010: 446–447; there is one non-formulary example in *Codex diplomaticus Cavensis* I, no. 95, from 882, stipulating one day's work a week for five years in exchange for a loan.

25. On penal enslavement and self-sale, see Rio 2017: 42–74 (and previously Rio 2008b, 2012, 2015).

26. *Formulae Andecavenses* no. 38 (translated in Rio 2008a).

27. Above, n. 3 for Salvian.

28. *Capitularia regum Francorum*, eds. A. Boretius and V. Krause, MGH Leges II, 2 vols. (Hanover, 1883–1897), no. 273, c. 34; see Rio 2017: 51–52.

29. Fortunatus, *Carmina* V, 4. Sometimes, as in the case of penal slaves, removal from the community seems to have been the point: Wihtred 26 (translated in Attenborough 1922).

30. *Capitularia regum Francorum* I, no. 33, c. 30.

31. *Sermo Lupi ad Anglos*.

32. *Pauli Sententiae* V.1.1; see Ramin and Veyne 1981; for further comment, Rio 2012.
33. Jankowiak 2017; McCormick 2001 and 2002 (arguing for very high volume of sales via western Europe as well).
34. Rio 2017: 19–41.
35. Graeber 2014: 171. The Roman Empire seems to be what is meant by the expanding commercial economy in the quote, given Graeber's chronology for the end of slavery (though he does acknowledge the later impact of the Viking presence, p. 422, n. 14); but the same terms could easily apply to the Muslim world in relation to western Europe as a whole during the early Middle Ages.
36. See, for example, Heers 1981, Blumenthal 2009, McKee 2008.
37. Rio 2017: 154–155.
38. On Roman convicts: Millar 1984.
39. Rio 2017: 230–236.

Bibliography

CHAPTER I

Acemoğlu, D., and J. A. Robinson. *Why Nations Fail: The Origins of Power, Prosperity and Poverty*. New York: Crown Business, 2012.

Bernard, S. "The Social History of Early Roman Coinage." *Journal of Roman Studies* 108 (2018): 1–26.

Boldizzoni, F. *The Poverty of Clio: Resurrecting Economic History*. Princeton, NJ: Princeton University Press, 2011.

Bowes, K. D. "When Kuznets Went to Rome: Roman Economic Well-Being and the Reframing of Roman History." *Capitalism* 2 (2021): 7–40.

Bowman, A. K., and A. Wilson. *Quantifying the Roman Economy: Methods and Problems*. Oxford: Oxford University Press, 2009.

Bresson, A. "Monnayage et société dans les mondes antiques." *Revue numismatique* 157 (2001): 51–68.

Bresson, A. *The Making of the Ancient Greek Economy: Institutions, Markets, and Growth in the City-States*. Princeton, NJ: Princeton University Press, 2016.

Bresson, A. "Silverization, Prices, and Tribute in the Achaemenid Empire." In *Aršāma and His World: The Bodleian Letters in Context*. Vol. 3, *Aršāma's World*, edited by C. J. Tuplin and J. Ma, 209–248. Oxford: Oxford University Press, 2020.

Campagno, M., J. Gallego, and C. G. García Mac Gaw, eds. *Capital, deuda y desigualdad: Distribuciones de la riqueza en el Mediterráneo antiguo*. Buenos Aires: Miño y Dávila, 2017.

Démare-Lafont, S., ed. *Debt in Ancient Mediterranean Societies: A Documentary Approach*. Geneva: DROZ, 2019.

Eisenstadt, S. N., ed. *The Origins and Diversity of Axial Age Civilizations*. Albany: State University of New York Press, 1986.

Elliott, C. P. *Economic Theory and the Roman Monetary Economy*. Cambridge: Cambridge University Press, 2020.

Erdkamp, P., ed. *Capital, Investment, and Innovation in the Roman World*. Oxford: Oxford University Press, 2020.

Graeber, D. *Toward an Anthropological Theory of Value: The False Coin of Our Own Dreams*. New York: Palgrave, 2001.

Graeber, D. *Fragments of an Anarchist Anthropology*. Chicago: Prickly Paradigm Press, 2004.

Graeber, D. *Lost People: Magic and the Legacy of Slavery in Madagascar*. Bloomington: Indiana University Press, 2007.

Graeber, D. "Debt, Violence, and Impersonal Markets: Polanyian Meditations." In *Market and Society: The Great Transformation Today*, edited by C. Hann and K. Hart, 106–132. Cambridge: Cambridge University Press, 2009a.

Graeber, D. *Direct Action: An Ethnography*. Edinburgh and Oakland, CA: AK Press, 2009b.

Graeber, D. *Debt: The First 5,000 Years*. New York: Melville House, 2011.

Hart, K. "In Rousseau's Footsteps: David Graeber and the Anthropology of Unequal Society." *Journal du Mauss* (January 2013). http://rousseaustudies.free.fr/articlema uss.pdf

Hart, K., J.-L. Laville, and A. Cattani, eds. *The Human Economy: A Citizen's Guide*. Cambridge: Polity Press, 2010.

Hobson, M. S. "A Historiography of the Study of the Roman Economy: Economic Growth, Development, and Neoliberalism." In *TRAC 2013: Proceedings of the Twenty-Third Annual Theoretical Roman Archaeology Conference, King's College, London 2013*, edited by H. Platts, J. Pearce, C. Barron, J. Lundock, and J. Yoo, 11–26. Oxford: Oxbow Books, 2014.

Humphrey, C. "Barter and Economic Disintegration." *Man* 20 (1985): 48–72.

Humphrey, C., and S. Hugh-Jones, eds. *Barter, Exchange, and Value: An Anthropological Approach*. Cambridge: Cambridge University Press, 1992.

Ingham, G. *The Nature of Money*. Cambridge: Polity Press, 2004.

Jaspers, K. *Vom Ursprung und Ziel der Geschichte*. Munich: Artemis-Verlag, 1949.

Jongman, W. M., J. P. A. M. Jacobs, and G. M. Klein Goldewijk. "Health and Wealth in the Roman Empire." *Economics and Human Biology* 34 (2019): 138–150.

Joseph, M. *Against the Romance of Community*. Minneapolis: University of Minnesota Press, 2002.

Joseph, M. "Theorizing Debt for Social Change." *Ephemera: Theory & Politics in Organization* 13 (2013): 659–673.

Jursa, M. *Aspects of the Economic History of Babylonia in the First Millennium BC: Economic Geography, Economic Mentalities, Agriculture, the Use of Money and the Problem of Economic Growth*. Münster, Germany: Ugarit-Verlag, 2010.

Jursa, M. "Babylonia in the First Millennium BCE: Economic Growth in Times of Empire." In *The Cambridge History of Capitalism*. Vol. 1, *The Rise of Capitalism: From Ancient Origins to 1848*, edited by L. Neal and J. G. Williamson, 24–42. Cambridge: Cambridge University Press, 2014.

Kron, G. "Comparative Evidence and the Reconstruction of the Ancient Economy: Greco-Roman Housing and the Level and Distribution of Wealth and Income." In *Quantifying the Greco-Roman Economy and Beyond*, edited by F. de Callataÿ, 123–146. Bari, Italy: Edipuglia, 2014.

Kurke, L. *Coins, Bodies, Games, and Gold: The Politics of Meaning in Archaic Greece.* Princeton, NJ: Princeton University Press, 1999.

Manning, J. G. *The Open Sea: The Economic Life of the Ancient Mediterranean World from the Iron Age to the Rise of Rome.* Princeton, NJ: Princeton University Press, 2018.

Manning, J. G., and I. Morris. *The Ancient Economy: Evidence and Models.* Stanford, CA: Stanford University Press, 2005.

Milanovic, B. *Capitalism, Alone: The Future of the System That Rules the World.* Cambridge, MA: Belknap Press of Harvard University Press, 2019.

Monson, A., and W. Scheidel. *Fiscal Regimes and the Political Economy of Premodern States.* Cambridge: Cambridge University Press, 2015.

Mooring, J. A., B. Van Leeuwen, and R. J. Van der Spek. "Introducing Coinage: Comparing the Greek World, the Near East and China." In *Money, Currency and Crisis: In Search of Trust, 2000 BC to AD 2000*, edited by B. Van Leeuwen and R. J. Van der Spek, 132–148. London: Routledge, 2018.

North, D. C. *Structure and Change in Economic History.* New York: W. W. Norton, 1981.

North, D. C. *Institutions, Institutional Change and Economic Performance.* Cambridge: Cambridge University Press, 1990.

North, D. C., and R. P. Thomas. *The Rise of the Western World: A New Economic History.* Cambridge: Cambridge University Press, 1973.

Ober, J. *The Rise and Fall of Classical Greece.* Princeton, NJ: Princeton University Press, 2015.

Payne, R. "Sex, Death, and Aristocratic Empire: Iranian Jurisprudence in Late Antiquity." *Comparative Studies in Society and History* 58 (2016): 519–549.

Peralta, D.-E. "Epistemicide: The Roman Case." *Classica* 33 (2020): 151–186.

Piketty, T. *Capital in the Twenty-First Century.* Cambridge, MA: Harvard University Press, 2014.

Piketty, T., L. Yang, and G. Zucman. "Capital Accumulation, Private Property, and Rising Inequality in China, 1978–2015." *Economic History Review* 109 (2019): 2469–2496.

Pirngruber, R. *The Economy of Late Achaemenid and Seleucid Babylonia.* Cambridge: Cambridge University Press, 2017.

Polanyi, K. *The Great Transformation.* New York: Farrar & Rinehart, 1944.

Purcell, N. "*Quod enim alterius fuit, id ut fiat meum, necesse est aliquid intercedere* (Varro): The Anthropology of Buying and Selling in Ancient Greece and Rome: An Introductory Sketch." In *Anthropologie de l'antiquité: Anciens objets, nouvelles approches*, edited by P. Payen and E. Scheid-Tissinier, 81–98. Turnhout: Brepols, 2012.

Schaps, D. M. *The Invention of Coinage and the Monetization of Ancient Greece.* Ann Arbor: University of Michigan Press, 2004.

Scheidel, W. "Quantifying the Sources of Slaves in the Early Roman Empire." *Journal of Roman Studies* 87 (1997): 156–169.

Scheidel, W. "From the 'Great Convergence' to the 'First Great Divergence': Roman and Qin-Han State Formation and Its Aftermath." In *Rome and China: Comparative Perspectives on Ancient World Empires*, edited by W. Scheidel, 11–23. Oxford: Oxford University Press, 2009.

Scheidel, W. "Physical Well-Being." In *The Cambridge Companion to the Roman Economy*, edited by W. Scheidel, 321–333. Cambridge: Cambridge University Press, 2012.

Scheidel, W. *The Great Leveler: Violence and the History of Inequality from the Stone Age to the Twenty-First Century*. Princeton, NJ: Princeton University Press, 2017.

Scheidel, W. *Escape from Rome: The Failure of Empire and the Road to Prosperity*. Princeton, NJ: Princeton University Press, 2019.

Scheidel, W. "Roman Wealth and Wealth Inequality in Comparative Perspective." *Journal of Roman Archaeology* 33 (2020): 341–353.

Scheidel, W., and S. J. Friesen. "The Size of the Economy and the Distribution of Income in the Roman Empire." *Journal of Roman Studies* 99 (2009): 61–91.

Scheidel, W., R. P. Saller, and I. Morris. "Introduction." In *The Cambridge Economic History of the Greco-Roman World*, edited by W. Scheidel, R. P. Saller, and I. Morris, 1–12. Cambridge: Cambridge University Press, 2007.

Seaford, R. *Money and the Early Greek Mind: Homer, Philosophy, Tragedy*. Cambridge: Cambridge University Press, 2004.

Shaw, B. D. "After Rome: Transformations of the Early Mediterranean World." *New Left Review* 51 (2008): 89–114.

Shaw, B. D. *Bringing in the Sheaves: Economy and Metaphor in the Roman World*. Toronto: University of Toronto Press, 2013.

Shaw, B. D. "Social Status and Economic Behavior: A Hidden History of the Equites." *Ancient Society* 50 (2020): 153–202.

Temin, P. *The Roman Market Economy*. Princeton, NJ: Princeton University Press, 2013.

Van der Spek, R. J., J. G. Dercksen, K. Kleber, and M. Jursa. "Money, Silver and Trust in Mesopotamia." In *Money, Currency and Crisis: In Search of Trust, 2000 BC to AD 2000*, edited by B. Van Leeuwen and R. J. Van der Spek, 102–131. London: Routledge, 2018.

Van Oyen, A. *How Things Make History: The Roman Empire and Its Terra Sigillata Pottery*. Amsterdam: Amsterdam University Press, 2016.

Van Oyen, A. *The Socio-Economics of Roman Storage: Agriculture, Trade, and Family*. Cambridge: Cambridge University Press, 2020.

Verboven, K. "Currency and Credit in the Bay of Naples in the First Century AD." In *The Economy of Pompeii*, edited by M. Flohr and A. Wilson, 363–386. Oxford: Oxford University Press, 2016.

Von Reden, S. *Exchange in Ancient Greece*. London: Bloomsbury Academic, 1995.

Von Reden, S. *Money in Ptolemaic Egypt: From the Macedonian Conquest to the End of the Third Century BC*. Cambridge: Cambridge University Press, 2007.

Von Reden, S. *Money in Classical Antiquity*. Cambridge: Cambridge University Press, 2012.

Von Reden, S. "Global Economic History." In *The Cambridge World History*. Vol. 4, *A World with States, Empires and Networks 1200 BCE–900 CE*, edited by C. Benjamin, 29–54. Cambridge: Cambridge University Press, 2015.

Weber, I. *How China Escaped Shock Therapy: The Market Reform Debate*. Abingdon, UK: Routledge, 2021.

Wittrock, B. "The Axial Age in World History." In *The Cambridge World History*. Vol. 4, *A World with States, Empires and Networks 1200 BCE–900 CE*, edited by C. Benjamin, 101–119. Cambridge: Cambridge University Press, 2015.

CHAPTER 2

Alster, B. *Proverbs of Ancient Sumer. The World's Earliest Proverb Collections*. Bethesda, MD: CDL Press, 1997.

Baßler, M. *Die kulturpoetische funktion und das archiv. Eine literaturwissenschaftliche text-kontext-theorie*. Tübingen, Germany: Francke Verlag, 2005.

Bresson, A. *The Making of the Ancient Greek Economy: Institutions, Markets and, Growth in the City-States*. Oxford and Princeton, NJ: Princeton University Press, 2016.

Brinkman, J. "Settlement Survey and Documentary Evidence: Regional Variation and Secular Trend in Mesopotamian Demography." *Journal of Near Eastern Studies* 43, no. 2 (1984): 168–180.

Campbell, J. K. *Honour, Family and Patronage: A Study of Institutions and Moral Values in a Greek Mountain Community*. Oxford: Oxford University Press, 1964.

Charpin, D. (2000), "Les prêteurs et le palais: Les édits de mîšarum des rois de Babylone et leurs traces dans les archives privées." In *Interdependency of Institutions and Private Entrepreneurs: Proceedings of the Second MOS Symposium (Leiden 1998)*, edited by A. C. V. M. Bongenaar, 185–211. MOS Studies 2, PIHANS 87. Leiden: Nederlands Historisch-Archaeologisch Instituut te Istanbul, 2000.

Clancier, P., P. Rouillard, P. Joannès, and A. Tenu, eds. *Autour de Polanyi. Vocabulaires, théories et modalités des échanges*. Paris: De Boccard, 2005.

De Zorzi, N. *La serie teratomantica šumma izbu. Test, tradizione, orizzonti culturali*. HANE/M 15, 2 vols. Padua, Italy: Sargon Editice e Libreria, 2014.

Diakonoff, I. "The Rural Community in the Ancient Near East." *Journal of the Economic and Social History of the Orient* 18, no. 2 (1975): 121–133.

Graeber, D. "Debt, Violence, and Impersonal Markets: Polanyian Meditations." In *Market and Society: The Great Transformation Today*, edited by C. Hann and K. Hart, 106–132. Cambridge: Cambridge University Press, 2009.

Graeber, D. *Debt: The First 5,000 Years*. New York: Melville House, 2011.

Hackl, J., M. Jursa, and M. Schmidl. *Spätbabylonische privatbriefe*. AOAT 414/1. Münster, Germany: Ugarit-Verlag, 2014.

Hudson, M., and M. van de Mieroop, eds. *Debt and Economic Renewal in the Ancient Near East: International Scholars Conference on Ancient Near Eastern Economies*, vol. 3. Bethesda, MD: CDL Press, 2002.

Jiménez, E. *The Babylonian Disputation Poems. With Editions of the Series of the Poplar, Palm and Vine, the Series of the Spider, and the Story of the Poor, Forlorn Wren*. CHANE 87. Leiden and Boston: Brill, 2017.

Jursa, M. "The Remuneration of Institutional Labourers in an Urban Context in Babylonia in the First Millennium BC." In *L'archive des fortifications de Persépolis. État des questions et perspectives de recherché*, edited by P. Briant, W. Henkelman, and M. Stolper, 387–427. Persika 12. Paris: De Boccard, 2008.

Jursa, M. *Aspects of the Economic History of Babylonia in the First Millennium BC: Economic Geography, Economic Mentalities, Agriculture, the Use of Money and the Problem of Economic Growth*. With contributions by J. Hackl, B. Janković, K. Kleber, E. E. Payne, C. Waerzeggers and M. Weszeli. AOAT 377 = Veröffentlichungen zur Wirtschaft sgeschichte Babyloniens im 1. Jahrtausend v. Chr., Band 4. Münster, Germany: Ugarit-Verlag, 2010.

Jursa, M. "Taxation and Service Obligations in Babylonia from Nebuchadnezzar to Darius and the Evidence for Darius' tax reform." In *Herodot und das Persische Weltreich. Akten des 3. Internationalen Kolloquiums zum Thema "Vorderasien im Spannungsfeld klassischer und altorientalischer Überlieferungen," Innsbruck, 24.– 28. November 2008*, edited by R. Rollinger, B. Truschneggand, and J. Wiesehöfer, 431–448. Wiesbaden, Germany: Harrassowitz Verlag, 2011.

Jursa, M. "Babylonia in the First Millennium BCE—Economic Growth in Times of Empire." In *The Cambridge History of Capitalism. Vol. 1, The Rise of Capitalism from Ancient Origins to 1848*, edited by L. Neal and J. Williamson, 24–42. Cambridge: Cambridge University Press, 2014.

Jursa, M. "Gift, Bribe and the Remuneration of Officials in Late Babylonian Sources." In *Individuals and Institutions in the Ancient Near East: a Tribute to Ran Zadok*, edited by U. Gabbay and S. Gordin, 146–159. Berlin and Boston: De Gruyter 2021.

Lambert, C. *Babylonian Wisdom Literature*. Oxford: Clarendon Press, 1960. Reprint, Winona Lake, ID: Eisenbrauns, 1996.

Liverani, M. *Prestige and Interest: International Relations in the Near East ca. 1600–1100 B.C.* History of the Ancient Near East/Studies I. Padova, Italy: Sargon, 1990.

Liverani, M. *Imagining Babylon: The Modern Story of an Ancient City*. Berlin and Boston: De Gruyter, 2016.

Nam, R. "Book Review of R. Pirngruber, The Economy of Late Achaemenid and Seleucid Babylonia." *Journal of Near Eastern Studies* 72, no. 1 (2019): 158–160.

Pirngruber, R. *The Economy of Late Achaemenid and Seleucid Babylonia*. Cambridge: Cambridge University Press, 2017.

Postgate, J. N. *Fifty Neo-Assyrian Legal Documents*. Warminster, UK: Aris & Phillips, 1976.

Scott, J. A. *Against the Grain: A Deep History of the Earliest States*. New Haven, CT and London: Yale University Press, 2017.

Skaist, A. *The Old Babylonia Loan Contract. Its History and Geography*. Ramat Gan, Israel: Bar-Ilan University Press, 1984.

Steinert, U. *Aspekte des Menschseins im Alten Mesopotamien. Eine Studie zu Person und Identität im 2. und 1. Jt. v. Chr*. CM 44. Leiden and Boston: Brill, 2012.

Steinkeller, P. "Mythical Realities of the Early Babylonian History (or the Modern Historian and the Native Uses of History Past." In *History, Texts and Art in Early Babylonia. Three Essays*, 167–197. SANER 15. Berlin and Boston: De Gruyter, 2017.

Stol, M. "Wirtschaft und Gesellschaft in altbabylonischer Zeit." In *Mesopotamien: Die altbabylonische Zeit*, edited by D. Charpin, D. O. Edzard, and M. Stol, 643–975. OBO 160/4. Fribourg, Switzerland: Academic Press; Göttingen, Germany: Vandenhoeck & Ruprecht, 2004.

Stolper, M. W. *Entrepreneurs and Empire: The Murašû Archive, the Murašû Firm, and Persian Rule in Babylonia*. PIHANS 54. Leiden: NINO, 1985.

Van de Mieroop, M. *Cuneiform Texts and the Writing of History*. London and New York: Routledge, 1999.

Van der Spek, R. J., B. van Leeuwen, and J.-L. van Zanden, eds. *A History of Market Performance from Ancient Babylonia to the Modern World*. London and New York: Routledge, 2015.

Van Driel, G. "The Murašûs in Context." *Journal of the Economic and Social History of the Orient* 32 (1989): 203–229.

Waerzeggers, C. "The Babylonian Revolts against Xerxes and the 'end of archives.'" *Archiv für Orientforschung* 50 (2003–2004): 150–173.

Waerzeggers, C., and M. Seire, eds. *Xerxes and Babylonia: The Cuneiform Evidence*. OLA 277. Leuven, Belgium: Peeters, 2018.

Winter, I. "Gold! Light and Lustre in Ancient Mesopotamia." In *Proceedings of the 7th International Congress on the Archaeology of the Ancient Near East: 12 April–16 April 2010*, edited by R. Matthews and J. Curtis, 2:153–171. Wiesbaden, Germany: Harrassowitz-Verlag, 2012.

CHAPTER 3

Berger, P. *The Sacred Canopy: Elements of a Sociological Theory of Religion*. New York: Doubleday, 1967.

Biardeau, M., and C. Malamoud. *Le sacrifice dans l'Inde ancienne*. Paris: Presses Universitaires de France, 1976.

Bodewitz, H. "Redeath and Its Relation to Rebirth and Release." *Studien zur Indologie und Iranistik* 20 (1996): 27–46.

Collins, S. *Selfless Persons: Imagery and Thought in Theravāda Buddhism*. Cambridge: Cambridge University Press, 1982.

Diels, H., and W. Kranz, eds. *Die Fragmente der Vorsokratiker*. Berlin: Weidmann, 1951.

Edmunds, L. "A Hermeneutic Commentary on the Eschatological Passage in Pindar *Olympian* 2 (57–83)." In *Antike Mythen: Medien, Transformationen, und Konstruktionen*, edited by U. Dill and C. Walde, 662–677. Berlin and New York: de Gruyter, 2009.

Gombrich, R. *How Buddhism Began*. London: Athlone, 1996.

Gombrich, R. *Theravada Buddhism*. 2nd ed. London and New York: Routledge, 2006.

Gonda, J. *Loka: World and Heaven in the Veda*. Verhandelingen der Koninklijke Nederlandse Akademie van Wetenschappen, Afd. Letterkunde, n.r. 73.1. Amsterdam: Elsevier, 1966.

Graeber, D. *Debt: The First 5,000 Years*. New York: Melville House, 2011.

Graf, F., and S. Iles Johnston. *Ritual Texts for the Afterlife*. London and New York: Routledge, 2007.

Halbfass, W. *Karma und Wiedergeburt im Indischen Denken*. Munich: Diederichs, 2000.

Heesterman, J. *The Broken World of Sacrifice: An Essay in Ancient Indian Ritual*. Chicago: University of Chicago Press, 1993.

Keith, A. B. *The Religion and Philosophy of the Veda and the Upaniṣads*. Two vols. Cambridge, MA: Harvard University Press, 1925.

Killingley, D. "The Paths of the Dead and the Five Fires." In *Indian Insights: Buddhism, Brahmanism and Bhakti*, edited by P. Connolly and S. Hamilton, 1–20. London: Luzac Oriental, 1997.

Krishan, Y. *The Doctrine of Karma*. Delhi: Motilal Banarsidass, 1997.

Lévi, S. *La Doctrine du sacrifice dans les Brahmanas*. Paris: Leroux, 1898.

Mourelatos, A. P. D. *The Route of Parmenides*. Rev. exp. ed. Las Vegas: Parmenides Publishing, 2008.

Obeyesekere, G. *Imagining Karma: Ethical Transformation in Amerindian, Buddhist, and Greek Rebirth*. Berkeley: University of California Press, 2002.

Olivelle, P. *Upaniṣads*. Oxford: Oxford University Press, 1996.

Seaford, R. "Immortality, Salvation, and the Elements." In *Harvard Studies in Classical Philology* 90 (1986): 1–26.

Seaford, R. *Money and the Early Greek Mind*. Cambridge: Cambridge University Press, 2004.

Seaford, R. *Cosmology and the Polis*. Cambridge: Cambridge University Press, 2012.

Seaford, R. "The Interiorisation of Ritual in India and Greece." In *Universe and Inner Self in Early Indian and Early Greek Thought*, edited by R. Seaford, 204–219. Edinburgh: Edinburgh University Press, 2016.

Seaford, R. *The Origins of Philosophy in Ancient Greece and Ancient India*. Cambridge: Cambridge University Press, 2020.

Tull, H. W. *The Vedic Origins of Karma*. Albany: State University of New York Press, 1989.

CHAPTER 4

Andreev, V. N. "Some Aspects of Agrarian Conditions in Attica in the Fifth to Third Centuries B.C." *Eirene* 13 (1974): 5–46.

Asheri, D. *Distribuzioni di terre nell'antica Grecia*. Turin, Italy: Accademia della Scienze, 1966.

Asheri, D. *Leggi greche sul problema dei debiti*. Pisa, Italy: Pisa University Press, 1969.

Bertrand, J.-M. "De la stasis dans les cités platoniciennes." *Cahiers du Centre Gustave-Glotz* 10 (1999): 209–224.

Blümel, W. "SGDI 5727 (Halikarnassos): Eine Revision." *Kadmos* 32 (1993): 1–18.

Bogaert, R. *Banques et banquiers dans les cités Grecques*. Leiden: A. W. Sijthoff, 1968.

Bresson, A. "Les cités Greques et leurs emporia." In *L'Emporion*, edited by A. Bresson and P. Rouillard, 163–225. Paris: De Boccard, 1993.

Bresson, A. *The Making of the Ancient Greek Economy: Institutions, Markets, and Growth in the City-States*. Princeton, NJ: Princeton University Press, 2016.

Bruce, I. A. F. "The Corcyraean Civil War of 427 B.C." *Phoenix* 25 (1971): 108–117.

Brucker, G. A. *Renaissance Florence*. New York: John Wiley & Sons, 1969.

Burford, A. M. *Land and Labor in the Greek World*. Baltimore: Johns Hopkins University Press, 1993.

Canevaro, M. *The Documents in the Attic Orators: Laws and Decrees in the Public Speeches of the Demosthenic Corpus*. Oxford: Oxford University Press, 2013.

Cecchet, L. "Debt Cancellation in Classical and Hellenistic *Poleis*: Between Demagogy and Crisis Management." *The European Legacy* 23 (2018): 127–148.

Chankowski, V., and L. Domaradzka. "Réédition de l'inscription de Pistiros et problèmes d'interprétation." *Bulletin de Correspondance Hellénique* 123 (1999): 246–258.

Clark, C., and M. Haswell. *The Economics of Subsistence Agriculture*. 2nd ed. London: Macmillan, 1966.

Cohen, E. E. *Athenian Economy and Society: A Banking Perspective*. Princeton, NJ: Princeton University Press, 1992.

Cohen, E. E. "The Wealthy Slaves of Athens. Legal Rights, Economic Obligations." In *Monde antique et les droits de l'homme*, edited by H. Jones, 105–129. Brussels: Université libre de Bruxelles, Centre de droit compare et d'histoire du droit, 1998.

Davies, J. K. *Athenian Propertied Families, 600–300 B.C.* Oxford: Clarendon Press, 1971.

Davies, J. K. *Wealth and the Power of Wealth in Classical Athens*. New York: Arno Press, 1981.

Davies, J. K. "Temples, Credit, and the Circulation of Money." In *Money and Its Uses in the Ancient Greek World*, edited by A. Meadows and K. M. Shipton, 117–128. Oxford: Oxford University Press, 2001.

Davies, J. K. "Classical Greece: Production." In *The Cambridge Economic History of the Greco-Roman World*, edited by I. Morris, R. P. Saller, and W. Scheidel, 333–406. Cambridge: Cambridge University Press, 2007.

de Ste. Croix, G. E. M. *The Class Struggle in the Ancient Greek World: From the Archaic Age to the Arab Conquests.* Ithaca, NY: Cornell University Press, 1981.

Ehrenberg, V. *The Greek State.* New York: W. W. Norton, 1964.

Ehrhardt, A. "Parakatatheke." *Zeitschrift der Savigny-Stiftung für Rechtsgeschichte. Romanistische Abteilung* 75 (1958): 32–90.

Eich, A. *Die politische Ökonomie des antiken Griechenland (6.–3. Jahrhundert v. Chr.).* Cologne, Germany: Böhlau Verlag, 2006.

Finley, M. I. *Studies in Land and Credit in Ancient Athens, 500–200 B.C.: The Horos Inscriptions.* New Brunswick, NJ: Rutgers University Press, 1951.

Finley, M. I. "Debt-Bondage and the Problem of Slavery." In *Economy and Society in Ancient Greece,* edited by B. D. Shaw and R. P. Saller, 150–166. London: Chatto & Windus, 1981. First published 1965.

Finley, M. I. *The Ancient Economy.* 3rd ed. Berkeley: University of California Press, 1985.

Fisher, N. R. E. "Independent Slaves in Classical Athens and the Ideology of Freedom." In *From Captivity to Freedom: Themes in Ancient and Modern Slavery,* edited by C. Katsari and E. Dal Lago, 121–146. Leicester, UK: Leicester University Press, 2008.

Forsdyke, S. *Slaves Tell Tales and Other Episodes in the Politics of Popular Culture in Ancient Greece.* Princeton, NJ: Princeton University Press, 2012.

Frier, B. W., and D. P. Kehoe. "Law and Economic Institutions." In *The Cambridge Economic History of the Greco-Roman World,* edited by I. Morris, R. P. Saller, and W. Scheidel, 113–143. Cambridge: Cambridge University Press, 2007.

Fuks, A. *Social Conflict in Ancient Greece.* Jerusalem: Magnes Press, Hebrew University; Leiden: Brill, 1984.

Gabrielsen, V. "Banking and Credit Operations in Hellenistic Times." In *Making, Moving and Managing: The New World of Ancient Economies, 323–31 BC,* edited by Z. H. Archibald, J. K. Davies, and V. Gabrielsen, 136–164. Oxford: Oxbow Books, 2005.

Gallant, T. W. *Risk and Survival in Ancient Greece: Reconstructing the Rural Domestic Economy.* Oxford: Polity Press, 1991.

Garlan, Y. "Le travail libre en Grèce ancienne." In *Non-Slave Labour in the Greco-Roman World,* edited by P. D. Garnsey, 6–22. Cambridge: Cambridge Philological Society, 1980.

Garlan, Y. *Les esclaves en Grèce ancienne.* 2nd ed. Paris: F. Maspero, 1995.

Garnsey, P. D. A. *Famine and Food Supply in the Greco-Roman World: Responses to Risk and Crisis.* Cambridge: Cambridge University Press, 1988.

Gehrke, H.-J. *Stasis. Untersuchungen zu den inneren Kriegen in den griechischen Staaten des 5. und 4. Jahrhunderts v. Chr.* Munich: C. H. Beck'sche Verlagsbuchhandlung, 1985.

Gillis, D. "The Revolt at Mytilene." *American Journal of Philology* 92, no. 1 (1971): 38–47.

Goldthwaite, R. A. *The Economy of Renaissance Florence.* Baltimore: Johns Hopkins University Press, 2009.

Graeber, D. *Debt. The First 5,000 Years.* New York: Melville House, 2011.

Gschnitzer, F. *Abhängige Orte im griechischen Altertum.* Munich: Verlag C. H. Beck, 1958.

Halstead, P. "Traditional and Ancient Rural Economy in Mediterranean Economy: Plus Ça Change?" In *The Ancient Economy*, edited by W. Scheidel and S. von Reden, 53–70. Edinburgh: Edinburgh University Press, 2002. First published 1987.

Harris, E. M. "A New Solution to the Riddle of the *Seisachtheia*." In *The Development of the Polis in Archaic Greece*, edited by L. G. Mitchell and P. J. Rhodes, 103–112. London: Routledge, 1997.

Harris, E. M. "Did Solon Abolish Debt-Bondage?" *The Classical Quarterly* 52 (2002): 415–430.

Harris, E. M. "The Legal Foundations of Economic Growth in Ancient Greece: The Role of Property Records." In *The Ancient Greek Economy: Markets, Households and City-States*, edited by E. M. Harris, D. M. Lewis, and M. Woolmer, 116–146. New York: Cambridge University Press, 2015.

Hinsch, M. *Ökonomik und Hauswirtschaft im klassischen Griechenland.* Berlin: Franz Steiner Verlag, 2021.

Homolle, T. "La loi de Cadys sur le prêt à intérêt." *Bulletin de Correspondance Hellénique* 50 (1926): 3–106.

Hopkins, K., and P. J. Roscoe. "Between Slavery and Freedom. On Freeing Slaves at Delphi." In *Conquerors and Slaves*, edited by K. Hopkins, 133–171. Cambridge: Cambridge University Press, 1978.

Horden, P., and N. Purcell. *The Corrupting Sea: A Study of Mediterranean History.* Oxford: Blackwell, 2000.

Hornblower, S. *The Greek World, 479–323 B.C.* 3rd ed. London and New York: Routledge, 2002.

Isager, S., and M. H. Hansen. *Aspects of Athenian Society in the Fourth Century B.C.* Odense, Denmark: Odense Universitetsforlag, 1975.

Ismard, P. *La cité des réseaux. Athènes et ses associations, VIe–Ier siècle av. J.-C.* Paris: Publications de la Sorbonne, 2010.

Jameson, M. H. "Agricultural Labor in Ancient Greece." In *Agriculture in Ancient Greece: Proceedings of the Seventh International Symposium at the Swedish Institute at Athens, 16–17 May 1990*, edited by B. Wells, 135–146. Göteborg, Sweden: Swedish Institute at Athens, 1992.

Lane, F. C. *Venice: A Maritime Republic.* Baltimore: Johns Hopkins University Press, 1973.

Lewis, D. M. *Greek Slave Systems in Their Eastern Mediterranean Context, c. 800–146 BC.* Oxford: Oxford University Press, 2018.

Loomis, W. T. *Wages, Welfare Costs, and Inflation in Classical Athens.* Ann Arbor: University of Michigan Press, 1998.

Lopez, R. S., and I. W. Raymond. *Medieval Trade in the Mediterranean World: Illustrative Documents.* New York: Columbia University Press, 1955.

Loukopoulou, L. "Sur le statut et l'importance de l'emporion de Pistiros." *Bulletin de correspondance hellénique* 123, no. 1 (1999): 359–371.

Lycos, K. *Plato on Justice and Power: Reading Book I of Plato's Republic.* Basingstoke and London: Palgrave Macmillan, 1987.

Meier, M. "Die athenischen Hektemoroi—eine Erfindung?" *Historische Zeitschrift* 294 (2012): 1–29.

Meiggs, R. *The Athenian Empire.* Oxford: Clarendon Press, 1972.

Millett, P. C. "Maritime Loans and the Structure of Credit in Fourth-Century Athens." In *Trade in the Ancient Economy*, edited by P. D. Garnsey, K. Hopkins, and C. R. Whittaker, 36–52. London: University of California Press, 1983.

Millett, P. C. *Lending and Borrowing in Ancient Athens.* Cambridge: Cambridge University Press, 1991.

Millett, P. C. "Aristotle and Slavery in Athens." *Greece and Rome* 54 (2007): 178–209.

Morris, I., and J. G. Manning. "Introduction." In *The Ancient Economy: Evidence and Models*, edited by S. W. Manning and I. Morris, 1–44. Stanford, CA: Stanford University Press, 2005.

Morris, S. P., and J. K. Papadopoulos. "Greek Towers and Slaves: An Archaeology of Exploitation." *American Journal of Archaeology* 109 (2005): 155–225.

North, D. C. *Institutions, Institutional Change, and Economic Performance.* Cambridge: Cambridge University Press, 1990.

Ober, J. *The Rise and Fall of Classical Greece.* Princeton, NJ: Princeton University Press, 2015.

Osborne, R. G. *Classical Landscape with Figures: The Ancient Greek City and Its Countryside.* London: G. Philip, 1987.

Osborne, R. G. "Social and Economic Implications of the Leasing of Land and Property in Classical and Hellenistic Greece." *Chiron* 18 (1988): 279–323.

Partner, P. *Renaissance Rome, 1500–1559: A Portrait of a Society.* Berkeley: University of California Press, 1979.

Pernin, I. *Les baux ruraux en Grèce ancienne.* Lyon: Maison de l'Orient et de la Méditerranée, 2014.

Schütrumpf, E., and H.-J. Gehrke. "Anmerkungen." In *Aristoteles. Politik, IV–VI.* Werke in deutscher Übersetzung, 9: 3, 207–665. Berlin: de Gruyter, 1996.

Seaford, R. *Money and the Early Greek Mind.* Cambridge: Cambridge University Press, 2004.

Shipton, K. M. W. *Leasing and Lending: The Cash Economy in Fourth-Century BC Athens.* London: Institute of Classical Studies, 2000.

Sombart, W. *Warum gibt es in den Vereinigten Staaten keinen Sozialismus?* Tübingen, Germany: J. C. B. Mohr, 1906.

Todd, S. C. "Lady Chatterley's Lover and the Attic Orators: The Social Composition of the Athenian Jury." *Journal of Hellenic Studies* 110 (1990): 146–173.

Trevett, J. *Apollodoros, the Son of Pasion.* Oxford: Clarendon Press, 1992.

Urban, R. "Das Verbot innenpolitischer Umwälzungen durch den Korinthischen Bund (338/37) in antimakedonischer Argumentation." *Historia: Zeitschrift für Alte Geschichte* 30 (1981): 11–21.

Van Wees, H. "Mass and Elite in Solon's Athens: The Property Classes Revisited." In *Solon of Athens: New Historical and Philological Approaches*, edited by J. H. Blok and A. P. M. Lardinois, 351–389. Leiden: Brill, 2006.

Walser, A. V. *Bauern und Zinsnehmer. Politik, Recht und Wirtschaft im frühhellenistischen Ephesos.* Munich: C. H. Beck, 2008.

Weber, M. *Die Stadt. Max-Weber-Gesamtausgabe*, vol. 22,1. Tübingen, Germany: Mohr Siebeck, 1999. First published 1921.

Weber, M. "Agrarverhältnisse im Altertum." In *Zur Sozial- und Wirtschaftsgeschichte des Altertums. Schriften und Reden, 1893–1908. Max-Weber-Gesamtausgabe*, edited by M. Weber, 1:320–765. Tübingen, Germany: Mohr Siebeck, 2006. First published 1909.

Welwei, K.-W. "Ursache und Ausmaß der Verschuldung attischer Bauern um 600 v. Chr." *Hermes: Zeitschrift für klassische Philologie* 133 (2005): 29–43.

Welwei, K.-W. "Ursprung, Verbreitung und Formen der Unfreiheit abhängiger Landbewohner im antiken Griechenland." In *Unfreie und abhängige Landbevölkerung*, edited by E. Herrmann-Otto, 1–52. Hildesheim, Germany: Olms, 2008.

Whitby, M. "The Grain Trade of Athens in the Fourth Century BC." In *Trade, Traders and the Ancient City*, edited by H. Parkins and C. Smith, 102–128. London and New York: Routledge, 1998.

Whitehead, D. *The Demes of Attica, 508/7—ca. 250 B.C.: A Political and Social Study.* Princeton, NJ: Princeton University Press, 1986.

Winterling, A. "*Arme* und *Reiche*. Die Struktur der griechischen Polisgesellschaften in Aristoteles *Politik*." *Saeculum* 44 (1993): 179–205.

Zelnick-Abramovitz, R. *Not Wholly Free: The Concept of Manumission and the Status of Manumitted Slaves in the Ancient Greek World.* Leiden: Brill, 2005.

Zelnick-Abramovitz, R. "The Status of Slaves Manumitted under *Paramonē*: A Reappraisal." In *Symposion 2017. Vorträge zur griechischen und hellenistischen Rechtsgeschichte*, edited by G. Thür, U. Yiftach, and R. Zelnick-Abramovitz, 377–402. Vienna: Austrian Academy of Sciences Press, 2018.

CHAPTER 5

Aarts, J. G. "Coins, Money and Exchange in the Roman World. A Cultural–Economic Perspective." *Archaeological Dialogues* 12 (2005): 1–27.

Ando, Clifford. *Roman Social Imaginaries: Language and Thought in Contexts of Empire.* Toronto: University of Toronto Press, 2015.

Andreau, Jean. *La vie financière dans le monde romain: Les métiers de manieurs d'argent (IVe siècle av. J.-C.–IIIe siècle ap. J.-C.).* Rome: École française de Rome, 1987.

Andreau, Jean. *Patrimoines, échanges et prêts d'argent: L'économie romaine.* Rome: Bretschneider, 1997.

Andreau, Jean. *Banking and Business in the Roman World.* Cambridge: Cambridge University Press, 1999.

Andreau, Jean. "Sur les choix économiques des notables romains." In *Mentalités et choix économiques des romains*, edited by Jean Andreau, Jérome France, and Sylvie Pittia, 71–85. Pessac: Ausonius Publications, 2004.

Arena, Valentina. *Libertas and the Practice of Politics in the Late Roman Republic.* Cambridge: Cambridge University Press, 2013.

Arena, Valentina. "Debt-Bondage, Fides, and Justice: Republican Liberty and the Notion of Economic Independence in the First Century BC." In *The Past as Present*, edited by Giovanni Alberto Cecconi, Rita Lizzi Testa, and Arnaldo Marcone, 621–646. Turnhout: Brepols Publishers, 2019.

Aubert, Jean-Jacques. "The Republican Economy and Roman Law: Regulation, Promotion, or Reflection?" In *The Cambridge Companion to the Roman Republic*, edited by Harriet Flower, 167–186. Cambridge: Cambridge University Press, 2014.

Barlow, Charles Thomas. "Bankers, Moneylenders, and Interest Rates in the Roman Republic." PhD diss., University of North Carolina, Chapel Hill, 1978.

Beck, Hans, Martin Jehne, and John Serrati. *Money and Power in the Roman Republic.* Brussels: Éditions Latomus, 2016.

Beckby, Hermann. *Die Sprüche des Publilius Syrus. Lateinisch-Deutsch.* Munich: Heimeran, 1969.

Becker, Wilhelm Adolf, and Joachim Marquardt. *Handbuch der römischen Alterthümer nach den Quellen.* Leipzig: Weidmann, 1844.

Bernard, Seth. "Debt, Land, and Labor in the Early Republican Economy." *Phoenix* 70, no. 3/4 (2016): 317–338.

Bernard, Seth. "The Social History of Early Roman Coinage." *Journal of Roman Studies* 108 (2018a): 1–26.

Bernard, Seth. *Building Mid-Republican Rome: Labor, Architecture, and the Urban Economy.* Oxford: Oxford University Press, 2018b.

Billeter, Gustav. *Geschichte des Zinsfusses im griechisch-römischen Altertum bis auf Justinian.* Leipzig: Teubner, 1898.

Blanton, Thomas R. "The Benefactor's Account-Book: The Rhetoric of Gift Reciprocation According to Seneca and Paul." *New Testament Studies* 59, no. 3 (2013): 396–414.

Blösel, Wolfgang. "Die Demilitarisierung der römischen Nobilität von Sulla bis Caesar." In *Von der militia equestris zur militia urbana. Prominenzrollen und Karrierefelder im antiken Rom*, 55–80. Stuttgart: Steiner, 2011.

Blösel, Wolfgang. "Provincial Commands and Money in the Late Roman Republic." In *Money and Power in the Roman Republic*, edited by Hans Beck, Martin Jehne, and John Serrati, 68–81. Brussels: Éditions Latomus, 2016.

Burnett, A. "The Beginnings of Roman Coinage." *Annali dell'Istituto Italiano di Numismatica* 36 (1989): 33–64.

Burnett, Andrew. "Early Roman Coinage and Its Italian Context." In *The Oxford Handbook of Greek and Roman Coinage*, edited by William E. Metcalf, 298–314. Oxford: Oxford University Press, 2012.

Burton, Paul J. "Amicitia in Plautus: A Study of Roman Friendship Processes." *American Journal of Philology* 125, no. 2 (2004): 209–243.

Burton, Paul J. *Friendship and Empire: Roman Diplomacy and Imperialism in the Middle Republic (353–146 BC)*. Cambridge: Cambridge University Press, 2011.

Carlà, Filippo and Maja Gori. *Gift Giving and the "Embedded" Economy in the Ancient World*. Heidelberg: Winter, 2014.

Coffee, Neil. *Gift and Gain: How Money Transformed Ancient Rome*. Oxford: Oxford University Press, 2017.

Crawford, Michael H. *Coinage and Money under the Roman Republic: Italy and the Mediterranean Economy*. London: Methuen, 1985.

Crawford, Michael H. *Roman Statutes*. Vol. 1. London: Institute of Classical Studies, 1996.

Crawford, Michael H. "Where Were the Coins We Find Actually Used?" In *The Economic Integration of Roman Italy: Rural Communities in a Globalising World*, edited by Tymon De Haas and Gijs Tol, 407–413. Leiden: Brill, 2017.

Dahlheim, W. *Struktur und Entwicklung des römischen Völkerrechts im dritten und zweiten Jahrhundert v. Chr.* Munich: Beck, 1968.

Damon, Cynthia. *The Mask of the Parasite: A Pathology of Roman Patronage*. Ann Arbor: University of Michigan Press, 1997.

de Ligt, L. "Demand, Supply, Distribution. The Roman Peasantry between Town and Countryside. Rural Monetization and Peasant Demand." *Münstersche Beiträge Zur Antiken Handelsgeschichte* 9, no. 2 (1990): 24–56.

Deniaux, Élizabeth. *Clientèles et pouvoir à l'époque de Cicéron*. Rome: École Française de Rome, 1994.

Diouron, Nicole. "Sénèque et Publilius Syrus." In *Traduire, transposer, transmettre dans l'Antiquité gréco-romaine*, 167–178. Paris: Editions Picard, 2009.

Dixon, Suzanne. "The Meaning of Gift and Debt in the Roman Elite." *Échos Du Monde Classique* 37 (1993): 451–464.

Dondorp, J. H. "Partes Secanto. Aulus Gellius and the Glossators." *Revue internationale des droits de l'antiquité* 57, no. 2010 (2011): 131–144.

Duckworth, George Eckel. *The Nature of Roman Comedy: A Study in Popular Entertainment*. Princeton, NJ: Princeton University Press, 1952.

Eberle, Lisa Pilar. "Making Roman Subjects: Citizenship and Empire before and after Augustus." *TAPA* 147, no. 2 (2017): 321–370.

Eilers, Claude. *Roman Patrons of Greek Cities*. Oxford: Oxford University Press, 2002.

Finley, M. I. *The Ancient Economy*. Berkeley: University of California Press, 1999.

Frederiksen, M. W. "Caesar, Cicero and the Problem of Debt." *Journal of Roman Studies* 56 (1966): 128–141.

Freyburger, G. *Fides. Étude sémantique et religieuse depuis les origines jusqu'à l'époque augustéenne.* Paris: Belles Lettres, 1986.

Gabrielli, Chantal. *Contributi alla storia economica di Roma repubblicana.* Como: New Press, 2003.

Ganter, Angela. *Was die römische Welt zusammenhält: Patron-Klient-Verhältnisse zwischen Cicero und Cyprian.* Berlin: de Gruyter, 2015.

Giancotti, Francesco. *Mimo e gnome: Studio su Decimo Laberio e Publilio Siro.* Messina: G. d'Anna, 1967.

Giuffrè, V. "Sulla cessio bonorum ex decreto Caesaris." *Labeo* 30 (1984): 90–93.

Graeber, David. *Debt: The First 5,000 Years.* New York: Melville House, 2011.

Graeber, David. *Debt: The First 5,000 Years.* New York: Melville House, 2014.

Greenidge, Abel H. J. *Infamia: Its Place in Roman Public and Private Law.* Aalen, Germany: Scientia Verlag, 1977.

Griffin, Miriam. "De Beneficiis and Roman Society." *Journal of Roman Studies* 93 (2003): 92–113.

Gruen, Erich S. *Studies in Greek Culture and Roman Policy.* Berkeley: University of California Press, 1996.

Haltenhoff, Andreas. "Wertebewußtsein und Lebensweisheit bei Publilius Syrus." In *O tempora, o mores! Römische Werte und römische Literatur in den letzten Jahrzehnten,* edited by Andreas Haltenhoff, Andreas Heil, und Fritz-Heiner Mutschler, 187–197. Munich: de Gruyter, 2003.

Harris, William V. "A Revisionist View of Roman Money." *Journal of Roman Studies* 96 (2006): 1–24.

Harris, William V. "The Nature of Roman Money." In *The Monetary Systems of the Greeks and Romans,* edited by William V. Harris, 174–207. Oxford: Oxford University Press, 2008.

Harrison, Alick R. W. *The Law of Athens.* Oxford: Clarendon Press, 1971.

Hellegouarc'h, Joseph. *Le vocabulaire latin des relations et des partis politiques sous la République.* Paris: Belles Lettres, 1963.

Herz, Zachary. "The Effect of Bankruptcy Law on Roman Credit Markets." *Business & Bankruptcy Law Journal* 2 (2015): 207–249.

Hölkeskamp, Karl-Joachim. "Fides–deditio in fidem–dextra data et accepta. Recht, Religion und Ritual in Rom." In *The Roman Middle Republic. Politics, Religion, and Historiography,* edited by Christer Bruun, 223–250. Rom: Institutum Romanum Finlandiae, 2000.

Hölkeskamp, Karl-Joachim. *Libera res publica: Die politische Kultur des antiken Rom— Positionen und Perspektiven.* Stuttgart: Franz Steiner Verlag, 2017.

Hollander, David B. *Money in the Late Roman Republic.* Leiden: Brill, 2007.

Howgego, Christopher. "The Supply and Use of Money in the Roman World 200 B.C. to A.D. 300." *Journal of Roman Studies* 82 (1992): 1–31.

Ioannatou, Marina. "Le code de l'honneur des paiements: Créanciers et débiteurs à la fin de la république romaine." *Annales. Histoire, Sciences Sociales* 56, no. 6 (2001): 1201–1221.

Ioannatou, Marina. *Affaires d'argent dans la correspondance de Cicéron: L'aristocratie sénatoriale face à ses dettes.* Paris: Editions De Boccard, 2006a.

Ioannatou, Marina. "Liens d'amitié et opérations de crédit à la fin de la république romaine." In *Le crédit: Hommage à Marina Ioannatou*, 11–40. Dijon: Faculté de droit et de science politique, 2006b.

Jehne, Martin. "The Senatorial Economics of Status." In *Money and Power in the Roman Republic*, edited by Hans Beck, Martin Jehne, and John Serrati, 188–207. Brussels: Peeters, 2016.

Jolowicz, Herbert F. *Historical Introduction to the Study of Roman Law.* 2nd ed. Cambridge: Cambridge University Press, 1961.

Jory, E. J. "Publilius Syrus and the Element of Competition in the Theatre of the Republic." *Bulletin of the Institute of Classical Studies* 35, no. S51 (1988): 73–81.

Kaser, Max. "Infamia und ignominia in den Römischen rechtsquellen." *Zeitschrift der Savigny-Stiftung für Rechtsgeschichte: Romanistische Abteilung* 73, no. 1 (1956): 220–278.

Kaser, Max, and Karl Hackl. *Das römische zivilprozessrecht.* Munich: Beck, 1996.

Kay, Philip. *Rome's Economic Revolution.* Oxford: Oxford University Press, 2014.

Konstan, David. *Friendship in the Classical World.* Cambridge: Cambridge University Press, 1997.

Kurke, Leslie. *Coins, Bodies, Games, and Gold: The Politics of Meaning in Archaic Greece.* Princeton, NJ: Princeton University Press, 1999.

Lavan, Myles. *Slaves to Rome: Paradigms of Empire in Roman Culture.* Cambridge: Cambridge University Press, 2013.

Leigh, Matthew. *Comedy and the Rise of Rome.* Oxford: Oxford University Press, 2004.

Lentano, Mario. "Il dono e il debito. Verso un'antropologia del beneficio nella cultura romana." In *O tempora, o mores! Römische Werte und römische Literatur in den letzten Jahrzehnten*, edited by Andreas Haltenhoff, Andreas Heil, and Fritz-Heiner Mutschler, 125–142. Munich: de Gruyter, 2005.

Leppin, Hartmut. *Histrionen: Untersuchungen zur sozialen Stellung von Bühnenkünstlern im Westen des römischen Reiches zur Zeit der Republik und des Principats.* Bonn: Habelt, 1992.

Lintott, Andrew. "Electoral bribery in the Roman Republic." *The Journal of Roman Studies* 80 (1990): 1–8.

Lowe, J. C. B. "Plautus' Choruses." *Rheinisches Museum für Philologie* 133 (1990): 274–297.

Maehle, Ingvar B. "The Economy of Gratitude in Democratic Athens." *Hesperia* 87, no. 1 (2018): 55–90.

Millett, Paul. *Lending and Borrowing in Ancient Athens*. Cambridge: Cambridge University Press, 1991.

Mommsen, Theodor. *Römische Geschichte. Von Sullas Tode bis zur Schlacht von Thapsus*. Leipzig: Weidmann, 1889.

Morley, Neville. "The poor in the city of Rome." In *Poverty in the Roman World*, edited by M. Atkins and R. Osborne, 21–39. Cambridge: Cambridge University Press, 2006.

Nörr, Dieter. *Die Fides im römischen Völkerrecht*. Heidelberg: Müller, 1991.

Pakter, Walter. "Roman Bankruptcy." In *Die Bedeutung der Wörter*, edited by M. Stolleis, 327–339. Munich: Beck, 1991.

Pakter, Walter. "The Mystery of 'Cessio Bonorum.'" *Index* 22 (1994): 323–342.

Pina-Polo, Francisco. "*Cupiditas pecuniae*: Wealth and Power in Cicero." In *Money and Power in the Roman Republic*, edited by Hans Beck, Martin Jehne, and John Serrati, 165–177. Brussels: Éditions Latomus, 2016.

Prichard, A. M. "The Origin of the *legis actio per condictionem*." In *Synteleia Vincenzo Arangio-Ruiz*, edited by Antonis Guarino, 260–268. Naples: Jovene, 1969.

Purcell, N. "The City of Rome and the Plebs Urbana in the Late Republic." In *The Cambridge Ancient History IX²*, edited by John A. Crook, Andrew Lintott, and Elizabeth Rawson, 644–688. Cambridge: Cambridge University Press, 1994.

Raccanelli, Renata. *L'amicitia nelle commedie di Plauto: Un'indagine antropologica*. Bari: Edipuglia, 1998.

Richardson, John. *Hispaniae: Spain and the Development of Roman Imperialism*. Cambridge: Cambridge University Press, 1986.

Richlin, Amy. "Talking to Slaves in the Plautine Audience." *Classical Antiquity* 33, no. 1 (2014): 174–226.

Richlin, Amy. *Slave Theater in the Roman Republic: Plautus and Popular Comedy*. Cambridge: Cambridge University Press, 2017.

Rollinger, Christian. "Kredit und Vertrauen in der römischen oberschicht." In *Gläubiger, Schuldner, Arme: Netzwerke und die Rolle des Vertrauens*, edited by Curt Wolfgang Hergenröder, 31–56. Wiesbaden: VS Verlag für Sozialwissenschaften, 2010.

Rollinger, Christian. *Amicitia sanctissime colenda: Freundschaft und soziale Netzwerke in der späten Republik*. Heidelberg: Verlag Antike, 2014.

Rotondi, Giovanni. *Leges publicae populi romani: Elenco cronologico*. Milan: Società Editrice Libraria, 1912.

Rouland, Norbert. *Pouvoir politique et dépendance personnelle dans l'antiquité romaine: Genèse et rôle des rapports de clientèle*. Brussels: Éditions Latomus, 1979.

Rowan, Clare. "The Profits of War and Cultural Capital: Silver and Society in Republican Rome." *Historia* 62, no. 3 (2013): 361–386.

Saller, Richard P. *Personal Patronage under the Early Empire*. Cambridge: Cambridge University Press, 1982.

Saller, Richard P. "Status and Patronage." In *Cambridge Ancient History XI²*, edited by Alan K. Bowman, Peter Garnsey, and Dominic Rathbone, 817–854. Cambridge: Cambridge University Press, 2000.

Satlow, Michael L. *The Gift in Antiquity*. Malden, MA: Wiley-Blackwell, 2013.

Seaford, Richard. *Money and the Early Greek Mind: Homer, Philosophy, Tragedy*. Cambridge: Cambridge University Press, 2004.

Shaw, Brent D. "Debt in Sallust." *Latomus* 34 (1975): 187–196.

Stewart, Roberta. "Who's Tricked. Models of Slave Behavior in Plautus's Pseudolus." In *Role Models in the Roman World*, edited by S. Bell und Inge L. Hansen, 69–96. Ann Arbor, MI: University of Michigan Press, 2008.

Tomulescu, C. "Origin of the *legis actio per condictionem*." *Irish Jurist (1966–)* 4, no. 1 (1969): 180–186.

Verboven, Koenraad. *The Economy of Friends: Economic Aspects of Amicitia and Patronage in the Late Republic*. Brussels: Editions Latomus, 2002.

Verboven, Koenraad. "Friendship among the Romans." In *The Oxford Handbook of Social Relations in the Roman World*, edited by Michael Peachin, 404–421. Oxford: Oxford University Press, 2011.

Viglietti, Cristiano. *Il limite del bisogno: Antropologia economica di Roma arcaica*. Bologna: Il Mulino, 2011.

Vlassopoulos, Kostas. "What Do We Really Know about Athenian Society?" *Annales. Histoire, Sciences Sociales: English Edition* 71, no. 3 (2016): 419–439.

von Premerstein, Anton. "Clientes." In *Realencyclopädie der classischen Altertumswissenschaft. Pauly-Wissowa. 7ter Halbband*. Stuttgart: Metzler, 1900.

von Reden, Sitta. *Exchange in Ancient Greece*. London: Duckworth, 1995.

Waldstein, Wolfgang. *Operae libertorum: Untersuchungen zur Dienstpflicht Freigelassener Sklaven*. Stuttgart: Steiner, 1986.

Wallace-Hadrill, Andrew. *Patronage in Ancient Society*. London: Routledge, 1989.

Yakobson, Aleksander. *Elections and Electioneering in Rome: A Study in the Political System of the Late Republic*. Stuttgart: Steiner, 1999.

Zehnacker, H. "Unciarium fenus (Tacite, *Annales* VI, 16)." In *Mélanges de littérature et d'épigraphie Latines, d'histoire ancienne et d'archéologie: Hommage à la mémoire de Pierre Wuilleumier*, 353–362. Paris: Les Belles Lettres, 1980.

Zimmermann, Reinhard. *The Law of Obligations: Roman Foundations of the Civilian Tradition*. Cape Town: Juta, 1990.

CHAPTER 6

Akerloff, G., and R. J. Shiller. *Animal Spirits: How Human Psychology Drives the Economy, and Why It Matters for Global Capitalism*. Princeton, NJ: Princeton University Press, 2009.

Bang, P. F. *The Roman Bazaar: A Comparative Study of Trade and Markets in a Tributary Empire*. Cambridge: Cambridge University Press, 2008.

Bang, P. F. "The Ancient Economy and New Institutional Economics." *Journal of Roman Studies* 99 (2009): 194–206.

Bannon, C. "C. Sergius Orata and the Rhetoric of Fishponds." *Classical Quarterly* 64 (2014): 166–182.

Barbier, E. B. *Scarcity and Frontiers: How Economies Have Developed through Natural Resource Exploitation*. Cambridge: Cambridge University Press, 2011.

Bernard, S. "The Social History of Early Roman Coinage." *Journal of Roman Studies* 108 (2018): 1–26.

Bresson, A. *The Making of the Ancient Greek Economy: Institutions, Markets, and Growth in the City-States*. Chicago: University of Chicago Press, 2016.

Brown, N. G. "A *Res Rustica* for All the People? Varro, *Villatica Pastio*, and the Villa Publica." *Transactions of the American Philological Association* 149 (2019): 317–351.

Burnett, A. "The Beginnings of Roman Coinage." *Annali dell' Istituto Italiano di Numismatica* 36 (1989): 33–64.

Cartledge, P. "The Economy (Economies) of Ancient Greece." In *The Ancient Economy*, edited by W. Scheidel and S. von Reden, 11–32. Edinburgh: Edinburgh University Press, 2002.

Diederich, S. *Römische agrarhandbücher zwischen fachwissenschaft, literatur und ideologie*. Berlin: de Gruyter, 2007.

Edwards, C. *The Politics of Immorality in Ancient Rome*. Cambridge: Cambridge University Press, 1993.

Elliott, C. P. *Economic Theory and the Roman Monetary Economy*. Cambridge: Cambridge University Press, 2020.

Gildenhard, I. "*Frugalitas*, or: The Invention of a Roman Virtue." In *Roman Frugality: Modes of Moderation from the Archaic Age to the Early Empire and Beyond*, edited by I. Gildenhard and C. Viglietti, 237–346. Cambridge: Cambridge University Press, 2020.

Gildenhard, I., and C. Viglietti, eds. *Roman Frugality: Modes of Moderation from the Archaic Age to the Early Empire and Beyond*. Cambridge: Cambridge University Press, 2020.

Graeber, D. *Towards an Anthropological Theory of Value: The False Coin of Our Own Dreams*. New York: Palgrave Macmillan, 2001.

Graeber, D. *Debt: The First 5,000 Years*. New York: Melville House, 2011.

Hollander, D. S. *Money in the Late Roman Republic*. Leiden: Brill, 2007.

Jiménez, A. "Money and Its Interpretation: Archaeological and Anthropological Perspectives." In *A Cultural History of Money in Antiquity*, edited by S. Krmnicek, 123–140. London: Bloomsbury Academic, 2019.

Launaro, A. "Finley and the Ancient Economy." In *M. I. Finley: An Ancient Historian and His Impact*, edited by D. Jew, R. Osborne, and M. Scott, 227–249. Cambridge: Cambridge University Press, 2016.

Kahneman, D. *Thinking, Fast and Slow*. London: Allen Lane, 2011.

Kronenberg, L. *Allegories of Farming from Greece and Rome: Philosophical Satire in Xenophon, Varro and Virgil.* Cambridge: Cambridge University Press, 2009.

Lewis, D. "Behavioural Economics and Economic Behaviour in Classical Athens." In *Ancient Greek History and Contemporary Social Science,* edited by M. Canevaro, A. Erskine, B. Gray, and J. Ober, 15–16. Edinburgh: Edinburgh University Press, 2018.

Mann, M. *The Sources of Social Power.* Vol. 1, *A History of Power from the Beginning to AD 1760.* Cambridge: Cambridge University Press, 1986.

Marx, K. *Grundrisse* [1857–8]. Translated by M. Nicolaus. Harmondsworth, UK: Penguin, 1973.

Marzano, A. *Harvesting the Sea: The Exploitation of Marine Resources in the Roman Mediterranean.* Oxford: Oxford University Press, 2013.

Morley, N. *Metropolis and Hinterland: The City of Rome and the Italian Economy, 200 BC—AD 200.* Cambridge: Cambridge University Press, 1996.

Morley, N. "Markets, Marketing and the Roman Elite." In *Mercati periodici e mercati permanenti nel mondo romano,* edited by E. Lo Cascio, 211–221. Bari: Edipuglia, 2000.

Morley, N. *Antiquity and Modernity.* Malden MA & Oxford: Wiley-Blackwell, 2009.

Morley, N. "The Return of Grand Narrative in the Human Sciences." *Crooked Timber* (book event on David Graeber's *Debt: The First 5,000 Years*), February 22, 2012. Accessed May 17, 2021. https://crookedtimber.org/2012/02/22/the-return-of-grand-narrative-in-the-human-sciences/

Morley, N. "Frugality and Roman Economic Thinking in Varro's *Rerum Rusticarum.*" I *Quaderni del Ramo d'Oro Online* 10 (2019): 41–54. Accessed May 17, 2021. http://www.qro.unisi.it/frontend/sites/default/files/Morley%20QRO%2010.pdf

Nafissi, M. *Ancient Athens and Modern Ideology: Value, Theory and Evidence in Historical Sciences: Max Weber, Karl Polanyi & Moses Finley. BICS* Supplement 80. London: Institute of Classical Studies, 2005.

Nelsestuen, G. A. *Varro the Agronomist: Political Philosophy, Satire, and Agriculture in the Late Republic.* Columbus: Ohio State University Press, 2015.

Nicolet, C. "Pline, Peul et la théorie de la monnaie." *Athenaeum* 62 (1984): 105–135.

Ober, J. *The Rise and Fall of Classical Greece.* Princeton, NJ: Princeton University Press, 2015.

Padilla Peralta, D. "Italy at Knife-Point: Reading Varro *De Re Rustica* 1.69.2–3." *Classical Philology* 112 (2017): 482–486.

Radkau, J. *Nature and Power: A Global History of the Environment.* Translated by T. Dunlop. Cambridge: Cambridge University Press, 2008.

Roselaar, S. K. *Rome's Economic Revolution: Integration and Economy in Republican Italy.* Cambridge: Cambridge University Press, 2019.

Scheidel, W., I. Morris, and R. P. Saller. "Introduction." In *The Cambridge Economic History of the Greco-Roman World,* edited by W. Scheidel, I. Morris, and R. P. Saller, 1–12. Cambridge: Cambridge University Press, 2007.

Seaford, R. *Money and the Early Greek Mind: Homer, Philosophy, Tragedy*. Cambridge: Cambridge University Press, 2004.

Sedlacek, T. *Economics of Good and Evil: The Quest for Economic Meaning from Gilgamesh to Wall Street*. Oxford: Oxford University Press, 2011.

Spencer, D. *Language and Authority in* De Lingua Latine: *Varro's Guide to Being Roman*. Madison: University of Wisconsin Press, 2019.

Viglietti, C. *Il limite del bisogno. Antropologia economica di Roma arcaica*. Bologna: Il Mulino, 2011.

Vivenza, G. "Roman Economic Thought." In *The Cambridge Companion to the Roman Economy*, edited by W. Scheidel, 25–44. Cambridge: Cambridge University Press, 2012.

von Reden, S. *Money in Classical Antiquity*. Cambridge: Cambridge University Press, 2010.

CHAPTER 7

Allen, M., L. Lodwick, T. Brindle, M. Fulford, and A. T. Smith. *The Rural Economy of Roman Britain*. London: The Society for the Promotion of Roman Studies, 2017.

Ando, C. "Decline, Fall and Transformation." *Journal of Late Antiquity* 1 (2008): 31–60.

Ando, C. *Imperial Rome AD 193 to 284: The Critical Century*. Edinburgh: Edinburgh University Press, 2012.

Ando, C., and M. Formisano, eds. *The New Late Antiquity: A Gallery of Intellectual Portraits (19th Century through Present)*. Heidelberg: Universitätsverlag Winter, 2021.

Bagnall, R. S. "Landholding in Late Roman Egypt: The Distribution of Wealth." *Journal of Roman Studies* 82 (1992): 128–149.

Banaji, J. *Agrarian Change in Late Antiquity: Gold, Labour, and Aristocratic Dominance*. Oxford: Oxford University Press, 2007.

Bernard, S. "The Social History of Early Roman Coinage." *Journal of Roman Studies* 108 (2018): 1–26.

Bowden, W., L. Lavan, and C. Machado. *Recent Research on the Late Antique Countryside*. Leiden: Brill, 2004.

Brandt, H. *Zeitkritik in der spätantike: Untersuchungen zu den reformvorschlägen des anonymus de rebus bellicis*. Munich: C.H. Beck, 1988.

Bransbourg, G. "Currency Debasement and Public Debt Management at the Time of the Second Punic War." In *FIDES: Contributions to Numismatics in Honor of Richard B. Witschonke*, edited by P. G. Van Alfen, G. Bransbourg, and M. Amandry, 141–158. New York: The American Numismatic Society, 2015a.

Bransbourg, G. "The Later Roman Empire." In *Fiscal Regimes and the Political Economy of Premodern States*, edited by A. Monson and W. Scheidel, 258–281. Cambridge: Cambridge University Press, 2015b.

Bresson, A. *The Making of the Ancient Greek Economy: Institutions, Markets, and Growth in the City-States*. Princeton, NJ: Princeton University Press, 2016.

Brown, P. R. L. *Poverty and Leadership in the Later Roman Empire*. Hanover, NH: University Press of New England, 2002.

Brown, P. R. L. *Through the Eye of a Needle: Wealth, the Fall of Rome and the Making of Christianity in the West 350–550 AD*. Princeton, NJ: Princeton University Press, 2012.

Brown, P. R. L. *Treasure in Heaven: The Holy Poor in Early Christianity*. Charlottesville, VA: University of Virginia Press, 2016.

Cameron, A. D. E. "The Date of the Anonymous *De rebus bellicis*." In *De rebus bellicis Part 1: Aspects of the* De rebus bellicis *(Papers Presented to Professor E. A. Thompson)*, edited by M. W. C. Hassall, 1–10. Oxford: Oxford University Press, 1979.

Carrié, J.-M. "Un roman des origines: Les généalogies du 'colonat du bas-empire.'" *Opus* 2 (1983): 205–251.

Carrié, J.-M. "Diocletien et la fiscalité." *Antiquité Tardive* 2 (1994): 33–64.

Carrié, J.-M. "Solidus et crédit: Qu'est-ce que l'or a pu changer?" In *Credito e moneta nel mondo romano*, edited by E. Lo Cascio, 265–279. Bari: Edipuglia, 2003.

Carrié, J.-M., and A. Rousselle. *L'Empire romain en mutation*. Paris: Seuil, 1999.

Clark, E. A. *Taxation and the Formation of the Late Roman Social Contract*. Unpublished PhD thesis, University of California, Berkeley, 2017.

Collins-Elliott, S. A. "A Behavioral Analysis of Monetary Exchange and Craft Production in Rural Tuscany via Small Finds from the Roman Peasant Project." *Journal of Mediterranean Archaeology* 31 (2018): 155–179.

Crawford, M. H. *Coinage and Money under the Roman Republic: Italy and the Mediterranean Economy*. Berkeley, CA: University of California Press, 1985.

Decker, M. *Tilling the Hateful Earth: Agricultural Production and Trade in the Late Antique East*. Oxford: Oxford University Press, 2009.

De Ligt, L. "Demand, Supply, Distribution: The Roman Peasantry between Town and Countryside: Rural Monetization and Peasant Demand." *Münstersche Beiträge zur antiken Handelsgeschichte* 9 (1990): 24–56.

Di Cosmo, N., and M. Maas. *Empires and Exchanges in Eurasian Late Antiquity: Rome, China, Iran, and the Steppe, ca. 250–750*. New York: Oxford University Press, 2018.

Dodgeon, M. H., and S. N. C. Lieu. *The Roman Eastern Frontier and the Persian Wars*. London: Routledge, 1991.

Dossey, L. *Peasant and Empire in Christian North Africa*. Berkeley, CA: University of California Press, 2010.

Drinkwater, J. "Maximinus to Diocletian and the 'Crisis.'" In *The Cambridge Ancient History XII: The Crisis of Empire (A. D. 193–337)*, edited by A. K. Bowman, P. Garnsey, and A. Cameron, 28–66. Cambridge: Cambridge University Press, 2005.

Duncan-Jones, R. *The Economy of the Roman Empire: Quantitative Studies*. Cambridge: Cambridge University Press, 1982.

Edwards, M., ed. *Optatus: Against the Donatists*. Liverpool: Liverpool University Press, 1997.

Elm, S. "Sold to Sin through *Origo*." *Studia Patristica* 98 (2017): 1–21.

Esmonde Cleary, A. S. *The Roman West, AD 200–500: An Archaeological Study*. Cambridge: Cambridge University Press, 2013.

Fernández, D. *Aristocrats and Statehood in Western Iberia, 300–600 C.E.* Philadelphia, PA: University of Pennsylvania Press, 2017.

Giannecchini, M., and J. Moggi-Cecchi. "Stature in Archaeological Samples from Central Italy: Method Issues and Diachronic Changes." *American Journal of Physical Anthropology* 135 (2008): 284–292.

Gowland, R., and L. Walther. "Human Growth and Stature," In *The Science of Roman History*, edited by W. Scheidel, 174–204. Princeton, NJ: Princeton University Press, 2018.

Graeber, D. *Debt: The First 5,000 Years*. New York: Melville House, 2011.

Grey, C. "Contextualizing Colonatus: The Origo of the Late Roman Empire." *Journal of Roman Studies* 97 (2007): 155–175.

Grey, C., and A. Parkin. "Controlling the Urban Mob: The Colonatus Perpetuus of CTh 14.18.1." *Phoenix* 57 (2003): 284–299.

Harper, K. *Slavery in the Late Roman World, AD 275–425*. Cambridge: Cambridge University Press, 2011.

Harper, K. "People, Plagues, and Prices in the Roman World: The Evidence from Egypt." *Journal of Economic History* 76, no. 3 (2016): 803–839.

Harper, K. *The Fate of Rome: Climate, Disease, and the End of an Empire*. Princeton, NJ: Princeton University Press, 2017.

Heather, P. *The Fall of the Roman Empire: A New History of Rome and the Barbarians*. New York: Oxford University Press, 2006.

Hobson, M. S. *The North African Boom: Evaluating Economic Growth in the Roman Province of Africa Proconsularis (146 B.C.–A.D. 439)*. Portsmouth, RI: JRA Supplementary series, 2015.

Ingham, G. *The Nature of Money*. Cambridge: Cambridge University Press, 2004.

Izdebski, A. "The Economic Expansion of the Anatolian Countryside in Late Antiquity: The Coast Versus Inland Regions." In *Local Economies? Production and Exchange of Inland Regions in Late Antiquity*, edited by L. Lavan, 343–376. Leiden: Brill, 2013.

Jongman, W. M. "Re-constructing the Roman Economy." In *The Cambridge History of Capitalism*, Vol. 1, edited by L. Neal and J. Williamson, 75–100. Cambridge: Cambridge University Press, 2014.

Jongman, W. M., J. P. A. M. Jacobs, and G. M. Klein Goldewijk. "Health and Wealth in the Roman Empire." *Economics and Human Biology* 34 (2019): 138–150.

Kelly, C. M. *Ruling the Later Roman Empire*. Cambridge, MA: Harvard University Press, 2004.

Kosso, C. *The Archaeology of Public Policy in Late Roman Greece*. Oxford: Archaeopress, 2003.

Laniado, A. *Recherches sur les notables municipaux dans l'empire protobyzantin*. Paris: Association des amis du Centre d'histoire et civilisation de Byzance, 2002.

Lavan, L. *Local economies? Production and Exchange of Inland Regions in Late Antiquity*. Leiden and Boston: Brill, 2015.

Lenski, N. "Captivity and Slavery among the Saracens in Late Antiquity (ca. 250–630 CE)." *Antiquité Tardive* 19 (2011): 237–266.

Leone, A. *Changing Townscapes in North Africa from Late Antiquity to the Arab Conquest*. Bari: Edipuglia, 2007.

Lepelley, C. *Les cités de l'Afrique romaine au bas-empire*. Paris: Institut d'études augustiniennes, 1979.

Lepelley, C. "Liberté, colonat et esclavage d'"après la lettre 24*: La jurisdiction épiscopale 'de liberali causa,'" In *Les lettres de Saint Augustin découvertes par Johannes Divjak*, edited by C. Lepelley, 329–342. Paris: Institut d'études augustiniennes, 1983.

Liebeschuetz, J. H. W. G. *The Decline and Fall of the Roman City*. Oxford and New York: Oxford University Press, 2001.

Mallan, C., and C. Davenport. "Dexippus and the Gothic Invasions: Interpreting the New Vienna Fragment (*Codex Vindobonensis Hist. gr.* 73, ff. 192^v –193^r)." *Journal of Roman Studies* 105 (2015): 203–226.

Manning, J. G. *The Open Sea: The Economic Life of the Ancient Mediterranean World from the Iron Age to the Rise of Rome*. Princeton, NJ: Princeton University Press, 2018.

Mattingly, D. J., V. Leitch, C. N. Duckworth, A. Cuénod, M. Sterry, and F. Cole, eds. *Trade in the Ancient Sahara and Beyond*. Cambridge: Cambridge University Press, 2017.

Mazzarino, S. *Aspetti sociali del quarto secolo: Ricerche di storia tardo-romana*. Rome: L'Erma di Bretschneider, 1951.

McCormick, M. *Origins of the European Economy: Communications and Commerce, A.D. 300–900*. Cambridge: Cambridge University Press, 2001.

Meier, M. "Das späte römische Reich ein 'Zwangsstaat'? Anmerkungen zu einer Forschungskontroverse." *Electrum* 9 (2003): 193–213.

Merrills, A., and R. Miles. *The Vandals*. Chichester: Blackwell, 2010.

Rapp, C. *Holy Bishops in Late Antiquity: The Nature of Christian Leadership in an Age of Transition*. Berkeley, CA: University of California Press, 2005.

Rathbone, D. *Economic Rationalism and Rural Society in Third-Century A.D. Egypt: The Heroninos Archive and the Appianus Estate*. Cambridge: Cambridge University Press, 1991.

Rathbone, D. "Monetisation, not Price Inflation, in Third Century A.D. Egypt?" In *Coin Finds and Coin Use in the Roman World*, edited by C. E. King and D. G. Wigg, 321–339. Berlin: Gebrüder Mann Verlag, 1996.

Reece, R. *Roman Coins from 140 Sites in Britain*. Cirencester: Cotswold Studies, 1991.

Reece, R. "British Sites and Their Roman Coins." *Antiquity* 67 (1993): 863–869.

Rostovtzeff, M. I. *The Social and Economic History of the Roman Empire*. Oxford: Oxford University Press, 1957.

Sarris, P. *Economy and Society in the Age of Justinian*. Cambridge: Cambridge University Press, 2006.

Sarris, P. *Empires of Faith: The Fall of Rome to the Rise of Islam, 500–700*. Oxford and New York: Oxford University Press, 2011.

Scheding, P. *Urbaner Ballungsraum im römischen Nordafrika: Zum Einfluss von mikroregionalen Wirtschafts- und Sozialstrukturen auf den Städtebau in Africa proconsularis*. Wiesbaden: Reichert Verlag, 2019.

Scheidel, W. "Quantifying the Sources of Slaves in the Early Roman Empire." *Journal of Roman Studies* 87 (1997): 156–169.

Scheidel, W. "Physical Well-Being." In *The Cambridge Companion to the Roman Economy*, edited by W. Scheidel, 321–333. Cambridge: Cambridge University Press, 2012.

Scheidel, W. *Escape from Rome: The Failure of Empire and the Road to Prosperity*. Princeton, NJ: Princeton University Press, 2019.

Scheidel, W., and S. J. Friesen. "The Size of the Economy and the Distribution of Income in the Roman Empire." *Journal of Roman Studies* 99 (2009): 61–91.

Schmidt-Hofner, S. "Der defensor civitatis und die Entstehung des städtschen Notabelnregiments in der Spätantike." In *Chlodwigs Welt: Organisation von Herrschaft um 500*, edited by M. Meier and S. Patzold, 488–522. Stuttgart: Franz Steiner, 2014.

Schmidt-Hofner, S. "Barbarian Migrations and Socio-Economic Challenges to the Roman Landholding Elite in the Fourth Century CE." *Journal of Late Antiquity* 10 (2017): 372–404.

Shaw, B. D. *Sacred Violence: African Christians and Sectarian Hatred in the Age of Augustine*. Cambridge: Cambridge University Press, 2011.

Shaw, B. D. *Bringing in the Sheaves: Economy and Metaphor in the Roman World*. Toronto and Buffalo: Toronto University Press, 2013.

Sirks, B. "The Colonate in Justinian's Reign." *Journal of Roman Studies* 98 (2008): 120–143.

Tedesco, P. "Note sulla genesi e l'evoluzione dell'autopragia demaniale nei secoli IV–VI." In *Ricerca come incontro: Archeologi, paleografi e storici per Paolo Delogu*, edited by G. Barone, A. Esposito, and C. Frova, 3–18. Rome: Viella, 2013.

Thompson, E. A. *A Roman Reformer and Inventor, Being a New Text of the Treatise* De rebus bellicis. Oxford: Oxford University Press, 1952.

Trommenschlager, L., and G. Brkojewtisch. "La circulation monétaire des villae médiomatriques: Analyses méthodologiques, numismatiques et archéologiques." In *Monnaies et monétarisation dans les campagnes de la Gaule du nord et de l'est, de l'âge du fer à l'antiquité tardive*, edited by S. P. Martin, 119–139. Paris: Ausonius éditions, 2016.

Vera, D. "Strutture agrarie e strutture patrimoniali nella tarda antichità: L'aristocrazia romana fra agricoltura e commercio." *Opus* 2 (1983): 489–533.

Vera, D. "Forme e funzioni della rendita fondiaria nella tarda antichità." In *Società romana e impero tardoantico 3*, edited by A. Giardina, 367–447, 723–760. Rome and Bari: Laterza, 1986.

Vera, D. "Massa fundorum: Forme della grande proprietà e poteri della città in Italia fra Costantino e Gregorio Magno." *Mélanges de l'École Française de Rome* 111 (1999): 991–1025.

Veyne, P., and J. Ramin. "Droit romain et société: Les hommes libres qui passent pour esclaves et l'esclavage volontaire." *Historia* 30 (1981): 472–497.

Von Reden, S. *Money in Classical Antiquity*. Cambridge: Cambridge University Press, 2012.

Von Reden, S. "Global Economic History." In *The Cambridge World History*. Vol. 4, *A World with States, Empires and Networks 1200 BCE–900 CE*, edited by C. Benjamin, 29–54. Cambridge: Cambridge University Press, 2015.

Vuolanto, V. "Selling a Freeborn Child: Rhetoric and Social Reality in the Late Roman World." *Ancient Society* 33 (2003): 169–207.

Wallace-Hadrill, A. "The Golden Age and Sin in Augustan Ideology." *Past & Present* 95 (1982): 19–36.

Ward-Perkins, B. *The Fall of Rome and the End of Civilization*. Oxford and New York: Oxford University Press, 2005.

Weber, M. *The Agrarian Sociology of Ancient Civilizations*. Translated by R.I. Frank. London and Atlantic Highlands, NJ,: NLB, 1976.

Whittaker, C. R. "Late Roman Trade and Traders." In *Trade in the Ancient Economy*, edited by P. Garnsey, K. Hopkins, and C. R. Whittaker, 163–180, 208–211. London: The Hogart Press, 1983.

Wickham, C. *Framing the Early Middle Ages: Europe and the Mediterranean 400–800*. Oxford: Oxford University Press, 2005.

Wickham, C. *The Inheritance of Rome: A History of Europe from 400 to 1000*. London: Allen Lane, 2009.

CHAPTER 8

Alram, Michael and Rika Gyselen, *Sylloge Nummorun Sasanidarum: Paris–Berlin–Wien, v. I Ardashir I.–Shapur I*. Vienna: VÖAW, 2003.

Arnason, Johan P. "The Axial Age and Its Interpreters: Reopening the Debate." In *Axial Civilizations and World History*, edited by Johann P. Arnason, S. N. Eisenstadt, and Björn Wittrock, 19–49. Leiden: Brill, 2005.

Arnason, Johan P. "Rehistoricizing the Axial Age." In *The Axial Age and Its Consequences*, edited by Robert N. Bellah and Hans Joas, 337–365. Cambridge, MA: Harvard University Press, 2012.

Banaji, Jairus, "Aristocracies, Peasantries and the Framing of the Early Middle Ages." *Journal of Agrarian Change* 9 (2009): 59–91.

Bellah, Robert. "What Is Axial about the Axial Age?" *Archives Européennes de Sociologie* 46 (2005): 69–89.

Brown, Peter. *The Ransom of the Soul: Afterlife and Wealth in Early Western Christianity.* Cambridge, MA: Harvard University Press, 2015.

Brown, Peter. *Through the Eye of a Needle: Wealth, the Fall of Rome, and the Making of Christianity in the West, 350–550 AD.* Princeton, NJ: Princeton University Press, 2012.

Brown, Peter. *Poverty and Leadership in the Later Roman Empire.* Hanover, NH: Brandeis University Press, 2002.

Bulliet, Richard. *Cotton, Climate, and Camels and Early Islamic Iran.* New York: Columbia University Press, 2009.

Callieri, Pierfrancesco. *Architecture et représentations dans l'Iran sassanide.* Paris: Association pour l'Avancement des Études Iraniennes, 2014.

Canepa, Matthew P. "Technologies of Memory and Early Sasanian Iran: Achaemenid Sites and Sasanian Identity." *American Journal of Archaeology* 114 (2010): 563–596.

Canepa, Matthew P. "Building a New Vision of the Past in the Sasanian Empire: The Sanctuaries of Kayānsīh and Great Fires of Iran." *Journal of Persianate Studies* 6 (2013): 64–90.

Caner, Daniel. "Toward a Miraculous Economy: Christian Gifts and Material 'Blessings' in Late Antiquity." *Journal of Early Christian Studies* 14 (2006): 329–377.

Colditz, Iris. *Zur Sozialterminologie der iranischen Manichäer: Eine semantische Analyse im Vergleich zu den nichtmanichäischen iranischen Quellen.* Wiesbaden: Harrassowitz, 2000.

Crone, Patricia. "Kavad's Heresy and Mazdak's Revolt." *Iran* 29 (1991): 21–42.

Crone, Patricia. "Zoroastrian Communism." *Comparative Studies in Society and History* 36 (1994): 447–462.

Crone, Patricia. *The Nativist Prophets of Early Islamic Iran: Rural Revolt and Local Zoroastrianism.* Cambridge: Cambridge University Press, 2012.

Daryaee, Touraj. "Ethnic and Territorial Boundaries in Late Antique and Early Medieval Persia (Third to Tenth Century)." In *Borders, Barriers, and Ethnogenesis, Frontiers in Late Antiquity and Middle Ages*, edited by Florin Curta, 123–137. Turnhout: Brepols, 2005.

de Jong, Albert. "Religion in Iran: The Parthian and Sasanian Periods (247 BCE–654 CE)." In *The Cambridge History of Religions in the Ancient World*, edited by Michelle Salzman, 23–53. Cambridge: Cambridge University Press, 2013.

Dagron, Gilbert. *Empereur et prêtre: étude sur le "césaropapisme" byzantine.* Paris: Gallimard, 1996.

Déroche, Vincent. *Études sur Léontios de Néapolis.* Uppsala: Uppsala Universitet, 1995.

Dossey, Leslie. "Wifebeating and Manliness in Late Antiquity." *Past & Present* 199 (2008): 3–40.

Fromherz, Allen James. *The Near West: Medieval North Africa, Latin Europe and the Mediterranean in the Second Axial Age*. Edinburgh: Edinburgh University Press, 2016.

Garsoïan, Nina. "Sur le titre *Protecteur des pauvres*." *Revue des études arméniennes* 15 (1981): 21–32.

Gnoli, Gheradro. *The Idea of Iran: An Essay on Its Origin*. Rome: Istituto Italiano per il Medio ed Estremo Oriente, 1989.

Graeber, D. *Debt: The First 5,000 Years*. New York: Melville House, 2011.

Gyselen, Rika. *Sasanian Seals and Sealings in the A. Saeedi Collection*. Louvain: Peeters, 2007.

Henkelman, Wouter. *The Other Gods Who Are: Studies in Elamite-Iranian Acculturation Based on the Persepolis Fortification Texts*. Leiden: Nederlands Instituut voor het Nabije Oosten, 2008.

Huff, Dietrich. "Beobachtungen zum Čahartaq und zur Topographie zum Girre." *Iranica Antiqua* 30 (1995): 71–92.

Janes, Dominic. *God and Gold in Late Antiquity*. Cambridge: Cambridge University Press, 1999.

Jany, János. "The Idea of a Trust in Zoroastrian Law." *Journal of Legal History* 25 (2004): 269–286.

Jany, János. "The Jurisprudence of the Sasanian Sages." *Journal Asiatique* 294 (2006): 291–323.

Jany, János. "Criminal Justice in Sasanian Persia." *Iranica Antiqua* 42 (2007): 347–386.

Kellens, Jean. "Les Achéménides entre textes et liturgie avestiques." In *Persian Religion in the Achaemenid Period*, edited by Wouter Henkelman and Céline Redard, 11–19. Wiesbaden: Harrassowitz, 2017.

Khatchadourian, Lori. *Imperial Matter: Ancient Persia and the Archaeology of Empires*. Oakland: University of California Press, 2016.

Lavan, Myles, Richard E. Payne, and John Weisweiler, eds. *Cosmopolitanism and Empire: Universal Rulers, Local Elites, and Cultural Integration in the Ancient Near East and Mediterranean*. New York: Oxford University Press, 2016.

Lincoln, Bruce. *"Happiness for Mankind": Achaemenian Religion and the Imperial Project*. Leuven: Peeters, 2012.

Lommel, Herman. "Die Elemente im Verhältnis zu den Ameša Spentas." In *Zarathustra*, edited by H. Schlerath, 377–396. Darmstadt: Wissenschaftliche Buchgesellschaft, 1970.

Macuch, Maria. *Das Sasanidische rechtsbuch "Mātakdān i hazār dātistān" (teil II)*. Wiesbaden: Harrassowitz Verlag, 1981.

Macuch, Maria. "Eine alte bemessungsgrundlage für die 'Tagesration' in den Pahlavi-schriften." In *Salaires, prix, poids et mesures*, edited by Rika Gyselen, 139–142. Paris: Association pour l'Avancement des Études Iraniennes, 1990.

Macuch, Maria. *Rechtskasuistik und Gerichtspraxis zu Beginn des siebenten Jahrhunderts in Iran: Die Rechtsammlung des Farroḥmard i Wahrāmān*. Wiesbaden: Harrassowitz Verlag, 1993.

Macuch, Maria. "Die sasanidische Stiftung 'für die Seele'—Vorbild für islamischen *waqf*?" In *Iranian and Indo-European studies: Memorial Volume of Otakar Klima*, edited by Petr Vavroušek, 163–180. Prague: Enigma, 1994.

Macuch, Maria. "Herrschaftskonsolidierung und sasanidische Familienrecht: zum Verhältnis von Kirche und Staat unter den Sasaniden." In *Iran und Turfan: Beiträge Berliner wissenschaftler, Werner Sundermann zum 60. Geburtstag gewidmet*, edited by Christiane Reck and Peter Zieme, 149–167. Wiesbaden: Harrassowitz, 1995.

Macuch, Maria. "The Function of Temporary Marriage in the Context of Sasanian Family Law." In *Proceedings of the Fifth Conference of the Societas Iranologica Europaea v. I: Ancient and Middle Iranian Studies*, edited by Antonion Panaino and Andrea Piras, 585–597. Milan: Mimesis, 2006.

Macuch, Maria. "Judicial and Legal Systems III: Sassanian Legal System." In *Encyclopedia Iranica*, edited by Ehsan Yarshater, 181–196. New York: Routledge, 2009.

Macuch, Maria. "Incestuous Marriage in the Context of Sasanian Family Law." In *Ancient and Middle Iranian Studies: Proceedings of the Sixth European Conference of Iranian Studies*, edited by Maria Macuch, Dieter Weber, and Desmond Durkin-Meisterernst, 133–148. Wiesbaden: Harrassowitz, 2010.

Macuch, Maria. "The *adwadād* Offense in Zoroastrian Law." In *Shoshannat Yaakov: Jewish and Iranian Studies in Honor of Yaakov Elman*, edited by Shai Secunda and Stephen Fine, 247–270. Leiden: Brill, 2012.

Macuch, Maria. "Legal Implications of Mazdakite Teaching According to the Dēnkard: The Great 'Restoration' of Husraw I." In *Husraw Ier reconstructions d'un règne: Sources et documents*, edited by Christelle Jullien, 155–174. Paris: Association pour l'Avancement des Etudes Iraniennes, 2015.

Macuch, Maria. "Pious Foundations in Byzantine and Sasanian Law." In *La Persia e Bisanzio: Convegno internazionale, Roma 14–18 ottobre 2002*, edited by Antonio Carile et al., 181–196. Rome: Accademia Nazionale dei Lincei, 2004.

Macuch, Maria. "The Talmudic Expression 'Servant of the Fire' in Light of Pahlavi Legal Sources." *Jerusalem Studies in Arabic and Islam* 26 (2002): 109–129.

Macuch, Maria. "'This Is the Law of the Persians'—An Allusion to the Sasanian Law of Surety in the Babylonian Talmud." *Iran Namag* 1 (2016): 18–27.

Marlow, Louise. *Hierarchy and Egalitarianism in Islamic Thought*. Cambridge: Cambridge University Press, 1997.

Miller, Nathaniel. "Tribal Poetics in Early Arabic Culture: The Case of Ashʿār al-Hudhaliyyīn." PhD diss., University of Chicago, 2016.

Morony, Michael. "Population Transfers between Sasanian Iran and the Byzantine Empire." In *La Persia e Bisanzio*, edited by Antonio Carile, 161–179. Rome: Accademia Nazionale dei Lincei, 2004.

Morris, Ian and Walter Scheidel eds. *The Dynamics of Ancient Empires: State Power from Assyria to Byzantium*. Oxford: Oxford University Press, 2009.

Patlagean, Évelyne. *Pauvreté économique et pauvreté sociale à Byzance, 4e–7e siècles*. Paris: Mouton, 1977.

Payne, Richard E. *A State of Mixture: Christians, Zoroastrians, and Iranian Political Culture in Late Antiquity*. Oakland: University of California Press, 2015.

Payne, Richard E. "Sex, Death, and Aristocratic Empire: Iranian Jurisprudence in Late Antiquity." *Comparative Studies in Society and History* 58 (2016): 1–31.

Payne, Richard E. "Territorializing Iran in Late Antiquity: Autocracy, Aristocracy, and the Infrastructure of Empire." In *Ancient States and Infrastructural Power: Europe, Asia, and America*, edited by Clifford Ando and Seth Richardson, 179–217. Philadelphia: University of Pennsylvania Press, 2017.

Pigulevskaya, Nina. "Zarozhdenie Feodal'nikh Otnoshenii na Blizhnem Vostoke." *Uchenie Zapiski Instituta Vostokovedeniya* 16 (1958): 5–30.

Rezakhani, Khodadad. "Mazdakism, Manichaeism, and Zoroastrianism: In Search of Orthodoxy and Heterodoxy in Late Antique Iran." *Iranian Studies* 48 (2015): 55–70.

Savant, Sarah. *The New Muslims of Post-Conquest Iran: Tradition, Memory, and Conversion*. Cambridge: Cambridge University Press, 2013.

Scheidel, Walter, ed. *Rome and China: Comparative Perspectives on Ancient World Empires*. New York: Oxford University Press, 2009.

Scheidel, Walter, ed. *State Power in Ancient China and Rome*. New York: Oxford University Press, 2015.

Schopen, Gregory. *Buddhist Monks and Business Matters: Still More Papers on Monastic Buddhism in India*. Honolulu: University of Hawaii Press, 2004.

Shaked, Shaul. "Administrative Functions of Priests in the Sasanian Period." In *Proceedings of the First European Conference of Iranian Studies: Part I, Old and Middle Iranian Studies*, edited by Gherardo Gnoli and Antonio Panaino, 261–273. Rome: Istituto Italiano per il Medio ed Estremo Oriente, 1990.

Shaked, Shaul. *Dualism in Transformation: Varieties of Religion in Sasanian Iran*. London: School of Oriental and African Studies, 1994.

Shaked, Shaul. "Zoroastrian Origins: Indian and Iranian Connections." In *Axial Civilizations and World History*, edited by Johann P. Arnason, S. N. Eisenstadt, and Björn Wittrock, 183–200. Leiden: Brill, 2005.

Shayegan, M. Rahim. *Arsacids and Sasanians: Political Ideology in Post-Hellenistic and Late Antique Persia*. Cambridge: Cambridge University Press, 2011.

Shayegan, M. Rahim. *Aspects of History and Epic in Ancient Iran: From Gaumāta to Wahnām*. Cambridge, MA: Center for Hellenic Studies, 2012.

Skjaervø, Prods Oktor. "*Tahādī*: Gifts, Debts, and Counter-Gifts in the Ancient
    Zoroastrian Ritual." In *Classical Arabic Humanities in Their Own Terms: Festschrift
    in Honor of Wolfhart Heinrichs*, edited by Beatrice Gruendler and Michael
    Cooperson, 493–520. Leiden: Brill, 2008.
Sundermann, Werner. "Commendatio pauperum: Eine Angabe der sassanidischen poli-
    tisch- didaktischen Literatur zur gesellschaftlichen Struktur Irans." *Altorientalische
    Forschungen* 4 (1976): 167–194.
Toral-Niehoff, Isabel. *Al-Ḥīra: Eine arabische kulturmetropole im spätantiken kontext.*
    Leiden: Brill, 2014.
Weber, Dieter. *Berliner Pahlavi-Dokumente: Zeugnisse spätsassanidischer Brief- und
    Rechtskultur aus frühislamischer Zeit.* Wiesbaden: Harrassowitz, 2008.
Wittrock, Björn. "The Meaning of the Axial Age." In *Axial Civilizations and World
    History*, edited by Johann P. Arnason, S. N. Eisenstadt, and Björn Wittrock, 51–85.
    Leiden: Brill, 2005.

CHAPTER 9

al-Bakrī, Abū ʿUbayd. *Muʿjam mā staʿjam.* Beirut: Dār al-kutub al-ʿilmiyya, 1998.
al-Kindī, Abū ʿUmar b. Yūsuf. *Kitāb al- wulāt wa-l-quḍāt.* Leiden: Brill, 1912.
al-Marzūqī, Abū ʿAlī al-Iṣfahānī. *Kitāb al-azmina wal-amkina.* Vol. 2. Hyderabad, 1914.
Azami, M. *On Schacht's* Origins of Muhammadan Jurisprudence. New York: Wiley, 1986.
Becker, C. H. *Vom Werden und Wesen der islamischem Welt;" Islamstudien*, 1:54–65.
    Leipzig: Quelle and Meyer, 1924.
Berg, H. *The Development of Exegesis in Early Islam: The Authenticity of Muslim
    Literature from the Formative Period.* Richmond, UK: Curzon, 2000.
Blachère, R. *Histoire de la littérature arabe des origines à la fin du XVe siècle de J.-C.* Vol.
    1. Paris: A. Maisonneuve, 1980. First published 1952.
Bonner, M. "The *Kitāb al-kasb* Attributed to al-Shaybānī: Poverty, Surplus and the
    Creation of wealth." *Journal of the American Oriental Society* 121 (2001): 410–427.
Bonner, M. "Poverty and Economics in the Qurʾān." *Journal of Interdisciplinary History*
    35 (2005): 391–406.
Bonner, M. "The Arabian Silent Trade: Profit and Nobility in the 'Markets of the
    Arabs.'" In *Histories of the Middle East*, edited by R. E. Margariti, A. Sabra, and
    P. M. Sijpesteijn, 23–51. Leiden: Brill, 2010.
Bonner, M. "'Time Has Come Full Circle': Markets, Fairs and the Calendar in Arabia
    before Islam." In *The Islamic Scholarly Tradition: Studies in history, law, and thought
    in honor of Professor Michael Allan Cook*, edited by A. Ahmed, B. Sadeghi, and
    M. Bonner, 15–47. Leiden: Brill, 2011.
Bonner, M. "Commerce and Migration before Islam: A Brief History of a Long
    Literary Tradition." In *Iranian Language and Culture*, edited by B. Aghaei and
    M.R. Ghanoonparvar, 1–27. Malibu and Costa Mesa: Mazda, 2012.

Brown, J. A. C. *Hadith: Muhammad's Legacy in the Medieval and Modern World*. Oxford: Oxford University Press, 2009.

Crone, P. *Roman, Provincial and Islamic Law*. Cambridge: Cambridge University Press, 1987a.

Crone, P. *Meccan Trade and the Rise of Islam*. Princeton, NJ: Princeton University Press, 1987b.

Crone, P. "Serjeant and Meccan Trade." *Arabica* 39 (1992): 216–240.

Crone, P. "Quraysh and the Roman Army: Making Sense of the Meccan Leather Trade." *Bulletin of the School of Oriental and African Studies* 70 (2007): 63–87.

Ghada, O. "Foreign Slaves in Mecca and Medina in the Formative Islamic Period." *Islam and Christian-Muslim Relations* 16 (2005): 344–359.

Gledhill, P. "Motzki's Forger: The Corpus of the Follower 'Aṭā' in Two Early 3rd/9th Century Ḥadīth Compendia." *Islamic Law and Society* 19 (2012): 194–199.

Goitein, S. D. *Studies in Islam and Islamic Institutions*. Leiden: Brill, 1968.

Goldziher, I. *Muslim Studies*, translated and edited by S. Stern and C. Barber, 2:17–254. Chicago: Aldine Atherton, 1971.

Graeber, D. *Debt: The First 5,000 Years*. Updated exp. ed. New York and London: Melville House, 2014.

Hallaq, W. *The Origins and Evolution of Islamic Law*. Cambridge: Cambridge University Press, 2005.

Heck, G. W. "Gold Mining in Arabia and the Rise of the Islamic State." *Journal of the Economic and Social History of the Orient* 42 (1999): 364–395.

Heck, G. W. *The Precious Metals of West Arabia and Their Role in Forging the Economic Dynamic of the Early Islamic State*. Riyadh: King Faisal Center for Research and Islamic Studies, 2003.

Heck, G. W. *Charlemagne, Muhammad, and the Arab Roots of Capitalism*. Berlin: De Gruyter, 2006.

Kister, M. J. "'God Will Never Disgrace Thee' (The Interpretation of an Early Hadith)." *Journal of the Royal Asiatic Society* no. 1/2 (1965): 27–32.

Koehler, B. *Early Islam and the Birth of Capitalism*. London, 2014.

Kuran, T. "The Absence of the Corporation in Islamic Law: Origins and Persistence." *American Journal of Comparative Law* 53 (2005): 785–835.

Lammens, H. "La république marchande de la Mecque vers l'an 600 de notre ère." *Bulletin de l'Institut Egyptien* 5th Series 4 (1910): 23–54.

Lecker, M. "King Ibn Ubayy and the *Quṣṣāṣ*." In *Methods and Theories in the Study of Islamic Origins*, edited by H. Berg, 29–71. Leiden: Brill, 2003.

Lombard, M. *The Golden Age of Islam*. Translated by J. Spencer. Amsterdam: North Holland, 2014. First published 1975.

Motzki, H. *The Origins of Islamic Jurisprudence: Meccan Fiqh before the Classical Schools*. Translated by M. H. Katz Leiden: Brill, 2002.

Motzki, H. "Der prophet und die schuldner. Eine *ḥadīt*-untersuchung auf dem prüf-stand." *Der Islam* 77 (2000): 1–83.

Motzki, H. "*Ar-Radd ʿalā r-radd*—Zur methodik der *ḥadīt*-analyse." *Der Islam* 78 (2001): 147–163.

Motzki, H. *Analysing Muslim Traditions: Studies in Legal, Exegetical and Maghāzī Ḥadīth.* Leiden: Brill, 2010.

Motzki, H. "Motzki's Reliable Transmitter: A Short Answer to P. Gledhill." *Islamic Law and Society* 19 (2012): 194–199.

Nana, M. F. *Al-Jūd wal-bukhl fi l-shiʿr al-jāhilī.* Damascus: Dār Ṭalās, 1994.

Rippin, A. "The Commerce of Eschatology." In *The Qurʾān as Text*, edited by S. Wild, 125–135. Leiden: Brill, 1996.

Rodinson, M. *Islam and Capitalism.* Translated by B. Pearce. New York: Pantheon, 1974.

Rodinson, M. "Les conditions religieuses de la vie économique." In *Wirtschaftsgeschichte des vorderen orients*, edited by B. Spuler, 18–30. Leiden: Brill, 1977.

Schacht, J. *The Origins of Muhammadan Jurisprudence.* Oxford: Oxford University Press, 1950.

Schneider, I. *Kinderverkauf und schuldknechtschaft: Untersuchungen zur frühen phase des islamischen rechts.* Stuttgart: Deutsche Morgenlandische Gesselschaft, 1999.

Schneider, I. "Narrativität und authentizität: Die geschichte vom weisen propheten, dem dreisten dieb und dem koranfesten gläubiger." *Der Islam* 77 (2000): 84–115.

Schneider, I. "Freedom and Slavery in Early Islamic Time." *Al-Qanṭara* 28 (2007): 353–382.

Serjeant, R. B. "Meccan Trade and the Rise of Islam: Misconceptions and Flawed Polemics." *Journal of the American Oriental Society* 110 (1990): 472–486.

Tripp, C. *Islam and the Moral Economy.* Cambridge: Cambridge University Press, 2006.

Watt, W. M. *Muhammad at Mecca.* Oxford: Oxford University Press, 1953.

Yāqūt al-Rūmī. *Muʿjam al-buldān.* 5 vols. Beirut: Dār Ṣādir, 1955–1957.

CHAPTER 10

Ando, C. "Decline, Fall and Transformation." *Journal of Late Antiquity* 1 (2008): 31–60.

Bagnall, R. S., and R. Cribiore. *Women's Letters from Ancient Egypt, 300 BC–AD 800.* Ann Arbor: University of Michigan Press, 2006.

Banaji, J. *Agrarian Change in Late Antiquity: Gold, Labour, and Aristocratic Dominance.* Oxford: Oxford University Press, 2007.

Boud'hors, A., and F. Calament. "Pour une étude des archives coptes de Medinet el-Fayoum (P.Louvre inv. E 10253, E 6893, E 6867 et E 7395)." In *From Bāwīṭ to Marw: Documents from the Medieval Muslim World*, edited by A. Kaplony, D. Potthast, and C. Römer, 23–58. Leiden: Brill, 2015.

Bougard, F. "Le crédit dans l'Occident du haut moyen âge: Documentation et pra-tique." In *Les élites et la richesse au haut moyen âge*, edited by J.-P. Devroey, L. Feller, and R. Le Jan, 439–477. Turnhout: Brepols, 2010.

Bransbourg, G. "Capital in the Sixth Century." *Journal of Late Antiquity* 9 (2016): 305–414.

Briggs, C. "The Availability of Credit in the English Countryside, 1400–1480." *Agricultural History Review* 56, no. 1 (2008): 1–24.

Briggs, C. *Credit and Village Society in Fourteenth-Century England.* Oxford, 2009.

Brown, P. *The World of Late Antiquity: From Marcus Aurelius to Muhammad.* London: Thames and Hudson, 1971.

Brown, P. *The Making of Late Antiquity.* Cambridge, MA: Harvard University Press, 1978.

Cameron, A. "The 'Long' Late Antiquity: A Late-Twentieth Century Model?" In *Classics in Progress*, edited by T. P. Wiseman, 165–191. Oxford: Oxford University Press, 2002.

Cameron, A. "Blame the Christians." *The Tablet*, September 21, 2017. http://www.thetablet.co.uk/books/10/11298/blame-the-christians.

Carrié, J.-M. "Solidus et crédit: Qu'est-ce que l'or a pu changer?" In *Credito e moneta nel mondo romano: Atti degli incontri capresi di storia dell'economia antica, Capri, 12–14 ottobre 2000*, edited by E. Lo Cascio, 265–279. Bari: Edipuglia, 2003.

Catsari, K. "The Monetization of Rome's Frontier Provinces." In *The Monetary Systems of the Greeks and Romans*, edited by W. V. Harris, 242–266. Oxford: Oxford University Press, 2008.

Davis, K., and M. Puett. "Periodization and 'the Medieval Globe': A Conversation." *The Medieval Globe* 2, no. 1 (2015): 1–14.

Dermineur, E. "Trust, Norms of Cooperation, and the Rural Credit Market in Eighteenth-Century France." *Journal of Interdisciplinary History* 45, no. 4 (2015): 485–506.

Dermineur, E. "Rural Credit Markets in Eighteenth-Century France: Contracts, Guarantees, and Land." In *Land and Credit: Mortgages in the Medieval and Early Modern European Countryside*, edited by C. Briggs and J. Zuiderduijn, 205–231. Cham: Palgrave Macmillan, 2018.

Drescher, J. "John Drescher, 'A widow's petition.' " *Bulletin de la Société d'Archéologie Copte* 10 (1944): 91–96, pl. I–II.

Feller, L., ed. *Calculs et rationalités dans la seigneurie médiévale: Les conversions de redevances entre XIe et XVe siècles.* Paris: Publications de la Sorbonne, 2009.

Fouracre, P., ed. *The New Cambridge Medieval History.* Vol. 1, *c. 500–c. 700.* Cambridge: Cambridge University Press, 2008.

Gerhard, D. "Periodization in European History." *American Historical Review* 61 (1956): 900–913.

Graeber, D. *Debt: The First 5,000 Years.* New York: Melville House, 2011.

Green, W. A. "Periodization in European and World History." *Journal of World History* 3 (1992): 13–53.

Harper, K. *Slavery in the Late Roman World, A.D. 275–425*. Cambridge: Cambridge University Press, 2011.

Hengstl, J. *Private Arbeitsverhältnisse freier Personen in den hellenistischen Papyri bis Diokletian*. Bonn: Habelt, 1972.

Hopkins, K. *Conquerors and Slaves*. Cambridge: Cambridge University Press, 1978.

Howgego, C. "The Monetization of Temperate Europe." *Journal of Roman Studies* 103 (2013): 16–45.

Humphries, M. "Late Antiquity and World History: Challenging Conventional Narratives and Analyses." *Studies in Late Antiquity* 1 (2017): 8–37.

James, E. "The Rise and Function of the Concept 'Late Antiquity.'" *Journal of Late Antiquity* 1 (2008): 20–30.

Jördens, A. "Öffentliche Archive und römische Rechtspolitik." In *Tradition and Transformation: Egypt under Roman Rule*, edited by K. Lembke, M. Minas-Nerpel, and S. Pfeiffer, 159–179. Leiden: Brill, 2010a.

Jördens, A. "Nochmals zur Bibliotheke Enkteseon." In *Symposion 2009: Vorträge zur griechischen und hellenistischen Rechtsgeschichte (Seggau, 25.–30. August 2009)*, edited by G. Thür, 277–290. Vienna: Verlag de Österreichischen Akademie der Wissenschaften, 2010b.

Joseph, M. *Against the Romance of Community*. Minneapolis: University of Minnesota Press, 2002.

Joseph, M. "Theorizing Debt for Social Change: A Review of Graeber's *Debt: The First 5000 Years*." *Ephemera: Theory and Politics in Organization* 13 (2013): 659–673.

Joseph, M. *A Debt to Society: Accounting for Life under Capitalism*. Minneapolis: University of Minnesota Press, 2014.

Jussen, B. "Richtig denken im falschen Rahmen? Warum das 'Mittelalter' nicht in den Lehrplan gehört." *Geschichte in Wissenschaft und Unterricht* 67 (2016): 558–576.

Jussen, B. "Wer falsch spricht, denkt falsch. Warum Antike, Mittelalter und Neuzeit in die Wissenschaftsgeschichte gehören." In *Spekulative Theorien, Kontroversen, Paradigmenwechsel*, edited by M. Steinmetz, 38–52. Berlin: Berlin-Brandenburgische Akademie der Wissenschaften, 2017.

Keenan, J. G. "The Case of Flavia Christodote: Observations on *PSI* I 76." *Zeitschrift für Papyrologie und Epigraphik* 29 (1978): 191–209.

Kennedy, H. "Military Pay and the Economy of the Early Islamic State." *Historical Research* 75 (2002): 155–169.

Ledeneva, A., ed. *The Global Encyclopaedia of Informality*. Vol. 1. London: UCL Press, 2018.

Lerouxel, F. "Les femmes sur le marché du crédit en Égypte romaine (30 avant J.C.–284 après J.-C.)." *Cahiers du Centre de recherches historiques* 37 (2006): 121–136.

Lerouxel, F. "Le marché du crédit privé, la bibliothèque des acquêts et les tâches publiques en Egypte romaine." *Annales: Histoire, Sciences Sociales* 67 (2012): 943–976.

Lerouxel, F. *Le marché du crédit dans le monde romain (Égypte et Campanie)*. Rome: École française de Rome, 2016.

Marcone, A. "A Long Late Antiquity? Considerations on a Controversial Periodisation." *Journal of Late Antiquity* 1 (2008): 4–19.

Marrou, H.-I. *Décadence romaine ou antiquité tardive? (IIIᵉ–VIᵉ siècle)*. Paris: Éditions du Seuil, 1977.

Mishra, S. "Agrarian Scenario in Post-Reform India: A Story of Distress, Despair and Death." IDEAS Working Paper Series WP-2007-001, Indira Ghandi Institute of Development Research, Mumbai, India, 2007.

Naismith, R. "Gold Coinage and Its Use in the Post-Roman West." *Speculum* 89 (2014a): 273–306.

Naismith, R. "The Social Significance of Monetization in the Early Middle Ages." *Past and Present* 233 (2014b): 3–39.

Nixey, C. *The Darkening Age: The Christian Destruction of the Classical World*. London: Macmillan, 2017.

Papaconstantinou, A. "A Preliminary Prosopography of Moneylenders in Early Islamic Egypt and South Palestine." Special issue, *Travaux et Mémoires* (*Mélanges Cécile Morrisson*) 16 (2011): 631–648.

Papaconstantinou, A. "Les propriétaires ruraux en Palestine du sud et en Égypte entre la conquête perse et l'arrivée des Abbassides." *Mélanges de l'École française de Rome—Moyen Âge*, 124 (2012): 405–416.

Papaconstantinou, A. "The Rhetoric of Power and the Voice of Reason: Tensions between Central and Local in the Correspondence of Qurra ibn Sharīk." In *Official Epistolography and the Language(s) of Power. Proceedings of the 1st International Conference of the Research Network Imperium and Officium: Comparative Studies in Ancient Bureaucracy and Officialdom, University of Vienna, 10–12 November 2010*, edited by S. Procházka, L. Reinfandt, and S. Tost, 267–281. Vienna: Verlag der Österreichischen Akademie der Wissenschaften, 2015.

Papaconstantinou, A. "Credit, Debt, and Dependence in Early Islamic Egypt and Southern Palestine." In *Mélanges Jean Gascou: Textes et études papyrologiques (P. Gascou)*, edited by J.-L. Fournet and A. Papaconstantinou, 613–642. Paris: ACHCByz, 2016a.

Papaconstantinou, A. "Choses de femme et accès au crédit dans l'Égypte rurale sous les Omeyyades." In *Le saint, le moine et le paysan. Mélanges d'histoire byzantine offerts à Michel Kaplan*, edited by O. Delouis, S. Métivier, and P. Pagès, 551–561. Paris: Publications de la Sorbonne, 2016b.

Papaconstantinou, A. "Women in Need: Debt-Related Requests from Early Medieval Egypt." In *Living the End of Antiquity: Individual Histories from Byzantine to Islamic Egypt*, edited by S. Hübner, I. Marthot, M. Müller, S. Schmidt, and M. Stern, 195–205. Berlin: De Gruyter, 2020.

Pernoud, R. *Pour en finir avec le moyen âge*. Paris: Éditions du Seuil, 1977.

Rustow, M. *Heresy and the Politics of Community: The Jews of the Fatimid Caliphate.* Ithaca, NY: Cornell University Press, 2008.

Sadanandan, A. "Political Economy of Suicide: Financial Reforms, Credit Crunches, and Farmer Suicides in India." *Journal of Developing Areas* 48 (2014): 287–307.

Samellas, A. "The Anti-Usury Arguments of the Church Fathers of the East in Their Historical Context and the Accommodation of the Church to the Prevailing 'Credit Economy' in Late Antiquity." *Journal of Ancient History* 5, no. 1 (2017): 134–178.

Samuel, A. E. "The Role of Paramone Clauses in Ancient Documents." *Journal of Juristic Papyrology* 15 (1965): 221–311.

Sijpesteijn, P. M. *Shaping a Muslim State: The World of a Mid-Eighth-Century Egyptian Official.* Oxford: Oxford University Press, 2013.

Tillier, M. "Prisons et autorités urbaines sous les Abbassides." *Arabica* 55 (2008): 387–408.

Tillier, M. "Dispensing Justice in a Minority Context: The Judicial Administration of Upper Egypt under Muslim Rule in the Early Eighth Century." In *The Late Antique World of Early Islam: Muslims among Christians and Jews in the East Mediterranean,* edited by R. Hoyland, 133–156. Princeton, NJ: Darwin Press, 2015.

Tillier, M. *L'invention du cadi: La justice des musulmans, des juifs et des chrétiens aux premiers siècles de l'Islam.* Paris: Publications de la Sorbonne, 2017.

Tillier, M., and N. Vanthieghem. "Un registre carcéral de la Fusṭāṭ abbasside." *Islamic Law and Society* 25 (2018): 1–40.

Urbanik, J. "*P. Oxy.* LXIII 4397: The Monastery Comes First or Pious Reasons before Earthly Securities." In *Monastic Estates in Late Antique and Early Islamic Egypt: Ostraca, Papyri, and Essays in Memory of Sarah Clackson (P. Clackson),* edited by A. Boud'hors, J. Clackson, C. Louis, and P. Sijpesteijn, 225–235. Cincinnati: American Society of Papyrologists, 2009.

van Minnen, P. "Money and Credit in Roman Egypt." In *The Monetary Systems of the Greeks and Romans,* edited by W. V. Harris, 226–241. Oxford: Oxford University Press, 2008.

Veyne, P. "La 'plèbe moyenne' sous le haut-empire romain." *Annales. Histoire, Sciences Sociales* 55 (2000): 1169–1199.

Vuolanto, V. "Children and Work: Family Strategies and Socialisation in the Roman and Late Antique Egypt." In *Agents and Objects: Children in Pre-modern Europe,* edited by J. Hanska and K. Mustakallio, 97–112. Rome: Institutum Romanum Finlandiae, 2015.

Westermann, W. L. "The Paramone as General Service Contract." *Journal of Juristic Papyrology* 2 (1948): 9–50.

Wickham, C. *Framing the Early Middle Ages: Europe and the Mediterranean, 400–800.* Oxford: Oxford University Press, 2005.

Wilfong, T. "The Archive of a Family of Moneylenders from Jême." *Bulletin of the American Society of Papyrologists* 27 (1990): 169–181.

Wilfong, T. *Women of Jeme: Lives in a Coptic Town in Late Antique Egypt.* Ann Arbor: University of Michigan Press, 2002.

Yiftach-Firanko, U. "Comments on Andrea Jördens, 'Nochmals zur Bibliotheke Enkteseon.'" In *Symposion 2009: Vorträge zur griechischen und hellenistischen Rechtsgeschichte (Seggau, 25.–30. August 2009)*, edited by G. Thür, 291–299. Vienna: Verlag der Österreichischen Akademie der Wissenschaften, 2010a.

Yiftach-Firanko, U. "P. Col. inv. 131 recto: A Loan Contract with Paramonê Provision from Mid-First-Century CE Theadelphia." *Journal of Juristic Papyrology* 40 (2010b): 267–282.

CHAPTER 11

Attenborough, F. L. *The Laws of the Earliest English Kings.* Cambridge: Cambridge University Press, 1922.

Banaji, J. "Late Antiquity to the Early Middle Ages: What Kind of Transition?" *Historical Materialism* 19, no. 1 (2011): 109–144.

Bloch, M. "Les 'colliberti': Étude sur la formation de la classe servile." *Revue historique* 157, nos. 1–2 (1928): 1–48, 225–263.

Blumenthal, D. *Enemies and Familiars: Slavery and Mastery in Fifteenth-Century Valencia.* Ithaca, NY: Cornell University Press, 2009.

Bougard, F. "Le crédit dans l'Occident du haut moyen-âge: Documentation et pratique." In *Les élites et la richesse au haut moyen âge*, edited by J.-P. Devroey, L. Feller, and R. Le Jan, 439–477. Turnhout: Brepols, 2010.

Breatnach, L. "Forms of Payment in the Early Irish Law Tracts." *Cambrian Medieval Celtic Studies* 68 (2014): 1–20.

Carrié, J.-M. "Le 'colonat du bas-empire': Un mythe historiographique?" *Opus* 1 (1982): 351–370.

Coupland, S. *Carolingian Coinage and the Vikings: Studies on Power and Trade in the Ninth Century.* Aldershot, UK: Ashgate, 2007.

Coupland, S. "The Use of Coin in the Carolingian Empire in the Ninth Century." In *Early Medieval Monetary History: Studies in Memory of Mark Blackburn*, edited by M. Allen, R. Naismith, and E. Screen, 257–293. Aldershot, UK: Ashgate, 2014.

Crone, P. *Slaves on Horses.* Cambridge: Cambridge University Press, 1980.

Duby, G. *Rural Economy and Country Life in the Medieval West.* Translated by Cynthia Postan. London: Edward Arnold, 1968.

Feller, L. "Dette, stratégies matrimoniales et institution d'héritier: Sur l'élite paysanne lombarde au IXe siècle." *Revue historique* 646 (2008): 339–368.

Finley, M. I. *Ancient Slavery and Modern Ideology.* New ed. Princeton, NJ: Princeton University Press, 1998.

Fustel de Coulanges, N. D. *L'alleu et le domaine rural pendant l'époque mérovingienne.* Paris: Hachette, 1889.

Graeber, D. *Debt: The First 5,000 Years.* Updated exp. ed. New York and London: Melville House, 2014.

Grierson, P. "Commerce in the Dark Ages: A Critique of the Evidence." *Transactions of the Royal Historical Society 5th Series* 9 (1959): 123–140.

Heers, J. *Esclaves et domestiques au moyen age dans le monde méditerranéen.* Paris: Fayard, 1981.

Hendy, M. F. "From Public to Private: The Western Coinages as a Mirror of the Disintegration of Late Roman State Structures." *Viator* 19 (1988): 29–78.

Holmes, C., and N. Standen, eds. "The Global Middle Ages." Supplement, *Past and Present* 13 (2018).

Jankowiak, M. "What Can Trade in Saqaliba Slaves Tell Us about Early Islamic Slavery?" *International Journal of Middle Eastern Studies* 49 (2017): 169–172.

McCormick, M. *Origins of the European Economy.* Cambridge: Cambridge University Press, 2001.

McCormick, M. "New Light on the Dark Ages: How the Slave Trade Fuelled the Carolingian Economy." *Past and Present* 177 (2002): 17–54.

McKee, S. "Domestic Slavery in Renaissance Italy." *Slavery and Abolition* 29, no. 3 (2008): 305–326.

Millar, F. "Condemnation to Hard Labour in the Roman Empire, from the Julio-Claudians to Constantine." *Papers of the British School at Rome* 52 (1984): 124–147.

Naismith, R. "The Social Significance of Monetization in the Early Middle Ages." *Past and Present* 223 (2014): 3–39.

Ramin, J., and P. Veyne. "Droit romain et société: Les hommes libres qui passent pour esclaves et l'esclavage volontaire." *Historia* 30, no. 4 (1981): 472–497.

Rio, A. *The Formularies of Angers and Marculf: Two Merovingian Legal Handbooks.* Liverpool: Liverpool University Press, 2008a.

Rio, A. "High and Low: Ties of Dependence in the Frankish Kingdoms." *Transactions of the Royal Historical Society Series 6* 18 (2008b): 43–68.

Rio, A. "Self-Sale and Voluntary Entry into Unfreedom, 300–1100." *Journal of Social History* 45, no. 3 (2012): 661–685.

Rio, A. "Penal Enslavement in the Early Middle Ages." In *Global Convict Labour*, edited by A. Lichtenstein and C. de Vito, 79–107. Leiden: Brill, 2015.

Rio, A. *Slavery after Rome, 500–1100.* Oxford: Oxford University Press, 2017.

Sarris, P. "The Origins of the Manorial Economy: New Insights from Late Antiquity." *English Historical Review* 119 (2004): 279–311.

Sirks, A. J. B. "Reconsidering the Roman Colonate." *Zeitschrift der Savigny-Stiftung: Romanistische Abteilung* 110 (1993): 331–369.

Verhulst, A. *The Carolingian Economy.* Cambridge: Cambridge University Press, 2002.

Whittaker, C. R. "Circe's Pigs: From Slavery to Serfdom in the Later Roman World." *Slavery and Abolition* 8, no. 1 (1987): 88–122.

Wickham, C. *Framing the Early Middle Ages.* Oxford: Oxford University Press, 2005.

CHAPTER 12

Childe, V.G. "The Urban Revolution." *The Town Planning Review* 21: 3–17.

Fustel de Coulanges, N. *The Ancient City*. Translated by W. Small. New York: Dover, 2006.

Graeber, D. *Debt: The First 5,000 Years*. New York: Melville House, 2011.

Hegel, G.W.F. *Elements of the Philosophy of Right*. Edited by A.W. Wood and translated by H.B. Nisbet. Cambridge: Cambridge University Press, 1991.

Latour, B. *We Have Never Been Modern*. Translated by C. Porter. Cambridge, MA: Harvard University Press, 1993.

Lewis, A. *The Evolution of the International Economic Order*. Princeton: Princeton University Press, 1978.

Malthus, T.R. *An Essay on the Principle of Population*. Edited by G. Gilbert. Oxford: Oxford University Press, 1993.

Marx, K. *Capital: A Critique of Political Economy: Volume 1*. Translated by Ben Fowkes. London: Penguin, 2004.

Rousseau, J.-J. *A Discourse on Inequality*. Translated by M. Cranston. London: Penguin, 1984.

Simmel, G. *The Philosophy of Money*. Translated by T. Bottomore and D. Frisby from a first draft by K. Mengelberg. London: Routledge, 1978.

Index